ONE MAN'S COLD HEROISM
WAS THE MARGIN BETWEEN
VICTORY AND DEFEAT...

Owens stood there, conspicuously in the open, rallying a company by his own steadiness. The issue was being decided on the ground where Owens stood. If his platoon broke, the whole position was gone.

But the wear on the men and weapons reached the cracking point. He had at last but 14 men, and they were wavering. They kept saying to him, "We're through; we must get out." He answered them, "No, we will wait for orders."

Yet Owens was uncertain of his own decision; maybe the men were right. So he sent a runner over to Dolan to ask what he had better do.

Back to the survivors came the message. Dolan had written it out, these words scrawled in pencil: "I don't know a better spot than this to die..."

"A memorable account, stunning in its force and vast in its humanity...You will find no better writing on war than in...Night Drop."

—JOHN TOLAND,
bestselling author of *Infamy*

NIGHT DROP

The American Airborne Invasion of Normandy

S.L.A. MARSHALL

Brigadier General, USAR, Ret.
Chief Historian, European Theater of Operations

Illustrated by H. Garver Miller

A JOVE BOOK

This Jove book contains the complete
text of the original hardcover edition.
It has been completely reset in a typeface
designed for easy reading, and was printed
from new film.

NIGHT DROP

A Jove Book/published by arrangement with
The Battery Press, Inc.

PRINTING HISTORY
Battery Press edition published 1962
Jove edition/June 1984

ISBN: 0-515-07626-0

Jove books are published by The Berkley Publishing Group,
200 Madison Avenue, New York, N.Y. 10016.
The words "A JOVE BOOK" and the "J" with sunburst
are trademarks belonging to Jove Publications, Inc.

PRINTED IN THE UNITED STATES OF AMERICA

Contents

List of Illustrations

NIGHT DROP

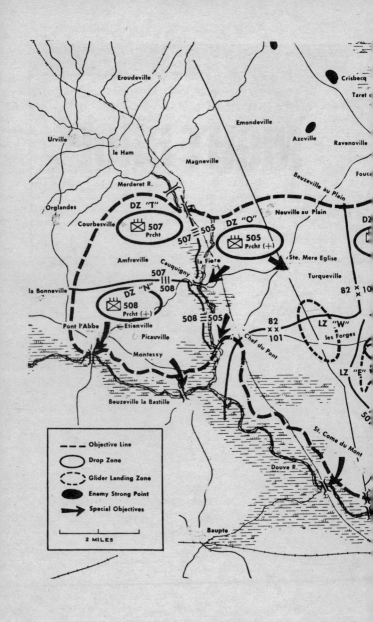

THE PLANNED AIRHEAD

Objectives of the 82nd and 101st
Airborne Divisions

Normandy June 6, 1944

Prologue

The repeats of history continue to fascinate people though, despite Ecclesiastes, there are ever new wonders under the sun. So to begin.

When in the year 1066 William of Normandy, confiding his duchy to his much-loved Matilda, assembled 696 ships, 13,000 men and 200 horses (the tanks of his day) around the mouth of the River Dives and set forth to conquer Harold and England, his way was softened by an appearance in the heavens.

It is chronicled that for seven nights there was a great to-do in the skies above the target area which "threw all that beheld it into consternation." Latter-day astronomers figured out that the Conqueror was helped by Halley's comet. So we have it that William was given overhead assistance after departing a harbor which was just off the acetate on which Allied planners grease-penciled a beachhead 878 years later. Other similarities between the two greatest invasions of the present millennium are not purely coincidental.

Landing unopposed, William took up strong ground next to a Roman wall near Pevensey. Having thereby secured his defensive base for operations, he turned to go against Hastings, which would give him communications by land and sea. The parallel shows how little military values change in a thousand years.

In 1944 the Allies had to have a main port. The mouth of the Dives, where William staged, and other neighboring shallows, wouldn't do. So the capture, clearing and use of Cherbourg at the earliest moment became the grand object. Even as it dominated all planning for Operation NEPTUNE, it regulated the movement of military forces, once Normandy became invaded. But as with William before Hastings, the business couldn't be rushed. The lodgment first had to be broad enough and pushed deep enough to be sure of holding. That done, the advance against Cherbourg could be pushed northward along with a westward drive to cut off enemy escape from the Cotentin Peninsula.

The initial scheme for the 1944 invasion did not provide for an assault against the Cotentin beaches. That was not because the planners scorned William's rule that main base should be fairly close to the object. The plan was written in 1943. The trouble then was that no one believed resources would stretch that far. So it was deemed wiser to concentrate forces against the east-west running coast between Grandcamp and Caen. Things changed when General Dwight D. Eisenhower took supreme command. He insisted that the invasion front be broadened to include the beaches on the Cotentin east coast, saying it was indispensable to success. And he had his way.

In the British sector, the assault front was lengthened eastward almost to the stream where William loaded his army, and westward to include the Cotentin beaches, code-named Utah. The original three-division assault was increased to five. More important still, enough lift became available to afford the dropping of two and two-thirds airborne divisions. Two were American. They were to hit in the flat hedgerow country inland from Utah Beach five hours before the small boats touched down. Their tasks were to seize the exits from Utah Beach and either seize or destroy the bridges and other crossings of the Douve and Merderet Rivers. So doing, they would reduce the heavy risks of the seaborne forces on the Allied right flank, which for a prolonged period would be separated from the mass of the invasion landing well to the eastward.

It was the task of U.S. VII Corps, landing at Utah, commanded by Major General J. Lawton Collins, to capture Cherbourg. The two airborne divisions were part of that corps. This is the story only of their first days when they fought nigh unhelped.

BOOK ONE

Against the Merderet

"So it came to pass in the first day of battle . . . men of the garrison spoke to Jonathan and his armour bearer and said: 'Come up to us and we will show you a thing.'"

— FROM THE FIRST BOOK OF SAMUEL

1

Into the Marshes

From the beginning, what threw the paratroopers and confused operations along the line of the Merderet River was the presence of the marshes.

This was not according to the script. It was known that where the Merderet joined the River Douve the flat valley was widely inundated and a man might drown there afar from the flowing stream. But the intelligence warnings were free of any hint that the Merderet might be equally treacherous. It was clean-billed—a modestly narrow stream, running clear through a well-defined trench between meadows which were flat and reasonably dry.

So when the sky soldiers dropped through the dark, either to bathe in mud where the marsh was shallow or to swim for life where it was deep, the shock of surprise told them that they had been jettisoned off course and were somewhere on the Douve.

Many drowned. Those more fortunate had equipment fouled and bodies worn nigh to exhaustion before they could shoulder arms. Twice a betrayer, the marsh, where it lost the grapple, lied to them about where they stood and which way to go. It blocked the concentration of thought as of men.

Yet all this came of curious circumstance. The waters had been there nearly one year. In July, 1943, the flood, backing up from the lock at La Barquette, reached the causeway west

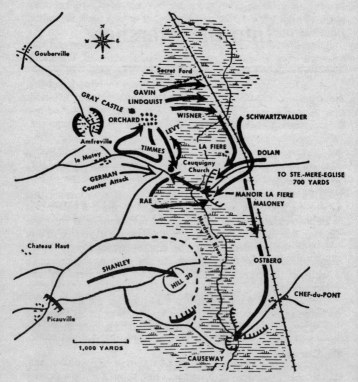

Figure 1. CONCENTRATION ON THE MERDERET

of Manoir de la Fière. By late summer the lake filling the valley on both sides of the Merderet was as deep as a man's chest. Reeds and tall grasses grew out of the water during autumn and thickened when spring came. They obscured the spread of the lake which at the La Fière causeway measured 650 yards from shore to shore. The lord of the Manoir, M. Louis Leroux, ruefully kept track of the rise because it turned back his cattle from their most lush pasture.

Untold woe may come to soldiers from map error and the vagaries of air reconnaissance. Here is a classic case. The sheet maps published by Company B, 660th Engineers, in April, 1944, define in perfect outline the limits of the flood, yet lift the curse from it with this label of understatement: "Ground here probably soft." In the weeks which followed, Allied reconnaissance planes braved the German flak to photograph the valley. In the pictures, it looks invitingly pastoral and firm. Whether owing to the tall grasses or to some freak of lighting or a trick by the camera, the waters remained hidden. The secret came unlocked when at last soldiers jumped out of the night to fight.

One other accident of ground partly offset the unexpected jeopardy. Dropping into the black pit, stopping, yet not landing, struggling with the waters and with harness while experiencing that first awful doubt about their bearings, they were drawn to one spot as by a magnet.

Directly above La Fière the railroad right of way cuts diagonally across the shallow Merderet valley. But the stream also bends at that point so that for two and one-half miles between there and Granville the rail embankment stands up boldly like a dike commanding the marshland. In dark or day it dominates the landscape—the one solid object in an otherwise uncertain situation.

When paratroops are misdropped by night into combat and become lost, instinctively they react like water and flow downhill. Reassembly comes about because, automatically, many men drift toward the drainage lines. Here is a simple biological urge (a child lost in the dark and ridden by fear would probably react the same way), which was unapplied as a tactical principle until the data from the Normandy drop illuminated it.

Similarly, the transcendent value of the valley railroad went unappreciated by the planners. Not knowing the marsh was there, they could not foresee that men, seeking escape from its clutch, must struggle toward that object which by bulk and line promised solid footing and a chance to start afresh.

Most of the paratroops dropped into the marsh were off course. The cloud bank, the enemy flak and that dulling of the senses which swiftly follows the high excitement of loading up had fogged judgment, limited observation, scattered the carrier formations and unnerved some of the pilots. When the green light flashed on, signaling that men had to jump, they were on average two miles from their proper drop zone. The strays included the command elements of 508th Parachute Regiment, many of its combat people, a great part of 507th Parachute Regiment and Brigadier General James M. Gavin's group. Most of them belonged to Force "A," which eight minutes after crossing the coast line was scheduled to arrive at its drop zone west of the Merderet and move at once to seize the two main crossings and hold them so that U.S. VII Corps would have thoroughfare.

But the eight minutes passed and Colonel Leroy Lindquist, of the 508th, looking out, saw only a wide expanse of water ahead of the plane. He said to himself, "That's the Prairie." The map had so labeled the wide flood plain where the Merderet joins the Douve. Then the green light flashed and he jumped. Tracer fire boiled up around him even as the chute opened and followed him down. He landed softly in two feet of water amid deep grasses. The fire kept coming. So he lay prone with his shoulders on a hummock and tried to work free of his harness. Amid the struggle, a large flight of carriers crossed the sky to the southward of him, and the tracers lifted to seek the larger target. Ten minutes after the drop he was mobile and splashing through the marsh not far from the landmark which the paratroopers later dubbed the "Gray Castle," though he still thought he was miles south of it on the Douve.

Suddenly a small blue light winked on amid the black of the horizon. His heart leaped up, for he knew the assembly beacon of his regiment. To his eye it looked nigh a mile distant but was in fact less than half of it. Then came the sharp command, "Halt!" It proved to be the voice of his own orderly, who had heard the splashing and was taking no chances. They went along together. Twice the walk was broken where the water shelved off sharply and they went in over their heads ... their introduction to the drainage canals which run roughly parallel to the Merderet.

Twenty men were already at the blue light when Lindquist got there. He could hear others splashing around in the marsh Runners were sent in all directions to round them up. They came back with a few members of the regiment, quite a body of 507th men and some artillerymen of Force "A." But the equipment checkup was dismal. The blue light had already gone out, short-circuited by the wet ground. Most of the supply bundles had been swallowed by the marsh, and of the three retrieved on high ground, only one had a radio.

One man spoke up: "While in the water I'm sure I saw a railroad bank just a little to the west of us." Hearing that, Lindquist for the first time knew his location. He said to the others, "Stay with me and we'll soon move that way." In this way was begun one of the major assemblies along the Merderet but on the wrong shore of it to nail down the bridgehead.

Gavin landed not far from Lindquist, but on solid ground within an apple orchard. Amid the trees cattle grazed contentedly. That they paid him no heed surprised him less than that they were not sleeping. Like Lindquist, he had looked out just before the green light went on and seen only an expanse of water. When he jumped, he had the same mistaken idea about where he was coming down. His descent drew rifle fire from the ground. Hardly out of his harness before he ran into his personal aide, Lieutenant Hugo V. Olsen, he collected his whole stick without leaving the orchard. The last few men were found at the edge of the big marsh. Some were in the water dragging supply bundles from the muck. Out beyond was the sound of splashing as new arrivals hit the lake. But there was no further sign of the enemy, though the banks were dug with foxholes and prepared gun positions.

Twenty minutes after the party assembled beside the marsh a red light shone from the far shore—the 507th's beacon. Then Gavin saw the blue light go on not far from it. Olsen was sent scouting for other men on their side of the water. In two hours he collected a force equal to a rifle company—all 507th men except for one planeload from the 508th. Returning, he told Gavin that he had seen a railroad embankment on the far shore and believed the men could make it by wading. Then for the first time Slim Jim knew where he was.

Heavy gunfire built up to the eastward. Gavin guessed that the sounds came from Ste. Mère-Église. At about 0430, Lieutenant Colonels Edwin J. Ostberg and Arthur Maloney, of the

507th, came into the orchard with 150 more men. On that impulse, Gavin decided tentatively that he must strike for the La Fière bridge and causeway and do it before full light. It was either that or face the ugly prospect of advancing 600 yards through a shallow lake in the face of enemy weapons after collecting more people. But if he moved toward the railway, he would be quitting ground on the decisive side of the river while risking full engagement merely to win the nigh side of a bridgehead. As a maneuver, that was doing it the hard way. But some instinct must have warned Gavin that there was not enough collectable American force west of the barrier to be sure of holding anything.

While he thus reflected, Lindquist was leading his 100 men to the railway bank. He had in mind the same object as Gavin. He knew that La Fière and the bridge were the mission of 1st Battalion, 505th Regiment. But he guessed that it, too, had been misdropped (in which he was wrong). If he got to the bridgehead and found 505th covering, he would move through it and try to get to Étienville, his own objective. Of that he had as little chance as a whisper in a whirlwind.

Except for the groups already mentioned, the 507th Regiment was virtually *hors de combat*. So far scattered were its sticks beyond the irruption area that for three days it remained uncollected. The designated drop zone was 1000 yards north of Amfreville. Not a single stick made it. One single Pathfinder Team made it, held the ground briefly and then faded away.

One of the most forlorn and frustrating missions of D-day fell to Lieutenant Charles Ames. He and half of his team came to earth at 0200 not more than 200 yards from the Amfreville Drop Zone. But the light men and their beacon were lost on the drop and never found. There remained to him his Eureka man, a wire man and the section sergeant. They tried unavailingly to find the others, so with time running out, at 0220 Ames sent up the Eureka. Then ten minutes later, he saw the serials carrying his regiment come on, fly directly over his head, go on and unload their human freight far, far to the eastward.

Then he guessed what had happened, and cursed himself, though it was not his fault. In the absence of lights, the Eureka is supposed to signal where the zone lies. The blip is on the grid while the carrier is near the DZ (drop zone). It goes down the scale during the approach. Winking out as the plane goes over, it rises again at a little distance. The pilots were puzzled that they saw no lights. Their few seconds of doubt until the blip rose again were enough to dissipate the power of the regiment.

After the second serial came over and went on, Ames stayed there one-half hour. Then machine-gun fire nipped at the field and he judged it time to withdraw and look for larger company. Some of the sticks which he had dreamed would form on him were now crawling half-drowned from the marshes. Others had far overshot the mark, and getting the green light after they had passed over the Division area, came down isolated in enemy country. Their problem became one of evasion and survival. When Ames walked out in the direction they had taken, he was one of the wisest men in Normandy—the first to know that the 82nd Division plan had fallen apart.

Lieutenant John H. Wisner, the regimental S-2 (intelligence officer), landed on the east bank of the Merderet, saw the railway bank and moved to it through the marsh. En route, he picked up 30 men from 507th's 2nd Battalion. He saw how the rail line was pulling forces together when nothing else worked. Men came crawling to it from the marshes on both sides. He gathered more and more of them in, until he counted 100. By then, he had come to Lindquist's assembly on the railroad. The two forces joined and the column marched on La Fière.

While only these few groups were shaking loose from the grip of the marsh and preparing to fight on the east shore, there remained in their sector, on the west shore, one considerable remnant of American infantry power within smelling distance of a magnificent once-in-a-lifetime strategic opportunity. Whether because of a mental aberration or a bad guess about the direction of the American attack when it came, the Germans had signally failed to mount guard over the west end of the La Fière bridgehead. There lay the defile, but they did nothing about it. Hours passed after the carriers came over and they knew the invasion was on, and they still had done nothing about it, though their garrison at Amfreville was mounted up, not more than five minutes' run by motor from the decisive spot. Their extraordinary blindness would be more noteworthy but for the like failure of the Americans, then and in the hours which too swiftly followed, to act as if they understood the supreme importance of the ground.

In time, that gentlest of generals, Charles J. Timmes, was to become one of the best-loved figures in the Army, schooled in the law, a master of the Russian language, and still a paratrooper. But he shakes his head mournfully when he recalls that day when a great victory was in his fist and he didn't squeeze.

Lieutenant Colonel Timmes, commanding 2nd Battalion, 507th, dropping into the marsh, was all but claimed by it. The wind had his parachute full billowed and he couldn't collapse it. So he was pulled willy-nilly across the surface, struggling hard, much of the time with his head under water. His body took soundings during this weird journey and the depths chilled him. But whenever he felt close to drowning, the chute yanked him into shallow water. Thus he coasted 20 minutes, covering perhaps 300 yards. He was delivered onto a canal bank just as the wind died. After this happy coincidence, he rested briefly, then shook free of his harness and looked about.

The first thing he saw was the rail bank on the far side of the marsh. There were sounds of firing north and south. From these signs, while still in the muck, he guessed exactly where he sat—one mile to the east of Amfreville. The brain was working all right.

Moving along the marsh fringe in search of men, he found ten of them, all of whom had been through an ordeal not unlike his own. They went on through the dark together. At about 0400, while they still moved indecisively along the west shore, wondering what to do next, two gliders landed just in front of them. From them, he gained ten more recruits. But the glider descent had drawn machine-gun fire and for the first time his band had to seek cover.

When it lifted, the band moved out with Timmes leading and just before dawn wandered into Cauquigny. Mark and underscore the name. It is but a flyspeck on the map, falsely denoting the presence of a village. There is really nothing to Cauquigny but an ancient church, wide open to the sky where the roof should be, the altar shattered, the rock walls partway down—this wreckage wrought by an air bomb. Next to it is the graveyard, gentled by a patina of moss and mold. The spot is quietly desolate but still somehow beautiful. Seeing it the first time, the casual visitor must feel invited to rest and meditate. But to believe that it is the key ground, the dominant position commanding great operations in war, overstrains the imagination.

Yet Cauquigny is to the west shore of the Merderet as is the Manoir de la Fière to the east shore—the elevated place near the approach and overlooking one end of a decisive bridgehead. There it lay for the taking by anyone prepared to dig in and hold till hell froze over. Nothing interrupted study of the scene by this first group of Americans to view it. There were no Germans in the vicinity. Had even one grenade been tossed at them, that might have changed everything; they would have deployed, and probably have stayed to fight it out on the right line. But it was too peaceful to be meaningful. So though they looked, they did not see.

Dawn had come. With it rose the sounds of firing from the direction of Amfreville. They say that a soldier should march toward the sound of the guns. The rattle carried by the wind spoke to Timmes that Americans—probably his own battalion—must be fighting to the westward. So he prodded his little band and they walked away from the bridgehead toward the noise of fury.

Going via the main road seemed too dangerous. So they veered north from Cauquigny church and went cross-country, sticking close to the lateral hedgerows, or walking along the parallel ditches. Stranded paratroopers were as common in the orchards as cows. They doubled their numbers as they moved along before, at a group of farm buildings, they picked up Lieutenant Louis Levy, of 507th, with 30 more men. So doing, unwittingly, they found a hero whose fighting career was to be brief but beautiful.

Timmes formed his column with flankers out, and all hands marching combat-ready so that they would be able to hit in any direction. He figured that at Amfreville he would be moving in on the flanks and rear of a German force already engaged frontally. On that assumption, he weighted both flanks, so that he might bring off envelopment in a rush. In this way are oft perfected those best-laid plans which have no relation to the situation.

Just outside Amfreville, Timmes ran into a platoon of 507th men. But they were also reaching for a far horizon and were determined to march to their assigned objective on the other side of the Merderet. So he let them go. Within ten minutes after they had moved off at right angles to his own line of attack, he was in trouble.

The Germans, dug in, were positioned behind the hedgerows on high ground just outside Amfreville. They broke the news with a volley of well-aimed rifle fire at close range. And though Timmes listened hard, he could hear no other fire. He heard several of his people cry, "Aid man! Aid man!" (There was none present.) Then as he prepared to maneuver, he suddenly realized that his preconception was wholly wrong. There were no other Americans fighting at Amfreville. All fire from the village was being directed at him.

From the church steeple and the house roof tops, machine guns began to bear on his thin line. As he saw it, he was losing control of his own force (the men had jumped for cover) and doing no hurt to the Germans. It was time to withdraw and he shouted the order. He had lost eight men. The four killed had to be left on the ground. The Germans followed his people out, one machine gun displacing behind them hedgerow by hedgerow, as the Americans tried to slip away.

By 0930, Timmes and company had gone into defensive position in the same orchard where seven hours earlier Gavin had dropped, one mile north of Cauquigny church. There was no need to urge the men to dig deep their foxholes right by the hedgerows enclosing their perimeter. Rifle and machine-gun fire was already raking that field. But the German skirmishers, while persistent, were few in number, and superior weapon power was with Timmes.

Because of this disparity, the group could have picked up and moved out during the morning. Timmes, reluctant to depart the assigned area altogether, made the wrong choice. By midafternoon, when he would have moved, it had become too late.

Gavin and force had tarried on the west shore longer than that commander ever intended because one thing after another had intervened either to delay movement or mock his purpose. Fate's unkindest cut was that during the two hours when Timmes maneuvered to Cauquigny church and out again, doubling and redoubling along the west shore, Gavin and force were always within five minutes' walk of him, with no Germans in between. Yet neither one heard or saw sign of the presence of the other. Had it been wide-open country, they would have inevitably attracted one another. But the hedgerows act as a sound barrier against human voice and the sounds of movement, just as by interrupting the line of sight, they make it all but impossible to know surely that fire comes from enemy, rather than friend. So union of forces came about on that morning more through happenstance than by contrived design. And there was so little of it, when compared with the many and disparate movement of small parties under independent command, that the game became like hunting elephants with a scatter-gun.

Some cat-eyed soldier brought Gavin the news that he could see a body of men (Lindquist's force) moving down the railroad on the far shore. He was sure they were Americans. Gavin was ready to take off and join them. But he held the order when he saw two gliders sail down and settle on his side of the marsh, not more than one-quarter mile away. That was like manna out of heaven. Until then the Gavin group had been able to retrieve but one bazooka and three bundles of ammunition. They were starving for radios and heavy weapons.

So the march to the far shore was postponed and Lieutenant Graham went forth with a patrol of six men to reconnoiter the gliders. He was back in 30 minutes, saying that he needed 30 more men, and he added, "a little less firing across the surface of the marsh." The gliders were down deep in the mud. Inside one of them was a 57-millimeter antitank gun, a jeep in the other. Graham came back in one hour after a vain tussle. He said his crew couldn't budge the equipment, the fire was getting steadily hotter, and he wasn't at all sure that it didn't come from American trigger-happiness.

This time Gavin went. He found the men gone to ground in the old German foxholes along the marsh edge. Yep, the fire was heavy. Colonel Maloney was left there with orders to rout them out and either complete the task or give it up. Maloney tried. It was no go. They couldn't lift the heavy machinery out of the bog. After the jeep was pulled from the glider, it settled into the ooze of its own weight, and all their pushing and tugging made no change. So they destroyed both pieces and high-tailed it back to Gavin.

By now it was bright day, the time being 0600-0630. The frustrating fight to save the gun—the one chance to get a heavy weapon—persuaded Gavin he had no choice about where to fight. To the same point was the story told by the men about the build-up of enemy fire along the marsh, though not a few

American parties moved along the edges of the marsh on both shores in these hours without bumping into any deployed Germans.

On the basis of the evidence, Gavin decided that the enemy was in such strength along the western bank that it was impossible to march toward Cauquigny and gather in the bridgehead from its offensive side. So the column—now numbering about 300 men—splashed across the marsh to the railroad, there to turn south and follow it into La Fière. It waded the water unmolested, not one shot being fired. It was Gavin's idea that he would gather up any troops he found around the Manoir and attack across the causeway from the east after loosening the German hold on the west end with massed fires— if that word fits any action which lacks artillery.

And right at this time, Timmes and company were rooting around in the churchyard at Cauquigny, finding not one German there and no sentry at the bridge. Not a weapon forbade their passage. Then when they turned north for their roundabout go at Amfreville, they still found no Germans anywhere near the shore.

In this lies the irony. Great battles, like epic tragedies, are not always staged or the product of human calculation, and disaster is less likely to derive from one gross blunder than from reasoned calculations which slip just a little.

2

Soft Fall amid Tension

Lieutenant Colonel Edward C. Krause embarked for the night drop wearing rabbit's feet shod with horseshoes. Then his guardian angel jumped with him and handled the risers on the way down.

This fool for luck saw the green T's which marked the jump field while in mid-air. He landed softly in a small, cone-shaped garden patch shut in by hedgerows. Before he could shake clear of his harness, 15 of his own men were at his side. So he knew he had it made—and how! The corner of the field where his boots first kissed Normandy soil was the same spot which he had fingered on the map when saying to his men, "Right there will be our assembly command post."

For him, it was a last-minute choice, but so was the 82nd's whole mission. Hardly a week before, its orders had been changed. By the belated shift, Ste. Mère-Église, the dairy center of a pastoral countryside, became vouchsafed a bright niche in the American pantheon.

The division was to have dropped still farther to the westward, extended to block enemy traffic to and from Cherbourg. Then in mid-May SHAEF intelligence got word that the German 91st Division had arrived in the area. That made the longer cast too much of a gamble. At the month's end came the less ambitious plan. It cut the gap between Ridgway and Taylor forces and teamed them to crush enemy resistance from Utah Beach west to the Merderet. One more headache for the American tactical planners, the make-over was a knife in the heart to the German 91st.

With revision, the capture of Ste. Mère swiftly became the touchstone of success in the division fight. Without the town as a base, the 82nd couldn't surmount the Merderet barrier and clear the road for Joe Collins's VII Corps advancing from Utah Beach. Ste. Mère was the district headquarters of the German Army, hub of a network of hard-surfaced roads and midway station of a trunk cable linking Cherbourg with Carentan and the coastal town of lower Cotentin. It was also protection. Built on fairly high ground of stone-walled stores and dwellings, the town dominated its approaches all around. The prospect was that the 82nd would fight there in isolation for at least one day. By plan, Krause & Battalion, of the 505th, drew this choice assignment.

He said to his 15 men, "Go to the DZ, divided into four small patrols; then fan out in different directions. Stay within six hundred yards. When you find men, send them back to me on azimuth. Be back in forty-five minutes."

One hour later he counted the collection. One hundred and eight fighters from his own battalion. One drunk Frenchman. Going beyond instructions, one patrol had netted him as he reeled homeward. The shock of being dragooned had sobered him. He walked straight, he talked straighter, and he knew everything Krause needed to hear.

"There is only one German company in the town—service troops, covering headquarters, motor park and supply dumps.

"One infantry battalion was quartered here until a week ago. Now it is camped on high ground south of the town."

Then the hostage to fortune spoke his brightest line: *"Si vous doutez, suivez-moi; je sais un sentier."* Krause jumped at the invitation; if the Frenchman had a pet path, let him lead on. He wouldn't be volunteering if it wasn't safe.

The force was formed into two companies, G and H. The Frenchman was put up with the point, Captain Walter De Long walking beside him. The men walked forward, hugging the hedgerows on either side of the trail. Heavy clouds over Ste. Mère made the night pitch-black. Getting no fire, they pushed right along. The veterans among them stepped out willingly. Krause could hear the older NCOs cussing out the new men

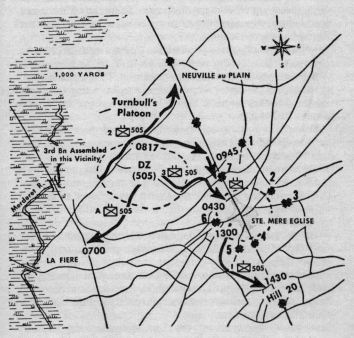

Figure 2. RIDGWAY'S BATTLEGROUND

for lagging; they tried to walk cautiously and kept their rifles at the on-guard position.

Thirty minutes after starting, they were in the outskirts of Ste. Mère. There Krause stopped them, saying, "I want no rifle firing until after daylight. Use grenades, knives and bayonets only." There was no good tactical reason for this, but it sounded hardboiled.

At the Montebourg road he pared off six small detachments. They were to move around the town and set up as many road blocks to east, west and north of it. That was a last-minute switch from his earlier calculation that he could depend on forces dropped nearer La Fière, Chef-du-Pont and Neuville to check the threat from these directions. Then with the Frenchman leading, the point slipped down the main road through the heart of town to establish the south-facing block. The main body trailed it as quietly as possible. As they took off, Krause told them, "Don't fight, if you can avoid it, for forty minutes; by then, we should have the road blocks set." Then unattended, he walked to the center of the sleeping town, found the cable point and hacked through the cable. That was one he wished to boast about later.

When it was done, so were the dark and the silence. He could hear rifles and machine guns going even as he saw first light. But by then, though he did not know it, all of his road blocks were set. Each member of the battalion had jumped with an M-1 antitank mine. Each carried a gammon (antitank) grenade. Enough bazookas had been retrieved to cover all blocks, which strengthened through the morning as additional men reported in.

But all hands felt a little let down. The big prize had fallen too softly. Cleanup squads went through the buildings; there was no house-to-house fighting. Having slept through the envelopment and penetration, the Germans snored on to be shaken from their beds. Thirty surrendered, eleven were shot dead and the uncounted remainder fled south through the dim light. Boringly efficient but hardly epic.

At 0500, Krause sent a runner to Regiment with this message: "I am in Ste. Mère-Église."

One hour later went a second runner with words more positive: "I have secured Ste. Mère-Église."

But Rowan didn't find the right Garcia. At the drop zone, he ran into General Ridgway and told him the news, without either saying that the message was intended for Colonel William E. Ekman or looking further for that gentleman. So Ekman continued in doubt.

By 0900, approximately 300 paratroopers were in Ste. Mère—more than enough to hold it. But because Ekman didn't know the situation there, things went awry.

According to plan, 505th's 2nd Battalion was to form a defensive perimeter at Neuville-au-Plain, giving Ste. Mère a buffer to the north. The commander, Lieutenant Colonel Benjamin H. Vandervoort, broke a leg on the jump and was being wheeled around in a small farm cart. By 0515, he told Ekman he had enough men to start, and was soon on his way. At 0616, being almost at Neuville, Vandervoort got a "halt in place" order from Ekman, no reason being given. At 0800, came a second message: "I've heard nothing from 3rd Battalion." At 0810, Vandervoort was told: "Turn back and capture Ste. Mère-Église." At 0816, came this: "Proceed to Neuville; I think 3rd Battalion is in Ste. Mère-Église." At 0817, the entry was completed: "Disregard the last order; move on Ste. Mère-Église." These stops and starts came of Ekman's quandary; he was still looking for light and not getting it, because of a lazy-minded runner.

Vandervoort turned in his gocart and led the battalion south. Then on hunch he hedged his bets. One strong platoon under a strong officer, Lieutenant Turner B. Turnbull, was detached from Dog Company and sent north to do the job at Neuville. Vandervoort said to him, "If there are Germans in the village, mop them up. Mine the road north of it. Set up a defensive position on the most favorable ground. Then hold."

So it was done. By the alteration of plan, Ste. Mère became doubly garrisoned and morale was uplifted. But it is impossible to find proof that the move was otherwise felicitous and conservative of Division power.

At 0930, Krause was counterattacked from the south by two infantry companies supported by three light tanks and two self-propelled guns. The thrust pointed at the southern road block. It was preceded by a dousing of mortar and machine-gun fire. Enemy skirmishers came down the main road herding cattle ahead of them for cover. Private Dominick de Tullio, in an outguard position beyond the block, after first turning the cattle into a field by waving his jacket (a gentle fellow), then grenaded the Germans who were driving the cows, killing one man, wounding a second and stampeding the rest. Krause rushed to the scene of fire. Seeing small groups of skirmishers swinging wide to get around the road block, he ordered more men up from the center of Ste. Mère to man the gaps between blocks. Then a shell fragment hit him in the lower right leg just hard enough to break the skin and pain like a double kick in the shin.

Vandervoort & Battalion arrived. He said to Krause, "It's your town; tell me what you want done." Thereafter they worked as a team, with Krause having the deciding voice. Vandervoort's strength was distributed around the perimeter where needed to round out the circle. Easy and Item Companies were kept as a mobile reserve inside the town. The arrival of this power and the accuracy of the American fire soon quelled the enemy drive from the south. Maintained two hours, it had failed to dent the outpost line.

But the heavy supporting fires did not diminish. From the direction of Hill 20, mortar and artillery shells, fired in salvo, continued to rock the town. Lieutenant William E. Wilson turned his own 81-millimeter mortars against it, getting off 70 rounds. But from Ste. Mère he had no line on the opposing batteries, because of the interposition of hedges along the high ridge. Looking down the main road, Krause saw a German convoy of five trucks moving toward the ground where he thought the enemy guns were based. He ordered Item Company to make a wide swingout to the right, then cut back to Hill 20 and deny its use to the Germans. It was easily said.

But orders uttered on impulse, rather than guided by reason, are seldom practical. Hill 20 afflicted Krause; therefore he wanted it out. The thing was as simple as that. He had, however, reckoned the German artillery strength at two batteries (probably an exaggeration). The Frenchman had told him an enemy battalion was camped to the south and he had estimated the German force in the counterattack at two rifle companies. The gun pits atop Hill 20 were so well obscured by the foliage that he could not judge where the German emplacements were centered. At the last moment he had seen a convoy moving fresh supply into the position. It might have been a routine assignment for a platoon of supermen, but it was far beyond the drive and cleverness of a tired, half-strength company of American paratroopers.

Still, Krause reacted in the traditional way. He was a better-than-average commander, and his ebullience won the admiration of his troops. Vandervoort had joined him at the last minute; he had the town, and an extra battalion was there to be used. If it even occurred to him that now was the time, deference still stopped him.

Item Company—80 men and five officers—went flankward to one-half mile west of the main road, then tried to cut back diagonally to the high ground where Krause had pointed. The difficulty was that in going out and cutting back, it took a zigzag course to conform to the lines of the embankments and ditches. Said one officer, "It cost time. Worse yet, we lost

sense of distance and direction. Almost two hours after the
start, we were back to ground next the main road one mile
south of town. That was far short of the goal. We discovered
too late that we were approaching on a line which put us directly
in front of the mortars we were supposed to be outflanking. It
was like a kick in the groin."

Coincidentally with the ranging-in of the mortar fire, Item
Company was hit from its right rear by well-aimed small-arms
fire. Captain Harold W. Swingler was killed by the opening
volley. Seven of his men were cut down. The formation temporarily dissolved as the men jumped for the banks and ditches.
For the better part of an hour Item Company stayed there
flattened not because the cross fire was prohibitively deadly
but because, after Swingler died, no other leader took the initiative to make the men move out. The wait itself drained their
energy.

Finally, the German mortars quit. It became safer to move,
and out of convergence the company found itself again. Slowly,
the men squared around and formed a fire line facing south
toward Hill 20. Two more tries were made to get at the Germans
by probing for weakness in the enemy left flank. Each was a
platoon effort made halfheartedly. The platoon which stayed
at base did not supply covering fire. These were attempted
sneak plays.

Both maneuvers were stopped and kicked back by enemy
fire before getting to the base of Hill 20. In each instance, the
attack tried to swing wider and wider around the German left
end and thereby squeeze out the local defense. But wherever
the Americans circled out and then cut back, the enemy skirmishers were out beyond them in blocking position. Getting
the nasty feeling that they were outnumbered and outwatched
by an omnipresent force, the attackers called to one another,
"They must be counterattacking." "It looks like they're trying
to encircle us." It was an illusion, but believing it made it real
enough. So they yielded the fight without really getting hurt.
The platoon fell back on the company. The company fell back
on Ste. Mère.

The irony was that they could have won their side of the
hill for a day by waiting a little longer and doing nothing. In
this fantasy, things happened as they did because both sides
were thinking much the same thoughts and falling prey to their
imaginations. The German battalion from Hill 20 was not trying

to devour Item Company; it, too, was getting out, bent on taking up new ground. The reason the platoon attacks couldn't get around the flank is that there wasn't one. The enemy formation was an extended column in movement, the front of which was already beyond the arc of the Item Company maneuver. The omnipresent skirmishers existed only in fancy; they were the Germans who deployed to fire positions to ward off the threat to their own retirement. The Germans on Hill 20 concluded by early morning of D-day that the Americans had taken Ste. Mère-Église in overwhelming strength; they decided that the north slope couldn't be held. Part of the force therefore shifted to the south slope to hold briefly while doing much damage; the rest of the garrison side-slipped to the westward and crossed the Merderet in late evening between the 82nd's half-formed bridgeheads at La Fière and Chef-du-Pont.

The distortions of the little picture typify the larger battle. Veterans who fought at Ste. Mère-Église today recall it as an affair of blood-and-iron, filled with shock, suspense and crisis amid the constant threat of being overrun. Battalion and company officers felt that way about it while they fought to hold Ste. Mère. But neither the vital statistics nor the play-by-play record bears them out. It was won and held in a series of small alley brawls, and wreaths of laurel cannot make them larger.

3

Turnbull's Platoon

There was nothing for Private Edward Easton to do but get to Neuville-au-Plain and get out again as fast as he could make it, putting one foot in front of the other until he heard fireworks or someone cried, "Hold!"

Easton was the first scout of Turnbull's platoon, and behind him followed 41 Americans. Spaced out in parallel columns which hugged the hedgerows off the shoulders of the road, they moved at a half-trot right through the hamlet and to a line 40 yards beyond the last house, where the rise on which the cottages nested fell off sharply. There Turnbull ordered a halt. The lieutenant was a half-breed, the best half being Cherokee; and what he wanted was ever all right with the rest of them because he spoke and acted like a fighting man.

On right of the main road, a hedgerow running at right angles to it and bordering an oat field was suited to Turnbull's purpose. From it, he could see 600 yards north along the road and had a clear view for the same distance on his right. The earth bank was as thick through as the body of a truck, as high as a man's shoulders and topped by heavy foliage. On left of the road an orchard of flowering apples sloped downward for about 200 yards to a farmhouse beyond which there was a sunken road and then cleared fields for about one-quarter mile.

Here was the chosen position, and it was good enough. Their one machine gun and the platoon's main body were

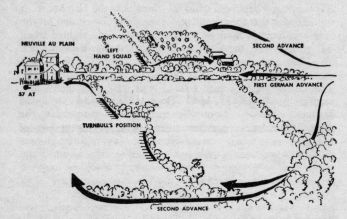

Figure 3. TURNBULL'S POSITION

spaced out behind the massive hedgerow. One squad was deployed to the left of the road. There was an ancient gate there flanked by a moss-grown stone wall, which was next to a manure pile. It made good resting. With one eye open, a rifleman reclining on the top could look forward through the gate and command the orchard. Just in case enemy armor should come from the north and break past the platoon line, a bazooka team (one man with a launcher and two riflemen to guard him) was sent back to the Neuville houses to serve as a road block. That was how they waited but their time was not long.

Not more than 20 minutes passed. The men behind the big hedge saw a company of Germans walking along the road toward them, in a column of twos, singing, whistling and carrying their weapons as lightly as if they were going to a Maypole dance. Turnbull's assistant, Lieutenant Isaac Michaelman, watched the approach for a minute or so nigh hypnotized, because it was so different from the way he had imagined the start of engagement. Then he crawled across the road to the squad behind the iron gate because he was worried that they would either miss it, or seeing it, would not take it seriously.

Under Michaelman, the squad advanced through the orchard 200 yards and deployed amid the barns next the farmhouse. It was his idea that they could stay there unobserved and hit the enemy column in flank as it came abreast. First sighted when 400 yards away, the Germans had almost drawn even when the squad took position. With Private Joseph C. Hudy, Michaelman moved to the loft of one of the barns for observation. That left Sergeant Robert Niland with four other men and a machine gun at ground level. They had been a mortar squad but had lost their weapons when the bundle blew up during the drop. The machine gun had been brought along in lieu of anything better, but it was not their dish of tea. Private Horace H. Brown handled it gingerly, withholding fire, awaiting the moment when the whole German company would be exposed broadside and he could blow it down with one traverse; such openings rarely arrive. His two covering riflemen, Privates John P. Slavierno and Harold Dunnegan, also held fire to permit Brown his big moment.

This tableau dissolved when the two squads behind the big hedge on the right of the road cracked down on the Germans. As the first bullet shattered the silence, the marchers dove headlong for the roadside ditches, whence they crawled to the hedges. But in the same instant occurred that which mystified Brown and his friends ever after. A bullet out of nowhere found Michaelman in the loft and drilled him neatly through both cheeks of his buttocks. Hudy yelled, "They got the lieutenant right through the tail." But the indignity to Michaelman was more easily suffered than the knowledge that they had all been suckered. In some way, while they had been arranging their surprise, the Germans had spotted them. Through gaps in the hedge Niland could see a handful of the enemy, from the rear of the column, racing across the fields on his side of the road as if to come at the squad from behind. He yelled the news to Brown, and the gunner fired four or five bursts in the direction he pointed, though he saw no targets. Private Stanley W. Kotlarz, who was covering the flank of the squad with a Tommy gun, out of sheer disgust because his weapon wouldn't carry the 200 yards to the enemy skirmishers, cried out, "Let's get the hell out of here!" Michaelman heard it, and the words hastened his decision to withdraw. He said, "We'll go back to the platoon," and he led off, hobbling along, using his carbine as a cane. An angling hedgerow covered their retreat.

At Ste. Mère-Église, Colonel Vandervoort had bested the handicap of his broken leg by borrowing crutches from a crippled French housewife. In a jeep taken from a glider, he rode to Neuville, with two 57-millimeter antitank guns in tow, guessing Turnbull might need them. It was a beautifully timed arrival. As he entered the hamlet, he could see his paratroopers on the road block frantically waving an orange flag forward—the friendly, welcoming sign. North along the road, Vandervoort could see what looked like a column of enemy troops.

"What are you doing?" he asked the signalers.

"Bringing them in," said one trooper. "This Frenchman here" (he pointed to a cyclist in civilian clothes) "just rode up to us. He was showing those other fellows the way. He says that's a body of German prisoners being brought in by an American detachment."

Before Vandervoort could parse this tall story, Turnbull's line opened fire on the "prisoners" with rifles, two machine guns and two BARs (automatic rifles), the Germans deployed to the ditches, Michaelman got hit through the tail, and in the excitement, the scurvy Frenchman got away. The enemy ruse—first casualty of the fight—was pretty clumsy, anyway. Vandervoort dropped one of the 57s at the Neuville road intersection. Then as he witnessed Michaelman's pullback, and feared it might mean that the whole line was cracking, he sent a runner to Turnbull, asking him, "How are you doing? Do you need help?" Turnbull returned the answer, "OK everything under control don't worry about me."

At that moment, facing his small group were 190 Germans. Yet the position on the high ground was snug. The squad on the left had refused its far flank slightly so as to cover the open fields in that direction. The AT (antitank) gun was sited to fire directly down the road and could blast anything from its surface for half a mile ahead. It was a respectable base of fire.

But even before Michaelman and squad got back to their gate, the platoon across the road felt the pressure rise. Mortar fire, in heavy doses, fell accurately along the hedge line, and though the bank and ditch were fair protection, there had been no time to dig foxholes. They could get no line on the mortar park; the big whammy seemed to come out of nowhere. That was what got them. A self-propelled gun appeared suddenly on the scene, sharp-shooting from 500 yards. Its second round knocked off the bazooka man on the road block. Its fifth round singed the 57 AT gun in Neuville and drove the crew to temporary cover amid the houses. In a few minutes, the crew came roaring back and with two well-placed rounds killed the German gun. Beyond it, looking through his field glasses, the gunner saw a Mark IV tank coming up. A few more rounds and it was hit and halted.

There was no equally ready answer for the enemy mortar fire. It built steadily upward, heavier in volume, increasing in accuracy. The first round which exploded into the line drew blood. Thereafter, hour by hour, casualties continued to mount, nearly all from the same cause.

The enemy wasted no time and lost no men trying to work the road. There was convenient cover on both sides of it. Confronting Turnbull's position, within a few yards of where the German column had been stopped, there is a large wood which runs obliquely southeastward until it comes almost even with the hedge covering Turnbull's men. This they made their main avenue of advance, but as they poked forward through the forest toward the American flank, they also sent out a small outflanking party far over on the left which stayed beyond reach of the American machine guns. (At more than 600 yards a gunner cannot see where the bullets are beating, and it is sheer accident when he delivers a killing or stopping fire.) The pincers in this broad envelopment moved forward together. While the mortars beat at the platoon, the infantry maneuver threatened that the survivors would be bagged whole.

Against the twin threat, Turnbull could do nothing but hold his ground, and simply by the act of holding, slow down the advance of the enemy toward Ste. Mère-Église. The shelling continued to thin the platoon's ranks. Its own return fire had no noticeable effect except to keep the flankers far out and make them move in a wider circle. That was the way the fight wore on through the morning and early afternoon. The advance was slow but even; on both flanks, it passed on beyond the American line. Still, Turnbull stuck it. By the time the enemy group working on the shorter bite and coming through the woods on the right was at the point of entering Neuville, the party which had moved out to the westward could, with one more bound, be across the platoon's line of retreat.

Signs that the noose was drawing tight came when the platoon line was hit by sniper fire from the Neuville buildings along its rear, and at the same time a machine gun cut loose on the hedge from among the barns forward which Michaelman had occupied earlier in the day. Private Clifford Keenan, a grenadier working on the right flank, turned to look at the Neuville houses where he thought the snipers were nesting. As he started to raise his carbine, he was shot dead by machine pistol fire.

Turnbull's men could see the forms of enemy riflemen wiggling along the ditches which ran next the hedgerows bounding their flanks. The nearest ones were not more than 60 yards away. But they were fleeting targets, and the mortar fire came in so steadily that the Americans couldn't prop to fire at them. Turnbull's force had dwindled to 23 men still capable of lifting a weapon. They were taking care of 11 wounded who were litter cases; the others were dead. The German fire had been beating on the asphalt of the roadway, barring evacuation of the casualties to Ste. Mère-Église. Now they were suddenly aware not only that the wounded were trapped but that it was probably too late to save anyone. The circle of enemy force was within 170 yards of closing to the rearward. Their last chance was slipping away while they looked at one another.

Turnbull pointed toward the enemy skirmishers crawling in the ditches. He yelled out to his men, "I have heard about spots like this. We're surrounded. That leaves one thing to do. Hit them in the center. So we charge them."

One private spoke up. "Sir," he said, "I'm ready."

Private Joseph Sebastian had just come back from prowling the right flank. There he had talked to Corporal Joseph Tremel, who had been with Keenan when he died. Tremel had said to him, "Some of the krauts are in the houses, but most of them are still one hedgerow short of it."

So Sebastian spoke up, saying to Turnbull, "I think you're wrong. We're not quite cut off yet. There's a chance that we can get out. And that's what we ought to do."

His protest shook Turnbull and he yelled out to the others, "What about it? Tell me what you want to do."

They chorused back, "He's right. Let's get out. There's still time."

So in a twinkling they got set. Turnbull said, "We'll have to leave the wounded."

Corporal James Kelly, the aid man, spoke up: "I'll stay here with the wounded and surrender them if I can keep from getting killed." Turnbull nodded. There were some weapons far over on the right which he knew he must abandon; the German skirmishers were now closing with a rush.

Then up spoke Sebastian again, saying, "I talked you into this withdrawal; OK, so I stay here and cover Kelly and the others with my BAR."

There wasn't time to argue with him. Sergeant Niland started toward one of the machine guns, intending to stay with Sebastian, along with Corporal Raymond Smitson, who, saying nothing, had taken his place beside the wounded, carrying a sack of hand grenades. Before he could touch the weapon, Niland was shot dead by a German who rushed him with a machine pistol.

Someone screamed, "Let's go! For Christ's sake, let's go!"

They went out at a dead run—16 of them all together—each man feeling certain that he would be shot down before he had moved a dozen steps.

But though they did not know it, there was help at hand. Getting back to Ste. Mère-Église after his quick reconnaissance, Vandervoort couldn't get the platoon out of his mind. Salvation came of his worry. Someone else in the command dispatched a runner to Turnbull saying that he should hold until he saw a white flare signal rise above Ste. Mère-Église. But that word was not passed to Vandervoort, and Turnbull had fought on through the fire-swept afternoon and into the evening, still looking vainly for the white flare. Sweating along with him, feeling at last that Turnbull's time had run out, Vandervoort ordered a platoon from Easy Company, 505th, to speed to Neuville and hold the back door open if the Turnbull force still lived.

Turnbull did not see the friendly force arrive. It reached the center of Neuville and deployed beyond the houses west of the road in the same minutes that he prepared his men to cut and run. In their flight, the 16 survivors dashed past this line with such speed that they missed seeing it. But they owed their escape to its lunge and to the covering fire from Sebastian and Smitson, who were captured. Turnbull's men ran all the way to Ste. Mère-Église. Nothing was said until they pulled up winded except an occasional cry from a noncom, "Keep scattered!" Having fired until Turnbull's party swept past, the Easy platoon also picked up weapons and ran clear out of range before the Germans could form and fire from the ridge of high ground running through the hamlet.

By its all-day stand, Turnbull's handful had kept the Ste. Mère-Église force from being hit simultaneously north and south during the most critical hours of D-day. Turnbull, who had been ready to stage his own little Balaklava at Neuville, but had been saved from it by Private Sebastian, gained this much from the respite—a few more hours in which to fight before death took him in action.

4

The Affair on Hill 30

As the plan so very neatly put it, all the 508th Parachute Regiment had to do was to drop in a body and gain control of the strategic ground in the angle formed by the Douve and Merderet rivers, where the waters meet en route to the sea.

The bridge crossing the Douve at Étienville was to be destroyed at once for protection, while offensively the regiment seized the causeway crossing of the lower Merderet for the swift passage of VII Corps in its advance westward from Utah Beach to cut the Cotentin Peninsula and isolate Cherbourg. The southern causeway at Chef-du-Pont, two miles distant from La Fière, is the main crossing, a broader and more solid roadway, affording entry to a much wider and more decisive area. It had to be the main concern of the regiment.

So it was planned that the 508th, dropping west of the Merderet and north of the Douve, would rendezvous on Hill 30, a steeply rising and orchard-crowned knoll overlooking the Chef-du-Pont causeway one mile distant. It was appleblossom time in Normandy and the flowering branches closed off all observation from this high ground, robbing it of military advantage. But soldiers ever seek high ground by habit.

The plan was frustrated by the bad drop which came of the beauteous sky and the fears of men. Some carriers became lost in the cloud bank. Others strayed because they disobeyed orders, taking evasive action to avoid a moderately heavy flak.

By two hours past midnight the 508th was far dispersed as it stood to jump into enemy country.

In consequence, most of the regiment dropped on the wrong side of the river and northward of the north crossing. Colonel Leroy Lindquist, the commander, set himself the task of collecting a part of his scattered force from the marshes bounding the Merderet and striking for the nearest object—La Fière.

By an odd twist, this undid the careful work of the one part of the carrier formation which had served the regiment faithfully and well. The serial carrying the 3rd Battalion had missed the cloud bank and ignored the ground fire. It flew undeviatingly to the drop zone, just northward of the village of Picauville, and its sticks unloaded at just the right second, to float down right on the button. So doing, they dropped into ground where, despite their best effort, they were to remain isolated during the four decisive days when the airborne forces were laying a carpet for VII Corps into the heart of Cotentin.

But the battalion's people momentarily felt nonetheless lost when their feet struck solid earth. Their commander, a youthful West Pointer, Lieutenant Colonel John B. Shanley, during his descent had seen the bundle light drop past him at the speed of a rock. He knew that its chute had failed to open. Still feeling his disappointment as he shook loose from his harness, he looked about him and saw the light gleaming in the distance. Making his way to it, he found that everything else in the bundle had been smashed to bits, but by a small miracle the light had survived the fall undamaged.

Eight of his men were already gathered around the light when he got there. They together decided that the ground was too low for the beacon. So the party moved out, looking for the nearest hill. When they found it, Shanley shinnied to the top limb of the one tall fir on its crown and there fixed the bundle light, tying flashlights to other branches until one man shouted, "They'll see it; it looks like Christmas."

Soon there were 30 men with him. He set the original eight for an all-around defense of two fields next the spangled fir. It was a simple outposting; where a cart trail cut through a hedgerow, there stood an American covering the portal with his hand weapon. The rest of the force was divided into five patrols and deployed to round up other men. Each party was sent forth on an azimuth or toward a specific hill or cluster of farm buildings with instructions that it would return to the position at a designated hour. As additional men were brought

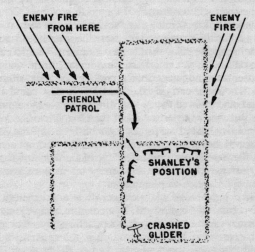

Figure 4. SHANLEY'S FIRST SKIRMISH

into the ground, they were distributed around the bordering hedgerows.

Of heavier weapons, dropped in the bundles, the patrols were able to retrieve only one machine gun. But help seemed to come to them out of heaven at the most propitious moment; an American glider sailed down and came to rest on the edge of one of their fields. They had watched its descent breathlessly after the C-47 which had it in tow had exploded directly over their heads.

Now they rushed it, certain that it was loaded either with heavy weapons or troops. But inside were only the pilot and his cargo—a baby bulldozer, than which Shanley needed nothing less. The pilot picked up a carbine and joined the defense.

Within the first hour one patrol got back with the word that it had reconnoitered the fringes of a nearby village which it took to be Picauville. Shanley, still uncertain of his position in relation to the drop zone, went the way the patrol had gone, took a bearing on a church steeple, and satisfied himself that he was standing on just the right ground. While walking back to his men, he stumbled across two bundles, one of which supplied him with a bazooka and the other with a command radio.

During all of this time, there was a German force of three infantry companies, one battery of artillery and four medium tanks in Picauville. They had been called out when the carriers came over and they knew they were under attack. One stick of paratroopers had jumped right into their bivouac area. Several of the Americans had been shot before they could unharness, and others had scrambled out of their clutches to temporary safety. But while the dark lasted, the Germans made not the slightest move against the forces assembling outside the village, reacting as if they were paralyzed by fear. This was not unusual. In fact, there is not one single example of German troops acting counter-offensively against the Americans in the night drop, though opportunities were numerous.

As first light broke, the position drew a scattering small-arms fire from the southward. It seemed to Shanley that this first contact came of enemy patrols punching in to feel out his location. Not more than a dozen rifles had spoken. Shanley judged that the nearest Germans were two fields away. But he had no idea of their numbers. So to save his scant ammunition, he ordered his men to fire only when they had a clear view of a live target, which was seldom. In this desultory manner, the action wore on for several hours, the enemy failing to press his advantage, and Shanley waiting and hoping to raise more strength before risking a full engagement.

Around midmorning, the German skirmishers began to press down along the hedgerows, and an accurate fire fell on the American foxholes, coming from the left flank. In time with it, a first friendly voice came over the SCR 300 radio. Lieutenant Norman McVicar had assembled 60 men in a field one mile northeast of Shanley. One of Shanley's patrols had wandered into McVicar's position, and McVicar at once set about raising Shanley on his own set. Shanley said, "You stay where you are, and I'll move to you."

By high noon the arrangements for this movement were complete, and Shanley was ready to give the order, sweating because by this time the Germans were extending their advance on both flanks. Then at the last moment he had to hold his hand. Approaching his left front, crouching low by the hedgerows, and apparently unaware of his presence, he saw another party of Americans. Shanley sang out to his men, "Direct all fire to the left!" He figured that he could pin the Germans on that side and that under the covering fire the friendly force could dash past the enemy and enter his lines.

Instead, as he opened fire, the approaching Americans returned it with all weapons, and two of his men were hard hit by the first volley. There was a quick waving of orange flags from within Shanley's lines, and the patrol, getting the friendly signal, came into the field on a dead run. It had been sent out on a general scouting mission by yet a third group of 508th men under command of Major Shields Warren, Jr., which was in motion not far from McVicar.

The concentration of fire toward the left to cover the patrol had had the unanticipated effect of cooling the German advance along that flank, and Shanley decided on the spur of the moment to make his withdrawal that way. It would pull him away from his assigned task—the blowing up of the Douve bridge at Étienville—but his force was small and he hoped that by joining the McVicar and Warren groups, he might pick up heavy weapons and explosives, lacking which there could be no demolition.

So the force started on its way, leaving behind ten of its number and one medical officer, all of whom had been either crippled during the jump or wounded in the action. They were dead weight and would have encumbered the party; the doctor was left behind to surrender them to the enemy.

Not until the moment when they stepped out, Shanley leading, was it seen that the glider, on settling to earth during the night, had blocked their only rearward exit from the two fields. Elsewhere on the left and rear boundaries the hedgerows and embankments rose solidly. Their thorned foliage was far too thick for there to be any thought of penetration.

The glider was too heavy to be moved. Shanley saw that the only escape was through the glider. One man at a time, they would have to run for it, climb into the door on one side, and exit on the far side. It would entail a terrible delay in the very moment when safety lay in swift movement. Shanley yelled out, "That's it; get going!"

The minutes dragged out. The force was halfway through this weird defile before the Germans on the right discovered what was happening and concentrated fire on the glider door.

Then the trickle of men stopped and Shanley, who was already in the clear, went back through the glider to see the cause. He found that the remaining men had formed a fire line inside the hedgerow and had abandoned all idea of trying to make the glider passage. He walked down the line, booting each man hard in the tail and yelling, "Get up! Move!"

Seven or eight jumped up and wiggled through the bull's-eye while bullets popped the frame. The others showed signs of following, and Shanley guessed—wrongly—that if he took off, they'd trail after. The others from this hesitant rear guard were never seen again. Whether they quit in the field or were shot going through the glider remains unknown. At least their presence stalled the Germans and from beyond the glider the withdrawal proceeded unharassed.

Hugging the hedgerows, Shanley's column marched to a point one-half mile east of Picauville. There it was stopped short by the spectacle of 200 American paratroopers sitting together in an open field doing absolutely nothing. No one had taken command. No orders had been given. So this considerable body of men had merely loafed for about twelve hours waiting for someone to happen along and tell them how to get started.

Shanley now divided his total force into three platoons, moved it to a promising hilltop and set up an all-around defense. He figured he had enough manpower for the mission, but for the rest of it, he had added only one .50-caliber and three .30-caliber machine guns to his heavy weapons array, and he still lacked explosives.

The time had come when he had to know what he would be up against if he pushed eastward to the Douve bridge. Four patrols were sent out, two to cut all wires in the vicinity, and the others to round up Frenchmen for information. They got what they went after. One farmer told them about the large German force garrisoning Picauville. Another said, "They're far stronger at Étienville and they're dug in." It was still early evening and Shanley's own force was continuing to build up. The Warren and McVicar groups had found one another, and after a brief brush with enemy skirmishers, had entered Shanley's lines. Even so, he doubted that he was strong enough to go against Étienville. He had not made radio contact with either the regiment or the other battalions. From the shreds of information supplied by the men he concluded that the drop had scattered the regiment far and wide and that there were no

American forces to west of Étienville save his own. (See end-paper map.)

This, as all subsequent information proved, was an inspired guess and it prompted an ineluctable decision—that he would proceed on the only mission given 508th which remained within his means, advancing to the high ground overlooking the Merderet River and the Chef-du-Pont causeway. Had he moved headdown against Étienville, his battalion would have been wiped out.

At 2100, Shanley organized his force into two companies, with Warren leading one and himself the other. In a two-hour march they got to Hill 30 without incident. It had looked fairly promising on the map. From the hillcrest there should have been a commanding view of the valley, the two causeways and Chef-du-Pont village. But the reality of the ground belied the promise. Hill 30 was crisscrossed by hedgerows of a particularly obtrusive sort. They were high-banked and thickly sown with tall shade trees. Also, the orchard ringed the crest. From the top of Hill 30, one had no sense of being on high ground. The world was closed off beyond the first fence. It was a favorable place for rendezvous, for it was plainly marked and dense with cover. But with the trees in leaf, it commanded nothing.

That night Shanley roughly shaped a position which he coordinated fully the next morning. His own company was formed in a crescent around the northern slope of Hill 30. Warren's was deployed so as to cover the approaches from the south. Thus disposed, Shanley's line was facing toward La Fière and Ste. Mère-Église a few miles distant, where already the main lodgment of the 82nd Division was under full siege. But the wind blew wrong to carry the news, and the oppressive silence atop Hill 30 stayed unbroken. Given the one situation wherein soldiers would be cheered by the noise of cannonading, Shanley couldn't raise any higher headquarters on his radio. For all that he and his men knew, they had become a lost outpost in an invasion which had failed. Yet while the quiet began to grip them, their sense of isolation was not complete, and their spirits stayed reasonably high. Their own affairs had gone well and they had suffered no real hardship.

The night was uneventful. On the second morning six patrols were sent out to look for supply bundles and clear the vicinity of enemy forces. Another group of strays from the battalion, bringing three machine guns, was led back to the hill.

This augmentation of strength encouraged Shanley to think of new enterprises, the opportunity for which was already at hand. On the SCR 300 radio, he heard from a friendly group on the far side of the Merderet that it had the Chef-du-Pont end of the causeway under control. All that he knew was that it was an American force of unknown size; more than that could not be put on the air. But as an aid to them, and as additional protection for himself, he decided to throw a road block across the highway running parallel to the Douve south of Hill 30. The block would face both ways, opposing enemy forces attempting to move east over the mile-long causeway, or coming against Hill 30 from either direction.

Yet curiously, when that block went into position that evening, while the block at Chef-du-Pont held, the Americans still did not have command of the southern bridgehead. Halfway across the marsh the causeway from Chef-du-Pont branched, its lower arm extending south into enemy territory around Beuzeville-la-Bastille and Montessy, on both sides of the Douve River. There was enough tree cover along the causeway so that enemy skirmishers from the two villages could move back and forth from the solid ground to the trunk of the upper causeway, which the Americans were attacking from both ends. The balance of forces was such that neither side was strong enough to dislodge the other, and thereby win the bridgehead.

One consequence of this unique deadlock was to confuse American thinking at the higher levels on a main question: Should the attitude toward the crossing be offensive or defensive? Shanley, sitting on the west bank, had already made up his mind. He was camped on the far side of a decisive bridgehead, and there he had to remain, since if he advanced his force to the nigh side, the Germans might blow the passage behind him, and the right of way might not be won again. It was his job to force the U.S. Army to march to him and to endure what he must until it did.

But to hold his ground, Shanley figured, he would have to keep the battalion buttoned up tight. Here's the shining example of the soldier acting defensively while thinking offensively.

On the other hand, the Americans on the Chef-du-Pont end of the causeway, having been badly mauled by the Germans on the first day, now wanted to blow up the Merderet bridge to keep the enemy from surging back. That would have can-

celed Shanley's purpose and changed his force from a linchpin
to a derelict.

There was one exception. A member of Shanley's battalion,
Second Lieutenant Francis J. Bolger, having dropped on the
wrong side of the river, had joined the group at Chef-du-Pont.
Hearing a division staff officer give the order to blow up the
bridge, Bolger decided on his own that the order was wrong
and immediately called Shanley by radio.

Because of Shanley's vehement protest, the order was first
suspended then later canceled. By that margin—a shavetail's
willingness to dispute higher authority—the bridge was saved
and was ultimately used to get the 90th Infantry Division and
other corps troops across the Merderet barrier.

Even so, Shanley was taking a shot in the dark. He was
still without knowledge of the general situation and had no
contact with higher headquarters. In these circumstances, it
might be a fair question whether his firmness about keeping
the bridge open came from a self-generated optimism or more
correctly from a reluctance to see destroyed the only link between himself and the one American party from which he had
heard.

The considerations were, in fact, joined. At this time, though
Shanley did not know it, his was the only American force being
employed tactically to the west of the Merderet. Elsewhere,
except for a few isolated and immobilized groups which were
simply awaiting rescue, the American forces had failed and the
enemy was in solid possession of the countryside. By instinctively camping on the objective, he was in fact fighting the
corps battle. But it was a close question whether, in the circumstances, he could hold out long enough to do the corps any
good. Word of his position had been relayed to Division. But
such were the pressure and flux of the hour, and so befogged
the view of stakes and forfeits, that the G-2 (military intelligence) rated Shanley's people a "lost battalion," a cipher in
the fighting situation, needing help but helping nothing.

That night the regimental commander jeeped to Chef-du-
Pont and talked to Shanley on radio. Lindquist agreed with
everything he had done and told him to continue holding Hill
30. It was easily said and hard done.

Ammunition was low. Food was nearly gone. Of medical
supply, the battalion had only personal first-aid packs. Casualties were mounting rapidly. The Germans had closed in.

The top of Hill 30 was getting an intense dousing of mortar fire from an attack pressed against the northern face of the perimeter. Rifle and Schmeisser fire bit at the foxhole line from the first hedgerows beyond.

The situation called for a quick toss of a lifeline from the east.

5

The Milling Crowd

In the advance of Able Company, 505th Parachute Regiment, against the La Fière position, there was nothing either accidental or casual.

It was the company's assigned target. Well set up for it, they moved to the mark, straight as an arrow. Never was an airborne unit more highly favored by fortune at the start.

The company parachuted to earth on the same drop zone serving the two battalions which were to fight in Ste. Mère-Église. Its assembly was the most perfect show in Operation NEPTUNE. Despite the dark, all but two men were accounted for within 60 minutes after the jump. They gathered while on the move, and the first squads were already under arms and marching toward La Fière when the last sticks hit the field. Faultless briefing by their own commanders and faultless performance by the carriers accounted for this phenomenon.

The spearpoint got to within 300 yards of the La Fière bridge. There at the road crossing east of the Manoir it came under sniper fire from its left flank. Then from somewhere among the farm buildings a machine gun opened up, and its first burst kicked up dust at their feet. After the men jumped for cover, Lieutenant George W. Presnell led one squad far over to the right, almost to the bank of the river, then tried to slip them leftward one at a time for a go at the farm buildings. Their maneuver had put them in defilade from the opening

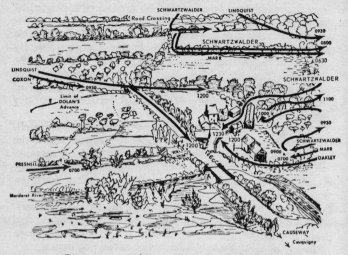

Figure 5. MOVEMENT AROUND THE MANOIR

enemy fire, and they figured they were on line to grenade the machine gun from in rear. Presnell pulled the pin and got ready to throw. At that moment a second machine gun opened fire from somewhere near the bridge.

Presnell hurled his grenade, more to get rid of it than from any assurance that he had the range, and in the same breath yelled to his men, "We'll have to get out." The weapons display had convinced him that discretion was the better part of valor; it was certainly no task for a squad.

But as he fell back on the company's greater strength, he contented himself with the twin reflections that he was the first man to have a go at the target and that he had made a satisfactory reconnaissance. This made his illusions complete.

A scout that morning wiggling along the several torturous approaches to Manoir de La Fière might have revealed a unique and discomfiting situation, had he but lived to tell it. Parties of fighting Americans were already pressing toward the same target from all directions, and at least one of them had already closed on it, engaged and shed blood. Not one was co-ordinated with any other, and none early sensed the presence of other Americans fighting in the vicinity. Of this lack of concert came much of the bitter hardship and unnecessary loss.

Again the boxlike compartmentalization of the countryside thwarted unity of action more direly than German fire. By shutting off sight and sound, the hedgerows worked for the defenders, multiplying their limited weapon power. La Fière is probably the bloodiest small struggle in the experience of American arms. But enemy numbers did not so make it. They were indeed few.

The ground itself must take its share of blame. But not all. In the nature of the circumstances, the Americans came to the contest piecemeal. Each element, apart from Able Company, 505th, was probing its way into an uncertain situation, unbriefed. There was never a time when the American side knew its own strength. The group-by-group character of the onfall, which occurred only because so many sticks had been misdropped in the vicinity of La Fière, enabled the enemy to deal with it in detail. Radio communication, which would have clarified the confusion, had been drowned in the marsh.

But there had escaped, by virtue of a lucky landing on the solid ground to the east of the railroad, a captain, then undistinguished, but several years later famed as Ben Schwartzwalder, of Syracuse, who became a national name because he took a football squad composed of indifferent material and by his genius created out of it a national collegiate champion. His eye was naturally attracted by straight lines, whether they were wooden uprights, the ten-yard markers of a greensward or the more carefully laid steel of a railroad right of way. So he moved by instinct to the embankment and there took over 44 men mainly of his own regiment—the 507th—who had won their scrimmage with the marsh. His gridiron of that early morning was crying for a coach who would sit back, watch the field and the players, determine where the defense was weak, then set up his own plays and let someone else carry the ball. But that was not his mood or mission. Someone higher up was running the show. In the absence of signals, he was a back raring for a plunge straight through center, and he didn't care a damn about cross bucks or Statue of Liberty plays. The opposing line was there; so blow the whistle.

Schwartzwalder's team first huddled just to the north of La Fière. It marched about 300 yards. There on the southern side

of the "Y" where two roads met near the Manoir, it was brought
in check by a heavy machine gun. Lieutenant John W. Marr,
who was leading the point 150 yards ahead of the main body,
looked back and saw that the company had stopped. When men
have gone to ground, a point becomes useless unless it can kill
the fire which has diffused and immobilized the main body.
Marr knew that. He swung his people far over to the left in
the hope that by coming at the Manoir from directly south he
could get at the gun which had stopped Schwartzwalder. So
moving, his group dropped behind the hedgerow closest to the
river. There fire broke around them from a number of positions
within the walled grounds of the Manoir. It was much too hot.
Marr yelled, "Follow me!" and led the point back to the company, his men running bent over and blessing the hedgerow
banks.

As they withdrew, the German gun which had made the
skirmish line flatten displaced forward hedgerow by hedgerow.
Its fire began to beat around Schwartzwalder at close range.
He ordered his men to attack along the hedgerow. They obeyed.
The gun and crew withdrew over the same line along which
they had advanced. The company accomplished nothing but
the killing of one sniper. But by this follow-through, the company got to the same ground where, a few minutes before, the
point under Marr was checked and turned back.

They were trail blazers on what was to become a beaten
path toward the causeway—the high road to American success—and in that precious moment it was also the key ground
to a juncture of force which might have clinched it cheaply.
For it occurred to Marr, as he watched, that half of the enemy
fire was being directed toward the opposite flank, though he
had no way of knowing that this was because the spear of Able
Company under Presnell was attacking from the opposite side.
It did not comfort him later to know that Presnell felt the same
sweat but lacked the hunch.

Schwartzwalder ordered Marr to move forward along the
nearest hedgerow and head for the stone wall bordering the
road leading to the La Fière bridge. Four men went with him.
Two were shot through the legs by a machine gun firing from
ten yards away as they dived toward the hedgerow. All went
flat. Technician Fifth Class Escobar, one of the wounded, cut
loose with his Tommy gun on the German position as he hit
the dirt. A German rose out of the ground with his arm cocked

to heave a potato masher. Corporal Lawton drilled him with his carbine. The German, not finished but wobbling, struggled to get the grenade away. Lawton and Private Parletto flung grenades right together. Their bombs wiped out the gun and three Germans. By then machine-pistol fire had made untenable the ground where the five men lay. Lawton, still looking for trouble though he was bleeding from two bullet wounds, shot a German officer who was casually regarding the scene through binoculars from beyond the La Fière bridge. Marr couldn't take what Lawton was going through. Convinced that already he had lost too much blood, Marr carried him out on his back with the rest of the point following.

Schwartzwalder and his people were two hedgerows to the rear. Of the diversion on their right flank—the first thrust forward by Able Company—they knew nothing. If the psychological moment had come and gone, they were unblissfully unaware.

The ground to the immediate south and east of the Manoir buildings—a terrain partly pasture, partly orchard and partly truck garden—is extremely irregular. The side road cutting in through the Manoir and used principally in servicing the establishment is bounded on the north by several large knolls, and on the south by orderly rows of large mounds, shaped not unlike the kitchen middens of Florida or the tells of the Middle East. The complex is crisscrossed by hedgerows. It was through these small hillocks and their surrounding hedges that Schwartzwalder made the first bid of the morning to seize the eastern end of the causeway. From the railway line westward the battleground rolls gently for a few hundred yards, then falls off sharply to the Merderet. Of this configuration, the unimpressive-looking mounds became a mass imposing itself between the flanks of any force attempting to envelop the Manoir position. The bulk of the Manoir itself compounded the difficulty. Here were not the usual French farm buildings. Massive stone-walled affairs, they average four stories in height, houses and barns. Where the buildings are not directly joined, they have connecting stone walls, higher than a man. The effect is like fighting on both sides of a block of apartments so stoutly built from foundation to outworks that heavy mortar fire could scarcely scar it. None but a very large force, perfectly joined, could bring off an envelopment of the Manoir from the eastward without risking rupture between the two flanks. These conditions were not present that morning.

Held for downs, Schwartzwalder took time out, still unaware, when on the other side of the property Presnell took his pasting and retired to the wings of Able Company, moving up under a born fighter, Lieutenant John J. Dolan. In that interlude, Slim Jim Gavin arrived on the scene, in the van of his band of 300. At La Fière village, while all was quiet, he talked briefly to Major Kellam, commanding 1st Battalion, 505th. Lindquist and party were not yet in contact with any of these forces.

Not yet knowing about the recoil, Kellam told Gavin that Able Company's point had worked forward almost to La Fière bridge. Kellam said, "We are lightly opposed, and I expect to have this position within one hour." It was a correct premise reasoned to a wholly wrong conclusion.

But on the strength of that report Slim Jim decided that his own duty was to head south just as fast as possible. The future U.S. Ambassador to France was not that day blessed with intuition. Chef-du-Pont had become the big question mark in his mind. What was happening there and around Hill 30, where the 508th Regiment was supposed to concentrate, had to be determined at once by personal reconnaissance. Lindquist, 508th's commander, and the people he had collected from the marsh were somewhere in the La Fière vicinity. That, at least, Gavin knew. Could his eyes but have penetrated the hedgerows, he would have seen Lindquist and Party at that moment working through the fields and along the hedges west of the railway with the object of attacking the Manoir from the southeast. But the fact that he was there somewhere spelled to Gavin that there was sufficient force present around La Fière to carry the day. That made it the less likely that anyone was rallying at Chef-du-Pont. So the men from 507th who were with Gavin seemed most available for the task at the other bridgehead. Aching for a fight, the force under Ostberg and Maloney was already swinging toward the La Fière bridge position while Gavin talked to Kellam. It took him some time to extricate them, re-form and get on the road to Chef-du-Pont.

In marching to La Fière, Lindquist, crossing Able Company's line of advance, had tried unsuccessfully to find Dolan. But someone in that unit told him, "We're attacking on the right side of the main road." Inaccurate information. Lindquist decided, on the strength of it, to advance his own force on the left of the road, thereby extending the general line.

The body was still in march column, off the road and hugging the parallel hedgerow, when it reached the road fork 200 yards east of La Fière bridge. There it came under machine fire from a gun near the river. One look at the foreground convinced Lindquist that the field of fire for the weapons defending the Manoir was so clear that farther advance on that line was prohibited. He pulled his forces back about 100 yards into defilade, organized them in columns of companies and then sideslipped them about one-quarter mile to the left so that his attack would go against the Manoir from south of the service road which wound down through the farm buildings.

Through this maneuver, his men became deployed in the area of the mounds, where a maze of hedgerows, in combination with the hillocks, promised advantageous cover for the advance of the skirmishers.

But these movements, made without Able Company's having any knowledge of them, effectively divorced Lindquist's force morally and physically from the undertakings on the right flank during the next few critical hours. Not more than 300 yards of compartmented fields separated the two commands at any time. Yet Dolan's company fought on through the morning without ever getting a sense that it was being helped or supported. Not one man in Able Company knew that any other American force was attacking the Manoir.

Though senior on the ground, Lindquist did not take command. He was filling in with an ill-assorted remnant at someone else's party and could not even know that he was senior. On the other hand, Kellam, whose battalion was supposed to capture La Fière, had only one company present, the others having been misdropped and scattered. So he properly left the tactical direction to Dolan. Because of these things, the attack remained uncommanded, unjointed, until near noon, when Matt Ridgway, jeeping into La Fière from his command post near Ste. Mère-Église, took one look. He forthwith directed Lindquist to take command and clean things up—which he did.

In the intervening hours, the advance of Lindquist's men through the hillocks had been tediously slow and unspectacular. They acted worn out. Harassed by a few snipers and an occasional burst of automatic fire, they succeeded only in raising that degree of caution which keeps down losses.

But over on the right Able was hurting. After Presnell had been kicked back, Dolan tried to soften the Manoir by smacking it with 60-millimeter mortar fire. The rounds got in there all right; but it was as futile as bouncing split peas off a tin helmet. When the bang-bang failed, Dolan thought of envelopment.

One patrol was sent far over to the right, to make a sneak play along the Merderet bank toward the bridge, with the hope either of catching the Germans on their blind side or of diverting them while they were smacked from another quarter. It was a wishful idea. The patrol was clipped and turned back by machine-gun fire before it had extended to the river.

The other patrol, under Second Lieutenant William A. Oakley, was sent far over to the left, for a sneak play up the riverbank from the south, with the same general object in mind. The mission reveals the sad state of Dolan's information and is eloquent of the confusions of the morning. Dolan's second patrol was being sent on an end run around Lindquist's flank as if that half of the property were wholly free of Americans.

Dolan then ordered Able Company's center to attack straight ahead over the ground flanking the main road—the same ground which Lindquist had looked at and called too deadly. Lieutenant Donald G. Coxon, who had the center platoon, was told, "Get your scouts out for the approach." The ground and hedges where the men lay prone were already being flailed by intense machine-gun and automatic-pistol fire.

Coxon replied, "Well, sir, if I must send someone out into that, I'll go myself." He crawled forward along the hedge, the first scout going with him. They made 100 yards. A bullet killed the scout. Another bullet wounded Coxon. He was pretty hard hit and he started crawling back. Then another bullet went through his back and opened the wall of his stomach. After that, he bled to death.

Second Lieutenant Robert E. McLaughlin took over the platoon. His radio operator, Corporal Frank Busa, moved on forward of him and was hit by a sniper's bullet. McLaughlin thought he was alive and crawled out to get him. Before he could reach Busa, a bullet hit him in the upper leg, went through the lower part of his stomach and came out of his buttocks. Dolan and Major James E. McGinity, the battalion executive, watched these men drop from beside the same hedgerow which McLaughlin had just quit. A sniper's bullet got McGinity through the brain; even as McGinity fell, Dolan got the sniper with a Tommy-gun burst that smashed his skull.

Then Dolan crawled forward and dressed McLaughlin's wounds. But he was in such pain that he cried, "Don't move me." Dolan crawled back to the hedgerow. It began to rain softly. Dolan crawled out a second time to cover McLaughlin with his raincoat. McLaughlin was dead.

Steadily, the German automatic fire built upward. But Able Company's ground was too exposed to permit suitable return. Already there were 10 dead and 21 wounded in Dolan's line. The able-bodied were willing to keep trying. But the center rush was plain suicide, and Dolan was worrying that if he maneuvered while the two patrols tried to return to his lines, he might shoot his own men. The hour was between 1000 and 1030. A few more men from the 507th were coming into the area and were taking positions in extension of Dolan's line between Able Company and the river. But for the time being they were unorganized and doing no hitting. So of this increase in manpower, Dolan could feel little or nothing. He knew only that his own outfit was battered and that he had better stop.

Shortly after 1100, Dolan sent a runner out to look for the patrol on the left. He ran into Lindquist and told him about McGinity's death and Able Company's losses. Ridgway had just arrived and told Lindquist to take over the sector.

Schwartzwalder's group had been met and absorbed by Lindquist during his left-end sweep. He now sent for Schwartzwalder and said, "I've got a mission for you." The plan he outlined was no novelty. Schwartzwalder was to attack the Manoir from the south over exactly the same route he had gone earlier that morning. At that moment anything was all right with Schwartzwalder. But he was still on a leash. Being a tidy-minded commander, Lindquist wanted to get things rolling by the numbers. There had already been too much random punching, only to fall flat. So all hands were to mark time briefly. Then at 1200, Dolan's people would hit the line again on the right, while Schwartzwalder's men went for a touchdown around the left. An officer was sent posthaste to Dolan to give him the signals.

By the book, the concept was flawless. Only two things went wrong. The officer carrying the word became lost among the hedgerows and never found Dolan. And Dolan's patrol on the left under Lieutenant Oakley swung so far over to the side lines that it missed Lindquist, Schwartzwalder and their people altogether and still arrived at the payoff ground itching to make a big score.

No one arose to block the drive but the Germans. Oakley and his group got to the river embankment, and then slipped, without being seen, to the first hedgerow by the Manoir, still without being seen. By then they were close enough to the enemy to end it all with a flying tackle. Machine-gun fire came against them, but they were already in tight against the hedge embankment and no one got hit. Using their rifles, Oakley and Sergeant Oscar L. Queen killed three Germans, one of whom had charged toward them firing a machine pistol. Then the patrol ran for the cover of the stone wall which runs from the southernmost barn of the Manoir almost to the bridge—a wall which figures heavily in operations still to come. They made it unhurt. From the wall, they were looking right into the rear of the German machine gun which had menaced the main road. It was a little out of range for grenading.

While the others fired weapons to cover him, Queen darted across the service road, running low, then ducked through a gate in the stone wall opposite. A grenade exploding near his feet stunned him and he pitched over. He heard a .45 pistol firing somewhere behind him. In the branches of a tree just above where he lay, he saw a figure stirring; Queen fired his carbine, and a German tumbled from the roost dead. Then Queen ran back across the road. Captain Dale Royden, who had just happened along and joined Oakley at the last moment, was still holding his pistol. He had emptied it on a grenadier heaving at Queen from one of the Manoir windows.

Next, the patrol's light machine gun was advanced to the stone wall, from where it took the enemy machine gun under fire and silenced it by killing the crew.

Now it was high noon, the minute set for Schwartzwalder and his people to make their rush. They came on. But it was a task for the scrubs. The Germans had had enough. Losing one man killed and two wounded, Schwartzwalder overran the Manoir. The Germans ran up a white flag. An American private stepped into the open to receive the surrender and was shot dead. Otherwise, the fire brigade was barely scratched. It had killed three or four Germans; it bagged eight prisoners.

Lest doubt remain about what had happened to the other forces of this resistance, the suspense needs be ended: there weren't any. The Germans who fought at Manoir de la Fière and stopped more than tenfold their own numbers have all been accounted for.

At 2300 the prior night, 28 German infantrymen had come to the Manoir, got M. Louis Leroux out of bed and told him they were outposting his property. He was startled; no such thing had happened before; no German had ever mounted guard over the Merderet crossing. Why they made the move just three hours before the American invasion hit is one of the mysteries. Possibly it was sheer coincidence. Be that as it may, Leroux counted the noses of his uninvited guests, and his account sheet should be good. When the firing started in early morning, Mme. Leroux and their three nippers wisely descended to the wine cellar. But M. Leroux, being more curious than thirsty or fearful, remained mobile and above ground. There is his word for it that no German reinforcements arrived. It is disconcerting.

After the Manoir fell, Second Lieutenants John G. Darling and Edward Keehan led an advance party as far as the bridge and were there halted by mortar fire coming from somewhere on their own side of the river.

Before it quieted, Schwartzwalder was already bound for the other side. This man loves a fight.

6

Levy and Patrol

Dug in among the apple trees, Colonel Timmes by midmorning began to have second thoughts about the position at Cauquigny church, from which he had walked away four hours earlier.

So he called Lieutenant Levy and said, "Take ten men, move south, dig in around this church (his finger pointed it out on the map) and make sure that your fire positions are sited to cover the west end of the causeway."

A man of few words, Levy took off at once. His group went armed with rifles, hand grenades, one Tommy gun, one BAR (automatic rifle) and a sack of antitank grenades, with launcher.

So began one of the bravest episodes in the Merderet battle. Its heroisms were sparked by the same enemy maneuver which robbed Gavin of his one chance for a swift, cheap victory.

Halfway to the church, Levy ran into Lieutenant Joseph Kormylo, of Dog Company, 507th, and 20 men, armed with rifles and one light machine gun. Kormylo had already been to the church and the La Fière bridge. In fact, not even Timmes had trudged over more French countryside.

Landing not far from where Gavin dropped, but somehow missing him, Kormylo had gone like a beagle on a hot scent straight for the bridgehead, collecting paratroopers as he moved. The first were glider pilots and antitankers; then he found a few of his own fellows, which made him feel better.

But after prowling the churchyard and scanning the bridge,

Kormylo decided that he had too few people to play around in
the open. Before fading back into the hedgerow cover, simply
to confirm his suspicions that he had arrived at the all-important
object, he snared a French farmer, led him to the bank overlooking the causeway, got out his phrase book, pointed his
finger and asked, *"Le pont La Fière?"*

The Frenchman said, *"Oui, le pont."* While they looked,
he could hear small-arms fire swelling on the far shore.

So he withdrew his gang northward a few hundred yards to
a well-screened field near the marsh edge. From there, he
sighted the light machine gun on the bridge and figured that
he was close enough to it to stop traffic. At first, he reckoned
that was the most he could do until he could find more people.
But the longer he looked at the bridge, the more the compromise
irked him. Finally, he said to his men, "This is wrong; we
better get back down there."

Right then, Levy and his group came along. The two lieutenants briefly discussed the situation, and together decided
that all of Kormylo's force, except the machine gun and crew,
should join Timmes in the orchard, while Levy continued on.
That Timmes had seen fit to send only ten men to the bridge
influenced this judgment.

Levy, the senior, was willing enough when Kormylo asked
permission to join the patrol. The hour was 1130 when they
started for the church; Kormylo did not expect any real trouble.
He had moved up and down the west bank twice without drawing fire. The sounds of fighting on the east shore were too
irregular to signal anything important.

Their plan was to take over the churchyard and dig in. Levy
reckoned it the key ground, the best place to hold, covering
the causeway, while still not committing them nakedly in the
open.

Their way, as they jogged along, was made rough only by
flurries of American fire from the east shore, which clipped
the branches around them and increased in volume and accuracy, until Levy first called a halt and then took them on a
roundabout detour west and south, to put a few more hedgerows
between them and the river.

It was exactly noon when the patrol took over the churchyard. After getting weapons set, they broke out rations. A
Frenchman appeared out of nowhere, bringing them milk and
cider.

The machine gun had been set up so that its field of fire ranged along the western bank, as well as covering the bridge. They could see Manoir de La Fière from where they sat. Beyond it, on the high ground, they could make out an American 57 millimeter gun. But the scene looked otherwise peaceful and they heard nothing suggesting that an attack was in progress. The distance from the church to the Manoir was about one-half mile.

As Levy finished lunch, two lieutenants from the 508th, leading 37 men, entered the churchyard. This group had collected on the west bank and had not yet fought. Both newcomers complicated Levy on his choice of position, one saying, "We hold this, and we've got it made." Their forces then built up on Levy. A light machine gun and crew were set to cover the road fork just below the church. The bazooka team was set to block the road from Amfreville. Feeling snug, Levy dispatched a runner to Timmes with the message: "We have secured the bridgehead."

Kormylo, scouting forward, noticed a sharp pickup of fire around the Manoir. Mortars were banging away; the rattle of automatic arms crescendoed. Men could be seen dashing from the hedgerows toward the causeway. Kormylo ran back to the church and with Levy spread the word: "Hold fire!" But despite their restraining effort, some of the riflemen continued to fire wildly toward the La Fière buildings.

Levy walked to the road and looked through his field glasses. "Kormylo," he yelled, "damn it, come see! Here's a paratrooper coming across the bridge."

Kormylo threw an orange smoke grenade into the middle of the road. At once came back an answering wave of an orange flag from a group of men crossing the bridge. These were small acts. In themselves, they were quite correct. But they helped build the tragic illusion. To all who beheld them, they signaled that the causeway fight was over and the 82nd Division had won the Merderet bridgehead at slight cost. Of the illusion came trouble unimaginable.

On the east bank the ball had been tossed again to Schwartzwalder, who one hour earlier had stood next to Lindquist's elbow when Ridgway said to him, "I want that bridge taken!" (That is how Schwartzwalder remembered it. According to Lindquist, Ridgway said, "I want this area cleared of all Germans and the bridgehead secured." The difference is one of

scope; the latter order would be all-embracing, and it sounds
more like Ridgway.) With Schwartzwalder, as the noon hour
came and passed, were 80 men. He knew hardly any of them
personally. Most of his own people accompanied Lindquist
when he took off, pursuant to Ridgway's order, to clear the
environs of La Fière. They were already purged of Germans,
but this he had no way of knowing. Of how things were on
the west shore no one on the east bank knew. No sign had
come their way of Americans holding at Cauquigny church.

Private James L. Mattingly, who had been appointed lead
scout for the causeway venture, looked at his watch. The time
was 1345. Just then Schwartzwalder said, "Let's go!" Marr
again commanded the point. He was apprehensive; a captured
German NCO had told him that manned rifle pits were strewn
out over the length of the causeway.

Walking erect in road center, Mattingly made 100 yards
without a shot being fired. Then from a pit at 20 yards' range,
a German rifleman fired and nearly winged him. Still standing,
Mattingly emptied his M-1 into the pit, then dived and heaved
a grenade. It hit fair, killing one German and wounding two.
Another pair jumped up, hands in air. Then five Germans in
a rifle pit, an arm's distance from Mattingly, arose in surrender.
Rifle empty, and weaponless, he waved them back toward the
main body. Two German crews, until then not even seen,
crawled out from positions along the embankments, quitting
their (MG-42) machine guns.

In this way, the Merderet causeway was first taken by the
enterprise of a solitary American rifleman. Only one paratrooper got hit during the crossing; from somewhere in the
marsh, a sniper got him with a bullet in the buttocks. Head
up, Mattingly walked on, followed by Private Johnnie K. Ward,
the second scout, and behind him, Marr.

From an observation window in the Manoir, Lieutenant
Wisner saw the exchange of signals when the orange smoke
was loosed at Cauquigny. But the trees prevented any clear
view of the marching column. He took it to mean that Schwartzwalder had reached the far side, guessed that his force would
have to go it alone from there on, and figured he had better
rally some support. Agitated, he talked it over with Captain
Dickerson, of the 507th, who answered, "Yes, we intend to
cross at once." So Wisner relaxed; the situation was in hand.

But the same circumstances had suffused Schwartzwalder

with a giddy optimism. He had expected to encounter stiff opposition along the causeway; instead the resistance had been beaten down by his energetic first scout. On top of that came the surprise friendly signal from the supposedly hostile battlement of high ground. He walked on, convinced that Americans were solidly in possession of the west shore and that his tour de force had hardly been needed. That impression was deepened when Levy and Kormylo came running to him while he was still marching, looking "happy as hell" and anxious to pump his hand.

They talked all too briefly. Then Levy continued on to the east shore where at the Manoir he talked to a staff officer, assuring him, as he had done Schwartzwalder, that he had the west shore secured. Within 15 minutes, Levy was back at the church. He said to Kormylo, "They promised me that a battalion of the 505th is on its way to take the bridgehead over."

Schwartzwalder and company still held beside the churchyard. But they had not deployed to ground. Marr was still out front with his point. From the way they were aligned, it looked to Levy as if they were not preparing to move west to extend the arc protecting the bridgehead but were poised to march north. So he raised the question with the older man. Schwartzwalder said he figured the bridge was already "captured" and that he had better get along to Amfreville—his original objective. Levy made no objection, but only this comment: "I was sent to hold the bridge, and I think I had better stick here." Until that moment, he had not thought to tell Schwartzwalder about Timmes and the people dug in among the apple trees. By this last-minute postscript, he again altered the course of the battle but may have saved Schwartzwalder for the football wars. When some few minutes later Schwartzwalder shoved off, it was not on a line plunge straight toward Amfreville but along a detour via Timmes and the apple orchard.

Worse luck, the noontide reinforcement of 508th people, which had stood by Levy at the churchyard, picked up and went along with Schwartzwalder, except for the two lieutenants and eight men. The others figured that the show was over along the Merderet and so vanished on hot heels, looking for a fight. With them went the bazooka team, scrapping the road block.

Lindquist in these minutes had been busier than three bird dogs. Completing his long sweep around the Manoir and finding the area "secure," he sent a force to organize his command post within the building. Then he double-timed to the west shore for one quick look. He saw Levy's group at the church and made a mental note that he would have to speed reinforcement to them. That Schwartzwalder had gone on hardly surprised him, though his visit and the other man's good-by were but a snap of a finger apart. His impression from the morning was that "Schwartzwalder was hell-bent on getting to a real fight." So Lindquist made his quick shuttle, found Cauquigny in dead calm, then laden with anxieties, ran back to the Manoir to order Company B to advance across the river and build up on Levy. "Company B" was the polite designation given to an ill-armed and motley medley of strayed artillerymen and headquarters hands, 40 people all told. Still, the move was made to tidy things up, and not because Lindquist, seeing his own vulnerable front, was suddenly ridden by a hunch that all hell was getting ready to pop.

At Cauquigny, the backs of Schwartzwalder's tag-end files had just disappeared beyond the first hedgerow, when Kormylo's attention became riveted in the opposite direction. At first he heard only rifle fire at far distance; then distinctly came the rat-tat-tat, rat-tat-tat of several machine guns. But the sounds were anonymous: they could be either enemy or friend. Then rose above the staccato chorus an unmistakable and spine-tingling rumble. Every moment it grew louder, and it came out of the west. Kormylo yelled, "My God! Tanks! That's German armor."

Quick like that, opposite him, a German ambulance bobbed out of the trail from south along the river. It veered west onto the Amfreville road. It stopped for a second. From the door a German waved a Red Cross flag. Before anyone made a move, it was away and speeding down the road. But the German had seen that there were Americans on guard in the churchyard.

Three minutes later, five shells exploded into the intersection. Others followed and searched north along the riverbank. Schwartzwalder, feeling them blister his tail, but not reading the meaning of the build-up, urged his men to move along faster. They ran at a double till they reached the sixth hedgerow north of the church. Still, some of the men thought they were taking the wrong direction. Marr long remembered that during a lull in the shooting he heard them whisper to one another, "Listen! Tanks! Listen! Tanks!" But Marr listened and he could not make himself believe.

Schwartzwalder pressed on. He felt he had to talk to Timmes. He wanted to hit Amfreville, but he wanted someone higher up to say, "Go!" So thinking, he unwittingly led his men into ground where a force equal to his own had remained immobile for hours under fire from north and west. Thereby he wasted himself. Joining Timmes, Schwartzwalder and company contrived but to share for the next 48 hours the paralysis of the people already under the apple trees.

Back at the church, Levy, Kormylo and the ten other men built up a line around the curving hedgerow enclosing the yard on the valley side and extending a few yards along the main road. The one machine gun was so placed that from the rear of the church wall it could sweep the road. The riflemen were spaced 15 yards apart, and the four lieutenants (two from the 508th) filled in among the enlisted men.

Thereafter, they waited. It wasn't long. But Levy, on his toes with excitement, couldn't stand still even the little minute. Kormylo was on one side of him, on the other an unidentified private, who would be killed that afternoon, nameless to his comrades in that hour, and still the Unknown Soldier. Levy grabbed the two of them, saying, "Come on along with me." Then he ran for a sunken lane bounding the church property and running at right angles to the Amfreville road. He said to Kormylo, "Maybe we can swing around their left and get in a few licks before they know what has hit them." He stationed himself in a shallow but heavily screened bay in the hedgerow bordering the lane and yelled to the others, "You move on a little; if it gets too rough, run, and I'll cover your retreat." They crept along the hedge to within one stride of the open road.

By now the roar from the tanks was deafening. Kormylo saw their turrets as they came into the intersection. Then a point of German riflemen crossed his front, moving obliquely from the left and turning their backs to him. Kormylo and the private emptied their M-1s into the group. But as the tanks drew even, the two Americans who had fired first got out at a dead run. As they dashed past Levy, he yelled, "Keep going!" Already another enemy group was setting up a machine gun just short of where the lane met the road; but it was on line to fire against the church. Kormylo glanced back. He saw Levy jump from the bay and lob a grenade over the hedge which landed plop on the gun and exploded. Its three crewmen were wounded; Levy jumped into the roadway and dispatched them with his rifle; his remaining bullets he frittered away on the lead tank, just as a gesture of contempt. By that time, the nameless private had doubled back and joined Kormylo, to help him cover Levy's withdrawal. He reached them, helmetless and "laughing like a maniac," which was his habit when the heat was on. His jacket was half torn away and his shoulder was bleeding. Kormylo remembered then that he had heard a second grenade go off.

The tanks were shelling the church, and the German infantry had closed right up by the hedgerow and were firing through it. Only six Americans still held their ground on the other side, fighting it out at five yards' range. The bank was too tall, the brush too thick, for rifle fire. So it was an ante-over duel with grenades. But it couldn't last; the German numbers were too great, and ammunition was running out. Kormylo saw first a helmet, then a shoulder, as one German tried to push through the hedge. He'd grabbed up a carbine a moment before; this he emptied into the German's skull.

Levy had momentarily disappeared. Kormylo thought he'd pulled out. But he had simply moved down the hedgerow and was standing near it, throwing hand grenades at the tanks. By then, only one other American—the nameless private—was standing the ground with them. Kormylo yelled, "Come on! Let's get the hell out of here!" Levy, now empty-handed, went with him, but the other boy was killed before he could get to the church wall.

With that exit, logically, the curtain should have rung down on the small drama at Cauquigny. But it was not mere bad taste in Private Orlin Stewart that he gilded the lily; he had been dealt out of the show, through no fault of his own, and that made him feel put upon.

Stewart was part (or so he thought) of the road block formed around the bazooka team, which had given Levy his noontime glow of confidence. He had been posted off to the right of the bazooka with his BAR and several gammon (tank-killing) grenades. He knew that he was supposed to cover the bazooka man, but he really didn't know anything about the gammons. When the bazooka team pulled out to accompany Schwartzwalder, it ignored Stewart, leaving him alone beside the road. He was still playing solitaire when the tanks rolled by. Here's what it took to end his reverie: the tanks went on to the intersection. Right then, the lead tank was hit by a rocket and set afire. The source of that rocket remained ever after a mystery; it may have come from the swamp; yet no American in or near the churchyard held, or knew about, any tank-killing weapon around him.

But when Stewart saw the lead tank (a medium) knocked off as if by magic, he acted like a man mad with power. He ran for the intersection. As he made it, two Renault tanks veered around the burning tank, headed for the bridge. Stewart, who had dodged behind a hedgerow but still looked straight at them not more than 30 yards away, had a queer feeling. It was as if he were repeating, "Why am I here?" over and over to himself, without finding any answer. Then he got the word: a private and a first sergeant whom he had never seen before (and they are still unidentified) came crawling down the same ditch where he was kneeling. The first sergeant said, "Hi!" He was loaded with gammon grenades; so was the private. The box hedge gave them partial cover. The Renaults came on by, broadside on; a Junior Leaguer could hardly have missed them. The top kick and his partner rose and pegged straight at the metal, one of them yelling, "Take that, you sons of bitches!" In sheer admiration, Stewart passed them his gammons and raised his BAR. There were five heavy explosions, so close together that Stewart was not certain he had counted right. And marvelously, the two Renaults clanked on a few yards, then stopped, disabled and in flames.

The crews tried to clear out. As the first two Germans jumped down, the sergeant blasted them with a fragmentation grenade. Stewart shot the third man as he ran. The second crew ducked back into the Renault. Right then, another medium tank rolled into the road fork, trailed by a large group of infantry. Stewart and company didn't waste a second glance on them; their grenades were gone; they ran back along the hedgerows leading north. But all they had done had been observed by a witness, Private Owen L. Darlington, the last man out of Levy's crew, who had watched without helping, being out of ammunition.

They fell in with Levy. The survivors got out carrying all weapons. The little fight, in which the bridgehead was lost, had lasted not more than ten minutes from start to finish. All other routes being closed to them, what was left of the patrol moved on to join Timmes under the apple trees.

But the first forfeit was exacted at Cauquigny while Levy and patrol were quitting it on the run. Company B, the rag, tag, and bobtail outfit which Lindquist had thrown together on the east shore and dispatched to help bulwark the far shore, was just arriving when the Germans swept past the church. The two leading squads had already reached firm ground and turned south along the shore preparatory to digging in when the blow fell. It caught them unaware, but the squads that followed fared far worse. The tank artillery shelled the causeway behind them, thereby cutting off their line of retreat; the enemy machine guns, banding against the twisting road, forbade any movement to the right. It was too late to advance, retreat or deploy. The men broke to the left and individually tried to wade, crawl and swim back through the marsh. But Germans and their weapons were thick on the western bank and were flailing the marsh with fire before the Americans had time to vanish into the rushes and reeds. Many of the fugitives were shot dead while wading in the muck next the west shore; more of them, wounded, struggled on, only to die by drowning in the river; if any escaped, report was not made of it.

Arrived at Timmes's orchard, Levy and Kormylo had a first breathing spell in which to compare notes. They agreed that had one paratroop company been dug in around the church, it would have beaten off the enemy and held the bridgehead. But the postmortems of practicing tacticians are worth little more than the might-have-beens of armchair strategists. There is no knowing what might have happened had that which happened not happened.

Before this last increment settled in, there were already 21 officers and 121 men under the apple trees. But the reinforcement, rather than helping the force, coincided with the main bid by the enemy to crush it in a vise. Earlier, Timmes might have gotten out little scathed. After Levy returned, he was fully besieged. Men knew this from the rising volume and swift spread of the fire until at last it covered every point. On the Merderet side, where no German stood, bands of automatic fire from the westward grazed the marsh surface, locking them in. Yet it was a wraithlike envelopment, for though they felt the pressure round the compass, they saw little or nothing of the living enemy.

During the next two days on this ground, one fourth of Timmes's people either were killed or suffered disabling wounds.

Adding to that score the toll of walking wounded, his casualties were nearer 50 per cent.

The squeeze on Timmes and the knockout of Cauquigny were twins of one general maneuver. The Germans knew about the underwater road which threads the marsh to the railroad line about 2000 yards northwest of the La Fière causeway, and were wary that the Americans would plumb the secret in time; when they stormed back to take the bridgehead, they were already committed to block the detour also. So a part of the force moved north to grab the ford; so doing, it collided with Timmes, holding the orchard just south of it. That produced the deadlock. The Germans couldn't get to the ford, nor could Timmes. They couldn't afford to pull back and he couldn't afford to break out.

That's where it stayed for several days, while Timmes was out of radio touch with everyone. His men had retrieved a 57-millimeter gun from the swamp the first afternoon; they used it to cover toward the north, along with two machine guns, thereby unwittingly keeping the Germans from the ford. Two bazookas also guarded in that direction; three 60-millimeter mortars and two more machine guns supported the perimeter on the south.

After getting the bad news from Levy, Timmes ordered vigorous patrolling toward the north, figuring that if there was to be an American rebound, it would probably be in a new direction.

"When our friends come," he said, "we want to be out there ready to help them."

It was a trifle optimistic.

7

Done the Hard Way

Slim Jim Gavin's dash to seize the lower crossing at Chef-du-Pont that first morning was ringed by luck, most of it bad.

Before leaving La Fière, he split his company to hedge his tactical bets, but of it came no advantage. With 75 men, Lieutenant Colonel Arthur Maloney was sent on a wide swingout east and south to see if a track could be found through the marsh south of the Chef-du-Pont causeway. The extra walk merely tired the men. Maloney had already vanished when Gavin heard from a Frenchman: "There are no Germans at Chef-du-Pont." So with Lieutenant Colonel Edwin J. Ostberg and 75 men, he took off straight down the railroad.

They beat Maloney to the village, but not the Germans. About four squads were guarding it. But they were not playing hero—yet. After token resistance among the houses, in which no blood was drawn, they sprinted for the causeway.

Its embankments were pitted with rifle trenches and machine-gun emplacements. With the paratroopers running behind, firing as they came, the Germans scurried to ground. The dikelike structure into which they settled runs flat, six feet above the level of the marsh. One hundred yards beyond its east terminus, the arched bridge over the Merderet obtrudes above the level of the road.

In this race for life, some of the enemy dived straight into the closest foxholes east of the bridge. Others braved the fire

65

Figure 6. Chef-du-Pont Causeway

longer to put the arching bridge between themselves and the Americans. From the embankment, Ostberg's rifles were pointing right down the throats of the closest Germans. But the hump in the bridge blocked the view of the road beyond, and the Germans who ran longest became relatively shielded.

After the running targets vanished, there occurred a two-minute hiatus in the firing. The pursuers quit shooting when they went flat, just short of the causeway. From within their cover, the Germans hesitated as if reluctant to resume action. Nobody said a word.

Then east of the bridge, one German rose out of the ground, hands high in air. He called, *"Kamerad!"* Before anyone could answer, a paratrooper, not more than 20 feet away, shot him dead within clear view of the people on both sides. Bad enough, whether it was a slip or done in cold blood, it still was not final and fatal except to one German.

Another minute passed silently. Then from the same rifle pit, a second German rose, hands in air. An American shot him dead before he could take two steps.

Someone yelled, "You son-of-a-bitch, you've killed us."

That was how they all felt. They knew that the second time there could be no excuse. The cries of "Cease fire!" were raised too late. One itchy trigger finger had fixed the situation. There might have been a chance for a deal: "We'll let you get away if you let us take the bridge." But since their eyes told them that they could neither escape nor surrender, the Germans would have to keep going now, staking their lives on this ground. Desperation would mount, and nothing could change it until the last man was gone from one side or the other.

Gripped by this bitter reflection, they stayed right there as if the tactical deadlock bound them to the foreground. There was no reconnaissance seeking an alternative to the point-blank duel. From their slight elevation, Ostberg's men picked off the Germans east of the bridge one by one. After they were dead, the bulge of the bridge intervened, and the enemy fire first went too high, then slackened.

So Ostberg organized a charge and led it. As he made the arch, running, a machine-gun burst crumpled him, and he pitched over into the marsh. The four or five men nearest him were also shot down.

Right after that, Maloney and company arrived. They were ambitious, not having seen Ostberg's fall. So they organized a second charge. It was stopped at the same point by a grenade shower, with much the same result, except that Maloney was unscathed.

Taught caution, the Americans crawled forward and slowly closed up on the bridge pit by pit, pulling the dead Germans from their holes to make room. But the nearer they got to the structure, the less they could see of the enemy movement beyond it, though things didn't seem to work that way with the enemy. A paratrooper would lift his head and shoulder to take aim; he would die with a bullet in his head before he could pull the trigger, as if an unseen German had a bead on that one foxhole. So they stayed low and continued the fight with grenades, most of which bounced off the bridge into enemy ground beyond. There were interspersions of rifle and burp-gun fire.

Things wore on that way until late afternoon, when Maloney and all but 34 of the Americans were recalled from Chef-du-Pont because the promise of easy victory at La Fière had proved a deception. When Maloney moved north, the command passed to Captain Roy E. Creek, a dour but determined soldier.

Not more than 15 minutes after the pull-out, the Germans brought up an artillery piece on the west shore and from 600 yards opened direct fire on Creek's ground. It all happened very quickly. The first round was a bull's-eye. By the time they slammed in a dozen more, the shellfire had taken fourteen of the defenders. Creek rushed around from foxhole to foxhole, counting his dead, seeing what could be done for the wounded. Making that round, he heard one of his paratroopers yell, "Hey, Captain, look there!" and saw him gesturing toward the rear.

Creek looked. Amid the farmhouses nested to the south of the village, he saw a line of German infantry rapidly deploying northward as if to close around his rear. It "looked like a hundred men" but might have been 50. They were still about 300 yards away. Creek guessed that they had hidden in the farm buildings all morning awaiting the open-and-shut opportunity which arrived when Maloney left.

So he was trapped now, the big gun battering his front, the rifle swarm enveloping his rear. Creek took it calmly. He reckoned that it would be another four or five minutes before the enemy infantry, at last fully extended, came forward firing. There seemed little point for the moment in turning his own people and weapons around to face the new threat.

Just then, help came out of heaven. An American glider carrying a 57-millimeter antitank gun nosed gently down and landed in dead center of Creek's position. They had not seen it till it was right on them.

His men jumped for the gun. Handling it like veteran artillerymen, they got it set, loaded, aimed and fired before the German infantry could react. Their second round hit the German artillery piece across the Merderet and smashed it. Then they swung the gun around and got away two rounds against the German infantry. Its line broke and ran for the swamp. The officers tried to turn them. Amid that effort, a division staff officer walked into Creek's position with a reinforcing platoon. Thereon the German infantry vanished wholly, still not having fired.

It was dusk. Creek had no intention of trying again for the bridge. He felt that his own 20 men were spent and he didn't care to rush the newcomers. But he wanted to find ground where the troops might spell one another for a few winks and still have greater safety through the night. So in search of a snugger position he walked north along the riverbank.

So doing, he found a narrow nub of solid land projecting for about 15 yards into the Merderet. Sighting from it, he could see that his weapons would put direct fire into the German position west of the bridge. It had been beckoning all day; but not one person had thought to scout round the bend.

One machine gun and a handful of riflemen firing from this coign for ten minutes swung the balance before dark came down. The Germans were picked off one by one. The end came when two last survivors rose from their foxholes and fled westward.

Creek then pushed the new platoon across the bridge to hold the diggings among the enemy dead. So seated, he had a loose grip on one end of the causeway but was still far from winning a bridgehead. The solid western bank was 700 yards away, and the expanse of marsh made the distance seem infinite.

Forty German corpses were counted among the foxholes and strewn along the embankments. Creek's own losses were 13 dead and 23 wounded.

Neither the box score nor the small victory made him feel any better. He was bitter most of all at himself, and raging that he had done things so badly.

He said to the others, "Who's the big damn fool? Look at me. Fight all day. Lose a lot of people. And at last I stumble into doing what any boy scout would have done in the first place."

Some of his seniors had also looked at the forest and missed the tree. But that knowledge didn't stop his brooding.

8

No Better Spot to Die

Of all that had happened since noontide around the La Fière bridgehead—the advance of Schwartzwalder's column, the stand by Levy's patrol, the German panzers' sweep of the west shore—the American force closest to the scene and most directly concerned knew nothing.

Still licking their wounds on the bloodied field, Lieutenant John Dolan's men, of Able Company, 505th, carried on little aware either that there were friendly troops near them or that a fresh enemy had them under his guns. Their immediate foreground, and their personal broodings, so monopolized their gaze and their thoughts that they scarcely glanced beyond the Manoir buildings to the river. Each individual knew that part of the battle which his eyes had seen. The company, as a whole, felt itself unhelped and unsupported, and was oppressed by a terrible feeling of loneliness.

When at last their front quieted and they felt free of fire on the local ground, they did not attribute their deliverance to other Americans having snuffed the German resistance. They thought, mistakenly, that the enemy had withdrawn across the Merderet. Knowing that they had tried to advance their own weapons to block the exit, only to be kicked back, they could not imagine that where they had failed, another unit had succeeded. Not knowing that Schwartzwalder had been there, they couldn't miss him when he pulled out.

Because the fire died, they automatically advanced to the shore rim by the Manoir, hard by the bridge. That filled the vacuum where Schwartzwalder and company had been, and in that sense they staged a relief without knowing it.

On the new ground their center faced the bridge, and its weapons pointed along the causeway. The flanks spread for 50 or more yards on either side, two platoons so deployed, while Second Platoon hugged high ground to the rearward at the turn of the main road. They cut their foxholes at once, because mortar, artillery and machine-gun fire was already periodically searching the embankment. This visitation signaled nothing special to Dolan and company, nor did the rumble of armor along the west shore. Not realizing that the Germans had not been there in strength all along, they heard no significance in the sound of the sudden build-up.

Four men moved out to establish a road block on the causeway beyond the bridge—Privates John D. Bolderson, Gordon C. Pryne, Marcus Heim, Jr., and Lenold Peterson—two bazooka men with two gunners to cover them. A slightly built Swede, Peterson spoke enough English to get by in military company. Taking over some of the pits from which Private Mattingly had pried the Germans an hour or so before, they deployed in depth with the bazooka on the left 25 yards to the fore. They had carried four antitank mines with them, and these they strung across the road. Last, a broken-down truck was dragged from the east bank and set broadside at the far end of the bridge—an indifferent shield covering the rear bazooka man. Ultimately (four days later), both the truck and the mines did their work. But they obstructed the wrong force.

Through the afternoon, Able Company dug deeper, for there was no respite in the fire. The word went buzzing around, "We're going to be counterattacked." At 1730 the Germans came on—two tanks close-trailed by a body of infantry. The lead tank got to the mines; the commander stood in the turret to take a look. From Able Company's left, Private Clarence Becker cut loose with a machine gun and killed him. In time with the burst, the bazookas let go against the hull, their fire mingling with the rounds from the 57-millimeter gun, perched on the high ground. Peterson, in the position far forward, had withheld fire till the last moment, not from boldness, but because the tree foliage of the causeway kept obscuring the column.

Quickly, he and Bolderson got off four rockets. All hit the metal, without seemingly hurting it. Still stopped, the lead tank swung its cannon around and fired. The round snapped a concrete telephone pole right by Peterson, and he had to jump for the open to avoid being crushed. Before he could fire again, the lead tank went up in flames. The second tank swung out and around the pyre, then turned sharply left, as if trying to ride out into the marsh. Peterson ran toward it about 30 feet so as to get beyond the screening trees. As fast as he could get them off, he put four rockets against the turret. Nothing happened. The tank's artillery followed him around as if bent only on pot-shooting one small man at 20 yards' range. Then he made a fair hit where the turret joins the body. When his next rocket shattered the tank's bogie wheel, Peterson ran forward another 30 yards, got on the tank's rear and banged one into the soft spot. The German still tried to back onto the roadway again, though one track was gone and the motor was dying. Peterson's last rocket breached the fuel tank, and the whole went up in flames, incinerating the crew. The tank action ended, Peterson ran back to his own lines crying, "Goot! Goot! I do her."

While the modern Horatius was thus performing, Able Company, from its main line, was concentrating fire on the German infantry that had followed the tanks. The marchers had lost their shield when the tanks veered during the bout with Peterson, and despite its sinuous line, the causeway was level and wide open to grazing fire from the machine guns anchoring Able's flanks. The effect was like "mowing hay." The Germans in the van were cut down in their tracks. The second company, which was still beyond the bend in the causeway, made no attempt to engage with weapons and scrambled back to Cauquigny. Practically unhurt, the Americans sniffed the sweet smell of success, and the spirit, bowed down in the morning, flamed high.

Under Major Kellam, the rest of Lindquist's force still east of the Merderet and deployed downstream from Dolan's men, heard the percussion in this symphony, but being out of sight, could not take part. Because they were out of sight, and Dolan did not know they were there, Able Company felt unsupported still.

The battle noise had also won the ear of Ridgway, and he had come posthaste to have a look. Able's agile defense cheered him; but the first appearance of the panzers on his lightly manned force was a warning. What concerned him far more was the 82nd's isolation; he had not heard one word from the seaborne expedition or any higher command; it was possible that the invasion had failed. He talked it over with Lindquist. Should the defense line break at the bridge, he said, all division forces might have to fall back on Ste. Mère-Église. In that event, it would be Lindquist's task to manage the withdrawal from the Merderet. So went the high-level talk, while at low level the Germans lunged and a Swedish private insured their defeat. Accordingly, Lindquist shifted Kellam's force from the river to the first hedgerow beyond the railroad and inside the "Y" formed by the two highways, so that if the worst happened, he would have a backstop. Kellam did not survive the move. A mortar burst hit him while he took his first look at the new ground, and he bled to death within a few minutes.

But the reaction continued to live and widen. General Gavin returned to La Fière from Chef-du-Pont, feeling sanguine enough, despite a rough day at the lower bridgehead. He had stayed at that spot, up among the weapons men, until he saw the situation turning in his favor. He had expected to find the upper crossing cooled off; instead, eyes, ears and instinct told him that the fight for it was just beginning.

No one at La Fière knew what had happened to Schwartz-walder's force or by what chance the Germans had banged back into Cauquigny. But the grievous hurt to his own side was unmistakable. Kellam, McGinity and six junior officers were now dead; Dolan, temporarily, was commanding the battalion. What impressed Slim Jim most was the intensity of the mortar and 88-millimeter gunfire pounding the Manoir area.

From the high ground, where Gavin observed, the die-hard solid stand of Able Company on the low ground was not clear to view. By error, someone in between went running back with the information that the Germans were lodged on the east shore with infantry, though the armor had been mauled and stopped. Though not a formal message from lower command, Gavin took it at face value. Coupled with the dwindling ammunition supply and the lack of medical care, that made a dire enough situation seem more desperate than it was in fact. At Gavin's command post near the railroad underpass, Ridgway met him to talk things over.

Next, Gavin sped an officer courier to Chef-du-Pont with

this message for Colonel Maloney: "Leave one platoon there with two machine guns; bring the rest to La Fière at once." If the forlorn platoon became forced to withdraw, it should head for La Fière.

While awaiting Maloney, Gavin walked forward along the road to the causeway. He ran into little knots of men talking excitedly while walking the road to the rear. He asked, "Why are you moving?" They said, "We hear a withdrawal is taking place."

Gavin swung over to Lindquist's position. He said something like this: "Make a quick reconnaissance toward the bridge. If the position seems near collapse, move your own force into the front line and stabilize it." Lindquist ran forward. He met a swarm of 505th men; they were not panicky, but they were bound for the rear. He grabbed hold of them, saying, "Come on, you're going back with me." They did so without a murmur. Then he ran into a pack of 507th men, idling near a hedgerow, back of the Manoir. He herded them forward and made them dig in right next the bridge. Shortly after these displacements were complete, Maloney came in with the force from Chef-du-Pont. That seemed enough stiffening for the moment. Lindquist dropped back to his group and brought them forward to ground where they had a better field of fire toward the river—just in case the Merderet line was crashed and all hands had to swarm back toward Ste. Mère-Église.

But Lindquist still hadn't made a foxhole-by-foxhole survey of Able Company's front or talked to Dolan; the steel was flying plenty and it was unhealthy enough up there for people burrowed in. So he had left Maloney with the instructions that he was "to attack forward, through 1st Battalion, 505th, and re-establish the position overlooking the bridge,"—this based on the assumption that the front had partly folded. Contrary to the signs, that was wrong. Maloney was also told that as soon as dark fell, antitank weapons would be rolled into the forward ground and dug in for line-of-sight fire.

When Maloney advanced, it was at once apparent that the local situation was less critical than imagined. It called for an over-all strengthening of the position rather than a rebulwarking of the center. Dolan's people had stuck like glue; what had happened was that the less-well-controlled small groups deployed in extension of Able Company's flanks had taken a run-out powder.

One strong company (mainly 507th men) of Maloney's Force, under Captain R. D. Rae, was put north of the bridge along the riverbank. The other half of Maloney's 200 was deployed south of the causeway along the marsh edge. But again, these reinforcements did not move through Able Company or make their presence felt, and that outfit continued to believe that it was carrying the weight of the world on its lonely aching back.

They were kept at full alert—needlessly, as it proved. The enemy did not come that night; but his fire never ceased. Six more Able men were wounded. There was but one aid man, Private Kelly Beyers, to attend them. So intense was the shelling that he could not evacuate them to the aid station 200 yards north along the river. Beyers carried them one at a time back to Gavin's command post by the railroad. This one man's fortitude and devotion to duty became a main brace to the rifle line.

Captain Rae's area drew no fire; his worst sweat was that his men were out of ammunition. At daybreak, a plane dropped bundles and relieved that worry. But the morning also made other changes in the situation. The signs mounted that the Germans were readying a main blow against Ridgway's north front near Ste. Mère-Église. All of Maloney's people were pulled away from the riverbank, and, joined to Lindquist's force, they marched east, on order from Gavin.

That loaded the defense of La Fière on the back of Able Company, as on the day before it had borne the brunt of the attack. Some drifters came into its lines from across the marsh in early morning—paratroopers who had missed all assemblies on the first day, but were at last drawn by the noise of the fight. They arrived sopping wet and blue with cold and, in that condition, were put into line. Others died in the attempt to cross. The Germans on the west shore had them directly in their sights. Their machine guns raked the surface of the marsh. Dropping all equipment, the Americans hunched low and, crawling through the muck and reeds, tried to stay as submerged as possible. But a score or more were shot dead, trying to make the shore, while Able Company watched.

Second Lieutenant William A. Oakley had the platoon guarding the bank to the right of the bridge. It was a poor position, barren of natural cover except for a few dwarf shrubs. The platoon had lasted only because its foxholes were deep. There had come to Oakley at dawn a squad from the 307th

Engineers, and combining the eight men with two machine-gun crews from Headquarters Company, he extended his flank until their weapons could fire crosswise over the length of the causeway.

When shortly after 0800 mortar shells in barrage volume broke upon the east shore, the worst of it was concentrated against Oakley's ground. He began to hear the cry, "Aid man! Aid man!" The enemy machine guns had also lifted fire from the marsh and were drilling the embankment. But their aim was too high. Only the mortars banged home.

Two hours of this, and the enemy attack came on, four Renault tanks in the van. The armor got only as far as the blackened hulls wrecked on the day before. Peterson and pals met it head on, helped by the 57-millimeter gun, now firing from just above the marsh line. It was nigh untenable ground for an antitank weapon, but no worse than the position of Corporal Felix Ferrazzi, a radio man filling in at a machine gun under Oakley. With his weapon, he had stationed himself right under the barrel of the 57-millimeter gun, so that both pieces could direct a synchronized line of fire on the bridge.

Other gunners begged him to move, yelling, "That's suicide; no one can take it." He shook them off. The blast of the 57 convulsed his body and made him gasp for air; he shook it off. One mortar burst showered him with fragments, cutting him terribly around his head and neck. But with blood already running from his ears, he kept firing. Some minutes later, a second mortar burst socked him again. He tried to pull the trigger. But one shard had also smashed into his weapon, disabling it. He flopped across the gun, and some kind rescuer in a rush pulled him to cover.

Together, Peterson's rockets, the 57 and Ferrazzi's fire had killed the front Renault. That piled up the German column. But in its last gasp, the Renault had run on past Peterson's road block position, to die next the wreck which the Americans had dragged onto the causeway the day before. Peterson and crew had lammed out and safely made the company line.

But though the enemy was blocked a second time, it was not a repeat performance. The pile-up of German armor in juxtaposition to the wreckage from the earlier fight threw a barrier (or shield) of metal broadwise of the causeway, and the enemy infantry sprang to make best use of it. Thereby the two sides became locked in a sudden death grapple at 35 yards' range, the Germans behind steel, the Americans partly helped by dirt banks.

The rain of mortar shell on the west bank doubled in intensity and, being aimed at the 57-millimeter gun, clobbered Oakley's ground. One burst felled Oakley, and he spouted so much blood that he had to be carried out; another burst wiped out the gun crew. When Oakley fell, the platoon command was taken over by Sergeant William D. Owens, a quiet little man, slow of speech, a Detroit punch drill operator turned soldier in his late thirties. As he rose to the task, Owens wasn't sure that he still had a line. Half the foxholes were empty and the remaining strength dwindled as he looked. Men limped or crawled away, jackets bloodied, arms shattered or faces ripped open. First Sergeant Robert M. Matteson, placing himself a few yards to the rear of the rifle pits to steer the wounded back, found them coming in such numbers that he "felt like a cop directing traffic."

But Owens stood there, conspicuously in the open, impressively imperturbable, rallying a company by his own steadiness. The moment had come when the example of one man's cold heroism was the margin between victory and defeat. Already, half the platoon were casualties; in Owens's own squad, three men remained. The rest of the company deployment, owing to the roll of the ground in relation to the line of the causeway, was not in position effectively to help the platoon. The men could fire; but they couldn't see the targets behind the wrecked German armor. The issue was being decided on the ground where Owens stood. If his platoon broke, the whole position was gone.

The strays who had come in that morning from across the river were the first to lam out—not all, but a few. Most of them were shocked and exhausted by their experience and, having no identification with the unit, responded to the instinct for self-preservation. Owens was too preoccupied with the fight to try to stop them, but he could measure the effect on his own men; they fired less, and more and more they glanced anxiously rearward. Matteson saw a lieutenant—stranger to the company—break for the rear, and tried to make him turn about. "To hell with it," said the officer. "I saw a whole battalion of Germans over there this morning. We can't stop them and it's time to get out." Matteson couldn't tell him to stay.

The machine-gun ammunition supply was now down to one box per weapon. The guns were kept fed by the persistence of

Supply Sergeant Edwin F. Wancio, who kept boring up to the line from rearward laden like a pack animal. There were no spare barrels for the guns. They were fired so continuously (the output was approximately 40 boxes per weapon) that, from overheating, when the gunners tried to hold fire momentarily, the guns kept spitting for 15 or 20 rounds. Two of the guns broke down from overusage; Lieutenant John Otto cannibalized them under fire, and one gun went back to work.

But the wear on men and weapons reached the cracking point. More of the strays crawled away. More of Owens's men crawled out bleeding. He had at last but 14 men, and they were wavering. They kept saying to him, "We're through; we must get out; let's go now." He answered them, "No, we will wait for orders. We haven't been told to go."

Yet Owens was uncertain of his own decision; maybe the men were right. So he sent a runner over to Dolan to ask what he had better do.

Back to the survivors came the message. Dolan had written it out, these words scrawled in pencil: "I don't know a better spot than this to die."

Owens shouted the answer aloud to his men. There were no cheers from the foxholes. But they had the word and they faced the river and resumed fire. In less than two minutes the crisis was over. Raising a Red Cross flag, the Germans asked for a half-hour truce to evacuate their wounded. Able Company rejoiced to take time out to succor its own wounded, though unaware that the enemy had quit. During the 30 minutes, the German bid to hold the Merderet barrier on both sides passed into eclipse. The enemy infantry did not come on again; under cover of the truce, what was left of the Renaults and rifle power faded back to Cauquigny.

That evening, Able Company was relieved by the 507th people under Captain Rae who had gone with Lindquist and company on the hurry call to the northern flank. Their run to the other side of Ste. Mère-Église had been an exhausting haul, but a wild-goose chase. The combined force had seen and killed but one German. Lindquist got back to the railroad line an hour or so after Dolan's fight had ended. With his people, he was ordered by Gavin to go at once to Chef-du-Pont, take charge of the fight to gain the lower bridgehead, and ultimately assemble his regiment in that vicinity.

Able Company was formed on the ground where it had

fought just before starting the march away from the river. It had been 147 able-bodied men the day before. Death and hard wounds had cut it to 81. When that number lined up facing Sergeant Matteson, 23 of them wore bandages or were still bleeding, while awaiting medical attention.

Matteson, whose face should have entitled him to play Quirt in *What Price Glory,* spit a quid from his mouth and said aloud, "If people still don't think that men get killed in war, they ought to take a look at this company."

9

Kickback at Hill 20

On Utah Beach in midafternoon, Colonel Edson D. Raff heard the news that 82nd Division had completed the capture of Ste. Mère-Église. It was just like getting money from home. He anticipated a speedy, uninterrupted run to where Ridgway awaited.

Paratrooper Raff's mission was to end Ridgway's isolation before dark closed on D-day, by hitting the road with a small tank-infantry column and getting to Ste. Mère at all possible speed. Called Howell Force, the relief column tarried next the salt water just long enough to de-waterproof its tanks. Within 90 minutes after finishing that detail, this mobile armored body—Company C of 746th Tank Battalion and one platoon of the 4th Cavalry Reconnaissance Squadron with 90 glider infantrymen from the 325th Regiment riding the tank hulls—was already in sight of Ste. Mère's church steeple. The column had breezed along through a contented landscape, made docile by the morning operations of the 101st Division and the westward advance of the 8th Infantry Regiment, which also carried a ticket reading from Utah Beach to Ste. Mère. The joy ride, Raff reflected, was suspiciously unlike war and possibly too good to last.

Where the roads cross at Les Forges, 2500 yards southeast of Ste. Mère, the column stopped with a bang. The noise came of enemy shellfire. One thousand yards ahead was Hill 20, whose defenders had just beaten back the outflanking maneuver by Item Company of 505th Regiment. Whether in recoil from that oblique pressure, or drawn by the smell of bigger game, the Germans had pulled up stakes on the northern slope, faced about, and moved to the other side of the hill where, solidly emplaced and supported by artillery, they met the attack of the 8th Infantry. The assault had stalled before Raff got there, and he had to size up the situation from what he saw, which wasn't quite enough. He could see concrete works near the crest of Hill 20. Colonel Jim Van Fleet's line infantrymen were nowhere in sight. Beside the road stood a tank sergeant, not of Raff's column. He said to Raff, "I got this far, and then some GI flagged me down; he said there's something on that hill that's stopping the infantry." Raff concluded that the 8th Infantry, fagged by the day's march, mentally pinned by a flash of local resistance, had resigned itself to waiting for an assist from its own artillery.

Raff couldn't wait. Halfway between his column and Hill 20 was Landing Zone W. The 82nd's artillery and other gliderborne units were due to touch down there at 2200. It was now 1700. So he had five hours in which to play do-it-yourself and, by overrunning Hill 20 with his own power, save the glider echelon from disaster. The added anxiety, coupled with his feeling that his own people were fresh while Van Fleet's were leaded by a day of battle, made him rush his fences, and possibly justified it.

Raff said to the lieutenant leading the reconnaissance platoon, "Take your scout car up the road and see what you can see." Then he beckoned to the sergeant of his nearest tank and said, "Go on along and cover him." The two vehicles advanced about 300 yards along the twisting highway. Then Raff heard two explosions close together and saw the tank pile up on the scout car. A few minutes later the lieutenant returned afoot. He explained that one shell had hit his car dead on and, failing to explode, had driven it back into the tank with such violence that the track had been stripped away.

Though no blood was drawn, the loss of two vehicles and the jittery reaction of the men who limped back convinced Raff that he had better move against Hill 20 full-armed or not try at all. But getting the column up and deployed in the compartmented ground was tedious and time-consuming. It was 1930 before he was regrouped and ready. The whole tank

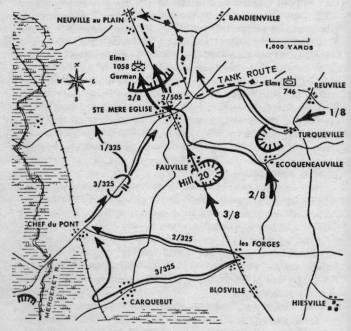

Figure 7. SECURING STE. MÈRE-ÉGLISE

company shoved off with the glidermen riding piggyback. The
armor had been instructed, "Move up the left, away from the
main road, use the cover of the hedgerows, move crossfields
and take the enemy in flank."

They tried, but it was no go. The two lead tanks made the
turn, crossed two fields and were then hit by a salvo of shells
and set ablaze; only three of the crewmen got out alive. The
following tanks ground to a halt at the nearest hedgerow. Raff
sped forward to survey the damage. The armor commander,
Captain Crawford, said to him, "That's eighty-eight fire. There

are several of them, and I'm sure the fields ahead of us must be well mined."

So again Raff temporized. While he had maneuvered, more of the 8th Infantry had closed on Les Forges. He sought out Colonel Van Fleet and proposed that the rifle companies go against Hill 20 from the left while the armor probed for a softer avenue on the right flank. Van Fleet would have none of it, though he agreed to support Raff with his cannon company. He reminded Raff that it was not his regiment's mission to boost the relieving column into Ste. Mère; the 8th's orders were to advance past the Les Forges crossroads and hold.

Though vain the try, there was no alternative for Raff but to get his own tanks moving again. By 2100, the force had advanced one more hedgerow and there stalled, with but one hour to go, as Raff figured it. From the new position, the tanks had a clear field of fire across Landing Zone W; that would help, if now the glider infantrymen could be realigned and sent up the hill aided by the armor's covering fire. For five minutes or so, Raff scuttled about, trying to arrange this forlorn mission. Then he heard a voice cry, "Look up there!" Directly overhead, at approximately 500 feet, was a serial of about sixty C-47s, towing gliders. They were winging into Drop Zone W, one hour ahead of schedule.

From there on, Raff was a shocked spectator helplessly watching an unparalleled spectacle. The carriers loosed the gliders directly above Hill 20. His companion of the day, Lieutenant Colonel Ralph Ingersoll, bore witness: "It was too small a landing field for so many gliders under any conditions. Only a few of them were able to make it. For desperate seconds they beat the air over our heads like monstrous birds. Then they crashed into trees and hedgerows on each side of us. They pancaked down on the road. They skidded crazily and stopped." It seemed to Raff that in an instant all of Hill 20 broke out with fire, as if to shame his own men for having been stopped by a token of resistance. He could hear rifles, machine guns, mortars, 88s and Schmeissers, all going at once. Some of the pilots veered off, sensing at the last second that the earth below was a live battlefield; their gliders crash-landed among the orchards behind 8th Infantry's lines. Those which kept the rendezvous, almost without exception, smashed on landing. If they escaped the gunfire, they were impaled on the antiglider poles with which the Germans had sown the field. One glider settled next Raff's still burning tanks; its riders jumped free before the glider, too, went up in flames. Another glider landed atop the enemy emplacement on Hill 20. Its crew, uninjured, rolled a jeep from the bird, methodically collected their equipment, and then sped right out of the enemy position, down the road and past Raff, as if repeating an everyday exercise.

"The battle of the glider landing," says the other eyewitness, "was over in ten minutes. It was without direction and there was really nothing anyone could do about it. The survivors filtered past us, supporting the limping, carrying the wounded. There were more still alive than seemed possible. Their officers began collecting them in the field behind the howitzers."

Dark had come. Having failed the attempt to win the field in time to save the gliders, Raff felt no compulsion to renew the attack on Hill 20. The try had accomplished nothing but the wasting of his own force. To order another trial would have been, in any case, a waste of breath. His men were shocked and sobered by the destructive side show they had watched from the front boxes. The lightning had struck just short of their boot toes, and they were not having any more of it tonight.

From all sides, reports were coming to Raff about the glider casualties. He had glimpsed some of the ruin—one pilot, crumpled in a ditch, both legs shattered; beside him, his group of infantry passengers so terribly stunned that when Raff tried to question them, they responded with hysterical laughter or babbled like infants. Also, he had learned something about gliders: the Horsas had splintered like matchwood wherever they landed, while the frames of the CG4As had taken far harder knocks and kept intact.

But he had seen enough, and he wanted no more of it. So he passed to his subordinates the task of collecting the human remnants from the landing for assembly at the Les Forges intersection. No doctors or aid men had come along with his column. Theirs was supposed to be a nonfighting mission, and they were not prepared to care for casualties. The medical attachments of 8th Infantry would have to dress the wounds, and its transport would have to do the evacuating.

So he recalled the tanks and combat cars to a hedge-bordered field safely out of Hill 20 range. There the vehicles formed a steel outer ring not unlike the covered-wagon laager of Indian-fighting days, and the men of Howell Force that night slept inside it. Raff closed off D-day still with no word of how the

82nd was faring within Ste. Mère and with no acknowledgment of any message from him. Should things look more hopeful when morning came, he would go against Hill 20 again. But orders would await a fresh view of situation. For now, his mind was centered on one simple plan—sleep—and he contented himself with the reflection that he had done all he could.

Thereby he slighted the most vital of all considerations—communications. In defending their block at Hill 20 and in holding the ridge at Ecoqueneauville, the Germans still possessed no more than a molehill in a vast landscape replete with horizontal and vertical cover ready to serve the evader. They blocked a main road; but their line was not continuous, and they were not spread through the fields and pastures. A small patrol could have gotten through to Ste. Mère by circling the defended ground and sticking to the ditches and cow tracks. A single runner, briefed on everything Raff knew about the situation, might have carried his knowledge to the besieged garrison in less than an hour.

More than reinforcement, more than the supply and the armor which traveled with Raff, that was what Ridgway needed—information about the general situation. It now sounds incredible: but through the afternoon and evening fight south of Hill 20, the Americans fighting in Ste. Mère gained not the faintest inkling of the near presence of either the 8th Infantry or Howell Force, less than three miles away. The clamor of a half-hundred gliders smashing amid a full-beat cannonade should have been heard in heaven; even so, it was missed in Ste. Mère-Église, within easy gunshot of the scene. The staccato of the local fight, which ringed them in, shut the heavier but more distant tumult from the ears of the paratroopers. All attention stayed riveted on their foreground.

As for why Raff did not send the word, he simply didn't know that Ridgway didn't know, and he couldn't conceive that the Ste. Mère force was hurting for news from the outside. Having heard from the division while on the beach, he took it for granted that a two-way circuit was operating. This is one of the commonest of battlefield errors in this era when soldiers, placing excessive reliance on the paraphernalia of modern communications, almost habitually neglect primitive precautions.

In the D-day twilight, the paratroopers covering the north and northeast sectors of the Ste. Mère perimeter saw a great flock of gliders drop down and attempt landings far outside their lines. This other serial arrived over the northern zone while the southern flock came to grief under Raff's eyes. So doing, it dropped into enemy country which would have been part of the friendly airhead had Vandervoort's battalion continued on to Neuville-au-Plain and stood there.

But the shrinkage of the position left the northern glider landing wholly exposed. Turnbull's Platoon had staved off the German thrust toward Neuville for nine hours only to be squeezed out a few minutes before the serial arrived. The enemy column had harried Turnbull right down the main road and was now shooting at Dog Company on the north outskirts of Ste. Mère.

Three gliders landed so close to Dog Company that its outposts collected the riders and brought them in before the Germans could interfere. Two hundred yards more or less was the difference between life and death. While the work went on, rescuers and rescued saw the more luckless arrivals shot from the sky by enemy machine guns along the hedgerows just beyond the outpost line. Other gliders crashed into the embankments or were spitted on the antiglider poles which spiked the meadows, with hard loss to their human cargo. Some members of the serial, by mere chance, swung over to the drop zone where 505th had dropped that morning and came to earth where they were relatively free of bullet fire.

So described, it was a bloody shambles, yes, but to the case-hardened garrison, bent on survival, it was a logistical offering which came like manna. Men had to think about it that way. There was no time or place for creature emotions; to feel pity was to quit. That was vital cargo out there and unless it was retrieved, it would fall into enemy hands. Some of the recovery task fell to Dog Company, but the lion's share was claimed by 88 men of Easy Company who, helped by a group of misdropped Screaming Eagles (101st Division men), systematically combed the fields, succored the crews and salvaged the freight.

The wounded and badly crippled were made as comfortable as circumstance permitted. The walking wounded and slightly halt were pressed into service. Hacking and smashing its way into the wrecked gliders, the company found the loads—food, ammunition, radios, jeeps, 57-millimeter antitank guns, bulldozers, shovels—almost invariably in showcase condition. They shifted it to inside the perimeter as fast as they could. The recovered vehicles made the command, for the first time, partly mobile. The 57s gave it a brace against enemy armor. One major supply difficulty—water shortage—remained uneased. It did not wax acute until the second day, when enemy artillery completed the wreckage of the Ste. Mère pumping system, thereby intensifying the misery of the wounded.

They were ready for the unexpected emergency of the night because the day had shown them that lightness of foot and constant patrolling was the way of salvation. Small detachments of German infantry were so numerous outside the perimeter that runner service between the defenders in Ste. Mère and the command posts in the drop zone had to be maintained through continuing patrol actions, the messenger going forth with several riflemen escorting him. When misfortune overtook the gliders, the onlooking fighters thought of it as just one more problem to be solved by deft patrolling.

Through the day, Ridgway had continued to move back and forth between Ste. Mère and the bridgehead abutments where his men were trying to force a crossing of the Merderet. The doubts arising from each local situation, along with the failure of any report from much of the Division manpower, were large enough to overwhelm a less redoubtable commander. More aggravating still, the General remained absolutely in the dark as to how the invasion was faring elsewhere. Modern technology failed this division completely. It had no radio link with anyone else in the expedition. Ridgway could not be sure that any relief was in prospect. He did not know whether Americans had taken the beaches or been thrown back into the sea. Sending messages, Division could not be sure whether it was heard by Corps or Army.

In his uncertain position, Ridgway decided to be sure of one thing—the Ste. Mère position. If the worst happened, if the morrow revealed that the seaborne forces had been beaten, leaving the 82nd's strength unequal to the task of fighting westward, what remained of the division would then fall back and strengthen the Custer ring formed round the town. Like Lieutenant Dolan at La Fière, he could think of "no better spot to die."

Late D-day evening, a patrol of Vandervoort's men prowled northeast from Ste. Mère and on coming to a crossroad near Beuzeville-au-Plain met a patrol of 12th Regiment infantrymen from the 4th Division. It double-timed back to town burning to tell the news. What it knew, however, added very little. The

12th Regiment infantrymen didn't know where their division stood or whether any relieving force was nearing embrace with Ste. Mère. They were just a patrol out roaming the countryside, seeking information, not carrying it.

Some hours afterward, that remarkable soldier, Lieutenant Walter F. Winton, Jr., an assistant G-3 (later Ridgway's right-hand man in Korea) struck off in the same direction, leading a patrol which included several men who had run the first mission. A fellow staff officer gave him a big shot of Benzedrine, saying, "You'll need it." Southeast of Beuzeville, Winton encountered more 12th Regiment infantrymen. But they knew nothing of the general situation. Winton there dropped his patrol because he could go faster alone. Several of the men had fallen asleep during the brief halt. At midnight he walked into the 4th Division command post and talked to Major General Raymond O. Barton. In a few minutes, he knew where Barton's regimental combat teams stood. Barton said he would push his tank destroyers into Ste. Mère come daylight. He gave the location of Raff and Howell Force as "somewhere south of Boutteville"—stale information but still better than anything 82nd Division knew. After downing hot coffee, young Winton (he was twenty-three) thought of beginning his return journey. But as he was many miles from Ste. Mère, it would mean threading strange country in the dead of night. The Benzedrine had worn off, and while he thought dazedly about the prospect, he toppled where he sat. Barton let him sleep. Another eight hours would pass before he could share his information with Ridgway. Dog-tired (he had moved all day on foot), that commander had at last wrapped himself in a cargo chute and gone to sleep in a ditch next the drop zone. Enemy bombers were overhead, doing their stuff, and throughout the night, Ste. Mère was pummeled by artillery fire. So a bed in a ditch was consistent with the situation, as appropriate to a night filled with boom-boom as to the end of a day charged with frustration. Seldom, if ever, has an American division commander been placed in a more futile position than was Ridgway's throughout D-day. Amid battle, his personal isolation was nigh complete. As a soldier, he was doing his part nobly; as a chief, he was almost devoid of power to direct anything, because of the collapse of communications. There was no channel to higher authority; his own people he could influence only as he physically touched them. He wrote of D-day: "There was little I could do toward exercising division control; I could only be where the fighting seemed the hottest, and thereby help my Battalion commanders."

But this was a unique personal burden, unshared by his forces in the combat line. By the close of D-day, approximately 140 of his men were hospitalized within Ste. Mère. All had been wounded in defense of the town. A larger aid station at the drop zone cared for other casualties. In the town fight, only seven men had been felled by bullets; the other wounded were down from artillery, mortar or grenade fragments. Numerically, the toll was light; it weighed heavily because men were dying who could have been saved but for the shortage of medical supply and surgical help. Too many bundles, too many doctors, had been lost during the drop.

Colonel Krause went reluctantly to the hospital that night, with a bullet in his left thigh, his third wound of the day. There he stayed 24 hours, when the surgeons got to him and cut the bullet out. Lying on his pallet, while coming out of shock, he reflected on a mystery: Why was it that the spirit of his enlisted men seemed so much more buoyant than his own? Though he groped, he couldn't find the answer. Other officers within the perimeter were baffled by the same question. It puzzled them that the men on the fire line never seemed to doubt for a moment that they would hold the town while the commanders, from their seats at the center, were ever uneasy and frequently felt that the whole position was going. Thinking of these contrasting attitudes, and asking himself why there was such a difference between the viewpoint of the command and the commanded in an operation of semi-siege character, Vandervoort at last glimpsed a truth which he stated to the others in these words: "In our position, the only accurate judges of the true situation are the men who are carrying the fight."

At last, a light had dawned. The commanders within Ste. Mère could hear fire from every quadrant of the perimeter. They were judging the pressure according to the volume of the noise. Sitting inside the town, what they heard made them imagine that uncontainable force was coming against them simultaneously from all sides. The same phenomenon which had deafened them to the reports of the glider battle at Hill 20 jammed their perception of the realities of what their own troops were experiencing. But riflemen along the perimeter knew in detail what they were engaging, and they had thus far seen or heard nothing which they felt they could not handle. The measure of danger was not how people felt about it in the command post but what was happening around the road blocks. Had line and rear been linked by radio and telephone, there would have been less phantasmagoria within Ste. Mère, but likewise the lesson would have been lost.

It remained for an interested bystander to underscore it. The Mayor of Ste. Mère had watched the fight throughout the day from a position inside the town. When at 1730, German artillery ranged in on the battalion command posts, starting the shelling which lasted all night, His Honor was still standing by. Then at 2100, the enemy made his last infantry thrust against Ste. Mère from the south. One road block crew met it and beat it back without feeling any impulse to cry for help. Reporting what they had overcome, they wrote, "It was hardly more than a strong patrol action."

In the archives of 82nd Division, there is a letter, remarkable for its simplicity, depth of feeling and hyperbole, which touches upon this same action. It came from the Mayor, and His Honor penned some days later, after liberation was complete. He wrote:

> On the evening of June 6, from the roadside ditch where at last I had taken cover, I heard the battle drawing closer to us. The Germans came back as far as the outskirts of the town. There was terrible hand-to-hand fighting.
>
> In the morning, I had heard your paratroopers say: "We are attacking; the forces coming by sea will be here in six hours." In the evening, however, the Germans came back and you still awaited reinforcement. One of your men told me: "The sea was too rough." The women around me cried and prayed. "Don't leave us!" One of your enlisted men replied with a laugh: "We will never leave you. Don't worry, lady, we are staying right here."

This touching memento from the war provides its own reminder that crisis, like beauty, is frequently in the eye of the beholder. The night fight at Ste. Mère had more of sound than of fury. Having spent most of their energy on the road, the attacking Germans had so little punch left that the relatively few Americans who manned the road blocks (and the fight was their personal affair) didn't even have to roll with it.

The enemy column which had chased Turnbull out of Neuville ultimately collided with one platoon of Dog Company under Lieutenant McLean just as the long twilight neared end. McLean knew the unpleasantness had arrived when small-arms fire, in moderate volume, broke around his position without drawing any blood. But this flare-up against the northeast road block must have been an exploratory probe by flankers because it cooled very quickly. McLean advanced four BAR men one field. They traded fire with the trespassers, just guessing where they were, for not more than ten minutes. When they stopped, nothing came back. Thereafter McLean was not molested.

The several road blocks covering the crossroads around the northern arc by this hour mounted, altogether, 80 people, three machine guns, five bazookas, two mortars, ten or so BARs and hand weapons. At each position, six or more mines had been sown in the roadway, with the heavy weapons deployed to their flanks along the hedgerows.

Soon after McLean's BARs shunted off the probe against Block No. 1, the German main body, massed solid in column and quick-stepping, almost marched over the mine field at Block No. 7. Sergeant Leonard Hodges had seen the column coming toward him from far off, but in the gloaming uniforms and arms were undistinguishable. He couldn't believe they were enemy soldiers because he credited Germans with more intelligence.

At the last second, as he was about to be overrun, he yelled, "Halt! God damn it, who are you?" The broad target vanished immediately as the Germans jumped for the hedges and ditches and opened fire.

Begun uncertainly, the foray ended in air. Hodges's people replied with rifles, grenades and bazookas, though they saw no targets. That defined the American position, and the first effect was that the Germans pulled back out of grenade range, and then tried to advance through the fields on the right flank. The ground was getting hotter all the time, with the solid embankments absorbing all the punishment; what amazed Hodges was that so much shooting could continue with no one getting hurt. The enemy's rightward swing was at last confirmed when three machine guns, tied together, zeroed in on the block from that flank and blazed away—range 100 yards.

Hodges said to the two men closest him, "Gather all the

grenades you can carry and come with me." They belly-crawled forward along the ditch on the opposite side of the road; it was good cover, but the ditch ran water and they spent an hour inching forward through the slop a mere 80 yards. That got them within 30 yards of the three guns. For several minutes they rested, flattened. Then Hodges whispered, "Now let 'em have it; throw everything." They rose and threw 30 grenades all together—fragmentation, white phosphorus and gammon— as fast as they could get them off. The shower killed all three guns and fended off the attack. Hodges crawled back to count noses. It was unbelievable; in three hours of skirmishing, not one American had been scratched.

From Block No. 7, the enemy bounced rightward into Block No. 6, commanded by Staff Sergeant Harry Yachechak. He knew they had come when his forward machine gun chattered away with no letup. Before the men around him caught their first glimpse of a target, an artillery shell landed square on the gun, killing weapon and crew.

Yelling to his 15 men, "Hold fire!" Yachechak made a swift recalculation. He had put the gun forward 120 yards, figuring it would double the strength of his position. The gun covered the approaches rightward of the road, being on a slight rise with a prolonged field of fire, while the rearward group (which had another machine gun) was spread behind a hedge on left of the road. He had echeloned them this way to conform with how the hedges ran. But now that the forward gun was knocked out, the question was whether to send the second gun forward. Where his right flank had been, he now had a gap through which the Germans could get on his rear. He said to the other men, "I think we're OK. I like it. Now, they'll get careless and swing wide and we'll nail them coming on. If they cut back, we're in trouble. Don't fire till I give the word."

The night had lightened and the field of buckwheat to their fore was vivid green, shimmering evenly. When the Germans streamed into the field, they marked the moon glint on their helmets. Yachechak waited until they were within 40 yards, then yelled, "Germans! Let 'em have it!" The one fusillade settled the issue at Block No. 6. They saw not more than a dozen of the enemy fall; the others ran back. The field covered by the forward gun was the only ground lost around Ste. Mère during the night, and it availed the enemy nothing. When Captain De Long, of H Company, came at dawn to check over his road blocks, he saw first the ruined gun and dead crew, and turned back to cry alarm that the line was broken. All the time, from behind the hedge, Yachechak and crew had been watching him, and he soon found them, doubled up with laughter at his error.

At first light, the enemy made another halfhearted pass at McLean's block. His platoon had been reinforced by survivors from the glider landing and three machine guns, with one 60-millimeter mortar. Though that was power enough to keep the enemy at a respectful distance, the fire fight lasted until 0800; the Germans pulled off to regroup just as McLean's people ran out of ammunition.

But it was just a coffee break and a chance to remove a dozen wounded to the hospital in Ste. Mère. The American perimeter had not been dented. Though they had performed feebly during the night fight, the Germans had not yet renounced the effort to smash it. In the circumstances, that was but proof of their folly.

10

One Pack of Strays

Around Picauville the countryside for days following the drop crawled with small bands of American paratroopers who could not get together. They had dropped in much the same manner as Shanley's force, and for many of the same causes that adversely influenced his operations, they were thwarted of any real chance to join their strength to some larger body.

Movement through the *bocage* country was much like wandering through a maze. The twisting hedgerows and sunken roads conformed to no sensible pattern, and main roads had to be avoided. Keeping men from sight of one another, the hedges and high banks also blocked out sounds and signals.

While the sounds of a skirmish several fields away might be heard, they conveyed nothing as to distance or direction. It was perfectly possible for these small groups to remain lost in themselves and lost to one another, though they wandered about and fought in the same area, separated by only a few fields, until sometime after the division cracked the Merderet barrier.

Once lost, as the sense of isolation increased, survival became their main drive, the desire to get back to the division a secondary objective. They fought when they were confronted beyond choice, and some of the results were spectacular.

Staff Sergeant Raymond J. Hummell assembled 36 strays not far from Picauville. None had a map; none could guess the location. This band was together four days. It killed 41 Germans

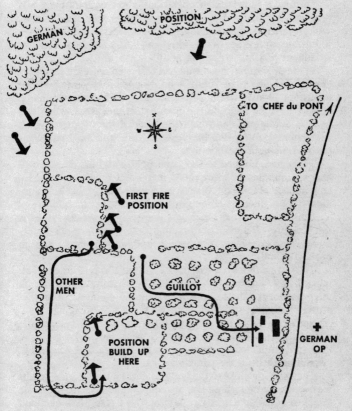

Figure 8.. THE FIGHT OF THE STRAYS

and destroyed one Renault tank. Ten of Hummell's men were killed during the fighting. Roaming around south of Shanley's force, Hummell was within easy walking distance of Hill 30. Yet he did not know it.

During its independent operations, the Hummell band was near another isolated group under Captain Jonathan Adams, which was having an equally rough go. Yet neither band ever felt the near-presence of the other, and of Shanley's movements Adams at first knew nothing at all.

In the beginning, his group had collected around Lieutenant Gerald P. Guillot, of 508th, who dropped 400 yards north of the River Douve within stone's throw of Montessy village. Guillot saw the river during his descent and was certain that he was coming to earth near the bank of the Merderet. That first impression twisted his sense of direction and started his party on its vain meanderings.

There had dropped in the same field with him six riflemen and six bundles of equipment in perfect condition—a rare coincidence among the misadventures of that night. The bundles yielded three machine guns and bountiful ammunition.

Guillot said to the others, "I know where we are. This is the Merderet. It's useless to mount these weapons with so few men. There are plenty of others around. I'll stay here. You go out and round them up."

They were gone two hours. The quest was fruitless—almost. They had found no men. But they returned loaded with three bazookas, another machine gun and a bundle of ammunition. The time was 0430 and first light was breaking.

Surfeited by heavy weapons, Guillot said to his people, "We've got no choice but to stash them and move out." So they stowed the heavy arms within the foliage of a hedgerow, swaddling them in the parachute silk.

Then staying close to the hedges, Guillot led his men southwest—the wrong direction. Having come to the river, he knocked at the door of a farmhouse. The farmer took one look and slammed the door in his face. At the next house, the Frenchman greeted the men effusively. After telling Guillot that the river was the Douve, he waggled a finger toward the far side of the road and whispered, *"Les Boches! Les Boches!"* Guillot asked, "How many?"

That conversation was broken off by rifle fire in the road.

The Americans ran out, but the action was over before they could reach the scene. Thirty more paratroopers had entered the village and jumped the German command post 40 yards away, killing four officers and capturing a clerk. The prisoner, shaking from fright, gave them full information about German deployments in the neighborhood. They had walked into a box. The greater part of a battalion was deployed to the east and north of them.

Guillot talked things over with Lieutenants Herbert L. Hoffman and Edgar R. Abbott. Before they could resolve a plan, mortar fire, in heavy volume, exploded amid the houses, and all hands began digging. While the entrenching went on, Guillot sent out three collecting patrols, with four men each, to search the near country. The shelling lasted four hours. The patrols came back with 50 more men, a third of whom had been injured on the jump. Two of the new arrivals were Captains E. L. Axelrod and John Thornwhist, Medical Corps. They set up an aid station for the crippled and wounded. Lieutenant Edward Napierkowski came in with eight 101st Division paratroopers dropped far short of their area. By midafternoon they counted nearly 100 men, and their position amid the farmhouses was fully organized.

In late afternoon Guillot raised the question, "Hadn't we better try to make Hill 30? That's where we belong." That object was about two miles distant. At the council of war, the officers concluded that they could slip past the enemy positions if they moved carefully.

So they struck forth, moving single file along the hedgerows with a point of five men out front. As they marched beyond Étienville, they met Captain Adams on the road, and being senior, he took command. With the column in motion, almost halfway to Hill 30, there was no time to exchange information.

The point started across an open field, heading toward a small forest. It had nearly entered the shade when fire broke out all along the line. Four men of the point were hit and killed instantly. The Germans were deployed just within the tree line— about two platoons of riflemen and four machine guns. It was a perfect deadfall, and the only thing that saved the American main body was that the point had pushed ahead too fast and too far.

As the column was pointed, it was broadside to the blast.

Flattened as it faced the fire, it was now in line with Guillot on the far right flank. Four riflemen near him had been shot down. He yelled to Axelrod, "Come help me!" The medico crawled over, and saved by a slight rise in the field, they worked together bandaging the wounded.

Adams, who was on the extreme left and had not yet entered the field, called to the other men, "Retire this way!" That would put an embankment between his men and the enemy line. Intent on their work, Guillot and Axelrod didn't hear the order and didn't see it executed. They stayed with the bandaging until it was finished; all four of the casualties had been struck in the legs or lower body.

At last, Guillot looked up and said, "By God, we're all alone." Axelrod told him, "You take off. But I'd better stay here with the wounded."

Guillot crawled rightward to the first hedgerow, then doubled back through an orchard. He picked up one companion— an unidentified sergeant from the 101st Division, who had stayed to bandage his own wound and was making his exit the same way. But they saw nothing of Adams's column; instead of fighting back from behind the hedgerow, it had departed.

Guillot said, "If we keep moving back toward the river, we may run into them again." But before he could find a hedge running the right way and affording fair cover, they came to a farmhouse. As they stepped into the open, rifle fire broke around them.

They jumped into a clump of lilacs.

Guillot whispered, "I think we'd better work through these bushes and into the house."

The sergeant nodded and followed him.

The place was unoccupied. They moved right up to the attic. As they settled and closed the trap door, Guillot heard a party of Germans enter the lower floor.

They stayed as quiet as mice. Below they could hear the enemy soldiers moving about, laughing and singing. Afternoon wore into evening. There was a clattering of dishes and pans from below, and the smell of meat cooking drifted up to them.

Darkness came. The house grew quiet. There was heavy snoring from below.

Guillot whispered to the sergeant, "If we don't get out now, we'll never make it at all."

The sergeant said, "Let's go."

They crept down to the ground floor, Guillot leading and carrying his Tommy gun. He was guided by the sound of the snoring. The Germans were sleeping in the kitchen. Looking in, Guillot saw two dark forms vaguely outlined on the floor.

Guillot took out his jump knife, crawled first to one man, then the other, and slit their throats. Neither struggled or tried to arise. He heard them gasp for air as he jumped for the door. The sergeant was already past him.

He asked, "Why didn't you shoot them?"

Guillot said, "Too much noise."

They took cover in an orchard and, surprisingly, soon found sleep. At 0630, they were awakened by a salvo of old-fashioned American profanity. It was Adams maneuvering along a hedgerow not far from them. They heard him before they saw his party of 14 men. The others had been scattered by the action of the afternoon before.

Guillot joined them, and the group returned to the field where Adams had made camp, en route stumbling across a bundle containing a radio. Soon Adams was talking to Shanley, who gave him the word: "Come on to Hill 30." In midafternoon, Adams and his party made a fresh try, the increment rolling up more strayed Americans as it moved along, hugging the hedgerows. For several hours Adams had heard no shooting, and the silence told him that the enemy must have gone. He said to Guillot, "I'm sure they've quit the ground they held yesterday."

So once again he marched his men at the forest, and once again, as the point drew nigh the trees, fire swept it clean. The only difference was that the Germans were firing from a wider front. That spelled out reinforcement, and so Adams withdrew his people to the same field where he had bivouacked, saying, "Maybe we'll make another try sometime tonight."

One hour later the Germans hit him there, attacking with a reinforced platoon. The Americans were breaking out K-rations at the moment. They jumped to their fire positions and turned the reluctant advance back after a few volleys. That first counterattack cost Adams and his group nothing, but snipers soon closed on the field while mortars pummeled it from the wood position, and losses began to mount. Adams's one mortar was down to its last ten rounds. Figuring he'd better hold that, he had nothing for effective reply. As the twilight ended, the Germans, in company strength, attacked again from a new direction. Adams's two machine guns were set exactly right to meet this thrust head on and spin it back. The only important effect was to convince Adams that he had best sit tight instead of conducting an excursion to Hill 30.

In early morning of D-day plus two, he heard on the radio from Shanley: "We must have blood plasma on Hill Thirty. Can you help us?" The group had collected 12 units. Adams called for volunteers. Lieutenant Henry Murray, Corporal Fred Green and Private Frank J. Circelli said they would try to break through.

They left one hour later via a route picked by Murray after studying the map. One-quarter mile away they were ambushed. Murray was killed instantly. Circelli was shot in four places, but came crawling back to Adams and told what had happened before he lost consciousness. Gone with the blood plasma was the hope that Murray would find a right of way reasonably free of Germans. The third man, Green, got lost among the hedgerows in trying to get back to Adams, hid for 11 days behind the German lines and finally rejoined his regiment.

In early afternoon a German three-man patrol wandered into Adams's field and were dispatched with hand grenades. In late afternoon, three more tried it and met the same fate. Private Joseph E. Atkins, a one-man road block, shot two of them with his M-1. The third German jumped into a hedgerow. Atkins saw his jack boots sticking out. So he blew up the embankment with a bazooka round. The routine continued. Mortar fire kept on pounding the position. To keep snipers back, the Americans sprayed the hedges and trees in their foreground with BAR and machine-gun fire. The Germans did not press tight again. There was plenty of ammunition for the light weapons, but by the fourth day the force had run out of food.

Next morning, the Germans broke into the nearby farmhouse and carried off the farmer, charging him with having helped the Americans. It was a bad rap with a lovely sequel. The wife came running to Adams, first to cry out the story, and then to add in French, "Now you can have all the food I've got." She brought over rabbits, chickens and finally a cow to be slaughtered, and there was a supply of milk for the wounded, some of whom could not take solid food.

The volunteer commissary was more than enough to see them through. American shellfire was laid on the field early the next morning, the first announcement that relief was coming their way. That flushed the Germans from the woods, and after they quietly pulled out, Adams and his party could arise and stretch.

11

Fate's Long Hand

Contrary to the Proverb, the darkest hours in Ste. Mère-Église followed dawn of the second day. That normal uplift which buoys the spirit of fighting men when, after the night's uncertainties, the sun also rises was for once lacking. Years later, we may well look back and wonder why. The torment of mind in the garrison, the feeling that it was up against forces far beyond its power, was little related to the reality of situation.

It is this diametrical contrast between fact and illusion, between the battle as fought and the struggle going on in men's minds, which makes the Ste. Mère passage-at-arms worthy of tedious reappraisal. Warriors are prone to say, "In combat, if you have perfect communications, you have everything." Though nearly an absolute truth, it still rings hollow. The flaw is that in battle the flow of pertinent information is always limited by human factors, even when all channels stay open and telephone, radio and runner remain whole and respond perfectly, which is rarely, if ever. Such is the traditional emphasis on the virtue of brevity in military messages that in battle it excludes the truly significant detail. The fear of sounding unsoldierly is as pressing as the fear of death. Yet brevity in speech may no more nourish the warrior spirit than curtness and formality elsewhere in life may promote a bond of fellowship. The rule keeps channels clear without clarifying what they should convey. Relay points may also become blocks, according to the emotions of men at varying levels. If the news has an upbeat and the sender-on is in an emotional downswing because of the pressure in his immediate environment, he will discount what he hears and will darken his own message accordingly. In combat messaging, man needs more than at any other time the touch of human nature which makes all men akin. It falls as blessedly as manna and as rarely.

In the closed circle at Ste. Mère, the reaction of the concentric circles of command, each upon the other, was as if they were separated by great distance and coping with three different problems. Their interdependence was absolute, which necessitated that all levels share as nearly as possible a common view of their resources and fighting experience. But because the physical apparatus of communications was at all times deficient and the human equation could not bridge the resulting gaps, each circle reacted according to its local environment and load of anxiety.

On the foxhole line next the road blocks, where stress normally would be greatest, it was least. During the night fight, they had met the enemy and thrown him back without sweat. Separately, they had good reason to message the command post in the town: "We can take these krauts in stride. We've proved it. They're hurting. Hallelujah, we've got it made." But they didn't. Soldiers are not inclined to minimize their battle chores. They're superstitious. It's like daring the lightning to strike in the next go.

Had the words held back been sent, they would have been a tonic to Krause on his pallet at dead center of the circle. He needed them at dawn when his morale hit bottom. The night-long bombardment by the cross-firing enemy artillery, the rebuff and exaggerated report of Item Company and his three wounds of the previous day combined to blacken his outlook. As rose the sun, so did his premonitions of disaster, his morbid reflection that this might be the last day for the battalion. He could not pass on what he didn't feel.

The want of bold tidings from that source was one more weight on Ridgway in his lonely seat at the summit. He could not be sure of Ste. Mère. At La Fière, the battle was going badly and getting worse. At Chef-du-Pont, a picket squad was clutching to a patch of ground by its fingernails. Division manpower remained far dispersed. Except in the 505th, his battle order was an agglomeration of cadres. From higher command, from forces elsewhere in the invasion, he still heard nothing. So all news was bad news. There was no warrant for optimism. Still, he did not waver. His decisions were based on one controlling idea—doing what he could with what he had. What there was of the 508th Regiment was accordingly ordered into Ste. Mère, while other forces at the La Fière bridge were given the precautionary instruction that if their line was breached, they should retire to main base. For reasons other than those which prompted him, he had maneuvered the 508th to the right spot. What came of it is eloquent proof that the gods of battle look with greater favor on a hard try than an ingenious plan.

Winton got back to Ridgway at 0800 and told him what he had learned from Barton at midnight. Still, that news by now was eight hours cold and nothing had come in direct from Raff's column, though it was tidying up mess kits in the next precinct. As if to rub it in, at 0920 Division got from the world outside its first radio message: "No info on your locations. All headquarters deeply concerned." That tone of injury in the irony of the circumstances made tempers rise until a message sergeant said, "It's like Sambo in the story. We ain't lost. We's here. We knows it. But wha's de Army?"

Within Ste. Mère, the artillery shelling, pounding down from the north, built up powerfully in early morning, and at last found a shining mark. One salvo smashed the water pump serving the block where the Americans were hospitalized. No reserve had been put aside. The wounded began to cry for water. The area of the other town pump was under heavy shelling; familiar with the target, the Germans were pouring it on at the most sensitive point.

Private Dominick de Tullio, the lad who had played cowherd the day before and thereby unmasked the enemy attack from the south, must have been born to the humbler tasks of life. In our battle line, such men not infrequently possess valor beyond understanding by the types who in action prefer to gun their way in noisy desperation. De Tullio said to Krause, "Leave it to me. I'll get through that. I'm a good water boy."

But the American Gunga Din didn't get very far. On his second trip a high-velocity shell exploded right behind his heels, shredding his body. He must have died instantly. The water pinch continued.

In his midnight tête-à-tête with Barton over coffee, Winton had done better than he knew. Convinced that the 82nd was hip deep in trouble and that joining hands with it at the earliest moment was imperative, Barton moved in to get the forces south of Hill 20 squared away for a combined attack. The 8th Infantry was to carry the heavy burden on the right of the main road helped by two of Captain Crawford's tank platoons, while Raff's one rifle company and the third platoon of Shermans would venture again over the same fields they had tried last night. Even before they jumped off, they knew it would be relatively a soft touch. Figuring Drop Zone W was still as hot as a pistol, Barton had sent an urgent signal that the touch-down of the 325th Glider Regiment be diverted elsewhere. But one serial, already airborne, came on. Some of the gliders settled to earth in no man's land amid the wreckage strewn by the enemy blast the night before. But no spectacle came of it. The Germans on Hill 20 reacted with a token fire; most of the men and machines got out whole-skinned. The greater part of the formation landed unscathed in the fields south and east of the Les Forges crossroad, strung out as far back as Utah Beach. Then as if thumbing their noses, some of the C-47s which had done the towing turned and flew straight into the teeth of Hill 20. It erupted with infantry weapons and at least one 88 gun. Two of the planes were blown apart in mid-air, their fiery remnants falling far scattered, while the waiting infantry watched open-mouthed from the departure line, more stupefied by the folly of it than grieved at the loss. To the doughboy witness, death in the sky, unaccountably, ever seems remote, unreal, depersonalized. But when a Navy ship is seen sinking, ah, that is quite a different thing.

So they knew before they pushed off that Hill 20 still re-sisted, though the weak welcome given the gliders also prom-ised them that the bold front of the night before was crumbling. All signs suggested that still more of the German garrison had sideslipped during the night opting the risks of tomorrow to the certainty of defeat today. But they were tough while they lasted. The Americans went at 0900. By 1030, with the aid of one battalion attacking via the short line out of Ecoqueneau-ville, Van Meet closed his noose from the left flank and crushed all organized fire on the height. A few snipers skulked in the hedges; there remained no other German resistance south of Ste. Mère. The 8th had moved at such a clip that Raff's people in this small fight were virtually freeloaders. Most of Colonel Lewis's 325th gliders had gone on to fields closer to Chef-du-

Pont. From him, Raff got the signal that by Ridgway's order, his column should take the low road to Ste. Mère, detouring via Chef-du-Pont. So he felt all dressed up with no place to go. But it was fair enough. Van Fleet had clinched the high road and was entitled to the grand entry.

Within Ste. Mère, McLean's platoon was relieved at its road block and sent southeast to meet the 8th Infantry and lead it into town. That was possible because, in the same hour that Van Fleet broke Hill 20, the Germans north of Ste. Mère made their final sortie, with consequences so conclusive as to bless citizens and guests with an almost workaday quiet. After a brisk preparatory barrage, approximately two companies of German infantry attacked straight down the road from Montebourg. The foot troops advanced by bounding along the hedgerows or moving on all fours through the ditches. While that left little to see, they were followed at less than a furlong by two self-propelled guns. Enemy skirmishers worked into the outlying houses in the 2nd Battalion area almost before the Americans knew they were beset. Where they could, Vandervoort's outposts fired a few rounds quickly and then fell back, not routed, but seeking better cover. One self-propelled gun came abreast of his command post, stopped and opened fire. Ignoring Vandervoort at the window, the enemy gunners shelled point-blank the 57-millimeter gun covering the north exit from Ste. Mère. At 150 yards' range, they still missed, but the opening burst drove the crew to cover.

Then Vandervoort saw one of his own soldiers (never identified) run from a building, take over the 57 gun, return the fire and in two rounds destroy the German piece, killing the crew. That incident, climaxed by the intrepidity of the unknown soldier, marked the high tide of the enemy advance and the start of the ebb. Waving a white flag, a German medical officer came forward to ask Lieutenant Waverly W. Wray, "May I have permission to carry out the wounded?" Not knowing the proprieties, Wray said, "Sure, go ahead." Having eavesdropped on the conference, Sergeant Charles Swan worked his way forward along a hedgerow to within 30 yards of a platoon of German infantry. He raised his Tommy gun; they were covered; he could mow 'em down. As he looked, they arose, took weapons, turned their backs and prepared to pull out under cover of the casualty evacuation. The itching of his trigger finger was offset by the doubt in his mind. Was it GI to maneuver tactical troops under cover of a mercy flag? But he didn't know the proprieties either, and so he didn't shoot. By noon the neighborhood had become so tranquil that Swan felt fit for a medal because of his self-restraint. He might have killed a few sitting ducks and not lived to tell it.

Just about then, "Lightning Joe" Collins closed his floating post aboard the U.S.S. *Bayfield* and landed on Utah Beach. The VII Corps general had extraordinary confidence that Ridgway and the 82nd would swim upstream whatever the current. But 34 hours after the drop, he was still waiting for solid information about how the fight went at Ste. Mère; and the longer he waited, the more he worried. So as he planted his flag ashore, there was an "I'll-go-see" set to his jaw. Right after hitting the road, he passed a tank park. Lieutenant Colonel D. G. Hupfer and his 746th Battalion (minus one company of Shermans) were getting their shore legs just prior to having a first go at Hitler. Collins said to Hupfer, "The 82nd may be in trouble at Ste. Mère-Église. In any case, they can use you. Get on the road fast and do what you can." Good offhand stuff—an act of inspired generalship—it was like shooting into a thicket not knowing the muzzle was pointed at a bear. (See map on page 94.)

The reaction of Big Matt Ridgway to Ste. Mère's noontide tranquillity, growing out of the German recoil, could only be one way. As nature abhors a vacuum, Ridgway loathes inaction in the face of a possible offensive opportunity. His generalship has no room for the housemaidenly rule that there must always be a pause to tidy up the field; he keeps going. Hard on soldiers? To the contrary, this perpetual drive, his habitual boring forward to the zone of personally aimed fire, his inquiring mind and his persistent question to any subordinate: "Do you know anything that will help me right now?" are among the virtues that endear him to people on the foxhole line. Americans detest wasteful generalship and instinctively recognize it. But they need to know that they are commanded by a Man—this above all.

Ridgway sat on the grass near his command post talking to Ekman and Vandervoort. The locale of that council of war stayed rooted in his mind through all the years that followed— for one reason. "We were right next the drop zone aid station where that wonderful Frenchman was caring for my casualties." But on that day they were speaking of other things than the

Good Samaritan. Surprisingly, Raff and his tank column had already hauled into Ste. Mère from their roundabout run, thereby beating the 8th Infantry to the "relief" of the isolated garrison, which meanwhile had worked free of the straitjacket. With only a couple of miles to go, Van Fleet's 2nd Battalion, as it approached Ste. Mère in the advance from Ecoqueneauville, came under artillery bombardment from batteries near Neuville, and swung eastward to dodge the fire, which prolonged their journey. It would be time enough to attack out of Ste. Mère when these wayfarers came abreast; 4th Division was committed to a south-north axis, while 82nd's course was westward according to the Big Picture; by that traffic pattern, the upcoming dirt-soldier battalion belonged on the right in the breakout effort, with the Montebourg road serving as the boundary between divisions. They discussed these prospects in general terms—Ridgway, the grave senior with an unstudied reserve; Ekman, whose bearing and speech were as rigid as if he had been machine-tooled; and Vandervoort, congenial, relaxed, with battle courage matched only by his wisdom. (He later lost one eye in combat and for that was retired, the Army thereby losing a file born for high command.) The show would be in Ekman's regimental sector, and his troops were tapped to help stage it. It followed that the further arrangements—arraying the forces and blowing the whistle—fell to him.

By midafternoon then, moving to a rendezvous at Ste. Mère were Van Fleet's troops, Lightning Joe Collins in his command car, and Ridgway, the first time that these names were ever linked in a fighting operation. None was then in the bracket of the Big Brass. The odds against their emergence exactly seven years later as the Army Big Three running the Korean war— Collins as Army's top man, Ridgway as Theater commander, Van Fleet as leader of the Eighth Army—would have been a neat parlay for the bookmakers who take bets on careers.

What eventuated proved once again not only that "the best laid schemes o' mice and men gang aft a-gley," as the pessimist said, but that when Heaven is kind, prayers will be answered anyhow. Ekman and Vandervoort had set it that Easy Company, 505th, would attack north on the east side of the Montebourg road, with McLean's temporarily absent platoon (it was out somewhere guiding the 8th Infantrymen) doing a shirttail job on the other side, and the newcomers extending west from his flank. The sense of it was that McLean's men already knew the ground and were therefore fitted for the accordion role—spreading or squeezing to keep juncture between forces not broken to team play. In theory, this tactical use of the "Lonesome End" was exquisite.

But battle operations, like radio programs, guide on the clock. Ekman perforce preset the hour for the kickoff, allowing what he thought more than sufficient time for assembly and deployment, then issued his orders accordingly to forces already present. There was no other way to do it and avoid utter confusion.

Thirty minutes before zero the German artillery came down smack on the deployment line and kept pounding. Easy Company had already toed the mark, crouched behind a hedgerow. The looked-for Van Fleet battalion was still awaited. Crawford's Shermans, which had arrived with Raff, maneuvered into position to support the infantry thrust up the Montebourg road. There was one-quarter hour to wait till go hour, 1715. That was the cue for the entry of the missing battalion—from the wrong wing. The head of the column appeared advancing straight toward the ground held by Vandervoort's battalion, still undeployed and well over to the left of Easy Company. It was too late now either to switch forces or to give way to the right so that the attacking line would have breadth and balance. As for McLean's platoon, that unit had somehow (not knowing of its attack mission) gravitated toward the rear of the arriving column instead of sticking with the van. So the right flank wasn't merely abbreviated; it was out.

No more delicate moment could be imagined for the arrival of the corps commander, and by a freak of timing, Lightning Joe showed up just then. According to the laws of chance and the rules of tactics, he'd earned a ringside seat at a classic operational foul-up. But never mind what the book says when Lady Luck can't read. Collins heard nothing of the misplays, and what he didn't know didn't hurt him. What his eyes saw he later described as "one of the most perfectly coordinated combined attacks laid on in Europe." Its unscheduled first round opened immediately after he shook hands with Ridgway—and it still wasn't blastoff hour.

Here's how magic took over. Colonel Hupfer and his tank column (Baker Company, the assault gun platoon and three Shermans from headquarters of the 746th) rode hard on Collins's heels from their park near Reuville. (A battalion skipper getting an order face-to-face from a corps commander isn't apt to drag his feet.) Then on turning into Ste. Mère's main street in Collins's wake, Hupfer, not stopping to ask questions, continued wholly unaware that an attack was about to be loosed and he might mess it up. The enemy was out there somewhere to be smitten. The armor nipped on, straight north along the Montebourg road right past the flank of Lieutenant James J. Coyle's all-wound-up paratroop company. The bolt from the blue shot by them approximately four minutes before they were due to jump off. They had still seen not a sign of the 8th Infantry, and having no desire to play Roland, they were agitated with doubt about whether the attack would go. The race-past of the armor was therefore not only a tonic but a signal. They were lifted by the feeling that the big power out front would smooth their way, and they read from the tank charge the meaning that everything was under control and ready to roll. (See map on page 82.)

So when their time came a few minutes later, they went. There was still no appearance of infantry support on their right or left. The battalion from 8th Infantry hadn't come into line, and McLean's platoon was missing. As they started, the artillery, which churned the ground around them, was joined by mortar shelling and intense machine-gun fire—proof of the enemy's far-forward observation. But the hedge embankments well shielded them. No preparatory fires had been laid on by the Americans; Ekman figured that the lines were too close-joined for that. Three of Crawford's Shermans moved out with Easy Company; the other three marked time, awaiting the 8th Infantrymen.

At the high ground north of Ste. Mère while still amid the houses on the town's outer fringe, Hopfer's column rode into line-of-sight gunfire, and he saw for the first time a body of German armor. Five medium panzers, five other armored vehicles, range 300 yards. From the lead Sherman, Lieutenant Houston Payne engaged, knocked off a self-propelled gun with his first round and set afire two of the panzers before running out of shells. Turning, he yelled to the commander of the second tank, "Now you get up there!" After twelve rounds and one hit, the second piece jammed. The demolition was completed by Major George Yeatts, Hopfer's executive riding the third tank. The German vehicles that could still go turned tail and ran north. For Hopfer's gang, it had been luck all the way.

Well-shelled, their only hurt was that the antiaircraft gun and part of a periscope had been blasted from Payne's tank. The rout of the enemy armor ended the heavy gunfire against Coyle's paratroopers right after they jumped off.

Pausing just long enough to get more ammunition from the tank with the jammed gun, Payne went chasing after Hopfer, who hadn't waited to watch his armor deliver its first haymaker. He was looking for a route by which to outflank Neuville instead of going at it headlong; finding a sunken road which angled off to the right, he zipped into it. Payne with two other Shermans tracked after. For a few minutes, the rest of the Baker Company tanks stayed put, firing along the main road on Neuville, then 2nd and 3rd Platoons also veered right and followed the leader. Wholly unaware, the few Shermans of 1st Platoon which tarried did Coyle's paratroopers an inestimable service simply by being there. They were right off the flank of the dug-in German infantry and so standing comprised one side of the box which was about to close. Where the 8th Infantrymen should have attacked, there was only a vacuum. That was the other oddity which made the perfect show possible.

Come to within 300 yards of Neuville, Payne saw another panzer near the village church before overtaking Hopfer, and engaging, destroyed it with his first three rounds. By then the enemy vehicles retreating from the first fight came abreast of him, but were already firing, having been warned by the killing of the tank next the church. They did better this time out of sheer desperation and the two other Shermans with Payne were hit and disabled. Lieutenant Frank Kogut's 2nd Platoon came up in the nick of time and finished the destruction of the enemy column. Kogut's force then nosed into Neuville, machine-gunning the hedgerows as it moved. Sixty German infantrymen were captured in the mop-up, and 18 of Ridgway's men were liberated within the village. There the tankers stalled for a while, not quite knowing what to do. They felt so far out on a limb that they could hear the wood cracking, and they didn't call for the infantry to come up, not knowing that it had ever started from Ste. Mère.

Compared to the run by Hopfer's armor, the advance by Coyle & Company was a mere nip. But in this fortuitously synchronized yet wholly unco-ordinated fight, that proved to be enough, thanks to the tanks having whacked the backside of the German infantry without knowing it was there. Coyle

used his head. Roads in rural Normandy have no more sensible
pattern than some of the modern designs wrought in American
suburbia. Having seen the tanks dash by on the highway to
Neuville, he realized he would make no killing by going that
way. Leading out from his left flank was an unimproved road
which meandered for a distance among the outlying houses of
Ste. Mère, at a rough parallel to the main road, and then cut
back to it. If the paratroops went that way, they might flush
their game toward the American tanks astride the escape route.
Just short of where the secondary road joins the Montebourg
road, it is crossed by a deeply sunken trail used chiefly for the
movement of cattle. But that seemed for the moment unimportant since its north-south line couldn't serve an enemy deployment.

Shoving off, the paratroops got almost to the intersection
of the trail and the secondary road without losing a man or
drawing flat fire. Then suddenly the bullets flew. On ahead,
Crawford's tanks, already feeling the buzz, had swung through
a gap in the hedgerow and moved up the field which the sunken
trail bounded so that they were above it and their guns were
pointing down into it.

But the automatic weapons were spitting fire, and this small
portion of a big war was at full boil. Coyle and his men came
on at a run, spread out in line in the spaces between the tanks
and poured more fire into the ditch. They had trapped a reduced
German infantry battalion in a cul-de-sac, and the slaughter
which came of it was grim and great. (The enemy was either
resting while awaiting orders or hiding, hoping to escape the
fight.) When first the armor moved in, a few of the Germans
had wiggled free and fled eastward. When Coyle's men closed
around the ends of the sunken trail, it became too late for the
others.

The overdue 8th Infantry Battalion also at last materialized
to join this fish-in-a-barrel shoot as it slackened. Done at spitting range, it was no contest, almost no fire being returned.
How long did it last? Possibly ten minutes.

The end approached when Coyle, who had been moving up
and down the line encouraging the tankers (who did most of
the killing), saw a white flag fluttering within the ditch. He
cried out, "Cease fire! Cease fire! Cease fire!" But his voice
carried feebly above the rattle of action and the screaming of
men. He ran up and down the line repeating the cry. American

fire dropped off. Then at the last moment a bullet from the ditch hit Coyle, and he went down and out. It was all over. From out of defiladed spaces within the ditch, 160 prisoners came crawling—many of them wounded—or stumbled into the open field, hands in the air. Coyle's 1st Platoon, trotting on to the Montebourg road, there to deploy facing westward as a catch basin for any fugitives, bagged the main prize—the German battalion commander.

McLean and his Platoon got to their jump-off ground rightward of the Montebourg road 15 minutes after Coyle attacked; they therefore strove all the harder to catch up. Coming to a large open field which was slotted with deep rifle pits (German-dug) in its foreground, McLean planted some of his BAR men in the holes; that was done to cover the advance of the rest across the flat, just in case the enemy should be waiting beyond the next hedge. This elementary precaution made the coup complete. The main body gained the embankment on the yon side without any harassment; in the holes, the BAR men awaited McLean's signal to come on.

Then just before the gap was to close between the forward line and the BAR men, Coyle's attack exploded against the Germans in the sunken trail several pasture lots beyond the other side of the Montebourg road. Seeking the only promising route of escape (some of Hopfer's tanks blocked the road to the north), the fleeing Germans streaked across the two pastures dominated by McLean's freak, half-unfolded deployment. In the rearward field the BAR men, seeing armed Germans running toward them, shot them down. In the forward field, the platoon sensed that the quarry was broken and, restraining most of its fire, motioned and yelled to the Germans to come in with hands raised. More than 100 prisoners were taken by McLean and his platoon.

So ended the fight. To the paratroopers, the whole thing had been ridiculously, mysteriously easy. They couldn't understand what had happened or divine the circumstances superinducing the enemy's surprising total collapse. If to the penned-in Germans it appeared that their undoing came of a neatly planned, skillfully executed envelopment, they were not made more blissful by their ignorance. Hopfer's accidentally timed intervention had made the decisive difference.

But Hopfer and his tankers in their far-advanced position were no wiser than victor and vanquished in their rear. At

Neuville they waited until 2100, hoping for an appearance by the American infantry. The scene was now quiet. The armor had won space which it was the foot soldiers' job to move up to and occupy before the dark closed. But nobody came. So tankers and tanks withdrew somewhat ruefully to their park at Rueville, which wisdom was the better part of too-long-sustained valor.

12

Through the Ford

To mention the secret ford which served Merderet operations adds a dash of mystery and romance, which is as it should be. Nothing else in the battle was ever revealed to as many people while remaining hidden.

On drop night, a French girl who dwelt in a house beside the railroad told Lieutenant Wisner all about the underwater passage through the marsh above La Fière leading to Amfreville. She even offered to lead him to it. But Wisner turned her down, possibly because, even in the dark, he could tell she was horse-faced. Trying vainly to find it himself, he finally gave up.

But for all her ugliness of face, he remembered the girl for her valiant spirit, as did scores of other paratroopers. With her mother and father, she spent D-night collecting lost troops and leading them to the railroad. She patrolled back and forth across the marsh in a small punt; her parents scouted the hedgerows and the water's edge. Together, they made possible the orientation of the greater part of two scattered battalions. Shortly, they vanished from that scene. Their work went unrewarded by the United States, for they were not afterwards located or identified.

The girl told almost every soldier she rescued about the ford. But even Wisner, who was an intelligence officer, attached no tactical significance to it and did not pass the infor-

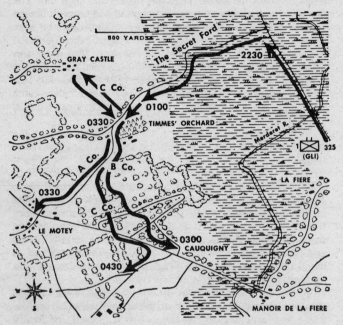

Figure 9. ATTACK THROUGH THE FORD

mation along to higher authority. Other paratroopers who had stumbled across the underwater cobbled road and walked it to the railroad bank after scrambling from the marsh also forgot to mention it. That it was finally found and used was hardly more proof of genius than that for three days it stayed missing and unsung.

By the morning of D plus two, Timmes felt hard-pressed in his orchard, the fire rising higher while vital supplies dropped to the vanishing point. The pinch would have been worse but that dairy cows may be cut up for steaks. Timmes again tapped Lieutenant Marr, one of those ubiquitous soldiers who pops up in the middle of every situation. Marr was to search through the swamp to the north for a possible escape route (he had never heard of the ford). That was his second such bid. The first time he had taken ten men along and had been clobbered with fire, losing half of them. So the second time, he took along one runner, Private Norman J. Carter, who found the ford by falling across it and barking his shins. The water was clear; they could see the sharp edge of the road bank. So the two-man patrol walked along testing whence the causeway led. East of the manse nicknamed the "Gray Castle," they came under machine-gun fire. But they were moving away from it, and the gun was too distant to be dangerous.

At the house by the railroad, they were embraced by the friendly French family, the ugly girl and her helpful parents. Pointing directly westward, the countryman said, "American! American!" Marr went to the roof and waved an orange flag. From ground beyond the marsh, an orange flag waved back. So the Frenchman put Marr in the punt and rowed him across the water to the bivouac of 1st Battalion, 325th Glider Infantry Regiment. From there, Marr started by jeep for the Division command post. But along the road he met General Ridgway and gave him the news about the ford. Big Matt attached so much importance to it that he turned around to discuss with his staff where the ford fitted into operations.

In this purely adventitious manner, a private's tumble into the drink altered generalship; and the late-arriving 325th Regiment was brought a bit too early to the unsolved problem of how to vault the Merderet. The 325th had flown into Normandy the second day (June 7). Its gliders were supposed to come to earth neatly in a fire-free landing zone already under firm control by other division troops. There was no such luck. The gliders of the regiment became scattered all the way from the Ste. Mère-Église-Carentan highway eastward to Utah Beach. The majority of them slid to earth in no man's land. That most of their human cargo escaped from the trap whole-skinned to join Ridgway's forces happened only because the enemy was already fully engaged in the head-down fight. Some glidermen were shot down before they could scramble to cover. During the landings, 160 men were either killed or disabled by glider crack-ups. All 35 who met death paid because they were riding the Horsa glider, which was a weak vessel; the riders in the CG4As were better favored. Otherwise, when the regiment assembled about five hours after landing, its condition was reasonably good. The men were still a little shaken, but the units were fully armed. For the next 24 hours, the 325th did much marching and countermoving, none of which radically helped the tactical situation, though the strategic outlook was brightened by its presence. Very late on D plus one (June 7), 1st Battalion was shifted to the reserve position beyond La Fière, where Lieutenant Marr found them the following day. Thus was set the stage.

Ridgway got to his CP (command post) with Marr in tow, so that he could tell the story of the ford. Among the listeners was Colonel Harry L. Lewis, commander of the 325th, a little man, rather old for airborne operations, with the disposition of a martinet and a manner which could be both vain and obsequious at one time. When Marr finished telling of his discovery and what he knew of the situation on the far shore, Lewis was ordered by Ridgway to "put a force exceeding not one battalion across the Merderet, hold the village of Amfreville and bring the western side of the bridgehead under control."

Perforce, the weight of this order fell directly on 1st Battalion, because it was on the right spot, and equally on Private Carter and Lieutenant Marr, because the coming of night and their knowledge of the ford made them indispensable.

Marr got back to Carter and told him, "You will return to Colonel Timmes with this message—a friendly force is coming in, and he must lift the mine fields covering the road north of the orchard." But that was only half of Carter's task. A party of engineers had been pared off to mark the edges of the ford with white tape so that the glidermen would not slip off into deep water; it was up to him to serve as pathfinder for this force. Two 325th riflemen were assigned him as escorts. The day was still bright when he started. From his entry into the ford until he got the word to Timmes in the orchard, he was under machine-gun fire all the way.

Dead beat, Marr reported to 1st Battalion at 1800, and contrived to get a few hours of sleep before, at 2300, with the last light gone, he started leading his new-found friends along the underwater road toward Timmes's position. The column was in midpassage when came the message from Ridgway, relayed by Lewis: "You will disregard that part of the order which applies to Amfreville and proceed immediately to the bridgehead with the object of capturing it before dawn."

Not one shot was fired while the battalion column walked

through the ford. Marr waited until the companies were deploying along the first hedgerow on the west bank, then walked on alone, seeking Timmes. He wanted to be sure that Carter had done his job and the mine fields had been lifted. So doing, he absented himself in the critical moment when his advice might have withheld the command from the initial error of which came cumulative diffusion. Suddenly the hedgerow was hit by machine-gun fire. Coming from the Gray Castle, it harassed but did not hurt. They were new at the game. Marr might have told them that the thing to do was keep going. But worrying about what might happen when the battalion broke into the open to make the turning move into the orchard, the commander, pivoting to the nuisance on his right, peeled off Charley Company to attack the Germans at the Gray Castle. That marched it away from the bridgehead. It also ignored the fact that Timmes and company were in position to keep that enemy force pinned to its ground.

Able Company was loosed to secure the road crossing at Le Motey so that no German thunderbolt loosed from Amfreville would smite the battalion in the rear when, squared around, it attacked toward the river. Baker Company was sent along to the main road to attack toward Cauquigny church. As promptly as Charley Company mopped up the Gray Castle, it was to turn and march to the support of Baker.

That was how Major Sanford explained his maneuver when he first met Timmes in the orchard. By the book, it was an orthodox plan, almost conservative, safe at every point, provided it was favored by time and tide everywhere. But these were green troops having a first go under fire on an overcast night.

Charley Company had already tarried overlong at the Gray Castle, and Marr was sent posthaste to extricate it and steer it to the main cockpit. This he did. The company was quite ready to leave, convinced that it had smashed the enemy. So they hit the trail, and the Germans, who had played dead dog, came right on behind, harassing them with Schmeissers from hedgerow to hedgerow. Marr kept yelling, "Keep moving! Keep moving!" fearful that the plan was already falling apart, which it was. The main effect was to feed the companies into battle piecemeal, unjointed, with no common front.

Lieutenant Levy had been sent as a guide with Baker Company, and Lieutenant Forman with Able. Charley jogged along in their wake and got to the main Amfreville-Cauquigny road without loss, the enemy burp-gunners having faded back into the scenery. No happening of that night is more amazing than that all three companies got right into the heart of the German main position without hearing more explosive noise than greets an average July 4 dawn.

As Charley Company turned the pivot, a runner from Baker Company arrived with the message: "We are attacking east along the north side of the main road. Come up at once on our right." On the spur of that invitation, the company commander at once deployed his platoons in line along a hedgerow, and the advance started with such a rush that it ripped off a snare of bell and horn alarms rigged by the Germans.

Marr remonstrated, "Don't you think you better make contact on your left before you commit everybody? You've got to know where the other people are." The commander answered, "You'll know that soon enough when we join flanks with them."

Almost as he spoke, the company line came to a road fork, and veered south along the hedgerow. Marr was certain that it had turned away from the main road but was helpless to make a correction. The company was already bounding ahead. That was the trouble with night fighting. Men couldn't see one another. Voices went unrecognized. Authority dropped to the vanishing point. What got started wrong was better left alone than surrendered to confusion. Knowing that already he had failed his job as pilot, Marr still went along.

The time was about 0330, and by now the overcast had thinned and the sky was starlit. Rifle fire punctured the silence as Charley Company crossed the first field. It came then to a sunken road, and looking through the thin hedge beyond, the men saw their target. They were right on top of a German artillery park. Twenty yards beyond the hedge they counted three 88s and one snub-nosed howitzer. Several score dark forms sprawled or stood among the guns.

The Germans saw them at the same time. As if paralyzed by surprise, they did not fire or move. Several voices cried weakly, uncertainly, *"Kamerad! Kamerad!"* and there were other words which the men didn't understand.

Along Charley's line went the cry, "Don't fire! Don't fire! The Germans are going to surrender." But the enemy did not come forth. A few shots were fired by the Americans; a few were returned. Marr yelled to the platoon with which he stood,

"We must advance and fire! Come on with me. We must move now or we've had it." Some of them answered, "That's right; let's go." But the majority were either confused by the shouting or doubtful of Marr's authority, so nothing came of it. As the minutes ticked by, more and more of them sprawled on the hedge bank or rested on their haunches.

In the center platoon, a German-speaking sergeant heard the enemy calling for an American to come over and talk surrender terms. Marr heard the platoon commander sing out, "All right, you go ahead." Marr ran to him, and said, "God damn it! You are sending that man to certain death. Don't do it. Now's the time to throw the book at the krauts." The officer said not a word, but the soldier stood fast. Then down the line was passed the order for the men to arise and close in.

From the cohesion, came a first spark of collected action. Rising, they started uncertainly toward the boundary hedge, a few of them firing. Right then, fire hit them from both ends of the sunken road. The German artillerymen had used the lull to deploy automatic gunners to both flanks and mount an almost perfect enfilade.

Marr couldn't see much of the execution; but right around him twelve men were cut down like ripe wheat. The shattered line recoiled into the oat field, and the German gunners displaced to punish them as they fell back toward the far hedgerow. Before they could reach that cover, an armored car swung into the sunken road and flailed them from the rear with its machine gun. The semiorderly retreat became a dead run, and the survivors didn't stop until they reached Timmes's orchard.

Instinctively, when the fire broke, Marr had gone flat. The company had fled before he knew it. He stayed there some time trying to help the wounded. So engaged, he collided with two of Charley's telephone linemen who had become stranded in the same way. The time was about 0530. They crawled along the hedgerows to the main road, where they were again pinned by fire. A German machine-gun crew had closed off that avenue with a band of fire directed toward the causeway. In the distance, from around Le Motey, came the sounds of a brisk fire fight, and Marr guessed that Able Company was in heavy trouble, also. One lineman with Marr still carried his EE8A phone. Proving that God helps those who try, when the lineman hit the dirt in ducking the fire, his hand closed on the company wire. Marr got on the phone and asked Lieutenant

Willard E. Young, who ran the mortars in the orchard, to barrage the edges of the road where he lay. He could see the German gun about 50 yards away. The shells came in accurately enough, and the German crew scampered away without waiting for a close one. Marr than crossed the road and found Baker Company. Its commander had already ordered a pull-out because he sensed that Charley Company had somehow failed the fight. Marr ordered more mortar fire, so placed as to cover Baker's withdrawal.

Then he walked on to Timmes's orchard. The scattered, battered elements of the glider battalion had all closed there by broad daylight. Their movements in, through and back again had lifted the fire pressure off Timmes's perimeter for the greater part of one night, but no lasting advantage came of the brief respite. The glidermen found positions under the apple trees, strengthening Timmes's force without really helping it. The German vise closed tight again, and the force stayed stagnant.

But at last and least, it had a telephone line to the far shore. Colonel Lewis got the bad news, and he relayed it to Matt Ridgway. The answer didn't relieve his feelings. Ridgway told him that he would have to take the available strength of his regiment the next morning and attack the causeway head on. The 90th Infantry Division was moving up to cross the Merderet, and no time could be lost.

All else having failed, there was no choice but to bull through.

13

Hill 30 and Millsaps' Patrol

On the third morning—D plus two—a patrol from the force in Chef-du-Pont came over the causeway, found it relatively free of resistance, and reported to Shanley's position on Hill 30. But the event, which should have cheered him, instead raised his wrath. For the patrol had come through Shanley's own road block without being challenged.

That Irish hothead—Shanley is a welterweight boxer with the brain of a nuclear physicist—charged down the hill to see what had gone wrong. One look showed him that his instructions on the organization of the position had been ignored. About 50 men had been assigned to the task of protecting the base of Hill 30 and stopping the east-west movement of German forces along the main highway. He had told them to set up two mine fields (they had found some enemy mines) so as to cover the approaches to the causeway from both sides of Hill 30. The force was then to be disposed on the most suitable central ground between the two blocks, acting as an "island of resistance" from which automatic fire could cover the blocks in both directions.

Instead, they had become widely scattered, without mutual support or central direction. So careless were the dispositions that a German column coming from the causeway could have knifed the position in half and taken both halves in the rear. Shanley set about reorganizing the position, and he gave detailed instructions on how to move the men and set the weapons in the central ground. After seeing them well started, he walked back up the hill.

While he was still climbing, and before the road block group could dig in on the new ground, a German attack mounted by approximately one infantry company drove down the hedgerows paralleling the road from the west. The American position was almost overrun before the Germans pulled the trigger. Their fire caught the road block crews right at the moment of dissolution, before one man had dug in on the new ground and while the heavy weapons were still on the move from the old positions. Shanley heard the rattle just as he reached Hill 30's perimeter and realized instantly that because of the orders he had just given to his men on the low ground they had been caught flat-footed.

He yelled to Warren, and together they rallied a platoon on the hilltop and charged southward down the hill, figuring they would move in on the left of the advancing Germans. So it was done. But no sooner had this enfilade begun to sway the enemy attack and bend it backward than Shanley's men heard the familiar sound of American rifle and machine-gun fire. Bullets grazed the ground on which they were fighting. There was a gap of about 300 yards between the road block men and the "fire brigade" which had charged down the hill. The former couldn't see what was happening, and Shanley had failed to advise them by runner of his intentions. He blamed himself that he was drawing a killing fire from his own men.

Taking one man with him, Shanley crawled back along the hedgerows to the road block crews, thinking that with a slight change in the direction of their fire, he could still get the best of it. The tedious move along a ditch took him at least ten minutes. Meanwhile the main chance had passed. The defense had withered; his people were huddled against the embankments. Heavy mortar fires were ranging all over the road block positions from German batteries located somewhere on the peninsula of solid ground around Montessy, thus taking in flank an unentrenched position already under bullet fire from its front. A number of men were hit while he sprawled there wondering what to do next. Then he ordered the road block crews to withdraw to the Hill 30 perimeter. Next, he worked west along the hedgerows, intending to lift the flanking platoon from its

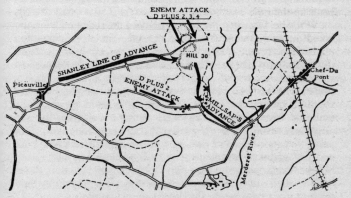

Figure 10. DEFENSE OF HILL 30

predicament. It was in his mind that the hill position was strong enough so that he would still be able to counterattack the Germans if the mortar fire lifted. He saw no advantage in wasting men's lives to defend ground which tactically meant very little at the time.

But he could not find the platoon which he had left with Major Warren, and wasting no time in search of it, he returned to Hill 30 and the main body. There he found Warren and the platoon. Warren's estimate of the situation had coincided with Shanley's and had been further stimulated by the fact that the mortar fire had begun to fall among his men.

The Germans moved in solidly and occupied the ground around the farm at the base for the hill. There was nothing Shanley could do about that for the time being. All along he had searched for mortars and had failed to find so much as one tube or base plate. With mortars he could have made the lower ground untenable. His bullet-firing weapons were invalidated by the surrounding hedgerows.

Tactically, the situation on the hill was now quite simple. The position was wholly surrounded and in a state of siege. Pressure against the perimeter had mounted throughout the day, and the attack was pressed with especial vigor from out of the northwest, following the enemy success against the road block in the southeast. The ridge line of which Hill 30 is a part extends in that direction, and the enemy mortar batteries were working from a level almost as high as the hill. The worst execution by their fire was among men who had already been removed to the first-aid station for lesser wounds. The men on the outpost line could see groups of Germans, as many as a platoon at a time, moving not more than a field beyond their own lines and trying steadily to advance their own fire positions along the cover of the hedgerows. But while the line took a beating and the losses from close-up small-arms fire rose until every fifth man was either dead or nursing a wound, the line did not bend.

Giving token encouragement to the defense, seven 75-millimeter M-3 guns from the 319th Field Artillery Battalion threw a few shells into the German ground periodically from their pits at Chef-du-Pont on the other side of the river.

Otherwise the situation was fully desperate. Food was gone, water was running short, and the bandages from the first-aid packs were already blood-sopped. Of other medical supply there was none. What hurt worst was the lack of plasma. Men were dying whose lives could have been saved. The other men knew it, and for infantry, there is no other personal torment, no blow to group morale, to compare with this. They begged the commanders to do something about it and cursed when they shook their heads. Shanley reckoned that the time for sending out search patrols was past and that he had no choice but to wait it out. His own discomfiture, and the morale of the defenders, were made the worse by the fact that three fourths of the men on the hill were strangers who had just happened into his command because of the bad drop. His own men were holding up better than the tails-down majority. At least, that is what he told himself.

That night Lindquist radioed Shanley that he was sending a convoy across the causeway to relieve Hill 30. However, there was first the detail of Shanley eliminating the Germans who held the position at the base of the hill. The convoy wouldn't start otherwise.

Lieutenant Woodrow W. Millsaps, an odd-ball type, volunteered for the task, saying, "I'll be damned glad to leave this hill." That afternoon Millsaps had worked among the wounded

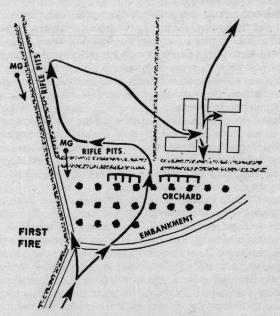

Figure 11. MILLSAPS' PATROL ACTION

and had heard them cry for water. Among them were a number of men suffering from chest wounds and others who had been hit in the stomach. Shanley had ordered that under no circumstances should they be given water; he thought that the effect might be fatal. But their crying got Millsaps down. While no one was watching, he divided what water was left in his canteen among the men who seemed to be suffering worst. To himself he kept saying, "Why not? They're going to die anyway." Whether this act of insubordination had pricked his conscience or he was sweating emotionally because of the inaction, there is at least his own explanation that he wanted to fight his way out because he was convinced that the Hill 30 force was spent and that the only chance for it was to open a line of communication to the east bank.

But he stuck on one point. To Warren he said, "I want my own men. I know by now that I can't control strangers." Warren was willing. Even so, the argument was lost when a roll call showed there weren't enough men left from Baker Company, able-bodied and carrying weapons, to fill out one squad. So he started out with a scratch force of 23 men picked up around the perimeter. Second Lieutenant Lloyd L. Polette, Jr., was his second in command.

It was about midnight when they left the hill. The arrangements were that they would proceed slowly and cautiously toward the position at the base. At 0230 hours they were supposed to be closed up on it. The seven guns in Chef-du-Pont would then drop 24 rounds on it. When the last round was fired, they would take it in a rush.

At 0230 the patrol was set and waiting. Three rounds of fire landed squarely on the German position. Then the artillery suddenly lifted and switched to the island mid-center of the marsh threaded by the causeway. This unexpected transfer nonplused Millsaps. He waited for the fire to switch back. Nothing happened. Meanwhile the men were growing restive. When at last the fire against the island died, Millsaps realized that the artillery was through for the night. So he moved on down the road with his men, Polette leading, and himself about two thirds of the way back in the column. He knew that if he ordered them to rush now, the enemy would be set and his own men wouldn't respond.

They had gone about 50 yards when a machine gun opened fire on them from directly ahead along the road. The front half of the column broke and "ran like dogs." Millsaps saw them coming back. He made a flying leap for one man and nailed him. He was a sergeant. Millsaps yelled, "God damn it, what are you doing?" The sergeant replied, "We're getting the hell away from that fire." Millsaps said, "God damn it, you've got a job to do even if there is fire. Go and collect those men!" He grabbed other men and yelled at them, "God damn it, stop! Everybody stop!" The sergeant had steadied and was now helping Millsaps check the flight. As for Polette, he had stood firm on the forward ground, and the three men closest him were sticking also. These four now came on back to assist Millsaps in getting the stragglers rounded up and started again. (At least one of them, Sergeant Royall Taylor, merits more than mention. Six years later, he wore silver leaves. There was no steadier battalion commander of infantry in Korea. But he had still not integrated. He said of himself, "I'm not the type for a Regular; I'm just a guy that likes fighting.")

There had been some scattering rifle fire and a showing of flares from the ground ahead. The road along which the patrol had come from Hill 30 branched right and left where the land flattened out. The fire had come at them from the left-hand road. In the fork of the road—the immediate foreground—there was an apple orchard to a depth of about 150 feet, and beyond the orchard, a solid cluster of French farmhouses.

Millsaps decided to move his men around to the right and advance through the orchard toward the houses. There was a solid bank of earth running around the orchard, but no hedgerow. It took about 30 minutes to swing the men around to the right, where they shaped a semicircular line, conforming to the curve of the embankment. During this time the German fire steadily increased. There were now three machine guns working, and they were all firing a great deal of tracer. Also, the enemy had increased the use of flares, and the whole scene was continuously illuminated. The German positions did not seem to be organized around any central base of fire but were scattered rather loosely along the hedgerows separating the houses from the orchard and covering a little side path which ran between them. Such was the light and such the noise that Millsaps could see the conditions were working on the nerves of his men, most of whom were engaging in an attack for the first time.

Millsaps passed the word down the line: "Keep moving till we close on them. Hold your fire till I give the word."

They went on through the orchard, moving right along until they reached the boundary hedgerow on the far side. This leg of the approach caught the enemy wholly unaware. The men were at the embankment before a voice, from not more than 20 yards in front of Millsaps, shouted a challenge in German. He fired at the sound with his M-1. His men had hit the ground immediately and were firing forward with all weapons. Several were firing Tommy guns. To Millsaps it seemed that the volume of fire built up in a flash second was tremendous. But getting the men to rise and go forward was another matter. They hugged earth. He kept yelling, "Get up, you damned sons-of-bitches! Now come on and go with me." But no matter how he cursed and begged them, they wouldn't budge.

Millsaps was acutely aware that if he could not get his men back on their feet he was lost. The Germans would come forward and build up fire frontally along the next hedgerow, or perhaps cut his line of retreat. Already he was drawing machine-pistol fire from his rear. Hugging cover, preoccupied with firing, his people seemed not to care what the enemy was doing.

So he let out a whoop and lunged a few yards forward through a gap in the hedge, crying for the others to follow. They stayed right where they were. He then crawled back to them, and went from man to man, saying, "God damn it, what's the matter with you? Yellow? No guts?"

Not a man would admit he was afraid. Each offered one excuse or another: he had been reloading his weapon, or bandaging a wounded man, or doing something else that tied him to the ground. But none resented the question. Millsaps knew that all of them were lying because he felt great fear himself. The palms of his hands sweated and his words blurred. He thought to himself how curious it was that in these circumstances his mind should be more occupied with the discoveries he was making about his men than with the movements of the enemy. But he chattered on for ten minutes without swaying them. Then suddenly and voluntarily Polette came to his aid, and together they bullied and prodded the men for another quarter-hour. Polette spoke more softly, but he booted their tails harder. Or was it that Polette's youth, shaming each man personally, made him the more effective catalyst in a situation where no one could really command? Millsaps wondered.

There is no answer. Men are neither lions nor sheep but a mixture. The man leading may turn them to either side of their nature. But until one other man joins him in desperation and anger, or in readiness to die on the spot, it is unlikely that the huddling instinct will be overcome.

As if a dam had broken, the psychological deadlock ended in one flash second. That quickly, the men were up and going through the gap in the hedgerow at a bound. The dozen or so Germans firing from rifle pits behind the next hedge were shot and grenaded as they tried to escape. Ignoring the buildings on the right, Millsaps's men swung left and back to the road. No command was given. But enemy flares made the scene bright as day, and the charging Americans veered toward another line of rifle pits on that flank. Germans jumped from the holes and tried to get away into the dark. They were Tommygunned as they fled. After emptying a Schmeisser into their ranks, Millsaps picked up an M-1 from one of his sergeants who had gone limp directly in his path, and continued to fire.

Five or six Germans had held their ground. Concussion and white phosphorus grenades fell among the attackers. Some were killed. Others were wounded. But those who remained on their feet acted as if oblivious to all danger or any sensation. Every act had become mechanical. When their comrades dropped beside them, killed or wounded, they paid not the slightest heed. And though they were wide open to counterattack from the farm buildings, no one guarded that way.

Millsaps was knocked down three times by grenades exploding next to him. But he remained unwounded, and the concussion didn't jar him. He saw some of his men stop long enough to shake phosphorus pellets from their clothing and then run on again.

When the last German along the road was dead, the Americans swung back to the houses. A thin line of riflemen and machine-pistol men were still defending them from behind the hedgerow. Millsaps's men charged through the gaps in the row, killing all who still held their ground.

With the last German dead, automatically they charged on into the barns, where they slaughtered the horses, cows and sheep. While this terrible orgy lasted, Millsaps watched dully, but without surprise, making no attempt to intervene. Vaguely he realized that they had all become victims of mass hypnosis and were behaving like men who had lost all reason. But the thought did not shock him.

The firing and frenzy died when there was nothing left to kill. Millsaps outposted the farm area; he thought there was a chance that other enemy forces might press in from the west. He had lost six men, who had been killed during the attack, and could muster only eleven who could still stand.

One badly wounded man was ordered to help outpost the road.

He said, "I can't, lieutenant, I'm dying."

Millsaps said, "I know you're dying. But God damn it, I'm dying, too. God damn it, everybody's dying. Go cover the road!"

He knew he was becoming hysterical because he found it difficult to think and talk clearly. The other men were even more overwrought. Some were laughing madly and others sobbed unrestrainedly. When he spoke, they responded with a stare. Millsaps could see numerous dead lying about, but in the half-light it was impossible to tell which of them were his own. The living seemed not at all interested in them.

Turning to Polette, Millsaps said, "You take over this position and hold it to your last man."

Polette merely nodded.

Millsaps then asked for volunteers to join him in crossing the causeway to Chef-du-Pont. Only one man said, "I'll go." He asked again. The others stayed silent.

So he started out with his one man, Sergeant William Kleinfelter, of Company B. A few hundred yards along the causeway they blundered into a German. Millsaps bayoneted him. Twice more they met enemy soldiers walking guard. Millsaps killed them. He felt he did not dare try to capture them or to encumber himself with prisoners.

During these killings Kleinfelter had lagged behind, and Millsaps resented it. Finally he said to him, "What's wrong with you? Can't you keep up?"

Kleinfelter said, "I don't know, but I think I'm shot."

Millsaps stripped off Kleinfelter's jump jacket and felt him over. The garment and undershirt were sodden and stickily warm. There were six bullet holes through his left arm and shoulder. By the time Millsaps had completed his examination, Kleinfelter was so weak that he could hardly rise. Millsaps had to carry most of his weight till they got to the American outpost line on the far side of the Merderet, where he dropped the wounded man and then went on, looking for Lindquist.

During this passage the causeway had taken a pounding from German mortars and artillery based south of the Douve. Millsaps was hurting enough from other problems that he scarcely noted it. But the American commanding on the east bank took a dim view and decided that it would be too costly to send a truck convoy across the causeway. Shanley was so advised by radio.

As dawn neared, Shanley withdrew Polette and his people from the farmhouse back to Hill 30. The decision was based on his feeling that they were not strong enough to hold there and it was folly to risk their lives to no good end.

At cross-purposes, Millsaps had begged and bullied the Chef-du-Pont command, describing the desperate plight of the Hill 30 force, boasting about his brave boys on the other end of the causeway and making light of the accuracy of the German fire. His persistence paid off—almost. Relenting, his host called Shanley on radio and said he would ready a convoy and get it across the causeway at once.

But Polette's men had already moved up the hill. With the light well up, Shanley feared that if he tried to advance in force toward the farm again, thereby to keep the door open to the convoy, he would bring on a fresh engagement. He asked that the column be withheld.

A little later he sent a patrol to Chef-du-Pont. It got there by wading the marsh one-half mile north of the causeway. When the patrol returned with a supply of blood plasma, it eased the main problem of Hill 30 prior to the arrival of the relieving force. This exploit showed that the enemy was no longer in position to interdict the valley with small-arms fire.

On the following day, Lindquist put another battalion of 508th across the river and established it on Shanley's right. Thereupon the enemy forces which had been crowding Hill 30 faded back. The whole situation along the Merderet had changed by this time. With both the Chef-du-Pont and La Fière crossings passing into American hands, the Germans on the west bank between the two bridgeheads came into full jeopardy.

They took it on the run, abandoning four infantry howitzers with their prime movers, 12 heavy machine guns and other matériel along the ground where they had confronted Shanley just to the north of Hill 30.

The reward for the veterans of that place was their knowledge that they had served under a Man. Elsewhere in the division, their stand was not immediately regarded as a stellar feat of arms. The wrong light was put on it by others who had moved and fired more while accomplishing much less. Eccentric mobility is more likely to take the eye than concentric steadfastness. What the main body remembered chiefly about Shanley's battalion was that it became isolated, did not join up with the others and had to be relieved by their means. So described, not even the toll of suffering makes the effort seem glorious.

But in view of its large strategic consequence and of the clear decisions of the commander which never deviated from the line most likely to produce the grand result, a good question is: Were they not the lodestar pulling the larger bodies on?

14

Charge of a Causeway

Second Battalion of the 325th Regiment started its advance to
La Fière on the fateful morning in a sullen and resentful mood.

Soldiers thrown into an attack are never as ebullient as
Rotarians. But there had to be another explanation for their
churlishness, since they did not know until they had almost
finished the approach and were in sight of the Manoir that they
were going into battle. While they swung along in column, the
bad news was passed back from squad to squad that they were
to charge across the causeway, which they saw below them,
and capture the shore beyond. They marked the line through
the trees by counting the enemy shells exploding into it. The
thing looked impossible.

But their grievance was more with Colonel Lewis than against
the Germans. An attached battalion, not organic to the regiment, they felt (as is common with combat troops in such a
status) that he favored his own people and slighted the orphans.
That gripe was not wholly without cause, and one incident
during the march-up intensified it.

Lieutenant Colonel Charles A. Carrell, who had brought
the battalion along, stayed with it just long enough to issue the
attack order, telling the officers, "You'll be going against a
reinforced regiment." A few minutes afterward, Lewis relieved
him of command and put in Major Arthur W. Gardner. It was
a little late for that, irrespective of the reasons. Gardner didn't

Figure 12. MERDERET CAUSEWAY FROM THE MANOIR

have time to take hold; the battalion was to go through its first and worst day of battle with no feeling of being directed from above.

George Company was first in column, followed by Easy, Fox, the heavy machine guns, the six 81-millimeter mortars and the other elements of Headquarters Company. While Carrell's final order was still being shouted back from unit to unit, the American preparatory barrage opened. It was a cannonade loosely coordinated in part, yet impressively powerful because of a last-minute break from one man's high initiative.

Brigadier General John M. Devine, commanding the 90th Division artillery, had landed at Utah Beach at noon the day before, to get the news that the invasion was running late; instead of heading for Cherbourg, the 90th would advance due west. By nightfall, some of the guns from two battalions were ashore, and without waiting further, he marched them to battery position near Reuville. At sunrise on June 9, though he had still heard nothing from Ridgway, he awakened with the uneasy feeling that the 82nd was in trouble. So he called the partly formed battalions and said, "Send your forward observers to Ridgway's CP right now and I'll meet them."

It was 0800 when he got there. Ridgway was just saying to his artillery officer, "We'll attack shortly, and we need 15 minutes of preliminary fire." The officer replied, "Sorry, sir, but I have no shells left." Then Devine presented himself, saying, "I'll haul ammunition for you; I'll support you; I'll do anything you wish." The effect was electric. Suddenly, everyone brightened.

But it was easier said than done. With Devine at the CP was Lieutenant Colonel Frank Norris, commanding the 345th Battalion, with six heavy howitzers. But by testing, they knew they were out of radio range of both battalions. So while Norris went forward with Gavin to get his first view of the causeway and Cauquigny beyond it, Devine sped back to establish radio relays, saying to his driver, "You've got to go like hell." By 1015, the relay for the heavies was set, and adjustment had been made after the registering fires. There was no time left to set up fire control for the light guns. Devine got to the 344th Battalion at exactly 1018 and said to Lieutenant Colonel Mervin Munson, "Lay on compass 4800 (due west) and fire; here's your target,"—fingering the map, he pointed to Cauquigny church and the road intersections near it. Two minutes later, the first light shells were on their way to target. These were the fires (supported by the cannon and machine guns of Able Company, 746th Tank Battalion, from hull defilade among the Manoir de la Fière buildings) that were loosed to clear the way for the glider battalion.

Sweating out the preparation, and the arrival of the infantry column, were Captain R. D. Rae and his battered crew of 507th men, who still held the foxhole line next the bridge, watching the minutes speed by. The word had been passed from man to man: "If the other people don't get here, we'll have to jump off right after 1000." When Rae heard the full orchestration in midmorning and he still had no order, he felt a little better, but not much. The signs told him that the 325th had arrived and would go; what kept Rae on the hook was Gavin's supplementary instruction: "Whether you go first or not, should the causeway attack waver, charge with your company and take over the assault."

Once begun, the thunder above the marsh swiftly doubled. The German answer, in kind, was full and immediate. Shellfire shook the ridge above the Manoir and crashed into the buildings. But its source was undeterminable, and there was no silencing counter-battery fire. From the ground around Cauquigny church came machine-gun fire of such intensity that it "beat like hail" on the walls and roads next the bridge. Rae's machine guns and rifles made full reply, but the spate did not slacken.

George Company, picked to brave this blast, kept moving to the rendezvous, hearing but not feeling the greeting. Until the last 160 yards, the road to the bridge runs at an angle, between high protecting banks. While the respite lasted, their anger rose higher against Lewis. He had promised them that the causeway and opposite shore would be "well smoked" before they charged. It wasn't his fault that there was no white phosphorus shell available. They could see at a glance that no curtain had been dropped along the Merderet. To the soldier's mind, a contract had been defaulted. The strong sulked; the weak saw an excuse for funking out.

They turned the last bend, and instantly fire swept over them from beyond the river. The men jumped to the ditches for cover. Captain Sauls saw them go down, decided that for the moment it was useless to call them to their feet again. The road ahead was a fire slot; flesh couldn't endure it. The sprawled company didn't have to imagine the danger of the passage. In the ditches with them were more than a score of dead of the 507th—most of them victims of shellfire. Mortar and artillery shells were exploding around the bridge end at ten-second intervals.

Sauls wondered if there wasn't a more protected approach. He asked a 507th officer who was glued to the same ground. The man said, "All I can tell you is we've taken a hell of a beating here for two days and there's a million Germans over there," which didn't help at all. So leaving the company, Sauls reconnoitered far over to the left, after circling the rear of the Manoir, and came out on the same side road which Schwartzwalder had taken on D-day.

It looked like a snugger jump-off point. The road approached the bridge at an angle. The ground was flat. A shoulder-high stone wall screened it during the last 40 yards, except where an enemy shell had breached it for seven yards, which meant that each man would have an instant of exposure moving to the final assembly. One enemy machine gun was beating on the breach. There was one other blemish. Rae's men were positioned along the river just forward of the wall. A half dozen of Rae's dead cluttered the road. Sauls called to one of Rae's sergeants, "Help me move these bodies so that my men won't see them just before they go." That done, he doubled back and brought the company up. Bounding one man at a time, they all made it past the breach in the wall. Beyond it, they waited crouched over, body to body, the first two platoons hugging the wall, compressed into a single line not more than 35 yards long. The guns were supposed to hold fire on the opposing shore until the last moment, then the barrage was to roll back as the infantry charged. The enemy shellfire fell just short of the wall. It didn't bother Sauls's people, but Rae's line was beginning to reel. Major Gardner came forward to see if Sauls was ready. The men were still grousing: "What about that Goddamned smoke?"

Sauls looked at his watch and called out, "Two minutes to go." To his amazement then, suddenly all hands shook the black mood. One man yelled, "Let's get to the other side; *beaucoup mademoiselles* over there; none over here." Everybody laughed. Sauls winked at the lead files, and those who caught his eye winked back. He felt better. Up front was Staff Sergeant Wilfred L. Ericsson, a towering man, and behind him,

Lieutenant Donald B. Wason. They'd set the pace.

It turned 1045. Sauls held 30 seconds extra, still praying for the smoke. Then he yelled, "Go! Go! Go!" From there on, what happened was up to the individuals. They had been told to go at a run, cross the 20-yard space between the end of the wall and the bridge at top speed, then peel off right and left, man after man, as they started across the 500-yard causeway at a fast trot, so that they would come to the far shore in parallel columns running along the roadway shoulders. That way, they would be closer to the embankment shrubbery; an infantryman always feels safer if there is a twig between him and an approaching shell.

At the last moment, on impulse, Sauls ran forward to become first man leading off on the left. Wason, outrunning Ericsson, broke trail on the right. Ericsson, overeager, swung in right behind him, followed by his entire squad. Wason yelled back, "Get over left." Ericsson got over—followed by his squad. In the wake, a few men alternated, until the whole thing drizzled out.

As this small spearpoint rushed, its pitifully few people marveled only that muscles would respond and men could live amid such fire. Every stride was a little victory. Mortar bursts from forward shook the roadway. Automatic fire came at them as if rising from the marsh. There was no time to look back and see if anyone was following. They ran straight up instead of stooping; they could run faster that way and save their wind.

No American charge into enemy country was ever pressed home by so few men. After Ericsson's squad, there followed but one BAR man and two soldiers with rifles. But everyone in this forlorn group made it to the far shore. What saved them was that the American artillery had not lifted. When they got to the far end of the causeway, the friendly barrage was still barring the road 25 to 30 yards beyond them. It was a barrier, but it was also a protection. Big Ericsson turned leftward along the first trail paralleling the march, not even stopping to see if his squad was following. It was. Sauls stopped where the trail intersected the main road, intending to serve as a semaphore, motioning the other men to follow Ericsson. It would be foolish to scatter one company. Some seconds—maybe a minute or two—passed before he recovered his wind and realized by another glance along the back trail, that no one was following. He and the handful of riflemen, which had already vanished into the scenery, composed the American bridgehead west of the Merderet.

Wason, having outrun both Sauls and Ericsson, had dashed straight up the main road. He had seen a German machine gun firing straight down the causeway as he came onto the west shore; he wanted that gun. Three or four men followed him. He yelled to them, "Stay back; I'll get the gun." His closing rush ended in a dead heat. Wason's grenade killed the gun just as one of the German gunners shot Wason dead. Sauls's runner, Private Frank Thurston, had watched it. He came running back to tell Sauls, adding, "Sir, there's a second gun beyond it; may I go get it?" Sauls said, "Sure, go ahead." Thurston was the cautious type. He crawled forward along a hedgerow, got to the road intersection, lay there in good cover, and killed the German gun crew one by one with his M-1. Then he crawled back to Sauls, laughing like a maniac. "Sir," he said, "I got all of those bastards."

By then, Sauls realized that the assault had miscarried. The causeway was empty. Of his company, he had three squads. By a fluke of battle, the breach in the stone wall at La Fière had betrayed the whole order of battle. Not all of George Company had managed to pass the hole and squeeze in next the wall. Most of the two rifle platoons were so collected when Sauls took off. But not all the members were nerved to follow him. The fainthearted cluttered the protected space while weapons platoon waited to dash past the break. No one said anything.

Private Melvin L. Johnson, in the lead, hesitated. Then he yelled, "Here I go." Midway across the gap, a machine-gun burst shattered his skull and he fell. That body, across the roadway, shocked the rest of the company and blocked the whole battalion. Hundreds of men stayed there, inert, unwilling, because of the effect of one bullet. The spot called for the re-energizing influence of a higher commander. None was present. Twenty minutes passed this way.

Then Lieutenant Frank E. Amino tried to break the spell. He arose yelling, "Follow me! Let's go kill the sons-of-bitches," and ran on past the gap. Not more than a dozen or so riflemen, among the stragglers whom Sauls had left by the wall, were shaken loose by his example. Once in the open, they tried to keep going. Most of the men they left behind stayed rooted.

But part of weapons platoon at least tried. Weighted as they were, the bazooka, Browning and radio handlers couldn't sprint like the riflemen. The charge had to die because they couldn't take the causeway in one dash. They moved tortoiselike, stopping every few feet to rest, looking vainly for some kind of dirt cover. Some, falling victim to the stopping habit, went flat on the bank and stayed there, though still unscratched. The more their numbers grew, the more intense became the enemy automatic fire along the roadway. Fully exposed and vulnerable, they simply waited for the fire to find them; then their bodies, dead or wounded, compounded the difficulty for men still mobile and trying to make the crossing. So began the choke-up; the longer the fight lasted, the deadlier became the passage.

Then amid the movement by George's weapons platoon, the first American tank tried to barge through. The mines which the Americans had sown beyond the bridge on D-day were still in place. Sauls had seen them as he ran past. But none of his men had stopped to clear the block. In trying to swing around the ruined German tank next the block, the Sherman exploded one mine. Without hurting the armor, it blew back, wounding seven men from weapons platoon. Staff Sergeant George F. Myers, section leader for the mortars, was struck by one fragment in the eye and half-blinded. Blood spurting from his face, he jumped up, yelling to the others, "Come on, now we've got to make it." He got to the far end of the causeway, then keeled over from loss of blood. Already there were 25 to 30 casualties—dead and wounded—strung out along the causeway.

Shallow drainage ditches ran along the embankments. Shortly these gutters were filled with the malingerers and the wounded. That eliminated the last trace of cover. Thereafter stagnation rapidly changed to paralysis. The more the casualties mounted, the heavier grew the fire, the more the roadway became blocked and the less became the chance that motion toward the enemy could be restored.

But the handful of Americans who had made the west shore were doing their utmost to redeem the battalion. Turning down the trail which ran left next the marsh, Sergeant Ericsson had motioned the BAR man, Private James D. Kittle, to move inside the hedgerow on his right and prepare to fire. Ericsson and his squad ran on down the trail; as he saw it, the Germans firing across the marsh from this flank must be in foxholes somewhere along the trail. He would blast them out of their

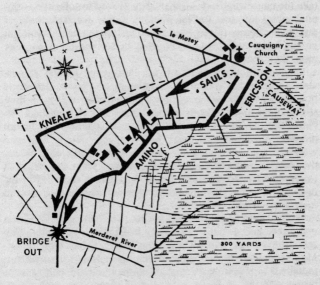

Figure 13. GEORGE COMPANY'S DEPLOYMENT

holes; they would try to escape rearward; then Kittle, keeping pace with him, could mow them down.

But Ericsson had overcomplicated it. At the beginning, two Germans popped out of the hedgerow with helmets rattling and hands up. Ericsson thumbed them back toward the causeway and yelled, "Get!" and they took off obediently, without guard. The squad moved on, grenaded the hedge, then ducked when potato mashers came back at them. The German bombs exploded weakly, encouraging Ericsson to yell, "Come on out!" Twelve more Germans came out of the hedge, hands in air. They were thumbed toward the causeway—and went. A few more grenades, and the exodus became general. Forty or so of the enemy quit the field where Kittle fired and the hedge where the squad bombed, having already thrown down their arms in surrender.

Sauls was still at the first intersection when Amino and his little gang arrived. That he had survived so long in the hot spot gave him a brief conviction of immortality. He sent this reinforcement—one and one-half squads—in the direction Wason had taken, saying to the men, "You are to establish a right flank for George Company." They set up a machine-gun position on the main road and directed its fire against Cauquigny church.

Out of Amino's group, Technical Sergeant John P. Kneale worked up to the road fork right next the church. He stood there in the open waving his arms like a traffic cop and yelling to the other men, "Come on! Come on! We've got the Goddamn bastards on the run." Sniper fire kicked up the dirt all around him. Paying no heed, he continued yelling. The men worked on up and passed him. Kneale stayed there, as if asking for a bullet. At last Sauls's nerve frayed from the strain of watching him. He ran forward and said to Kneale, "I'm ordering you to get the hell out of here and seek cover. You're driving me crazy."

After mopping up the trail position for 150 yards, Ericsson and squad had to withdraw. They had run out of ammunition and Ericsson saw that several of his hands, tiring, were beginning to dog it. He was almost back to the main road when a bullet hit him just above the left kidney and stopped him for that day.

Sauls saw him fall, and the loss shook him into a realization that he was overextending. George Company had been told to mop up on the left of the main road, and he was trying to do it all with less than a platoon. So he recalled Amino and some of his group to take over where Ericsson had left off. The rest of the men under Sergeant Kneale were to work along the second trail, which ran leftward. That would put the two groups on a roughly parallel but gradually converging course. Each force was to use its fire in such way as to provide a release for the other.

This simple maneuver was the beginning of order on the west shore. On the causeway the situation was still fully desperate. Fire beat upon the road from both flanks and front. The litter of dead and wounded along the embankments continued to thicken. Where men moved at all, they had to pick their footing slowly.

The German prisoners taken by Ericsson had tried to get back to La Fière. But once on the causeway, they fared no better than the Americans. Most of them were killed by their own fire as they moved westward.

Looking the scene over, after taking his bullet, Ericsson decided it was safer to bleed in a ditch than to attempt the passage. He flopped down in a shellhole near the head of the causeway and waited for conditions to change. More than two hours later, a friend, First Sergeant Harry B. Ready, found him there. Grown stiff and weakened by his wound, Ericsson could barely speak. But he motioned to Ready and shoved his own Tommy gun into his friend's hands.

"Take that with you," he said. "You won't need a carbine over here."

15

Struggle for Mobility

With 1st Platoon Leading, Easy Company was supposed to cross the causeway and clear the area around Cauquigny church of all Germans. Coupled with the sweep of George Company east of the road, that would break resistance and free the bridgehead of all fire but the enemy artillery.

Not waiting for his platoon, Lieutenant Richard B. Johnson took off to reconnoiter the west shore and pick a spot from which he could point his men into the action. He got there right after Amino and Kneale, with their people, had vanished into the hedgerows in their new deployment. So that left Johnson all alone amid the German army. He crawled forward to the hedgerow bounding the church, then squinted through the gaps in the hedge for whatever he could find. It was an unprofitable business. The graveyard was being heavily churned by American mortar bursts from the east shore. Bullets clipped twigs and blossoms from the apple bower above his head. But of a live enemy, he saw no sign.

Ten minutes passed before any of his men came up. With the best of intentions, Sergeant Henry W. Howell had stalled the movement. On getting beyond the bridge and finding the road blocked with George Company stragglers, he pulled up because he had been given no instruction about passing through the other outfit. His skipper, Captain Charles F. Murphy, might have resolved this dilemma. But at that moment, a mortar shell exploded next him, felling four other men and smashing Murphy's face. A bloody mess, Murphy staggered on toward the west shore hoping to find an aid man. His executive, Lieutenant Bruce H. Booker, had been put at the rear to herd the shirkers. So Howell, in the van, stayed put until the battalion S-3, Captain James G. Fogle, happened along and told him, "Get this platoon going or we'll all die here."

Howell and group picked their way like men doing a bending race in slow motion. It was no longer possible to walk fast, much less run. Stragglers, prisoners and wounded men were streaming back. Dead littered the pavement. Other wounded crawled along the embankment. Some of the men, still unhit but drained of their courage and shocked into immobility, sought cover behind the dead bodies, there being none other. Enlarging the cluster, they increased the congestion. Because intermittently all movement was blocked, and the willing hearts wished to take some positive action, the causeway willy-nilly became a general fire line.

Howell noted that the leader of his own machine-gun crew, Sergeant Larry S. Wilson, advanced his weapon about 30 yards at a time, and on each stop, set up and fired. Other heavy-weapons men did the same. Among the riflemen, the movement was slow or rapid, smooth or jerky, according to the example set by the squad leader. If he lost heart and fell away from the platoon, his men usually quit with him.

Lieutenant Booker had a double chance to ponder these things. Out of sheer anger, he moved up to the front of the company and reached the west shore even with Howell's men. Then aware that the main body had straggled, he returned to the bridge and made a personal sweep forward, prodding Sauls's malingerers as well as his own. On that round, he was hit through the calves of both legs and temporarily string-haltered. He sat down on the road shoulder to wait for a medico. While so tied, he kept waving his arms and yelling, "Come on, you bastards! Get up there! God damn it, get up there! That's where the fight is." That shamed a few of them into starting again, and the exhortation continued. Before he could get his wounds dressed, he saw a knot of Easy Company men coming from the west shore, quitting the fight. He pulled his pistol, then shouting and laughing, he fired six rounds just above their heads; he yelled, "Keep coming toward me and you see what happens." They turned back, and by then, they were laughing, also. That incident didn't close Booker's record for the day. He was simply waiting for his legs to cool off. Once bandaged, he resumed the role of driver up and down the causeway.

Howell kept his rendezvous with Lieutenant Johnson. He had lost 12 men—killed, wounded or strayed—during the passage. But the rest of the platoon caught up before he closed on the church. Howell stopped by his officer to get instructions. Before he could speak, a machine-gun burst crumpled him and shot away part of Johnson's shoulder. Staff Sergeant Frank C. Studant took over the platoon; two minutes later a bullet got him through the heart. These mortal wounds came from westward; but the survivors could also feel fire on their backs; Captain Rae's eager beavers, of the 507th, were covering them with a vengeance.

When, after fanning out along the paths and ditches, they swung into the churchyard, it seemed to them that from both directions all weapons were concentered their way. The Germans nested there had long felt it; the cross-fire had wholly unnerved them. They had dropped weapons. Some stayed flat, moaning piteously. Others bobbed up and down in their foxholes, like jacks from a box, crying, *"Kamerad!"* Thirty of them were captured in and around the church and waved on their way toward La Fière. Amid this surrender, one artillery shell exploded off the church wall, killing two, wounding five, of the Americans.

Nominally, 2nd Platoon had come up abreast by this time. That is to say, Lieutenant William G. Weikart had arrived with 12 men; the rest had fallen by the wayside. Despite the beginning of collapse in the German position, the main body of the company was still rooted to the causeway. Yet the heavy bleeding was forward. Of 148 Easy Company men who started, only 35 had been stopped by wounds on the causeway. More than that number had succumbed to fear. They said later that the passage drained them of body vitality. The day was not warm, but the heat seemed terrible. The slow march was more exhausting than the dead run. The first files had only to face fire; the followers threaded a gauntlet of agony. Able-bodied men stopped to give first aid to the wounded. The wounded stopped to tilt a canteen to the lips of the dying. Amid acts of mercy, the fire beat round.

Booker, leg wounds dressed, tried to rise. The legs wouldn't respond. He went forward, crawling, still begging other men to follow him. In a shellhole at the end of the causeway, he found one of Sauls's men, Private Alexander Hahn, bleeding copiously from an arm wound. Ripping his own jacket apart, he applied a tourniquet, which saved Hahn's life. By then his own wounds had opened again, and with strength slipping, he knew that he must find help or black out. So he crawled back across the causeway on hands and knees. But his spirit still sparked. He kept yelling to the people he passed, "Get on up there and fight." Crossing the bridge, he met a soldier going forward and scribbled a message for Easy Company. It got to Lieutenant White while he led the fight to clear the fields west of the church, and he read it to the men around: "Tell the company to give them hell, and I'll be back in a couple of days." The Hollywood touch comes naturally to the American soldier under combat pressure; in this way, real life, mirroring the sham, sublimates it.

On the forward ground, Easy Company's token force got to its objective line and held for 15 minutes. Then Weikart sent a six-man patrol along the trail running north from the church to search the nearby farm buildings. When the patrol shortly returned with 27 prisoners, Weikart too soon decided that his side of the bridgehead was cleared. Then he noted that the patrol was one man less. It had gone from building to building, prodding a few Germans from each one. Come to the last one, Staff Sergeant John N. Selmer was about to enter firing, when a voice from inside the barn spoke in clear English: "We have here only two wounded." Selmer lowered his rifle and walked in. From his rear, by the wall, a German officer shot him dead with a Schmeisser. The German was killed while still firing.

Lieutenant White, arriving late with 18 men, made a boo-boo, missed the side road to the church, and barged straight down the main road. Two hundred yards beyond the causeway, just inside a hedge, a German mortar crew was firing as rapidly as it could get off the ammunition. White and party got within five yards of the tube, still unobserved. The Germans were too engrossed in their work to look up. The Americans, looking on while five rounds were fired, could see that the mortar was plastering the causeway. Curiosity satisfied, Sergeant Samuel L. Webster tossed a grenade which exploded dead center amid the crew, killing all three men.

Covering all these movements, about 45 minutes had passed since Sauls sprinted toward the bridge. It was time for Captain

James M. Harney to lead Fox Company forth to mop up behind George and Easy and beef up the bridgehead's center. The assignment was based on the assumption that all had gone fairly well, the flanks had taken firm hold and the prime need was to close the main door against counterattack.

When Harney and company got to the riverbank, signs that the situation was subtly changing were already at hand. Rae's men were no longer firing from their foxholes but standing in the open, watching the battle. It looked as though the pressure was easing. Except for the one Sherman stranded on the causeway, the American tanks were in hull-down position among the Manoir buildings, firing at Le Motey, range 1700 yards. One of Rae's paratroopers said to Harney, "I'm glad you're doing it instead of us guys,"—an eloquent observation, but premature.

The difficulty in the higher-command position was that it had no idea how things were going. No information was coming back. Sounds of battle from the far side were so irregular that it was impossible to tell whether the 325th was making headway or suffering another repulse. Nothing could be seen of the fighting. The Americans were lost to sight among the ditches and hedgerows. Except for an occasional smoke puff or dust cloud, the opposite shore looked normal and motionless. The one positive sign of American success—the German prisoners—hadn't appeared east of the Merderet. Most of them had been killed trying to cross the causeway. Of how the advance fared there watchers from the east bank could see very little. The choke on the causeway made them believe that again the glidermen were losing out; they had no news of penetrations along the enemy front. The foliage of the poplar trees, the curve in the causeway, the dust and the smoke threw a curtain between the observers and the action, hiding to view everything truly significant. For these reasons, the immobilization in the rear was mistaken for a sign of tactical reverse up front.

There the problem was changing rapidly, though what the sergeants knew of it could not be communicated to the generals. An attack which had been at the point of failing for lack of men was already suffering from a congestion of fighters. The front was too narrow. The limit to the numbers which could advance along the ditches and hedgerows without presenting too broad a target to the Germans was quickly reached. Now the causeway choke was thickening because the forward ground could not absorb the relatively few men who made it to the other side. But of this traffic trouble, observers on the east shore got no hint.

At daybreak, Ridgway had committed the break-through operation to Gavin. Slim Jim, after talking it over with Colonel Maloney, of the 507th, tabbed Rae's company as a reserve to do the bulldozing task if the glider battalion bogged down. Worrying that the paratroops might, on the other hand, be caught up by the spectacle of the charge and prematurely join it, he said to Rae, "Don't go till I give you the signal." That precaution was taken lest a general recoil at the beginning be followed by German counterattack against the east shore. To observe chain-of-command procedures, Maloney stayed by Gavin 100 yards east of the bridge to take the signal and relay it to Rae.

For more than one hour, Gavin watched the unfolding of the operation, trying to determine where the balance lay. His instinct told him that the more the transcauseway movement slowed, the more likely would become a total reverse; the look of the thing, while deceptive, was therefore not assuring. By the time the Sherman tank hit the mine, piling higher the wreckage strewn next the bridge, he had become acutely concerned about the signs of buckling in the rear of the glider battalion. He did not forthwith conclude that the attack on the far shore had failed; but his eyes told him that the manpower needed to support it had stagnated along the road. The longer he watched, the surer he became.

In his moment of decision, he had left Maloney and was among Rae's men on the riverbank. He turned and said directly to Rae, "All right, go ahead! You've got to go." These intimate circumstances, disregarding the previous arrangement, gave Rae a conviction of unlimited urgency. He concluded mistakenly that the 325th had failed, that no penetrations had been made on the west shore, and that his paratroops would be going it alone once they crossed the river. That did not bother him particularly; like most jumpers, he sniffed at glidermen.

When Rae led off, 90 men followed. They got just past the bridge before they had to stop. Stragglers had knotted up around the ruined vehicles just beyond it. The solid wall of blackened steel and human flesh stretched from waterline to waterline, barring the way.

As Rae's column stalled, an artillery shell exploded on the

embankment, wounding four of his men. Rae's runner, Private Richard Keeler, had hit the dirt but was unhurt. Rae picked him up, saying, "Now listen, son, if you're going to get it, you'll get it, so you just keep walking this road with me." That seemed to strike Keeler as a new idea. Rae heard him repeating his own phrases, word by word, as Keeler walked around pulling other men to their feet. Then Keeler formed a flying wedge of about eight men, and as if hitting a football line, this formation bulled through the human huddle around the wrecked tanks, and the hole once opened, stayed.

Most of the men who had foundered amid the armor were out of Harney's company. There was no real excuse for them. They had simply goofed off at the first opportunity. Harney tried to get them ahead by booting them in the pants. Also, he cursed them a little. But it did no good; "they reacted as if they had their brakes set." He thought to himself that if he tarried to argue with them, in the end no one would move. Then anger filled him, and he pulled away from them, attended by a few personal retainers from his headquarters group. That departure put him just a few yards ahead of the point of Rae's column after Keeler made his power play. When Harney looked back and saw them come on, where he had hoped that some of his own people would be shamed into following, he concluded that Rae's paratroops weren't performing like Galahads, either. He could count only 35 men trailing after Rae. Two thirds of the company had fouled up, where Harney's people had stopped. It was his first knowledge that the 507th unit had been committed, and he judged from the early signs that nothing very helpful would come of it.

But he was dead wrong about that. Striding with Rae was a slender, pink-cheeked lieutenant, James D. Orwin, and when he walked the causeway, all things began to change. Various officers had tugged at the same human mass, but except for Booker, none had stirred it very much. Others knew the words, but they couldn't play the right tune. Rae, for one, pressed too hard; an intense man, he tried to counter hysteria by shouting orders more loudly. It didn't work. Harney, a brave man, but shy and taciturn, tried standing procedures, which became mumbo jumbo in an emotionally distrait situation. Then came Orwin who played through the grim scene as lightly as if he were attending a class picnic.

Twenty minutes earlier death had touched his elbow and

then passed on. The closeness of the call made him feel that his luck was running. If it did not supply his inspiration, at least it dressed him for the part he played. While he stood on the east bank, a mortar shell had exploded in front of him and blown his steel helmet apart without breaking his skin. He was not even stunned by it.

So now as he strode the causeway, there was a knitted cap on his head. Stuck in his hair, under the cap bill, were two red roses plucked from the Manoir wall. Many men still remember those roses over the years. Orwin walked along, head up, a broad grin on his face. Come to a group which had quit the fight and at first gazed at him dully, as if not seeing, he didn't raise his voice. He said to them, "And now we're all going to the other side. I think you had better come along. Things are good over there; it will be better for all of us. Walk with me, for I'm a lucky guy."

That was the only medicine he used. But they listened. And most of those who listened arose and followed. The causeway began to flow with life. Harney heard one of his own sergeants say, "It's as if they were watching Jesus Christ." But danger still suffused the scene. Lieutenant William H. Condon accompanied Harney, though he had broken a hipbone during the glider landing. Right after Orwin began work, an artillery shell came in, and Condon got one slug of it in his skull and another through his shoulder. To his comrades, it looked "as if the whole side of his face had been smashed in." Blood masked his features and drenched his shirt front. Too weak to walk forward, too stubborn to be evacuated, he stayed there, playing traffic cop, pointing after Orwin and saying to the others, "Get up and follow that man."

Instead of seconding Orwin, Rae and his leaders stepped out as rapidly as they could, feeling that the speed of their advance would help pull Orwin's strays along, and knowing that if they ever lost momentum, stagnation would return. But no such litter of battle may be cleared in one move. So while Rae and the main body kept advancing, Orwin and two assistants broke back to serve as beaters a second time, shooing stragglers forward to the column. To the eyes of Lieutenant Wisner, the intelligence officer accompanying Rae, the scene began to resemble "an escalator . . . two streams of men on the inside trying to run forward and on the outer side, streams of wounded trickling back." He was impressed with "the large number of wounded still able to walk or crawl back from a fight which remained so fresh that it was impossible to distinguish between the corpses and the litter cases when one passed them by." But Orwin's sweep, coupled with Private Keeler's line buck, was already having one other prime effect. At last the aid men could get through, and they were already running back and forth along the causeway bandaging the wounded as rapidly as they could get to them. As they cleared the embankments of a large number of litter cases for evacuation to the east shore, the movement further freed the vital passage.

Halfway to the west bank, Rae's men for the first time saw German prisoners coming back, hands lifted. But it made little impression on Rae, who, busy with other thoughts, failed to read it as a sign that the glidermen must be doing Trojan work in clearing the bridgehead of the enemy. Come off the causeway's west end, Rae's column drew rifle fire from Germans hidden along the edge of the swamp south of the road. That fixed Rae's impression that no other force had preceded his people to the cockpit. He joined battle, convinced that he was doing it pretty much alone, and weeks later, he still boasted that the paratroops had nailed the bridgehead virtually unhelped. Among soldiers, this is not an extraordinary illusion.

Harney and his headquarters group crossed the causeway in 17 minutes. By the time they had finished their run, the other elements of Fox Company, tagging behind Rae, had become so scrambled that squad and platoon organization had been lost. Leaders grabbed whatever men were closest to them and tried to command them. Harney's order read that at the west bank his platoons should peel off right and left and mop up behind the other two companies. But arriving first with a small group and guessing that if any main body of the company trailed after, it would probably be disorganized, he decided that unless he led straight forward against the center of the enemy ground, his followers might never find him. Rae, coming along behind him, decided on his own to take the same line, without knowing of Harney's decision, on the theory that by smacking the German center, he might collapse the flanks. In this purely random fashion, as the two groups began their deployments, the bridgehead came at last to have a center and to take form all around. The situation west of the Merderet was still a disjointed attack pressed by separate squads. Though the units were muddling through to the object, there was no American command on the ground. The battalion leaders had failed to take hold, and the generals were fully occupied elsewhere.

Colonel Lewis, the regimental commander, was back at the Manoir getting angrier by the minute because his infantrymen on the far shore were getting no help from the American armor. He ran on up the road toward the tank park to find out why and to give someone a tongue-lashing. Instead, he met General Ridgway along the road and dropped the problem in his lap.

Ridgway, instead of issuing an order outright, went to the bridge to take a look. What he saw convinced him that the wrecked metal beyond the bridge barred passage. Lewis had been looking at the barrier for several hours but had done nothing about it. Instead of ordering someone else, Ridgway stepped out on the causeway to see what must be done and to do it. For the moment he was a soldier intent on one thing— using his own hands to clear a right of way. Quite unaware, Gavin was complementing Ridgway's effort. He had gone back to the tanks, found them only partly fueled and almost out of ammunition, and was doing his best to get them squared away.

While the boss men thus toiled and sweated, Lieutenant Lee C. Travelstead's Heavy Weapons Company came marching down the main road toward the bridge to complete the battalion assignment. It had been so far back in the column that its people had no impression of how the battle had been going for two hours, knew nothing of the panic on the causeway, and hadn't even heard that the main-road approach was too dangerous. That was a break, since by the time of their arrival, it wasn't.

All of Travelstead's men were heavy-laden. He knew they had no chance to make a run for it; theirs would be a slow, back-breaking march. He said to them at the start: "Keep your heads. Keep your equipment. Keep moving. That way we'll make it." They listened well and they did it, moving solidly together, with no one pausing to fire.

Ridgway was still amid the wreckage, working alone, trying to loosen a cable from the partly crippled Sherman tank so that the other hulks could be pulled away. When they passed him, he neither looked up nor spoke. Ten paces beyond Ridgway, the mortar platoon was hit by a mortar shell, which killed one man outright, wounded four seriously and bloodied five others. With shell fragments in his skull, one arm, and one leg, Lieutenant Joseph I. Shealy staggered on, leading the platoon. Three others were lost to the litters. Ten yards from the carnage,

Ridgway stayed bent to his task. In him, it was a natural manifestation of practical courage; other fighting Americans loved him for it, this day at the Merderet bridge, as later in Korea. Shealy put it simply: "I had to go on; the steel in Ridgway offset the steel in my body." But at the far end of the causeway, Shealy collapsed from loss of blood and was laid in a ditch to await evacuation. By then two more of Travelstead's men had been killed by mortar fire, and two others had been put out of action by bullet fire.

The time was high noon. With the aid of a few enlisted men, Big Matt had completed his mechanic's task, and the wrecked metal had been shunted to the embankments. Having readied the tanks, Slim Jim herded them toward the river. The Shermans came down the hill and clanked across the causeway in the wake of Travelstead, firing their machine guns flankward to flush the remaining Germans from their nests amid the marsh. Most of the wounded had been cleared to the east shore. The few remaining infantry stragglers fell in behind the armor and trudged forward.

While the tanks made the run unscathed, by an ironic twist, Captain Lewis S. Mentli and his group, who might have used them as a shield, paid doubly for their ardor. Mentli was in charge of the battalion command's rear echelon. At the last moment, as a point of honor, he decided to take off ahead of the tanks. Mentli and comrades made it to the field beyond the first road intersection on the west shore. There the battalion command post was supposed to be set up and working. But Captain James R. Fogle, who had the assignment, had fallen on the causeway, badly wounded. Others in his party who made it to the field were routed and scattered by enemy fire. So Mentli and his fellows, drawing a blank, hacked their way through a hedgerow to get into the field and set up shop. They had just chosen the spot for it when the Shermans came along the main road and opened fire with the machine guns, felling five of Mentli's men. Instead of raising a CP, Mentli had to evacuate a stricken detachment. Soon after so doing, he was killed elsewhere in the battle.

In the communications section, Sergeants Ready and Morrison and Private Rumsey on the east shore awaited word that the CP was up and ready for a wire from Regiment. When it didn't come, they started across, laying wire as they moved. Just beyond the bridge, Morrison was hit in the thigh by a bullet and crawled over to the embankment to await a litter bearer. Ready and Rumsey made it to the west shore and got ready to operate. But it was no go. Mortar fire had cut the line behind them, and such was its intensity throughout the early afternoon that for the next two hours they shuttled back and forth along the causeway repairing breaks in the line.

At the tag end of the column was Lieutenant Clarence H. Knutson and his supply section, traveling on four loaded jeeps and trailers. The spectacle of the mortar shells exploding into the road was enough to give Knutson pause, as he crossed the bridge and braked to a stop beside Slim Jim.

Said Knutson, "Sir, can you tell me if any vehicles have crossed yet?"

Said Gavin, "What have you got?"

Said Knutson, "Ammunition, just ammunition."

Said Gavin, "Then get over there! I mean you get the hell over there."

They got the hell over.

16

Building the Bridgehead

By the time Captain Harney and his palace guard approached the main road intersection near Cauquigny church, the main body of Fox Company was not far behind, having been pushed across the causeway by the Sherman tanks.

But the near presence of this upcoming strength could not warm him because the foliage shut it from sight. So he was drafting help wherever he found it. At the crossroads stood four unemployed Americans, jellying on the pivot, as the old Army phrase goes.

Harney asked, "Who are you?"

One replied, "George Company men—three cooks and a radio operator."

Harney said, "Good. Will you three cooks deploy to the front and act as scouts? The radio man will stay with me."

They went to it. As the point of the whole Army, breaking fresh enemy ground every yard they moved, the three cooks fought with unusual gallantry through the afternoon. It was a typical incident.

West of the Merderet, the all-important VII Corps bridgehead gradually took shape because the relatively few Americans, who had closed on the enemy and by accident had fanned out until their distribution covered every path and ditch in the semicircle, kept pushing because some lieutenant, sergeant or private kept prodding them. Had they awaited orders from higher echelons, they might be waiting still. Through the afternoon, it was a soldiers' battle.

Still mistakenly believing that, virtually without help, his paratroopers had clinched the first lodgment, Rae was enough of a soldier to know that there had to be some central direction. At the crossroads, he voluntarily yielded to Harney, asking him, "Now what do you want me to do?"

Harney said, "Take all the men now moving on the left side of the road, regardless of unit, go by the trail leading left and try to make contact with George Company's left flank. When you find them, advance west to the high ground and take up a defensive position."

Within five minutes after Rae deployed, Harney overtook Lieutenant White and 18 men from Easy Company, who had also been advancing down the main road.

He said to White, "Take your people straight down the road which leads north from the church and try to get to the 1st Battalion." (The outfit which was still pinned down in the orchard with Colonel Timmes.) "If you make it, then with their help, clear the high ground to the westward and go into defensive position."

While Harney gave these orders, Lieutenant Travelstead came up with the heavy machine guns. Harney sent one section to the left to overtake Rae, and attaching the other to White's group, decided to go along with it.

Rae, after leaving Harney, second-guessed his orders, and splitting his force, sent half of it to make the contact on the left, while he led the rest of it straight down the main road to Le Motey, the most advanced ground of the day. With his arrival, it looked as if the bridgehead were well rounded out. But a pattern was emerging only because Harney, aware of the vacuum, was disposing like a battalion commander.

The most baffling figure in this battle is Colonel Lewis. Two of his battalions were now west of the Merderet, which meant that the honor of his regiment was irrevocably committed to the fight for the bridgehead. Yet, instead of becoming the linchpin when lower command failed, he was preoccupied with thoughts of how to re-establish the broken channels so that information would flow normally from front to rear. Of this personal aberration and the resultant lack of organization of the skirmish line, higher command had no sensing, since Lewis was keeping a stiff upper lip, and it was not the task of Gavin or Ridgway to scout his front to see how things lay.

In George Company's sector, south of the main road, Captain Sauls was satisfied with his progress, except that his ammunition was about out, and he had no communications except the man-to-man grapevine. He worried a little because two hours had passed and he had still heard nothing from Lieutenant Amino's group, sent to mop up along his right flank. His first knowledge that there was a more promising build-up behind him and west of the river came when a runner arrived, saying, "Colonel Lewis is at this end of the causeway and wants to see you."

He found Lewis sitting on a stone wall, talking to Ridgway. They were mulling over the advisability of setting up a regimental CP near the church. Lewis led Sauls aside and said to him, "I still have heard nothing from the battalion commander. If he can't be found, you are to take over. And I want you to establish a battalion CP right there," pointing to the spot.

While they talked, Private Kenneth Lynn came out of the orchard beyond the wall, herding 25 prisoners, overlooked by Easy Company in its sweep to the right. He had captured them within 200 feet of where Ridgway sat.

Getting the word, Sauls felt that he still had to double back to his own company, or leave it adrift in its moment of greatest weakness. That hunch paid off. Under Sergeant Kneale the outfit had been brought to a standstill by three enemy machine guns. When the other men wouldn't move, Kneale crawled alone 70 yards forward toward the strong point. There he was soon joined by two of Rae's officers who, sent to make the contact with George Company, became so engrossed in this fire fight that they forgot to send word of the contact to Rae and neglected to tell Sauls of their mission.

Kneale lay next a hedgerow embankment trying to get a line on the German guns when the two lieutenants flattened beside him. One said, "God damn it, man, we can't do this unless we get some fire power forward." As if to emphasize the point, two German antitank guns, from somewhere near the machine-gun nest, cut loose against the George Company front. The enemy base of fire seemed not more than 125 yards away.

Kneale crawled back to the company, calling for a machine-gunner. Private Will E. Dickens, with a light Browning, and two members of his crew went along when Kneale crawled forward again. Dickens set up in a corner of a field near where

Kneale had first reconnoitered. He fired for five minutes. The German fire slacked off. Kneale said, "By God, I think you've killed them."

As he spoke, a shower of potato-masher grenades came over the hedgerow right on them. The Germans, driven off by Dickens's fire, had used the interlude to close on the hedgerow where he lay. One grenade exploded under Dickens, and its steel shredded his body. He was still pulling trigger when at last he fell unconscious across the gun, and a few minutes later he died.

This was the moment when Sauls returned. One look convinced him that it was no task for light weapons. He sent a runner back to Sergeant Irwin, with whom he had seen setting up the 81-millimeter mortars near the spot where he had talked to Lewis. Back at the mortar position, the lost-or-strayed battalion commander, Major Gardner, appeared on the scene just long enough to countermand Sauls's order for a stonk on the German battery.

But it made no difference. Dickens had done his work before the grenade killed him. The German antitank guns did not fire again. Kneale and the two privates had stood to the hedge and blasted the German skirmishers back with their own grenades.

Sauls took a bullet through his hand and bled badly. Nothing would stanch the wound, but he tarried for a few minutes watching. The first tier of enemy guns had gone out, but as his men tried to advance, another tier opened from beyond. The ammunition supply had touched bottom; Sauls peeled one squad off and sent it rearward to seek resupply, saying, "If you can't find it anywhere else, strip it from the wounded and the stragglers." In this clutch, a Sherman tank overtook the company and moved with the riflemen, shooting up the hedgerows as it advanced. That extra wallop was needed. The hour of easy surrender had passed. These Germans were sticking until blown out of their foxholes.

Staff Sergeant Roger F. Bertolini prowled a slit trench in a field to the right of the road and came back with one German officer and five enlisted men. But they had quit because they were also munitionless and Bertolini had gathered them in with a machine gun already burned out. He ran back to the main road, scrounged a new gun from a straggler and got back to the fight just in time. The infantry was again moving without help from the tanks; the first one had quit when its machine gun jammed; a second Sherman appeared, stayed just long enough to draw a few rounds of mortar fire, then bugged out. That made it twice as hard for the rifle line to get going again. Rounding another bend in the road, Kneale and partners were stopped by a machine gun which, because of the angle, could singe both of the lateral hedgerows and stream bullets into the parallel ditches. When Kneale and the others wiggled ever so slightly, the gun spoke; when they held still, it stopped, so as not to reveal its position.

Bertolini got his gun going from behind a hedge but wasn't sure of the line. Trying to observe for him, Sauls twice got his helmet creased by bullets. Ten minutes and two cases of ammunition were wasted in this futile exchange. Then Sergeants James Malak and Leo Kohlreiser set up a 60-millimeter mortar at a hedge 25 yards behind Bertolini, opened fire at 100 yards, and on their second round smashed the German gun.

The men moved on without Sauls. Weak from loss of blood, he tottered back to the main road and at the end of the causeway ran into Lieutenant Knutson, still hauling ammunition. "Get it up to my company, or they'll have to pull out," said Sauls.

Knutson went barreling right down the lane toward which Sauls pointed. When he braked to a halt in front of Lieutenant Thomas E. Goodson (later killed), who had relieved Sauls, Knutson yelled, "Hey, what you firing at?"

Goodson replied, "Antitank gun and machine gun."

"How far away?"

"Eighty yards away."

"Well, for Christ's sake, get me out of here."

The trailer with the ammunition was dropped, and the riflemen turned it upside down for a quick unloading. Knutson, backing the jeep and making his turnabout in almost the same motion, was hooked to the trailer and on his way again before the Germans could react. They had the jeep in plain sight, and one round into it would have blown up Goodson & Company. Now the Americans had stuff to burn, and the 60 mortar quickly killed the antitank gun. The men walked on another 300 yards, then finding no enemy, returned to the main road. As they approached the church (the time was about 1530), they were pinned down by machine-gun fire from the orchard. Private Leonard Reel, going it alone, made a wide sweep around two fields to see if he could get at the gun from the rear, and ten minutes later was back, happy as a lark, herding 30 prisoners.

Amino and his party returned at about the same time, and George Company, moving via the hedgerows, took up forward ground on the right of the battalion perimeter.

Gavin figured that Le Motey village was the most likely rallying ground for the Germans. The main risk was that under cover of the buildings there reinforcements from Amfreville or farther west would assemble and counterattack the American groups scattered around the bridgehead before they were either dug-in or joined in support of each other. So, as insurance against that specter, the artillery was ordered to drop its fire back to Le Motey and hold on that target for an indefinite period, plastering the two main roads.

Harney took no account of what the guns might do when, on the spur of the moment, he decided to go for Le Motey instead of mopping up behind the other companies. First, he sent Rae and party there. Then after accompanying White partway on his sortie to Timmes's orchard, he swung back to the main road and headed for the village. Shortly he was in front again; and counting Rae's company, Travelstead's party, and Harney's own people, troops moving on Le Motey were strung out for 500 yards between the village and the causeway. No part of this force had any communication with the American batteries, and no information about the artillery plan was sped forward to the column.

Its rear elements were still shuffling forward when machine-gun fire from their right scattered and pinned them. Sergeant Joseph Sindad, who was on ahead with Travelstead, saw this rear guard of Rae's people hit the dirt and decided to help them. But he had a problem. He was armed only with a machine gun, without tripod or ammunition, his carrier having been blown up during the causeway crossing. So when Sindad heard the paratroopers yelling from the ditches, "Give us machine-gun fire! Give us machine-gun fire!" he left his gun, ran back 150 yards directly through the zone where they were pinned, found a box of ammunition, ran forward again, set up his gun on an embankment and provided the covering fire which enabled the last of the paratroopers to rise again and assemble on Rae. Then he joined the machine-gun crew of Sergeant Ernest Neinfeldt, and together they walked to the Le Motey crossroads.

As they arrived, a soldier unknown to Sindad offered him a tripod. Said Sindad, looking at the intersection, "A noble place for a gun—I'll set up right here."

Just as he finished fitting the gun to the mount, an American artillery shell exploded directly in front of it. Travelstead was felled, with five shards in his body. A second shell exploded dead on the gun, wrecking it. Two paratroopers who had stepped close to the gun got the full force of the blast, thereby saving Sindad. They were killed outright; so were two members of Neinfeldt's crew. In a twinkling, the shellfire was dropping all along the line. Harney and his men, who had moved out to the right with the intention of advancing to more favorable high ground, were midway of an orchard when the barrage dropped on them. One paratrooper was killed; four glidermen were wounded by the first shell. The other men ran back to the road and dived for cover behind the first hedgerow.

Travelstead, bleeding terribly but still self-possessed, sent three different runners rearward with messages to the artillery, before submitting to first aid and quitting the fight. Harney dispatched two runners, put a radio signal "lift fire" through one of the Sherman tanks and threw out orange smoke. None of it did any good. Harney redressed his line at the first hedgerow short of the zone beaten by the American gunfire. The friendly barrage continued to deny him the coveted high ground. One of Travelstead's gunners, Sergeant Harold J. Lowe, stayed with him to become the anchor of the right flank.

Rae had not had time to deploy. Being among the buildings of Le Motey when the shells dropped, his force lost only five or six wounded. He pulled out—21 able-bodied paratroopers with him—to look for a tank from which to message the artillery. As he fell back, he was rejoined by the group which had veered left looking for Sauls's flank, and in the excitement, they still failed to tell him about making the contact. The recoil carried him to Cauquigny church, where Ridgway and Lewis were in conversation. Sauls's presence fixes the time of the incident at about 1300. Lewis told Rae, "You will set up your force in the vicinity of the church and serve as a general reserve."

En route to Timmes's orchard, Lieutenant White and his 18 men had also run into the American shellfire, taken one look and recoiled to the edge of the marsh, just north of the church where Easy Company had bagged its Germans. So with White abandoning the effort to establish a front on the right, and a gap existing on the left, where Rae's people were supposed to join hands with George Company, Harney & Company were far out on a limb. Harney sensed his isolation, still not knowing what had happened and being too preoccupied with his command chores to find out. His front was drawing unremitting small-arms fire from the Le Motey buildings and his 60-millimeter mortars were doing their best to put it down. There was as yet no indication of enemy movement around his flanks, but he felt it must come soon and would find him vulnerable. So he counted noses: 50 men from Fox Company, 12 from George Company, 16 heavy-weapons men from Headquarters Company and 6 paratroopers. Except for nine walking wounded, the force was sound, but it wasn't enough. So Harney ran back to the churchyard, where by sheer chance he met the highly elusive Major Gardner and told him, "You had better get Company E forward and put them on my left if you expect the ground to be held." Then back to his own people, where the heavy build-up of enemy fire during his brief absence told him that more Germans had arrived at Le Motey.

It was too soon to expect Easy Company. But some move had to be made. Harney sent out a six-man patrol under Lieutenant Archie E. Noel. Their mission: to reconnoiter the fields and hedgerows off to the left and try to find Sauls's flank. Harney had no way of knowing that George Company was still a tightly compressed spearpoint beating against antitank guns and machine-gun pits along one narrow and distant lane. Its problems in the foreground excluded worries about juncture. Noel's mission was hopeless from the start.

Noel and his friends got just 150 yards. There the patrol was ambushed from out of houses which earlier had been searched and cleared by Rae's people. The job was nigh perfect—a little slam. Two men were shot dead and three were wounded. But all might have been lost had not Private Henry L. Henderson seen the patrol cut down, sprinted across the road in the face of machine-gun fire, picked up a BAR from the dead hand of Private Joseph W. Woodbury and poured on a covering fire so that Noel could crawl out of the trap and get back to warn Harney. Noel said, "I saw at least a platoon of krauts. They're moving, and they'll soon be on our rear."

It was wearing toward midafternoon. The strain of the long wait, the disaster to the patrol and Noel's warning, presaging counterattack, forced Harney's decision. On the way up, he had noticed a position about 200 yards to his rear, with strong embankments running along slightly higher ground, and less exposure for the flanks. Harney ordered a fall-back to that line. He said, "The mortars will go out first. Riflemen will follow, one-half squad at a time. Keep tight to the hedgerows. Then the BARs will go, and the machine guns will come out last." That was how they did it. No one rushed, though machine-gun fire, from the Germans who had ambushed Noel, was already flailing them from the left when the first elements withdrew.

Harney judged by the signs both that the men were feeling the pressure and that they remained under good control. In clearing away, several men in the first two squads had abandoned their ammunition. Harney said nothing about it. But he noticed that the last few officers and NCOs, before getting out, picked up the boxes and belts left by their comrades and carried them back to the new line. There they faced about and awaited the next enemy move, which was not long in coming.

Easy Company, given orders by Major Gardner, had lost more than an hour rounding up its men before starting forward. Its advance on the left coincided with Harney's withdrawal via his own right flank. Of this came much trouble. For it meant that Captain Murphy & Company went forward looking for a friendly flank that wasn't there while moving into ground already held by the enemy.

Having, in effect, traded missions with Easy Company for the time being, Captain Rae, on his own, also went to bat in place of Lieutenant White. Shaping up a strong patrol, he started it north from the church bound for Timmes's orchard.

But this time the mission was restricted. The patrol wasn't to seek new worlds to conquer. Finding Timmes, it should tell him that the Americans were in fairly solid on the west shore of the Merderet. Thereafter, the forces on the spot were to work out their own salvation and get to the bridgehead.

17

Misery and Grandeur

With neither sensing the other's presence, Easy and Fox Companies pivoted on each other like sections of a revolving door.

Harney did not know Murphy was advancing well over on his left; Murphy had neglected to send him word that he was coming up.

Murphy did not know that Harney was retiring on his right. Harney had made his decision and exit under such pressure that there was no time to tidy up the details.

As the columns passed each other within shouting distance, flankers sent out by either one would have revealed the disparate movements. It didn't happen. The banks and box hedges locked tight the secret of this strange maneuver and compounded the confusions growing from the holiday in the battalion command.

Without incident, Murphy got his men up to the hedgerow bounding the sunken road which leads into Le Motey, then with a swing of his arm directed them to form a fire line next the embankment. Seeing nothing of Fox Company, he sent a two-man patrol running to the next field on his right to "tie in the flank." In these same seconds, Harney's men were setting up weapons on the new ground two fields to the rear. The enemy fire had stopped. Not one sound warned Murphy that the Germans, having moved from Le Mortey on Harney's heels,

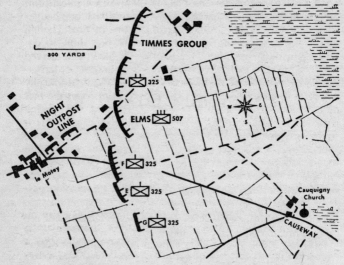

Figure 14. THE CONSOLIDATED BRIDGEHEAD

had boxed in the ground on which Easy Company was deploying.

Not more than two minutes passed. The skirmish line finished extending to the right. The patrol darted into the other field. Just then, from that same flank, a crashing and perfectly aimed enfilade fire by multiple machine guns ripped the length of the embankment where Murphy's men sought cover. To escape it, they flopped in the parallel ditch. At least three guns were raking the position from slightly higher ground not more than one hedgerow distant. Had not a bank obtruded so that the guns could not bear on the ditch, they all would have died. But in their inferior position, the Americans could not raise their heads to return fire. Several mortar rounds—smoke-loaded—landed in the road between the two positions. They read it as the forewarning of German counterattack.

Murphy shouted an order. The words were undistinguishable

above the tumult. Not one member of the company knew what he had said. Men of the 2nd Platoon, who were nearest him, took from his gestures that they should move back one hedgerow to slightly higher ground out of the line of fire. Though they were just guessing, it seemed like the best thing to do. So they made an exit, crawling via the left flank, and arrived whole-skinned at the new ground, still crawling but orderly.

But over on the right flank, 1st Platoon either read Murphy wrong or cracked wide open. The cry went up: "Get the hell out! Get the hell out!" "Go! Go! Go!" The yelling and the first wild lunge by a running man produced total dissolution. It started as an urge, turned into personal panic and became stampede. In a split second, all of 1st Platoon was on the main road tearing for the causeway, its leaders with the others.

George Company, having completed its first sweep of the day under Goodson and Amino and then having moved rightward looking for an open flank to latch on, had come forward far enough to see these things happen. Sighting Murphy on ahead when he moved into position, Goodson decided that the contact was complete. The company was halted, and Sergeant Malak set up his three 60-millimeter mortars. As Easy Company broke from the forward hedgerow, German shellfire and bullets found the George Company area. Malak fed his mortars frantically, at first centering fire on the orchard where the enemy machine guns seemed to be nested, then traversing along one line at 200 yards' range so as to cover the front of both companies. This one man, with one weapon, was the only effective counterforce in the decisive moments. At least the enemy did not come on.

Technical Sergeant Leonard Slater, of Harney's outfit, was on the main road moving a heavy machine gun when he saw the Easy Company stampede—about 30 men—come at him. He had no hand weapon. But he knew that the rout, if not checked, might sweep the whole front. Walking the road toward him, 40 yards away, was a paratroop lieutenant. Slater ran toward him, yelling as he moved, "For God's sake, stop them any way that you can!" When this happened, the runaways were already passing the hedgerow behind Harney's line. Harney's men had seen them, but Harney had stood there in plain sight with arms out and his squads had held their ground. Sergeant John M. Harrison, of Headquarters Company, who was with the big mortars next the road, saw them dash by. One man yelled, "It's counterattack and we're getting out." Harrison moved that way, looking for a few willing hands who would help him carry the mortars back.

Then Harrison saw the jumper lieutenant. He stood square in the road pointing his .45 at the runaways. They had stopped. He shouted so loud that Harrison could hear him above the other sounds of battle. He said, "You'll keep your God-damn asses right where they are. Some of my men are up there, and none of you are going to pull out. Now hold it, you sons-of-bitches." They looked around uncertainly. None tried to argue. Harrison tried to pass. The lieutenant at first blocked him, then agreed that it was all right to prepare to move the mortars back, should the panic show signs of spreading. He added, "But these riflemen are going to stay right here with me until they're ready to fight again." One hour later, under their own leaders, they were shepherded back to the ground where Murphy and his one platoon still held forth.

Through the evening the German mortars and artillery kept pounding the front. But the enemy infantry did not advance. There was no real change in the American position except that Harney moved two squads across the main road so that he would have some fire power and observation on his otherwise open flank.

Rae's patrol got to the orchard of containment to discover what it had already suspected—that Timmes no longer was in need of help. The forcing of the causeway had lifted the pressure from that embarrassing local situation. Quite suddenly the air above the foxholes was clear of everything but apple boughs. But now that all of the maneuvering in that direction was over, there was nothing to be done. The bridgehead had to be extended, and Timmes was correctly positioned to fill out the right flank. So he continued his sojourn in the orchard.

At sundown the Germans made their die-hard effort. The beat of mortar and machine-gun fire intensified, joined by the artillery. Then Harney & Company saw groups of infantry coming across the fields toward them on the right flank. Sergeant Thomas A. Strum, who had gone scouting that way, on his own, saw them first. Rounding a tree, he had physically collided with two German riflemen. There wasn't room to fire. He bashed in one German's skull with his Tommy gun, and the other man ran. Gun wrecked, Strum saw too late that other skirmishers had moved in between him and the company position. So he ran for the rear, figuring that he would summon help for the company.

Harney, waiting the onfall, for the first time felt shaky. He had just been back to tell Gardner, "You must get someone up to support me on the right, or the line won't hold," and Gardner had said to him, "I'll have plenty of help for you in just a few minutes." Now the crisis was at hand, no one had come, and Lieutenant Howard Hill, the artillery forward observer, was saying to him, "We have somehow lost radio contact with fire control." But having broken the bad news, Hill sprinted to another position 200 yards to the rear where he expected to find another SCR 610 radio. Harney made only one move. He withdrew the platoon which he had placed to the right of the road, fearing that it was overexposed and could be cut off. It was the only ground given up during the fight.

When the shellfire came down, Harney yelled to his men, "Get down!" They lay flat in the ditches, hugging the embankments, waiting for the storm to pass. Not a man was hit. Then as the German barrage stopped (lest it compromise the advancing infantry), Harney's men propped up against the hedgerows and met the onfall with rifles, machine guns and grenades. For five, or possibly ten, minutes, the standoff was maintained. Harney braced to the spectacle. Came the cry from his machine-gunners: "No more ammunition!" At that moment, into the scene rode Strum astride a Sherman tank. He had persuaded the crew to load with infantry ammunition and get up to the fight. The tank unloaded and went back for more. So hot was the road with fire that no open vehicle could have made it. The men marveled that Strum had survived. He continued the shuttle till the supply was ample. Then the Sherman settled next Harney's right shoulder, shelled the buildings forward and sprayed the fields on the right with machine-gun fire. The intervention was decisive. The fight was over before the American guns, summoned by Hill, could speak.

Yet these happenings, unattended by any misadventure to the engaged American infantry, were wholly misread by the command in the backwash of the battle. Colonel Lewis had collapsed from exhaustion, and his executive, Lieutenant Colonel Sitler, had taken over. He sat in the CP (command post) at Cauquigny church playing his part by ear. The place was shaking from the cannonade. When Sitler looked out, he saw a few infantrymen running toward the causeway. Seconds later he heard a tank rumble past, going the wrong way. Then after a brief spell, he thought he heard another tank headed rearward. He took no time to investigate. Better favored, he would have learned that it was Strum's tank hauling ammunition.

But imagination leaped and phantasmagoria built up higher in the mind of this normally stolid man. First, he started collecting a scratch force of engineers and headquarters people to make a last-ditch stand. Then he called Division to say that the situation was rapidly worsening and he needed whatever help he could get. So even as the outlook on the battle line brightened, the rearward view of it darkened steadily during the next hour.

Lewis had made one move just before he folded. He went to Captain Rae and said, "I am being counterattacked on both flanks" (which was not correct) "and I need more men on the fire line" (which was right enough).

Rae said, "Be specific; where do I put my men?"

Lewis said, "I can't say in detail. I haven't time. Go up, find a hole in the line and plug it."

That was what Rae did. He threw his 80 men in on the right of Harney and slightly to the rear, so that his position by nature became a refused flank. There they were punished by mortar fire, but they saw no German infantry. Harney's people had ended the close-up fight. Soon their flank on the right was extended by impressive reinforcement. From out of Timmes's orchard, 1st Battalion, 325th Glider Infantry, was at last in position along the main avenue of the American advance. (See map on page 168.)

By 1900, scattered groups of CP men had sifted into Harney's position. These were the scratch reserves which Sitler had shunted forward. Then came Lieutenant Knutson with 20 supply and communications men; they were given rifles and took their places in the hedgerow line. The effect on Harney's people was electric. They had not felt the arrival of Rae's company. One hundred yards distant, it might as well have been 'cross the river. But with the filling of gaps in their own line, their hearts leaped up. Harney was astonished to hear them ask, "When do we start moving again?"

On getting Sitler's disquieting message, Slim Jim Gavin raced to the front, armed to do his part in the foxhole line. When he got there, a quick reconnaissance told him that the emergency had passed. The situation was clearing. Gavin could tell the pressure was off because he heard no rifle fire. Though he saw that troops were digging in for the night, the time seemed ripe for hitting back, since his own perimeter was hardly half formed. Rae was bent over, digging a foxhole, when Gavin found him. The hour was 2100 and a wisp of daylight remained. Their talk was punctuated by mortar shells churning the foreground.

Gavin said, "Let's move; I want you to take your men and go forward."

Asked Rae, "How far do you want me to go?"

Replied Gavin, "Go to town!" It was hardly a military order. If to the brigadier it meant drive the bolt home, the captain still had his mind on Le Motey.

Before Rae could get his people in motion, Harney and Fox Company were ordered to join the attack. That insured the inevitable end to the story. These two outfits had to stay paired to the finish to write the anticlimax, which would have delighted the ancient Greeks. The ragged start by Harney & Company that morning, typical of the battalion pattern, had spurred the commitment of Rae & Company. The paratroopers were cast in the role of the tactical battering ram which the glidermen would serve as a mop-up force. But the perverse course of battle mocked the script. Through the day, Harney and his people had drawn enemy steel like a magnet and fought back till their magazines were empty. Rae and his people, uniquely among the forces which had charged the west shore, wandered from scene to scene but were always at the wrong spot, or too awkwardly disposed, to engage the Germans in a man-against-man fire fight. The illusion in Rae's mind that he had won the bridgehead persisted only because he had no idea of what had happened in other sectors

Fate stayed consistent. Rae went "to town." Through the late twilight he led his men into Le Motey, meeting no opposition en route, finding no Germans there. His men finished the day without seeing the enemy infantry. They remained nonengaged through the night, their fitful sleeping interrupted only by the banging of 88-millimeter shells against the roof tops, and there was too little glory in that.

In the adjoining sector on Rae's right, Harney moved along the main road, having at first the supporting fire of three Sherman tanks. So covered, the force met no resistance. The enemy seemed to have departed the neighborhood. So the tanks raced on alone to a sunken road which runs just short of Le Motey, bounding the field where the Germans had ambushed Murphy & Company in midafternoon. They sprayed its hedgerows all around with their machine guns, until, no fire being returned, they were satisfied that the enemy was either fled or dead. Then fearful of laagering in the forward ground, the tanks withdrew to a park near the church.

In command of Harney's right wing, Second Lieutenant Leo J. Fitzmartin walked through the gap in the hedge, expecting his men to follow him into the field. Four riflemen did so. The others missed his signal in the half-light. Fitzmartin gained the center of the field before becoming aware that he was almost unattended. At that moment, from opposite corners, two machine guns caught him in a perfect cross-fire. His four riflemen were shot dead. From the road, the platoon saw Fitzmartin fall and lay still. They were certain he died, also. But he was feigning it. He knew that if he stirred he would draw more fire. The fusillade had shattered his right leg. After dark closed, he tried to move but found that he was in too great pain to crawl away. Wisely, on getting the bad news, Harney called off the attack until morning. Fitzmartin lay there all night fully conscious. Back toward the river he could hear a rumble as of large forces gathering. At daybreak the Germans began to talk excitedly along the hedgerow 30 yards from where he lay. At 0600 he saw them shoulder arms and march away. At 0700 his own men advanced across the silent field and found him. There was no other excitement. When Fitzmartin was littered off, the last footnote was written, and the bridgehead fight was done.

Midway in Fitzmartin's ordeal, Colonel Sitler had heard by phone that escorts were wanted from his headquarters to guide the van of 90th Infantry Division across the Merderet. By dawn, 2nd Battalion of 357th Infantry Regiment was marching the causeway. The relief of the bridgehead forces was going forward while Fitzmartin watched the backs of the departing Germans, and when the stretcher bearers took him out he passed the upcoming columns. He knew then that the initial mission of his own division—the 82nd—was complete. The ground he had helped win was now the springboard to the further pursuit and destruction of the German armies in the west.

NIGHT DROP

Moving into St. Marcouf, France on June 8, 1944.

A stick of 501st PIR men prepare for departure for Normandy.

Joe Pastore and Ben Schaub (Co F, 502nd PIR.)

A paratrooper of the 101st Airborne Division killed by the Germans on D-Day.

Men of the 506th patrol a small town on horseback June 10th.

The 502nd PIR passes through St. Marie du Mont.

Typical infantry positions in the hedgerows.

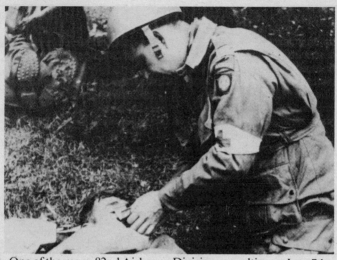

One of the many 82nd Airborne Division casualties on June 7th.

Dead Man's Corner.

A young Lieutenant of the 82nd briefs his commander
on the enemy situation.

Airborne wounded on deck of SS *Queen Express*
on way to England.

Sgt. Lazenby and Pvt. Rodrigues of the 505th PIR
after 37 days behind German lines.

BOOK TWO

Crossing the Douve

"Every man's sword was against his fellow and there was a great discomfiture."

— FROM THE FIRST BOOK OF SAMUEL

18

Pat Cassidy and Outfit

In the Normandy night drop, the place where the plan was most likely to split at the seams was right next Utah Beach.

The two United States airborne divisions were committed to the venture to insure that the beachhead would be won and tranquilized before the seaborne forces launched their small boat waves at the strand soon after dawn.

General Omar N. Bradley, who personally drew this part of the plan, insisted that things be done this way. To his tactician's eye, the ground permitted no alternative.

When, belatedly, Air Chief Marshal Sir Trafford Leigh-Mallory tried to stop the night drop, predicting it would result in an 80 per cent wastage of machines and men, Bradley said, "If there is no airborne attack, there can be no Utah assault." That put it up to Eisenhower, who weighed the decision alone in his tent, and then sustained Bradley.

The stakes in what happened right at the Utah corner were therefore highly personal. If the night drop went well elsewhere, but failed to win an open door for the 4th Infantry Division at Utah, it would miss at the decisive point.

The linchpin task—the splicing together of airhead and beachhead—fell to 2nd Battalion, 502nd Parachute Regiment,

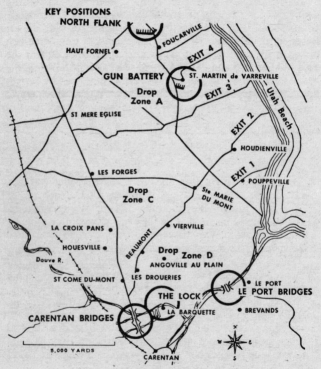

Figure 15. 101ST DIVISION'S OBJECTIVES

commanded by twenty-eight-year-old Lieutenant Colonel Patrick J. Cassidy.

They were to jump into Drop Zone A—a meadow chosen because it was the closest serviceable field to Utah. That done, they would cleanse the vicinity of Germans and form a front far enough north to shield the cross-the-beach landings.

Easily stated in its general terms, the mission was nastily complicated by the simplicity of the ground. The Normandy coast around Utah is depressingly flat except for sand dunes. Between the beach and the solid farmland is a mile-wide belt of salt marsh which would be awash at high tide but for the sand barrier. Dirt causeways topped with asphalt run from the beach to the farm country west of the marsh. Laced by hedgerows and grown with Lombardys and spare pines, which create an illusion of height, the cultivated area is also of such flatness that guns more than one mile inland could put direct fire on Utah Beach.

One enemy coastal battery lay just west of the village of St. Martin-de-Varreville; the Allied bombers had tried to blast it, but the results were unknown. The best causeway out of Utah—Exit No. 4—ran through St. Martin, past the battery and into the barracks area housing the German gunners, which garrison point was identified in the American plan as "Position WXYZ." A second causeway—Exit No. 3—linked Utah with the *bocage* country 700 yards south of St. Martin.

These features made the first-round assignments of the 502nd Regiment elementary. Overrunning of the battery and crushing of its garrison had to precede the clearing of the two vital causeways. Thereafter the Five-O-Ducks could think about attacking north, solidifying their own perimeter and eventually joining hands with the 82nd Division.

Mission and man were well met. Pat Cassidy was then an undistinguished Reservist who thought lightly of his command ability, and never having faced combat, was twinged by doubt that he could cut it. Probably no one ever told him that these things marked him as healthily normal. He knew that he was in tune with his men. He had great faith in them. He was not certain about much else. Cassidy always felt "scared as hell" and was ever ready to admit it with a grin. Maybe that was his beauty secret, for uniquely, he never looked haggard in combat.

The flight from England was peaceful. Cassidy was surprised that most of his men slept, though that was natural, since they were drained of energy by the excitement of mounting up. As the serial passed Jersey and Guernsey, Cassidy saw his first antiaircraft fire; but the bursts were far off. Then they crossed the Normandy coast, and tracers boiled up around the C-47. They passed into fog, and the ground fire ceased. Six minutes out from Drop Zone A, it picked up again, and when Cassidy saw the green light flash on and made his move, "it was like jumping into a Roman candle." Tracers from three or four machine guns converged directly over his head. First, the shock reaction, then the thought, "They must be firing at the plane," which somehow made him feel better. But they followed him all the way down, then lifted as he felt his chute snag in the top limbs of a tall oak. His boot toes barely scraped hard pavement. As he strained in space, the tree slowly yielded from his weight, and after minutes of struggle he fell flat near a road intersection.

One machine gun turned its fire toward him, and the bullets bounced off the pavement five feet from his head. Temporarily spent from his bout with the oak and still held by his harness, he couldn't wiggle away toward the ditch. A little strength returned, and he managed to work loose a grenade, thinking he would use it on the gun. Then another plane came over, the fire lifted from the road, he shook loose from his harness and, crawling over into a field, was ready to forget about the gun. From the flight of the plane, he judged his east-west directions, and crawled on about 20 yards. The gun resumed fire straight toward him. That shook him; the war was getting much too personal. So he lay flat awaiting more planes to draw the fire away. When they arrived, he saw other paratroopers jump— a little to the westward. He crawled that way hugging the hedgerow. In his first 20 minutes he made not more than 100 yards and heard no human sound except a horseman going past at a mad gallop. Mortar fire bracketed him—six rounds of it. More planes came over. The mortars quit. Then surprisingly, magiclike, in a second, full strength returned and he arose and walked.

As he swung along the hedgerow, he felt, rather than heard, the presence of some other person beyond it. Looking through a gap in the hedge bank, he saw the forms of two other men, backs turned toward him. So he snapped his mechanical cricket just once. The men went flat; there was no reply to his recognition signal. He wondered: Now what do I do? While he groped for the answer, a hand right under his chin (he had missed seeing the third man) snapped a cricket. All suspense was lifted.

Cassidy sang out, "Where in hell are you going?"

The man next him replied, "We're looking for Cassidy." It was his own radio operator. The others were his runner and a strange paratrooper. Cassidy said, "We're in business; so let's move."

In the next field they met Lieutenant Colonel Robert L. Strayer, hobbling on a wrenched leg, and four troopers from his stick. Cassidy saw silk billowing from the field beyond. There he found Lieutenant Jack Williams, his own machine-gun officer, down with a twisted ankle. But Williams had already rounded up a dozen men, sent them out to hunt bundles and retrieved two machine guns. The crickets kept cricking, and more men moved out of the shadows to join the party as they heard the signal.

They moved on to a road intersection where Cassidy halted the group and deployed a few riflemen outward for local protection while he collected more men and tried to get oriented. Williams, using a carbine as a cane, hobbled north in search of a signpost or friendly Frenchman. Five minutes passed; then they heard heavy rifle and machine-gun fire from the direction he had taken. As they waited and worried, Williams got back with Captain Fred Hancock, of Charley Company, who had collected 30 men (most of them strays) and Lieutenant Samuel B. Nichels, with a handful of Able Company men.

Hancock said, "Down that road a piece I saw a sign which reads: 'Foucarville—Two Kilometers.'" Cassidy checked his air oblique photo and got the location. He was only a short stroll from his objective, and the urge to get there was strong. But there was a slight problem: most of the 200 men now present belonged to the 506th, and Colonel Strayer was determined to hold on to his own people, and concentrate still more, before marching on his objective far to the south. The Irishman still kept his temper.

Cassidy said, "Then clear your people out so I can get organized. We're ready with what we've got." There were left to him the fragments brought in by Williams, Hancock and

Figure 16. AREA OF CASSIDY'S OPERATIONS

Nichels. To save time, they marched straight down the middle of the road. Halfway to St. Martin-de-Varreville, they met cigar-chewing Captain Frank Lillyman, leader of the division's team of Pathfinders, who had been the first American soldier to land in Normandy. Lillyman was bound west to pick up men he had left covering the lighted "T" on Drop Zone A.

Lillyman said to Cassidy, "I've got news for you. I scouted the coastal battery. It's thoroughly bombed out. No need to worry about that one."

Cassidy said, "In that case, pick up your men, move a little farther north and set up a road block just short of Foucarville." Lillyman listened on the run, and without asking one question, split from Cassidy and started north. The man had been born too soon; he belonged to the age of the astronauts, which opened 15 years later; he burned to be first in action since he was never first in the classroom; having beaten everyone else into Normandy, he was determined to close first on the enemy. So it is not surprising that Lillyman shagged his few men toward Foucarville as if going to a five-alarm fire; the irony is that he ran second best; that was more ridiculous than that he ultimately survived the war unscarred.

What was in the mind of Captain Cleveland R. Fitzgerald, who commanded Baker Company, is less easily explained. Cassidy thought of him as a steady type, though inclined to act on impulse. The psychologists might say that on D-night he was the victim of autohypnosis generated by excessive concentration on the object. That is a gentler way to put it than that he was compulsively bent on getting the whole thing over at the earliest moment.

He jumped clear and landed fair right next the drop zone. Aided by Lieutenant Harold Hoggard, he collected nine men, and over Hoggard's protest, refused to wait for more. This squad took off immediately for Foucarville. At 0200 or D-day (June 6) they entered it from the west side, thereby becoming the first American unit to attack Germans in the Normandy invasion. Leading his meager band, Fitzgerald wandered into a courtyard, not knowing that it served the enemy headquarters. The German sentry plugged him through the lung. Falling, Fitzgerald shot the German dead with his Tommy gun. There was no stir from within the building. Fitzgerald yelled back to the other men, "Don't come up!"

Hoggard sent a private forward to look over Fitzgerald; he made it by crawling and hugging the stone wall. Fitzgerald whispered to him, "Tell Hoggard not to worry about me; it's too late; I'm dying." He was a trifle premature; surviving the last battle in Europe, he was killed by a motor collision in Germany. But Hoggard took him at his word, withdrew the squad 700 yards to the south and waited for daylight.

By then, Hoggard counted 25 men and reckoned he was strong enough to have another go at the village. His scouts, Privates William Emerson and Orville J. Hamilton, were over-anxious. They rushed for the center of the village, not realizing Hoggard was swinging the main body around on a circle tour, and so lost the others. Making it to the German command post without drawing fire, Emerson found Fitzgerald and was told: "You keep going. Leave me alone; I'm finished." But Emerson no longer knew where to go. The scouts moved aimlessly to the next intersection, where they were joined by two other troopers who had split from the main body. It was the moment of German awakening. Suddenly, fire came against the Americans from all around. Grenades from out the buildings burst amid Emerson and his friends. The street blazed with rifle fire. Hoggard and his platoon on the outer circle were smitten from both flanks by machine-gun fire. Hamilton got a grenade slug through the back. Sergeant Olin L. Howard, one of the four at dead center, took a bullet through the wrist. Their companions dressed their wounds under fire, then helped them back to where Fitzgerald lay.

Hoggard, in his swingabout, had picked up two German prisoners before the automatic fire boxed him in. From them he got the news he wanted: about 150 Germans manned the fortified hill north of Foucarville, which for the moment was a few too many. Worrying about his missing scouts, he with-drew through the village, adding Hamilton and Howard to the wounded he was taking out. Fitzgerald, he did not touch. The captain said, "I'm too badly hit to be moved," and that was that. No stars adorned this rather awkward sortie; but it had driven the frightened enemy from Foucarville.

Daybreak and Hoggard's plunge at Foucarville coincided with Pat Cassidy's arrival at a French farmhouse next the German coastal battery. "That," said Cassidy to the others, "will be our command post." From within the house two wild rifle shots punctuated his comment. His soldiers rushed the place, searched it and reported, "We found no krauts." So Cassidy moved in. All that day two Germans stayed concealed in a closet right next him. His landlady later explained, "I hid them; they had been very kind to me."

Cassidy walked over to the battery. Sitting on a high knoll amid the ruins, waving an orange flag, was Lieutenant Colonel Steve A. Chappuis, commanding 2nd Battalion. He nursed a game right leg, twisted on the jump; but he had tarried just long enough to collect ten men and then gone straight to the target.

Said Cassidy, "Move over to the CP and we'll get you fixed up."

Said Steve, "I'd better stay put; more of my men are bound to come this way."

So before turning back, Cassidy briefed Chappuis on what he proposed to do. A wide defensive outguard would be thrown around the CP to block Germans from breaking through to Utah Beach. Charley Company would form a road block on the north, and Baker Company on the south. They would hold while the enemy artillery barracks were cleaned out. These things done, the battalion, having collected more people, would be ready to attack north.

Said Cassidy, "I've already sent a detail to attack the barracks. As more men come in, I'll chase them along. I think we'll handle that one." Great expectation! What Cassidy didn't realize was that he had dispatched to the key point a medley of 15 men, strays from almost as many different units, strangers to one another. Sky soldiers who don't know one another bond together under fire no better than line infantry. But on D-day this Irishman's luck ran stronger than the Utah tide. He had included in the detail one Staff Sergeant Harrison Summers, of Baker Company.

The average American paratrooper is born south of the tracks, and such gentleness as he knows in childhood comes of the love of his family. He volunteers for jumping because he yearns for bigger country and a little prestige. They get it in the service, and nigh invariably they return to civil walks the steadiest of citizens. Not every one is a Harrison Summers; were it so, the nation would have less need to worry about its defenses. In later life a mine inspector in West Virginia, Summers at the threshold of WXYZ was a slender, quietly bashful soldier, Laughing Boy in uniform, anything but a warrior type. In sending him along, Cassidy was unaware that he had just given orders to a second Alvin York, or that he had handed him an odd-ball crew. Summers knew at least half of it; he didn't recognize one of his soldiers.

Cassidy got back to his CP, quite pleased with himself and the clearing situation. According to Chappuis, part of the 3rd Battalion had marched past earlier, which meant that he had a buffer to the south of him. Thirty or more of his own men had reported in during his brief absence. Someone on his staff remarked, "There's quite a fight on at WXYZ." But he paid little attention to that. Though the German camp was but a stone's throw away, the intervening hedgerows deadened the sound, making the near situation seem less urgent. He was reassured also when a batch of prisoners entered the yard. Their guard said, "We got them at the barracks. The fight's hotter by the minute. But we don't need more men." That sounded good enough; and there was other work to do.

A runner arrived with the news that Fitzgerald and other Baker Company men had been hit at Foucarville. He added, "The captain is dying and can't be moved." Captain Frank Choy, the Korean surgeon, who was something of a battalion pet, was rushed north as fast as the "meat wagon" could travel.

No sooner had Choy gone than a stretcher party arrived, bearing one man shot above the heart, another drilled through both legs and Lieutenant Elmer F. Brandenberger, who had joined the fight against the barracks. A booby trap had exploded near Brandenberger's arm, and it was shattered and shredded. He said to Cassidy, "Sir, I'm sorry I got hit; I didn't do my job very well." Before Pat could either choke up or reply, a runner arrived with the message: "We're running out of ammo." Cassidy turned first to the problem of resupplying the force attacking the barracks, leaving his wounded to the medical sergeant, Eugene E. Forbes.

Shortly, Forbes came to him saying, "Colonel, I'm stuck. There are two units of blood plasma left. That private, shot above the heart, looks as if he will die anyway. Brandenberger is bleeding terribly. He'll have a fighting chance if we give him plasma now. Who gets the plasma?"

It was a question for Solomon. Without batting an eye,

Cassidy replied, "It goes to the man who needs it most right this moment. Do it, even if you think it'll be wasted. We can't choose between one life and another." So the private got the plasma and ultimately recovered. Brandenberger had to wait. But even as Cassidy made his decision, something flashed in the back of his mind, and he realized he was forgetting something important. He sweated but couldn't recall it.

On quitting Foucarville, Hoggard moved a few hundred yards west to the battalion's forward CP, set up by Major Thomas A. Sutliffe. Because Sutliffe had brought up an aid man, Hoggard went back with a half-squad to bring out Fitzgerald. They found a deserted village; all Germans had pulled out to the fortified hill position, and the French had fled to the fields for safety. The "meat wagon" arrived with Captain Choy aboard and, steered by Sutliffe, trailed Hoggard into Foucarville. Getting to Fitzgerald, Choy stayed by him in the courtyard for the next two hours administering plasma. Hoggard also stood fast but sent Private Pete Egic running back to Sutliffe with the message: "Send up more men and I'll resume the attack."

Choy's service to Fitzgerald raises a question. Now that a doctor had come, that individual quit talking about death. But Choy's prolonged absence to attend one patient, far removed from the fight, complicated Cassidy's command problem and multiplied the losses of the morning. The score would have been worse but for the cool judgment of Private Patrick J. Callery, a dentist's assistant who drove the "meat wagon." Dumping Choy at Foucarville, Callery continued on his rounds. His vehicle didn't come by its title as a classic jest. Cassidy had found a butcher's cart at the farm and pressed it into service as an ambulance. Under sniper fire, Callery plied the Normandy roads through the day, picking up wounded and drop-injured paratroopers for delivery to Cassidy's CP. The place was already jumping sufficiently without that traffic. Soldiers misdropped all the way from the ocean shallows to the Merderet marshes converged on it through the morning. Cassidy's adjutant sorted out these arrivals, using the CP as an impromptu division regulating station. More than 100 men from other units passed through his hands and were sent along to their assigned missions. Charley Company stayed in place covering the center position, turning to attack only when the snipers got too bold.

More POWs came in from the WXYZ fight. They told a strange story: all their officers had gone the evening before to a conference near Ste. Mère-Église, leaving the neighborhood leaderless in the hour when the Americans struck.

Somewhere around 0815, after many fruitless tries, Cassidy called 4th Division on radio and got a "Roger" back. His message was: "The enemy gun position near St. Martin is in American hands."

General Barton replied, "That's the best news I've had in many hours; now what about the causeways?" Cassidy couldn't tell him anything. The clearing of the exits was supposed to be 3rd Battalion's mission, and he still had no news from them.

Worrying about it, he sent along a patrol of 12 men under Sergeant H. J. Snyder with these instructions: "See what is happening along the causeway west of St. Martin. If the village isn't yet cleared of enemy, it's up to you. Pay special attention to the church steeple; they'll likely be using it."

Then a runner arrived to tell him, "We've got about 65 men to the north of here. Lieutenant [Wallace A.] Swanson wants to know what to do." They checked the map; Swanson and his party were concentrated on the exact spot where Cassidy had landed the night before. So Cassidy said, "Tell Swanson to establish road blocks all around Foucarville and hold until we're ready to attack." But Swanson had miscounted his men; he had 44 instead of 65, and so the assignment stretched him mighty thin.

After talking to wounded, stretcher bearers and prisoners, Cassidy still had no clear idea of how the barracks fight was going, or what had happened so agonizingly to prolong it. He figured he had sent enough men along. But the witnesses were most vague, as if they, too, were remote from the action. Cassidy wanted to go look, but having deployed his forces in four directions, he felt as though he were walking through glue at the center. He said over and over, "I don't dare leave here." He had expected to crush WXYZ within 30 minutes.

For a time he toyed with the idea of sending Charley Company to attack the barracks from the rear, then reluctantly abandoned it. He had to remain strong somewhere; there was no indication that any friendly force covered him to the westward. So he set up a weapons dump in the courtyard, the dregs of the American bundles and the captured German stuff. The spare hands—three draftsmen, one demolitions crew and an operations sergeant—were grouped under Lieutenant Richard Evers and sent to join the fight at WXYZ. Evers, shot and down, rode back on a stretcher almost before Cassidy realized he had gone.

Sergeant Snyder returned from St. Martin to say, "We found them in the church—about a dozen of them. We cleaned them up and lost nobody. The patrol is still there." They'd cleared the steeple of radios, range finders and telephones; hand grenades shattered the machinery without tilting the weathervane or rocking any plaster saints. Snyder was sent along to Baker Company, and a replacement took over the patrol with instructions to "set up road blocks and cover the causeway." Still without word from the other battalions, but satisfied with his own information, Cassidy called Barton again to say, "Exit No. 4 is now open and ready for your advance."

Forbes was back with a question. "I've tried to stop Brandenberger's bleeding. Nothing works. The bone is gone. The arm holds together with a few shreds of flesh. I can't get into the wound with compresses, and I have no plasma. Maybe I can save him by amputating the arm. But I can't make the decision. It's up to you."

They talked it over. By chance, Forbes mentioned the magic word "bundle." In that instant, Cassidy's mind cleared, and the elusive idea was snared. In early morning, on the last leg of his march to the CP, Cassidy had seen a bundle in some nearby field. It looked like a medical bundle. But his conscious mind was filled with other things, and he had passed it by. Going out of the CP on the run, he called to Sergeant Robert L. de Pinquertaine, "Bring a stretcher and follow me." Together they searched the near fields and soon found the bundle, complete with plasma, bandages and morphine, and near it an equally useful bundle of machine-gun ammunition. Portaging both bundles on the stretcher, they got back to Brandenberger in time.

Someone arrived with a third bundle, which disclosed an 81-millimeter mortar. There were no mortarmen on hand. So when a private volunteered with these words, "I think I can fire a mortar; I'm not sure, but I'd like to try," Cassidy sent him along to the barracks fight, saying this: "Report to Lieutenant Homer J. Combs. If he says use the weapon, then go ahead and try."

A little later, the meat wagon rolled in, with Choy aboard,

Fitzgerald and several other wounded, which lifted much of the pressure off Cassidy. He allocated a second farm cart to his ambulance and bundle-collecting service. But high noon came and went, and he still knew little or nothing of the separate actions in which he had lost officers and men. He was much too busy for that.

19

Roses All the Way

Even as the luck of D-night ran with Cassidy, dropping him where he should be and distributing his people so that as needed they could come to him in time to wage effective battle, it ran out on Lieutenant Colonel Bob Cole, commanding 3rd Battalion.

In this, there was a certain poetic justice. Cole and Cassidy had a Damon and Pythias friendship. A West Pointer out of San Antonio, Cole loved to ride Cassidy, and when loosened up by a few cocktails, would predict an unhappy fortune for the Reservist and his battalion, once the fighting began. Not even Cassidy sensed that Cole's hard way with other men screened an inner torment. Physically rugged, seeming to all who knew him the personification of confident courage, he was haunted by an unshakable nightmare that he would sometime fail his troops in battle. It drove him to spend his life gallantly, but much too soon. All that happened to him in the Normandy drop simply piled higher his feeling of frustration.

Cassidy's serial of 44 carriers (it included the Regimental Headquarters) had come in first. Cole's battalion rode the second serial of 36 planes, and his first stick jumped at 56 minutes past midnight.

Cole descended easily, saw no fire on the way down and landed sprawled amid a giant rosebush, with the thorns raking his face and snagging his clothing. For one-quarter hour he struggled with his harness only to become worse entangled. By then he had lost his helmet and was thorns from his scalp to his boot tops. Belatedly, he realized that if he was to escape the bush at all, he must get out his knife and cut away his field gear and some of his clothing. So he went to it.

As he broke into the clear and reached back for his jacket and weapons, he heard someone moving furtively along a nearby hedge. Cole snapped his cricket. From the dark came the answering snap—doubled. It was a soldier from Regimental Headquarters—another of the misdropped.

"Stick with me," Cole told him; "we'll get a gang and then we'll fight."

In less than five minutes they were joined by two battalion NCOs. They trudged along looking for "friendlies"—more men or a helpful signpost. Cole hadn't the faintest notion where he had struck earth.

Next, they ran into Lieutenant R. C. Pick, of Regimental Headquarters Company, who had collected five men.

"Where are we?" asked Cole, "and where are you going?"

Said Pick, "I have no idea where I am, but I intend to move along on my own mission."

Nettled by more than the rose thorns in his hide, Cole asked, "Well, if you don't know where you are, how in hell do you propose to do that?" and then walked away from Pick.

Cole tried to get his bearings by watching the course of the planes. But they seemed to be cutting in every direction. After another half hour of aimless wandering, they met Major J. W. Vaughn, Captain George A. Buker, and two paratroopers. Vaughn was the supply officer; Buker was operations. The first said to Cole, "We've found no bundles." The second added, "I'm just as lost as you are."

Taking command, Cole also moved to the front as point and first scout. After the excitement of the drop, the other men had gone listless. They didn't wish to move along, and to make them do it, one had either to kick their tails or lead out.

At first, Cole took them cross-lots, staying close to the hedgerows. It proved too slow, because he had to search for the gates in the dark while his companions sat down to rest. So reluctantly he swung over to the highway. They picked up a few more men as they marched, mainly paratroopers from the 505th, 507th and 508th Regiments—the first warning to

Cole that he had dropped into the wrong stretch of country, though he was still unaware that he had settled this fate on himself by taking the wrong direction.

For one hour, they went west instead of east, looking for a signpost or a town, and they must have covered several miles. Ahead they saw buildings, silhouetted by the flash from anti-aircraft guns, and they marched that way till they closed on the first houses.

Cole beat on the door of the first home. A woman's voice answered in excited French. The door stayed closed.

Near Cole stood a private from the 505th. He said, "She tells us to go away, that she's afraid. I speak good French. I think I can sweet-talk her into changing her mind."

He got on with it. Finally, the private turned to Cole and said, "According to her, we're in Ste. Mère-Église." Cole said, "Holy hell, then we've got to get out of here." The door opened. Another 82nd Division man shoved a map at the woman. She pointed out exactly where the party was standing. It was necessary for Cole to backtrack the way he had come.

They were now about 30 men. They took off on a road running slightly northeast, and after 40 minutes ran into several of the battalion's officers standing at an intersection. The column rolled up more men as it moved along, becoming 80. The reinforcers had been lying idly in the fields or hiding in the deep shadows next the hedges. When they heard the column trudge by, they were drawn to the noise.

The rout march ended with the noise of wagons coming toward them.

A loud German voice cried, "Halt!"

A man stood in the lead cart, fired a few wild rounds from a machine pistol, then jumped from the cart, running.

There were five carts in the procession. The riders fled to the ditches. Cole's men prodded them out, killing a few and capturing ten. The carts were loaded with field mines, saddles and other leather goods.

Cole said to Vaughn, "Get them emptied right now; we can use them to collect bundles."

Cole thought that he had just about come to his objective. But he wanted to be sure. So alone, he moved off some distance to the right. According to his map, he would find a chapel there, and that would be his check point.

From behind, as he started his walk, he heard a machine gun firing. But he paid little heed. He found the chapel and returned to his men.

The carts had not been emptied, and the men were standing idle.

Hot as a hornet, Cole shouted, "Where in hell is Vaughn? Why don't you comply with orders?"

Pointing down the road, one soldier said, "Major Vaughn went that way to look at the carts. We didn't get any orders."

Cole said, "Then go get Vaughn."

Out of the dark, another soldier had come running just in time to hear the words. He said, "It's too late now; Vaughn is dead."

Cole walked back with him to check on the story. The Germans had set up a machine gun in a ditch just beyond the last cart. Vaughn was shot at ten yards' range as he walked into it. Near his body were two dead Germans. In his dying moment, he had closed on the gun and killed the crew which had ambushed him. For Cole's battalion, this otherwise useless death was the fleeting wisp of glory on D-day.

The German wagons in tow, the column marched south a short distance, then turned east at a point which would enable the force to deploy south of the coastal battery. Right there, at the pivot, Cole met two officers and 30 men from Item Company.

Someone of this group said to him, "Don't bother about the gun position; it's a wreck, and Steve Chappuis is sitting on it."

The force was then split three ways. Under Lieutenant Robert G. Burns, one group, including all of the strays, was sent south to contact the 506th Regiment.

The second group, under Captain Clements, headed for Exit No. 4 to hold the causeway for the advance of the 4th Infantry Division. It marched through St. Martin-de-Varreville without drawing a shot, somehow missing the Germans later mopped up by one of Cassidy's patrols.

Cole led the third group to mount guard over Exit No. 3. As he drew nigh to the village of Audoville-la-Hubert, he heard a few rounds of rifle fire and thought he smelled action. The promise was never fulfilled. By 0730, his fighters were "in position and ready to slaughter any Germans fleeing westward under pressure from the beach." But nothing heroic or spectacularly sanguinary came of this stand. It was not Cole's day.

Two hours later, under pressure from the Utah landing, the Germans tried to beat back across the causeways, and walked directly into Cole's two blocking positions. Well covered by the ditches and the hedge banks, the Cole and Clements groups killed about 75 Germans without getting one American scratched. It was no more contest than a turkey shoot.

Annoyed by the washing-out of his main missions, through circumstance and earlier intervention by other forces, Cole didn't even bother to set up a command post. That's how it happened that he was not sending along the information for which Cassidy was sweating.

20

Summers at WXYZ

When Harrison Summers left Cassidy to attack the German barracks on the Reuville road, 15 men followed him in squad column along the sunken trail which led that way.

They were not his people. They responded somewhat sullenly to the order. They started without any group feeling, and they stayed that way. It was a formation only in the sense that they walked close together for so long as they met no fire.

Summers knew not one man by name; no one spoke; there was no time to shake hands all around and get acquainted. Before getting a first view of what they were up against, Summers decided that it would be easier to start the assault single-handed than to attempt giving orders. Either they would join because he was setting the strong example or they would withhold because they didn't have that kind of stomach, in which case it was too late to do anything about it.

So here was one man setting himself against a position which was supposed to be the target of a battalion. When he committed himself in the first five minutes, though it was full-length, he had no idea of the magnitude of the task.

The barrack tier was set in a vegetable garden about 200 feet off the Reuville road and extended the distance of a city block. The intervening ground was soft and slippery. The column pulled almost even with the first building unobserved. Then Summers sprinted for the door and kicked it in. Not one

Figure 17.   WHERE SUMMERS FOUGHT

American followed him. The Germans inside were now firing through ports in the side of the building and had driven the other men to cover. When Summers burst in on them, firing a Tommy gun, four fell from the fire, and the other occupants, including a number of enemy civilians, escaped through the back door and fled to the third building. The second barracks, located diagonally across the street, Summers also charged alone. But when he broke in the door, the birds had already flown and he only wasted his breath.

From almost in front of the second house, Private William A. Burt set his machine gun to fire on the third house—range 50 yards. Through the slots, the Germans replied with rifles and machine pistols. But Burt's sweeping fire, trained on the ports, made them keep their bodies down, and their shooting was wild.

Brandenberger had come up; when Summers charged this time, the lieutenant was drawn along with him. But his luck went out like a light. As they closed in next the wall, Brandenberger's shoulder triggered a booby trap, and the explosion knocked him down, shattering his arm. Summers let him lie there and kept going. Again he kicked the door in, firing as he entered. There were six Germans inside—that is, six that he could see. They were busy at the ports, crouching low, but still firing toward the road somewhat aimlessly. He shot them all down with one sweep of the gun. When Summers emerged, Brandenberger was already gone; but two other men had been hit while trying to help him clear away. The skulkers were not in sight. Where they made any contribution, they stuck in the roadside ditch and provided some covering fire. But their timidity did not save them. As reinforcements came along, they built upon this stagnant line, with a few gallant exceptions.

Summers was winded now, and he rested next the building wall for about half an hour—the picture of a fellow needing a friend. As he stood to try it again, an unknown captain wearing an 82nd Division patch joined him, saying, "I'll go with you." Before they had bounded 20 yards, a sniper plugged the captain through the heart, and he died without Summers ever learning his name. The sergeant ran on, kicked in the door, and shot down six more Germans. Others who had fled through the back door circled the buildings with hands raised and surrendered to the Americans in the ditches.

But the captain's death had shaken Private John Camin. He could no longer bear seeing one man go it alone. He came to Summers asking, "Why are you doing it?"

Said Summers, "I can't tell you."

Then from Camin: "What about the others?"

Summers: "They don't seem to want to fight, and I can't make them. So I've got to finish it."

Camin: "OK, I'm with you."

As a team, they charged the next five houses, stopping between each run to rest a bit. From house to house, they changed weapons, one covering with the carbine (Camin's weapon) while the other broke the door in and blasted with the Tommy gun. Every house was stone-walled and fire-slotted. The enemy weapons stayed pointed at the road. Private Burt moved his machine gun along in pace with Summers and Camin, shooting up the embrasures. They took no prisoners because no chance afforded, but firing and fighting, saying nothing to one another, they flushed some of the game toward the flattened net of skirmishers. Thirty Germans were killed in the five houses.

Next, they came to a larger building, charged it and kicked the door open. It was the garrison mess hall. Incredible as it sounds, there were 15 German artillerymen at the tables, munching food and seemingly paying no heed to the fighting. As they started to rise, Summers mowed them all down, having no choice.

After one more respite, the group—Summers and Camin and the men who had stuck to the ditch—came to the last building. This was the main barracks, a stone-walled two-story structure.

A high hedge with a thick bank obtruded between building and road. Without sweat, the Americans closed on the bank. Confronting them was a perfectly flat and open field 75 yards wide. While they paused at the bank, glooming at the prospect, a sniper cut loose on them from somewhere on their right rear, picking off several men who were trying to approach the barracks through an orchard to one side of it. This countersurprise stampeded them forward, and they broke through the hedge, headed for the building. Fire crashed against them from the slotted walls and from another sniper's nest on the right. Four men were killed; four were wounded. That stopped the rest, and they recoiled to the road, leaving their unknown dead behind.

Near the barracks was a haystack, and near the haystack, a shed. Burt burned tracers into the hay till it flamed high. The fire spread to the shed, which was stored with ammunition, and the stuff started exploding. That didn't shake the barracks, but Germans came pouring out of the shed. They were shot down—about 30 of them—as they tried to flee across the open space.

The virginal volunteer with the 81-millimeter mortar never showed and nobody ever found out why. But for extra insurance, Cassidy had also sent along Staff Sergeant Roy Nickrent with a bazooka. Nickrent, a talkative *bon vivant* from Chicago, got there as the shed began to blow up. Nickrent made his sneak run down the inside of the hedgerow on the far side of the road. Then coming opposite the barracks, he kicked holes in the embankment so that he could stand on it, got in behind a tree, and opened fire. His first six rounds exploded through the barracks roof. As he saw it, there was no use trying to penetrate the walls. The 60-millimeter mortars also cut loose at this time, but the action was too close-joined for effective use of the weapon, and the shells exploded far beyond it. When his seventh round crashed through the roof and black smoke spiraled from the hole, Nickrent dusted off his hands, said, "That ought to take care of that," and returned to the CP.

During the rocket attack, some of the men had crawled back from the road and resumed fire from behind the hedgerow. They saw the last round set the upper story ablaze. Watching also was Lieutenant Evers, who had just arrived, with his makeshift crew, thrown in by Cassidy as the final reinforcement. Evers sprinted from the road to join the skirmishers along the hedge line; a bullet felled him just as he took off; his participation lasted a split second. Lieutenants Combs and Theodore S. Richards came up in time to see Evers shot down, and their contribution, if less dramatic than his, added little more. There was no longer need for command along the hedge line, and to brave the bullet fire in the middle ground would have been foolhardy. In torching the building, Nickrent's bazooka had both burned out the Germans and reduced the barracks fight to a last glowing ember.

Summers was still in there firing, Camin beside him, but except for his trigger finger, he was beaten down. Small wonder. For more than five hours, he had carried the frontal attack either alone or moving with men marked for quick sacrifice, and then at last he had paired with an inconspicuous private who led an equally charmed life. The sheer physical exertion, had it been done in a field exercise apart from danger, would have folded an average soldier. Outbursts of blind bravado in combat are relatively paltry, though the fighter who reacts explosively, under some fleeting compulsion which transcends his reason, is usually medaled for "valor above and beyond the call of duty."

There was none of this in Summers. He did consciously, step by step, and as a matter of course, everything that the situation and the default of other soldiers required of him. For endurance, for sustained courage hour after hour, and for blessings from on high which made his luck run immortally, his performance is without parallel. At the end, his body was bruised all over from collision with the walls and the impact of the doors, but his skin was as unscarred as his mind.

From along the hedge line, someone cried, "They're coming

out now!" And they were. The Germans poured from the building, fleeing the flames. They came in such numbers that though the Americans from behind the bank loosed fire with all weapons, and never slackened, some of the fugitives got away for a few moments to the westward. The other half—approximately 50 men—were shot down in the foreground during the breakaway.

The others escaped the fire for the frying pan, having made their sortie at the worst possible moment. The hour was 1530. The spearhead of the 4th Infantry Division was just then advancing into the position on its westward march from Exit No. 4, while on the far side of the barracks, moving east along the Reuville road, was the regimental assembly party of the 502nd under Lieutenant Colonel John T. Michaelis. With the converging of these two bodies, what was left of the enemy became ground between the upper and nether millstones. The point of the Michaelis party, under Captain James H. Hatch, saw some of the fugitives huddling in a field west of the barracks. Hatch yelled back, "Send forward a machine gun." The Germans started to run, and Hatch's first scout, Private Stanley Gruber, cut loose with his M-1. Their Parthian volley drilled Gruber through both legs. As the enemy vanished into the scenery, his playmates hoisted Gruber in a shelter half and carried him toward Cassidy's CP. But Gruber's only bullet had killed their flickering resistance, which gave him the last laugh. As the party slogged along, 31 Germans came out of the shrubbery with hands raised. It was the postscript to the affair at WXYZ.

Summers and his beat-up party reclined in the last house next the burning barracks.

He said, "I guess it's time for a smoke."

Someone asked, "How do you feel?"

He said, "Not very good. It was all kind of crazy. I'm sure I'd never do anything like that again."

Spoken like a soldier but hardly like a prophet, the closing remark proved only that Summers had yet to know himself.

21

Road Blocks at Foucarville

Not knowing that Hoggard had beaten him to Foucarville, when Swanson found him there, he got sore as hell and lashed out at his fellow lieutenant.

Part of it may have been pique that Hoggard, who had done the fighting while Swanson was collecting men, had already harvested much of the credit. But in his circuitous approach to the village, Swanson saw Germans moving about rather freely on the high ground north of Foucarville before he ran into the Hoggard party. So he took it out on Hoggard for not anticipating the orders which he, Swanson, had only lately received from Cassidy.

He asked, "Why in hell didn't you set up road blocks?"

Hoggard simply shrugged him off. There was no point in explaining that he had been rushed into Foucarville by Fitzgerald with only nine other men, that he had used his limited power to beat the enemy back from the village, that there was no time for anything else, and that one does not set up road blocks with the enemy at his back.

Taking two men, Swanson went forward to reconnoiter the ground for Blocks 1 and 2, east of the village, and Block 3, to the north. The other men were deployed to root out snipers from within the houses. The ease of the reconnaissance, coupled with the fact that the snipe hunt bagged nothing, said mutely that Hoggard and his party had fought effectively, thereby

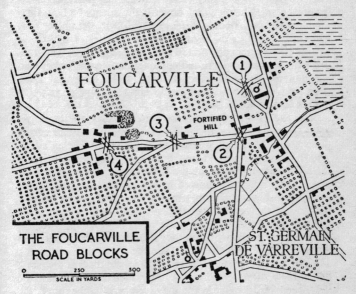

Figure 18. FOUCARVILLE ROAD BLOCKS

giving Swanson a pass to first base.

Their reward for it when Swanson got back from his half-hour look at no man's land, was that they were named to maintain the two meanest blocks, those which faced eastward. Sergeant Cecil Thelan and helpers mounted Block 3. The groups moved out during the noon hour deploying in skirmish line to their areas, and by an hour or so later, all were set and ready.

At Block No. 1, three riflemen, a rifle grenadier and a machine-gunner covered the intersection. They got to ground just in time. The pressure of the American infantry moving across the causeways from Utah Beach was now such that fugitive small groups of Germans were flooding inland. Through the afternoon, Block No. 1 was continuously engaged in rifle action from the eastward, while from the Foucarville church steeple, snipers peppered its rear.

Directly confronting the German strong point north of the

village, Block No. 2 had six riflemen, one grenadier and a bazooka team. The men took cover in the ditches on both sides of the road and, finding some German wire, strung a rude barricade. Forty yards beyond them was a sea of barbs, enclosing the German position. The slope facing them was studded with concrete shelters and pillboxes, and in the background was a motor park well screened by tall trees. In several of the trees were well-hidden platforms nesting machine guns which poured fire on Block No. 2.

The fire exchange droned on through early afternoon. At 1500 the Germans on the hill tried to get on the rear of the three blocks by slipping down a hedgerow on Thelan's left. The first warning was a heavy build-up of fire down the main road. The sneak play along the flank might have been missed had not the attackers shouted at one another in exhortation. Looking that way, Thelan's men could see German helmets bobbing as they passed the thinned spots in the hedge. Two machine guns and 12 rifles were ready. The gunners rushed toward the embankment. But they had dropped their tripods so that they could work the guns from the top of the hedge bank and still have fair cover. The riflemen joined them at the bank; under this well-protected volley fire, which caught them in the side at ten yards' range while they were still on the move, the Germans wilted and retired uphill screaming.

The bank itself had served to shield the Americans against the supporting bullet fire from the hilltop. But then an antitank gun from the high ground, closer to them than the infantry weapons, found their line. Its shells cut through the foliage and earth.

Saying nothing to anyone, Private John T. Lyell left Thelan's party and crawled uphill to go after the gun. A few of the riflemen saw him start, and they trailed after. At the military crest, Lyell found the gun, positioned between two dugouts. For the moment, it had ceased fire, and he saw no one around. He yelled, "Come on out and *kamerad!*"

Three Germans emerged from the nearest shelters with hands raised. A fourth came behind them, and Lyell saw his arm swing up and over; as the missile was loosed, he threw his own grenade. The Germans were killed by Lyell's grenade and by rifle fire from behind him. One fragment of the potato masher shattered his shoulder and he went down. Privates Richard P. Feeney and James Goodyear tried to get up to him, but the open space just ahead of them buzzed with bullets. Goodyear at last made it, with Feeney and Staff Sergeant Thomas Wright laying back and providing the covering fire which stopped the enemy rifles. Goodyear gave Lyell a shot of morphine. By then it was no longer possible to carry him out, because an enemy machine-gunner had come up, joined the fight and driven Feeney and Wright back. Just under the grazing fire, they lay there together in a defiladed hollow until the day was almost done. Then Goodyear dragged Lyell into an abandoned German communications trench, where several hours later he died from loss of blood.

By late afternoon, the church-tower snipers had winged four men on Block No. 1. Emboldened by the action, more Germans had come out of their holes and were sharpshooting from the roof tops and windows of the village houses. But having put most of his men on the blocks, Swanson didn't feel he had enough strength in reserve to risk lives in a house-to-house search. Of this came the day's rarest touch of poetic justice. In late afternoon, four Germans who had sniped from the steeple tried to steal away from the church via a side door. An 82nd Division private, who had lain quietly in a hedgerow facing the door through most of the day because he felt more like resting than like fighting, saw them emerge and shot them down with a Tommy gun.

That still didn't restore the premises wholly to the godly. At the roadblocks, the Americans hung on, facing a vastly stronger force on their immediate front, and harassed by occasional bullets from the steeple. Swanson had distributed the people in his reserve through German dugouts and fire trenches within the village which were handy to his purpose. But word got to them from the road block crews that they were getting shot in the back and didn't like it. They didn't like it, either. On their own, in late evening, Sergeants Willis Zweibel and Charles Assay and Private Leroy Nicolai decided to rush the church. They saw one German duck from the building, and they shot him as he tried to plunge through a hedgerow. From under the belfry, they could hear a rifleman working the floor above. Zweibel said, "Let's either kill this son-of-a-bitch or drive him crazy." So they stood right under the bell and fired through the planking until there was nothing left to shoot. Every time a bullet clanged the metal, Assay yelled, "That's for whom the bell tolls." When at last the church was silent, they walked out. They weren't sure they had killed the German, but they didn't give a damn about climbing up to see.

Coupled with the mark-time look of the big German force on the hill, the extermination of the snipers in the village emboldened Swanson to extend his force. He threw out a fourth road block to the west, at the center of a nearby hamlet, so small that it didn't bear a name. Twelve riflemen, two machine guns, two bazookas and 15 pounds of explosives gave it power. Without realizing it, Swanson had made his happiest move of the day.

Of these developments, Cassidy knew only the barest outline. He sent Lieutenant Nichels to Foucarville to "see how Swanson is making out." On reporting, Nichels saluted (in combat, paratroopers are the salutingest men in American uniform) and asked, "Sir, how are things getting along?" Swanson said, "We are engaging several hundred Germans in defensive position north of here." It looked like an interesting fight; Nichels asked permission to stay and, on getting it, sent another runner back to Cassidy to repeat what Swanson had just told him. On receiving the news, Cassidy remarked wryly, "It looks as if Company A will be able to take care of itself." Since there was no call for help, he would tend his own knitting.

When Michaelis and his column arrived, Cassidy and his people were already in a field next the CP. A final sorting-out was in process, and men were moving to the four corners, according to their units. Michaelis now had the regiment, having relieved the veteran Colonel George Van Horn Moseley, who had broken his leg on the jump. It was a great break—the first of many which made Michaelis a celebrated name in the Army.

"Pat" said to "Mike," "Sir, if you can take over getting the wounded to the beaches and aboard the LSTs, I think I can handle the rest of the problem." So it was agreed. Demanding service for the wounded, like other problems, is lubricated by rank.

Cassidy next ordered Charley Company to march on Beuzeville-au-Plain (west of Foucarville) and set up four road blocks around it. That done, the battalion would complete the line of barricades covering the northeast corner of VII Corps's beachhead. By 1730, the wounded were on their way to the LSTs in some captured trucks.

Cassidy said, "Now I'd like to move on Foucarville."

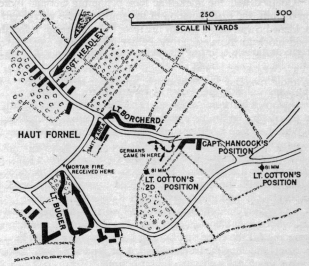

Figure 19. AT HAUT-FORNEL

Michaelis answered, "Get going."

The battalion party marched north at 1800.

Going to Beuzeville, Charley Company veered from the main road at St. Germain-de-Varreville and followed a dry stream bed, which was probably a mistake. Out in front 250 yards, the point of 23 men was led by Lieutenant Morton J. Smit. Looking ahead, Smit saw on the skyline a church amid a cluster of houses. Just then a runner got up to him from the skipper, Captain Hancock, with the message: "Push into Beuzeville and set up road blocks east and west of it." (Having moved out in too great a rush, Hancock was improvising on the run.)

Lacking a map, Smit concluded that the village ahead was his target. So he pointed his scouts that way, and the scouts moved into and through Haut-Fornel, 150 yards in advance of Smit and his party.

Though they drew no fire, Smit, seeing a large barrackslike building, concluded too late that he should have conned the village. He ducked into the barracks and found it strewn with Lugers, caps, belts, canteens—beautiful souvenirs. As he started shoving the treasure into a German B-bag, he heard rifle fire from the direction the scouts had taken. Private Harold F. Boone, who was covering him at the inner door, shouted, "Hey, I can hear krauts talking."

Through the window they saw a truck stop and a squad of Germans unload. They dashed for the barracks entrance. A second truck had come alongside, and the soldiers were already in the street. To Smit's eye they looked "scared, excited and unwilling to move." Boone emptied his Tommy gun into them —range 40 yards—and saw "about ten men fall." Smit foolishly spent his ammunition firing his carbine at the truck wheels and saw one tire go flat. A few bullets buzzed round the door, but it was wild shooting. They retreated down the hallway, out the back door and into a paved walled courtyard.

Out of ammunition, they still didn't worry until potato mashers, lobbed over the wall, exploded around them, the fragments bouncing off the stone and hurting just enough to draw blood.

Smit, watching the barracks back door, said to Boone, "Look for the gate; that wall's too high to climb."

Boone was back in a moment, saying, "There isn't any gate."

Beyond the barracks, from the direction of the street, they heard the rattle of rifle fire. Smit guessed that his men had deployed among the houses and were fighting back. After 30 minutes there was profound silence. They wondered how the thing had gone. Then they heard men walking along the barracks hall—but it was the heavy tread of jack boots.

So they sprang for the wall and made it, with Boone standing on Smit's shoulders and pulling him up. But it was too late. From both sides they heard the yelling of Germans rounding the building to head them off.

Twenty yards beyond the wall was a hog wallow, thick with garbage, the penned animals still unfed.

Smit said, "Into the slop; bury yourself."

They did it methodically, lying side by side, one man helping the other to a perfect shroud of stinking waste until at last only their lips and snouts were sticking out. That was how they rested for the next hour, communicating with one another by a finger poke in the ribs. Germans prowled all around them, occasionally looked in the wallow, and then moved elsewhere.

Finally, they heard voices—American voices—distant at first. Some of Smit's own men, beaten back from the village, had reformed and come at it again. Smit knew it when Private John Lesinski (who was a better looker than the Germans) stood above him tickling his ribs with a bayonet, ready to shove it home.

Smit yelled, "Lesinski, what in hell took you so long?" then rose from the reek, shedding garbage as he stood.

Lesinski said, "My God, look at the lieutenant!"

With Lesinski was Sergeant Charles H. Tinsley. They heard more firing from the street, toward which a hedgerow ran from the wallow. Smit said to Tinsley, "You scout forward on one side of it, and I'll take the other." But he didn't say how they would get together at the other end, and since only Tinsley was loaded, this was important. Tinsley had picked the right side; nothing happened to him. But on the inside of the row, as Smit neared the street, a column of Germans, recoiling from the American attack at the other end of the village, came crawling along the ditch straight toward him.

Turning before they saw him, Smit knew Hobson's choice. Along with Lesinski, he and Boone got back in the garbage again. American mortar fire came over the barracks and exploded around the courtyard. The Germans flattened out, scattered all around the hedge line and wallow. Dark came. Firing stopped. The enemy soldiers moved into the barracks. Smit led his troops—both of them—out of the garbage and into a wooded area. He said, "Nuts to the war. This isn't my day. Right here we stop." So they flopped under the pines, tried to sleep and got sopped by a gentle rain. Within 15 feet of where they lay, hidden from view by a clump of lilacs, were two set-up empty German squad tents, with a cache of food and water. It was the climactic D-day entry in their string of misadventures, not yet ended.

Captain Hancock couldn't imagine what had happened to Smit's point and wasn't given time to go see. From the firing, he reckoned that Smit had bumped a hornet's nest. But that had to be Smit's business. His entry into Haut-Fornel had aborted an enemy battery—two self-propelled 88s—which came riding, with their crews, straight towards Hancock's front when the small-arms firers engaged. Capture of the guns, which had halted a furlong away, became Hancock's prime concern, and he figured it would be easy.

He split his force three ways. Lieutenant Bernard C. Bucior, with 17 men, started on a wide sweep to the left, which would get him to the edge of the village on the rear of the guns. Lieutenant Jack Borcherd took another 17 men to the right; moving on a smaller arc, he was to come in close and pinch out the battery. Hancock and his few remaining hands strung out, ready to fire, behind a hedgerow.

After leaving Hancock, Borcherd, without authority, hedged his bets, split his force, and sent the other half, under Sergeant Harold Headley, to make a wider end run and come in on the far side of Haut-Fornel. With his nine men, Borcherd got to within 75 yards of the battery—grenade-launching range. In addition to the two 88s, he could now see a half-track, an ammunition truck and about one platoon of German infantry. It was too late to recall Headley, who was on his way. Borcherd's few men bellied up to a hedge bank and opened fire on the battery group with rifles, rifle grenades and machine gun. One truck caught fire. Another truck, pulling a small piece of artillery, moved into the scene. The truck stopped when the crew bailed out, but the vehicle didn't burn. A few of the Germans had fallen from the fire; most of them ran for cover.

At that point, from excitement, Borcherd's men forgot their mission. They were still unscathed, and the battery was little hurt. Still, they broke through the hedgerow and ran on to search the houses of Haut-Fornel, neglecting the guns, and speeded on by machine-pistol fire from their rear.

Headley's simultaneous run toward them from the far end of the village was less blessed. Straight off, Sergeant Curtis DeWitt was shot through the back. Two comrades picked him up, and the group came on. Three Germans emerged from a house, hands raised. Midway of the village, the patrol heard someone shout a loud command in German. The three POWs broke and ran but were shot down before they could reach cover.

At that moment, Borcherd, moving toward Headley, saw a German infantry platoon marching straight into the intersection where he stood. There were only four riflemen with him; his machine gun was too far back to do any good. He yelled, "We got to get the hell out!"

When he and the others ran out, they left Headley unwarned

and moving at right angles directly into the German platoon. Headley hadn't seen it because of the houses. But his men were already tense because of the steady fire build-up along the street. Private William Kelley jumped into a German truck, waved his arms, and yelled, "Lieutenant! Lieutenant!" not knowing that Borcherd had already come and gone. Missing the lieutenant, plagued by the fire, not knowing a superior enemy force was about to cut them off, they deployed into the houses.

But Private Kelley knew his business—at least, partway. One German 88 had returned to the cover of the village, accompanied by a truck. The other gun had vanished to God-knows-where. Kelley ran to the house opposite the gun, fired two rounds from his bazooka through a window—and destroyed the piece.

That done, he darted across the street to see what was in the truck. It was piled high with German odds and ends—prime souvenirs. So he jumped aboard and began rummaging. Someone yelled, "Don't touch it! It's booby-trapped." Kelley jumped out again.

Two Germans came running from the house where he had plied his bazooka, and he shot them dead with his other weapon—a Tommy gun. As if that had loosed the storm, the street became a gut of fire. Two of Headley's men were killed by bullets; two others were wounded. This fusillade came from the late-arriving enemy platoon, which had also taken to the houses.

It didn't stop Private Garland Hatcher, who, not knowing the odds, figured his patrol could still swing it. He stood in the middle of the street, bawling, "Come out you God-damned krautheads! Get the hell out of those houses before I blast you!"

The other men were clearing out, leaving Hatcher behind, still yelling. Then Headley and Kelley turned back to help Hatcher, or make him move. But they lost sight of him when another left-behind comrade came running from back of a garden wall, got a bullet in the leg as he intersected them, and falling, sent them sprawling. When they arose, Hatcher had disappeared. They backed up against a hedge bank. Machine-pistol fire from the two-story house opposite them clipped the bush above their heads.

Kelley had one bazooka round left. Headley said, "Give it to them!" So he moved once more into the street and with his last rocket fired the building. Then he threw the tube away, jumped for the hedge and got wedged tight. Headley bulldozed him through with his shoulder and followed through the hole. They were in a vegetable garden. Germans held the fields on three sides of it. So they sat there, back to back, among the cabbages for the next 90 minutes, one guarding with an M-1, the other with a carbine. Headley, also, had been carrying two weapons.

Headley watched a cabbage leaf shaking back and forth and, wondering at the phenomenon, called Kelley's attention to it. Kelley whispered, "You damn fool, it's against your knee." That was the only conversation they later remembered in an otherwise silent vigil.

The rest of the patrol got back to Hancock; he had no reason to believe there were other survivors. So he had both the 60s and the 81s shell Haut-Fornel for more than an hour. About 70 rounds were fired. Much of it fell in the fields around Headley and his friend or near the hog wallow where Smit and fellows rested. The pair in the cabbage patch crawled away at dusk. By then the mortar explosions had torched the village, and most of the Germans were fighting the fires.

Before following along with Bucior's patrol on the left, one aside is necessary to clarify this weird battle, arising from a meeting engagement, owing to the error which put Smit on the wrong road into Haut-Fornel. Hancock's arrival there had coincided with the march-through of a German artillery column en route to support the Foucarville strong point. Borcherd's patrol had intercepted only the tail end of the column. The rest of it, which had cleared Haut-Fornel before the Americans first sighted it, sped on toward Block No. 4 west of Foucarville. The crew at the block saw the convoy far off. They set the demolition and lit the fuse as a quarter-ton truck, in the van, raced toward the block. It was bull's-eye. The explosion lifted and wrecked the pilot car, and its flaming debris barred the road. There were four trucks behind, all loaded with artillery-men. The two machine guns couldn't miss this broad target; the two bazooka men got off four rounds. The vehicles blazed. The surviving Germans had already jumped for cover. Some of them rebounded to Haut-Fornel, adding to the confusions of that scrambled action. Others took to the ditches and came on against Block No. 4. The crew felt too hard-pressed and sent a call to Swanson for help. This happened at 1730. Swanson sent them Lieutenant Delmer Idol with five men. Aided by this powerhouse, the crew steadied.

With the best of intentions, Bucior and his patrol got caught way out in left field. Their route lay along the proverbial long lane which for them had no turning. By the time they were ready to angle back to Haut-Fornel and a path availed, there was a large farm on their rear, and they thought they saw Germans moving in the yard. Bucior dropped a machine gun with two men there to block for him, and by the time the gunner had killed his first two Germans (they walked right into him from the farm), Bucior and the others were moving along a sunken lane toward the village. But they soon stopped. Where the lane intersected the first road, the barrel of an 88 crosswise of it barred the way like a sign reading: "Please Detour." So they carefully scouted forward. There were at least two squads of Germans around the gun; having put out flankers, Bucior's own party numbered seven.

They had already been spotted and fired on, and they guessed the Germans had outposted the gun. But because it was too late to recall the flankers or warn them, they moved forward, on their bellies, staying in the ditches. That was how it was when Borcherd's patrol began shooting up the village.

By the time their crawl got them to the edge of the road ahead, the German 88 and party had moved from the intersection. Bucior said to Private William Haas, "Cross the road and sort of feel things out; if you see any Germans, fire at them and then let's see what happens."

These were not the best possible military instructions, but Haas was game. He crossed the road, saw, and was seen by, a party of about 12 enemy 50 yards up the road and closer to the village. Haas dutifully fired his M-1, and straightaway got creased in his skull by a bullet. With his face a bloody mess, he crawled back across the road to Bucior, and said, "Well, I did it."

Bucior tried to put rifle fire and hand grenades on the enemy from behind the hedge bank. One was too long; the other fell short. One attempt to move by the open field met such a hail of bullets that Bucior cried, "Back to the lane!" He moved the way he had come, then tried to go at Haut-Fornel on a wider arc. The route took the men through an orchard toward a stone wall. From behind the wall, a sharpshooter fired. The bullet ripped a gaping hole in Bucior's shoulder. Gone flat, the men grenaded over the wall till the rifle fire stopped. They were so close to the Germans that otherwise they could not have evacuated Bucior. Privates Donald L. Matthews and Philip Sangenario helped him along, not resting until they got with the machine gun near the farm. The patrol rested and lit cigarettes. Sangenario dressed the wound. Bucior said, "Oh, hell, we can't sweat it out here; follow me!" So they tried the lane again. As they slipped along, a German patrol came straight toward them on the inner side of the hedge.

Matthews, in the lead with his dismounted machine gun, saw them and fired first. Three were killed; the others scattered to cover, but soon opened fire. Sangenario noticed that Bucior was bleeding heavily and moving jerkily at the tactile pace of a blind man.

He said, "Lieutenant, you've got to let me take you back."

Bucior said, "Hell no, hell no, hell no, keep going."

With the party now were these three, two riflemen and an 82nd Division trooper armed with a Schmeisser. They lurched another 50 yards. Private Warren Hicks saw a German foxholed in a field on the right, and shot him with his M-1. Bucior said to Sangenario, "That's a machine-gunner; crawl out and get the weapon." As Sangenario crawled, heavy fire came from the bordering orchard. He came out with the piece, test-fired it, jammed it after three rounds and hurled it back into the field crying, "Aw, to hell with it!" Thirty yards farther along, the trooper with the Schmeisser saw movement in the hedge, fired into it and killed a sniper.

They reached the intersection a second time. There were no enemy soldiers around. They saw a house blazing high in the village. The man with the Schmeisser whispered, "Look out!" From his spot on the right, he had seen an enemy platoon advancing through a field straight toward them. Matthews stood by him next the gate. Standing erect, they let the crowd have it, with the machine gun and Schmeisser. When Matthews's gun ran dry, Hicks took his place. Two squads of Germans were cut down and did not move after they fell.

Uncertain, they marked time there for ten minutes. Then a mortar shell exploded into the road, fair amid them. Hicks got a slug in the leg. The man with the Schmeisser was hit in the back. Came quickly two more rounds. Bucior was hit in six places. Matthews got fragments in his chest and shoulder. Private Bernard Ormsbee was wounded in the hand. That left only Sangenario unhurt.

Bucior said, "I guess we better drag our ass down the road."

Hicks said, "I can't; I can't move my leg."

Ormsbee said, "You better damn well move it, or you never will again."

He pulled Hicks to his feet and shoved him. Bucior started to walk, took two steps and then reeled. The others grabbed him and in relays helped him along; they fell back haltingly to the farm, and how they made it from there to the hospital none could later remember. But there was no deliverance for Bucior.

Getting fragments of information about these happenings as he moved north with his headquarters people, Pat Cassidy felt more and more like a man shoveling sand against the tide. Unexpected front-line fury has an echo which too often amplifies going rearward from echelon to echelon. Major Sutliffe at the forward CP didn't make Cassidy feel any better. Able Company was "catching hell at Foucarville." Charley Company had put its nut in the wrong cracker at Haut-Fornel. Cassidy ordered telephone wire strung to the two fighting sectors. Machine guns were deployed in an arc to cover the CP's right and rear. Lieutenant Rance Cotton and his one 81-millimeter mortar were placed in a small stream bed behind the CP to give what help he could. These signals read that the bind was getting tighter, as Cassidy viewed it.

Next, he walked west to con Hancock's situation. En route, he ran into Bucior's shot-up patrol, which, missing the company flank, continued on its way, tottering along, looking for aid from anyone who would give it. Blood-drenched and inarticulate, Bucior had become a dead weight on the others, and they staggered under the load. Here is the grimmest, most heartbreaking spectacle of the battlefield. It is far more shocking to see unhelped wounded reeling aimlessly to the rear, unguided and with no certain destination, than to tramp over acres laden with the newly dead, looking at each body to determine the cause of death.

There could not have been a worse torment for Cassidy than his chance meeting with Bucior. One man who was sustaining the lieutenant said, "The company is still catching hell. It's awful hot up there. We can't figure it out."

Coupled with the ghastly appearance of the patrol, the words shook Cassidy. Every natural impulse prompted him to deliver this shocked band to safety. But he felt he had to leave them to shift for themselves while he continued frontward to see if the outlook for the battalion was as dark as it seemed.

Weighed in cold blood, it was the right decision. If its aftermath raises a question, that's because fighting men have emotional natures as well as tidy minds. The figures are supposed to balance; what is not present should at least be accounted for. Somewhere between the spot where Cassidy left him and the beach Bucior vanished. That is it; he was taken, and nobody knows how or where. His unexplained fate is one of the most haunting mysteries of Normandy.

But for Cassidy, finding Hancock wasn't easy. Hancock had decided to pull Charley Company away from that multi-loaded booby trap, Haut-Fornel, and take up new ground facing northwest, breaking off engagement if possible, but continuing to block. He was in movement when the patrol passed by and Cassidy came up.

Looking for a fight and not being able to contact the Foucarville force, Lieutenant Cotton had quit the stream bed and brought his one 81 mortar forward to ground directly behind Hancock's re-forming line. He was in time to see Bucior's forlorn crew reel past at a distance and to get off a few rounds against the German machine guns which badgered Hancock during the shift of position. Then German snipers pressed in close and picked on Cotton—the wrong man. He shagged three of his crewmen out to drive off the snipers while he personally took over the feeding of the tube.

Hancock's new CP and most of his wounded had folded to within a French farmhouse. Automatic fire was plunking into the thatch of the roof. Cotton wondered where the enemy machine guns could be located that they were still finding Hancock. So he scouted forward through the field ahead of Hancock's position, about 150 yards, to have a look. He reached the far embankment just in time to see a platoon of Germans turn the corner of the same hedgerow and lunge toward the CP, which, not yet outposted, was unalert to the danger.

Cotton had two grenades. The quarry was beyond throwing range. Still, he went straight for the platoon at a dead run, yelling, "You God-damn Krauts! We got you! We got you!" the words rising and dissolving into a war whoop. Still running, he heaved both grenades—and was wild with both throws. It didn't matter. The platoon broke and scattered like quail. Some of the Germans ran back into the field beyond Cotton. He heard them coming along the hedge. Through gaps in the foliage, he emptied his carbine into them and saw four men fall. The others, including two that Cotton had winged slightly, bolted across the field. Drawn by the noise, Hancock came up at that moment and found Cotton "doubled up and laughing like crazy."

Together, they moved to the far end of the second field. The ground tapered off, ending in a narrow hollow. Out of the defilade, a white flag fluttered, and they saw three or four helmets bobbing. Cotton waved his arms with the "come on in" motion. Thirteen Germans came out of the hole. Hancock and Cotton herded them back to the CP. The paratroopers said, "Let's shoot these bastards now." Hancock answered, "Don't you think we've had enough shooting for one day?"

Cassidy, moving rapidly in and out of these scenes, had them register on his mind in about the same way that a marathoner, running past a head-tall picket fence, would get the give-and-take of a garden party on the other side. This is one of the hair shirts of battalion command; when operations are in flux, there is no such thing as reading the score infallibly. It's blindman's buff in quicksand. What impressed Cassidy was that Hancock had fallen back and the Germans were still rushing him. Already hurting bad, his own people were being crowded.

Fire from the enemy 88s was now beating around Cassidy's CP. At dusk the battle noise rose ominously. Cassidy had no artillery support; the 377th Battalion, which had parachuted into the same area with him, had lost all but one tube on the jump. The gap between the Able and Charley Company sectors was a maze of hedgerows wide enough to afford entry to a regiment well spread. Through the afternoon, limited counterattacks had been thrown at both company sectors. The 88 shelling gradually shifted from the CP area to the unguarded middle ground. If the limited assaults against the two dangling flanks were a feeling-out process preparatory to an all-out drive through center, now would be the time. That's about how Cassidy thought it out as he came to the end of his Perfect Day, and though he didn't have the wind up, it wasn't wholly down, either.

First, he ordered Baker Company, which was protecting the CP area, to move forward and take a position within the gap, facing half left so that it could give some support to Hancock.

Then he called Michaelis and said, "Now I must have help."

Michaelis said, "As fast as I can round up people, I'll get them along to you."

Collecting the spares around the CP—15 men armed with rifles and carbines—Cassidy led them to a forward hedgerow in the center which was roughly in line with his flanks.

Michaelis, finding him there some minutes later, said, "I'll have a few more squads up to you shortly. Now, how do things look?"

Cassidy answered, "The enemy seems to be well organized. I think he has enough strength to break through us."

Yet even while he spoke these words, the decision was his, and the breaking situation was about to be delivered fully and finally into his hands. Cotton's small sortie in front of Hancock had stopped the enemy's last gasp. The remaining Germans were pulling out of Haut-Fornel. In front of the fortified hill at Foucarville, it seemed to Swanson that all of his pounding had been in vain. He had steadily barraged the works with the 60-millimeter mortars and had scrounged machine guns from the other positions to concentrate fire power in Headley's group. But there was not a sign that any softening had occurred.

Then just after 2200, the German weapons on the height went suddenly silent. Seconds later, a white flag was raised over the position. There emerged into the open, with hands raised, 87 Germans and one Frenchwoman—widow of a German fighter who had died that day.

As this group moved downhill, the ground behind them erupted. Other Germans could be seen trying to flee the position in the opposite direction, while midway stood a gang of American paratroopers gunning down the fugitives.

From below, Swanson & Company watched this weird tableau, bug-eyed, baffled at what was happening, and too startled to move. The mystery was solved later. All day long, 17 of General Taylor's men had been held prisoner by the Germans on the hill. Misdropped far to the north of the assigned field, they had been rounded up by the Germans in Foucarville and marched to the fortified hill. One genius among them, who remained ever after anonymous, said to his fellow prisoners, "Let's tell these krauts that at 2230, according to plan, there is scheduled an artillery concentration that will blow this hill plumb to hell." A tall story, invented on the spur of the moment, they got it in circulation early and kept repeating it. As the clock ticked on, the German garrison grew steadily more nervous.

The greater number decided to give up. The die-hard minority planned a breakaway to the north. This, too, the POWs knew. Then as the Germans started their run, the Americans were all ready and set for it. They grabbed the arms dropped by the surrendering Germans in time to blast the getaway. Some of Headley's men guessed what was happening, rushed the hill and joined the shoot. About 50 Germans were killed in this *coup de grâce*. Swanson's people took over the enemy fortifications that night, finding them well littered with silk stockings and lingerie.

Before hearing of the collapse at Foucarville, Cassidy already knew that he had it made. A major from the 22nd Infantry Regiment arrived at the CP. He waved his arms in the direction of the gap between Able and Charley Companies and said, "Some of my men are moving there right now. Over to their left, the 12th Regiment is advancing. Another battalion of the 22nd has come up on your right at Foucarville." Soon after the major departed, Cassidy got an order from Michaelis to withdraw slightly and reorganize, so that 502nd's 2nd Battalion could move through and take over the sector. By midnight the front was quiet, and at daybreak the battalion moved back.

Lieutenant Smit and his two strays awakened in the wood near Haut-Fornel just about then. They started in what they thought was the direction of the battalion, but making a 180-degree bad guess, they headed for Bandienville, another enemy strongpoint. They knew it when they ran into fire from a German nest mounting two machine guns. Smit and Lesinski crawled along a ditch to get on the flank of the position, and from 30 yards' range, gunned down both crews. While they waited there, congratulating one another and wondering what to do next, they heard a large body of men coming through the hedgerow on their rear.

So they crawled on along the ditch. Reaching a dead end,

they turned, prepared to make a stand. Then a man popped through the hedge right next them; he was an American infantryman.

Smit asked, "What are you doing here?"

The boy said, "I don't know. But I can tell you what you're doing. You're fooling around in front of the 12th U.S. Infantry during an attack."

It was time to get out and return to the battalion which had done the one best job for America on D-day.

22

The Man and the Lock

In the assignment of targets for the Normandy invasion, the perfect coupling was the choice of Colonel Howard R. "Skeets" Johnson to take and hold the La Barquette lock.

They fitted as did Horatius his bridge. A new Macaulay might write an epic around it.

The regimental commander of 501st was a flamboyant warrior, a fire-eater and gasconader, who orally thirsted for German blood and ruled training with the intensity of a varsity coach evoking the Rutgers spirit between halves. In this strange character, high courage was well met with showmanship. But the one made the other less credible.

"We are the best!" So yelled the regiment. The men got it from Johnson spoon-fed. It was one of his ideas in toughening troops. He intended to win the war with his regiment. The odd part is that at the finish, the 501st had as good a claim on so doing as any outfit, though Johnson did not live to see it.

Men didn't soldier for Johnson out of love, or because they knew that in combat he would prove a peerless leader with unerring judgment. He was a brittle taskmaster, and his demands, no less than his eccentricities, inspired more fear than respect. One of his own staff wrote of him: "He was the friend of any man who could bite his own teeth and go on till he was blind. The utmost—the impossible—those were his goals." The regiment thrived and hardened because his domineering was tempered by a retinue of younger officers whose superb

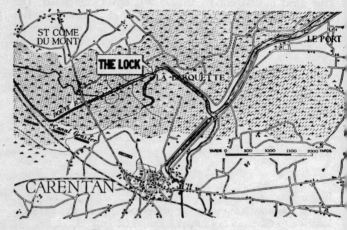

Figure 20. Carentan Bridgehead

capacity for battle leading was probably unequaled elsewhere in the Army. Several were marvelously mature and mellow for their years. Owing to this cushion, the command was solid.

So was the stone-walled lock which Skeets was sent against. But the lock also was inscrutable as a military value, being but one feature of an inordinately complex battleground toward the worsening of which man and nature had collaborated through the ages.

Long ago the Contentin peninsula was an island. Less long ago, it was again spliced to Normandy through the raising of the old sea bottom. This remarriage by the land would be plainly revealed by the map but for the man-made barriers which hold the sea back. The meadows flanking the narrow trenches of the Madeleine, Taute, Merderet and Douve rivers for two thirds of the way across the base of the peninsula are below the level of the sea at high tide. But for the barriers, the Bay of Grand Vey would reach west past St. Saveur-le-Vicomte.

Bonaparte tried to re-engineer the neighborhood, taking advantage of these features. Having in mind the Isle of Wight with relation to Southampton, he planned to convert Carentan into a fortified island covering the base of the Cotentin and securing Cherbourg from being taken in flank. The digging of the great moat around Carentan was never completed. The Napoleonic works are still in evidence, clearly defined. But they appear only as deep and useless bays in a modern canal system developed, not as an aid to navigation, but to drain the tidal flats.

Normandy's hedgerow system grew of agricultural necessity. It enabled a society of small farmers to provide themselves with both herbage and trees while conserving the little tillable ground. The hedged-in farm plots—commonly only a fraction of an acre—are given over to orchards, truck gardens, hay growing and some pasturing, though the cattle graze mainly in the lush bottom lands bounding the rivers.

Drainage of the sea-flooded valleys, enriching the Cotentin, was sealed with the building of the La Barquette lock almost a century ago. Where it stands, about four miles south of Brevands, all the eastward-flowing streams become one, which for the rest of the distance to the Bay of Grand Vey is called the Douve. By opening or closing the lock, according to the tides, its guardian may either regulate the flow of fresh water to the sea or turn the Carentan marsh areas into a shallow salt lake.

There are three of them—the Carentan, the Baupte and the marsh of St. Côme-du-Mont. The Baupte marsh is a peat bog. The other two drain readily during summer and may be traversed easily by the foot traveler. In winter the rains pile up water to the depth of a foot or more. Duck hunters love this region. The local farmers cope with the winter waters by paddling around in small boats. From April to November, the bottoms are fairly firm again.

Invading Normandy in 1940, the Germans did not tamper with the La Barquette lock for two years. It remained closed against the tide. The cattle grazed in the familiar low ground. Then in November, 1942, the enemy took over, and sea water began to fill the Baupte marsh within ten miles of Carentan. Thereafter the lowlands were filled as rapidly as the push of the tide permitted, the lock being closed at low tide to prevent draining.

British observation planes saw and reported these inundations. But the expanse of water was not great, and it was surmised that the Germans were only experimenting. Months later there were more flights. The waters, said the observers, had subsided. Yet this was illusion, the explanation of which was not forthcoming until too late.

The waters continued to spread as rapidly as the enemy could let the tide in. Before the autumn of 1943 had passed, the flood had reached full height along the river valleys, and thereafter the level remained constant. But in England the photo interpreters saw the tall reeds and missed the deep waters. Nature's own camouflage well served the Germans.

Not knowing that the enemy had already filled the cup, the invasion planners became fascinated with the lock as a night-drop target until their fertile imaginations far overrated its strategic importance. They saw it as a prize which, quickly won, might turn the battle. If the German forces to the westward rebounded strongly against the beachhead, the marshes around Carentan could be turned into a lake, imposing an extra barrier between the enemy and the invaders. Later, the lake could be drained when the expedition was ready to ride again. The blowing up of the bridges along the causeway crossing the Douve east of Carentan was part of the same concept. It was the one avenue across the flood plain. The enemy was expected to stand at the lock for a final death grapple, like Davy Crockett at the Alamo.

To take them on was a mission not more desperate than noble. In the grand scale of total war, it was an enterprise not unlike that of the legendary Dutch urchin who kept his finger in the hole of the dike and defeated the North Sea. No other task could have been more to the liking of Colonel "Skeets" Johnson. The extreme hazard was that if the enemy wasn't really concerned about dying for the lock, he would be stuck naked in the bottom lands, and the Germans would murder him from the high ground. But if Skeets dwelled on that possibility, he confided it to no one. Blood in his eye, he was hell-bent on action. Just before the mount-up in England, he assembled his regiment and said, "What we do tonight and tomorrow will be written in history." Then he whipped out his jump knife, raised it high and screamed, "I swear to you that before to-morrow night this knife will be buried in the back of the blackest German in Normandy!" Corny stuff? It is reported that at that point his troops screamed back.

Good luck did not load with this regiment. Its 3rd Battalion was designated the Division Reserve. The 1st Battalion was so badly scattered in the drop that it could not form. Its commander was killed, its executive and staff were missing, and every company skipper was gone. So what might have been a regiment at zero hour became the 2nd Battalion minus, with here and there a few fighting fragments, whose members got better breaks than the other hostages to fortune.

Among them was Skeets, riding the lead plane of the serial. Being with Johnson, the other occupants remained awake. They were ready when they sighted the French coast; everybody arose with Skeets and let out a war whoop. There followed a final adjustment of equipment as the plane flew on through showers of flak. Came the warning signal, then the green light. It flashed through the astral dome from the lead plane to the others, and the men jumped—all except those who rode with Skeets.

A K-ration bundle blocked the door to the open air and wouldn't budge. So they struggled with it 30, 40, 50 seconds while the plane raced on, covering perhaps two miles. When at last the bundle dropped into space, they followed in a rush, cursing that they had overshot the mark. They should have been thanking Heaven for the K-ration bundle. Its intervention corrected the pilot's error and delivered them onto Drop Zone D. Only one other planeload of the serial, which was also blocked by a bundle, made the station on time.

Tracer fire boiled up around Skeets as he jumped. In his struggle with the bundle he had loosened his reserve chute. When it bloomed, he knew that he was too big, too slow a target. So he cut the chute away in mid-air. Hitting the ground, he was instantly fired on by a rifleman from behind a hedge 25 yards away. With his .45 he fired two shots toward the flash and heard a scream, followed by silence. Then he lay quiet for five minutes before cutting away his harness, afterwards rolling over and over till he got within the shadow of a hedge bank.

He went through its gate on his belly. Then he rested for some time in a roadside ditch, reflecting. He was at a crossroads, and opposite him was a large building with the silhouette of a château. His first impulse was to go there and ask directions. But some deeper instinct warned him—or possibly the brush with the hidden marksman—that he had "dropped on something hot" and was already fighting for his life. So he decided not to go, and thereby spared himself to be killed by enemy artillery in Holland. The building was the local German headquarters, and he was in the center of a well-prepared position.

Skeets wiggled out of this one, after first stripping himself of everything he thought he could spare. The load felt heavier than he had anticipated, or maybe he was weaker. When he crawled off, staying in the hedgebank shadow, it was on hands and knees and sometimes on his belly.

Beyond the château he came to a small stream and started to crawl through it. The water was way over his head, and for minutes he foundered, gasping, carried by the water, feeling nigh to drowning.

He had forgotten to look skyward for other planes or dropping men, thereby to get directions. The fire from the unseen enemy had distracted him and kept his gaze pinned to earth. So he crawled around blindly for about 20 minutes, though always he moved downhill. This was a response to instinct, rather than training, for there was one principle vital to assembly which was unknown before the Normandy night drop. In the dark, lost paratroopers involuntarily respond to gravity, move as water moves, and by following drainage lines, empirically find one another.

Johnson had overlooked no one. Only the No. 2 man of his stick had come down near him. Later his chute and pack were found high in a tree behind the German headquarters. He must have dangled for a few minutes before cutting himself loose. But his bullet-riddled body was found in front of the building. The mournful conclusion is that he heard the exchange of fire, came on the run to help Johnson, and so met death.

Mortar fire found the field through which Skeets was crawling. It exploded on all sides of him, as if a rattled enemy were indiscriminately shelling just on the chance a soft target might be there. Then came machine-gun fire. Above the roar and rattle he heard a larger blast from skyward, looked up in time to see a double glare in the sky, and knew that two of the C-47s had collided. Out of the night came prolonged screaming which died in crescendo, as if a man had been bayoneted.

Now he was crawling down a steep bank and into swampy ground, away from the sounds of the fighting. His compass said he was going south. He figured he must be headed toward the Douve. So for 20 minutes he stayed with the hedge shadows as they descended parallel to the stream bed. The moon was bright. He decided to wait, hoping that men would come to him. Another quarter-hour passed. Then a cricket chirped very close. He reached for his own cricket; it was gone with the gear jettisoned at the château.

Skeets called, "Flash!"

Someone in the dark yelled, "Thunder!"

Then he cried out, "Welcome!"

Never before had he felt the sensation of utterly joyous relief. Every foot of the way, he had known fear.

It was a party of 15 paratroopers, most of them members of 506th's 3rd Battalion, straining to keep their assignment with the Douve bridges near Le Port. But they were still wandering unoriented. Johnson said, "I think we better keep moving south right along this hollow." They were willing enough, and so he took command and led the way. The cricket was the chief means of drawing other men to them as they stumbled along.

By dawn, 150 men followed Skeets as he closed toward rendezvous with the lock. But the approach march had been rugged, because of the swampy ground. They splashed through streams, sometimes chest-deep. When a man went down, the others pulled him up. No one said a word. Following the leader, they stayed shy of roads and worked fields. As they moved into the bottoms, mortar shells exploded into the marsh. The shells were so far overhead that Johnson grew confident his force was not detected. He had insisted that the force stay together, irrespective of unit, and he said to the others, "Wait till you are sure of your location! Wait till we have strength!"

But now that they were within short reach of La Barquette, and the men recognized the ground from having studied small models of it in rubber relief, there was no longer room for doubt or time for waiting.

The lieutenant from 506th said, "I want permission to leave now; I must go on to Le Port."

Skeets said, "Then go."

They split up shortly after 0400. The lieutenant led his 30 men east along the canal bank. Johnson already had his scouts out. They moved as far as the first road intersection, then came back and reported, "Yes, that's the lock up ahead." The light was coming fast. They could see the canal banks distinctly and the cluster of buildings beyond. Johnson decided to split his force and hit at once. About 50 men would charge the lock directly; the others would build up a defensive base between the main road and the canal, to hold the fort if the charge was repulsed.

The lock task force made it in one dash. Not even a sentry covered the vital object. The lock itself was deserted—no Germans, not even a curious Frenchman to say *"Bienvenu; comment allez vous?"* They pulled up short, a little crestfallen.

Yet even the quiet was ominous. Looking beyond the far bank they saw 50 yards away some fire pits and hutments. But if an enemy lurked there, he must have been asleep. In any case, it was their job to hold the lock, not to conduct excursions from it. So they dug in where they were, and they dug deep. Then mortar fire broke around them and with it random rifle and machine-gun fire. They didn't determine its source or truly try.

If there were Germans close at hand, they made no effort, then or later, to wrest away the prize by counterattack.

Skeets had watched the denouement from 300 yards off. After the lock party went to earth, they were no longer visible to him. But he knew they were all right. When the people with him finished digging in, patrols went out to prowl the nearby houses. They found no one. Still, Johnson fretted because his position was no good. The force was staked out in a hollow; the Germans could blast it from the ridges around St. Côme-du-Mont. But he figured he could risk tarrying a little while, though the enemy seemed not to covet the lock. More men would gravitate to him: then he could push on and blow up the Douve bridges.

Soon after 0600, he heard the rattle of a continuing small-arms fight to the northward. It was the first sign that other friendly forces were operating near him. The wait otherwise was vain. No more men came to him. His patrols, sent this way and that, reported that after 200 yards or so in any direction, they were stopped by fire. Strongest guarded was the causeway into Carentan.

Shortly a strange patrol arrived, bringing the word that Major R. J. Allen, regimental S-3, was at Bse Addeville on the high ground to the north, a fair-sized force with him. They didn't know his situation or if he was fighting: they only knew his location.

Still lusting after numbers, Johnson picked up his 50 men at the perimeter and marched on Allen—a fire-water exercise through the canals and ditches, with snipers constantly harassing the column from cover on the flanks. The journey took two hours; the crow-flight distance was about two miles. Near the end one paratrooper lagged behind and was felled by a bullet. Dropping his weapon, Lieutenant Edley Craighill (later killed) crawled back across the fire-swept field and brought the man to safety on his back.

There were almost 100 men with Allen, including Lieutenant Farrell, USN, who had trained as a paratrooper so that he could direct supporting fires from the ships off Utah Beach. The force was heavily embattled within the houses by Germans sticking to the hedgerows north and west of the hamlet. Allen stayed there, hoping to attract enough Americans to attack St. Côme-du-Mont. His was a polyglot collection, counting men from every unit in the division. Rounding up farm carts and animals from the nearby barns, Allen had moved them out, with covering patrols, to collect bundles and jump-injured paratroopers. One fourth of his men had sprains or breaks. Bullet and mortar fire around Addeville had cost him 12 or 15 casualties. He had set up a first-aid station, which was already overflowing. Now, as Johnson arrived, he had at last begun to feel that he was holding his own. But it had been an exhausting morning.

Allen had no news to tell Johnson apart from what he had seen, heard and felt of things right around him. How the other airborne forces elsewhere were faring, he had no idea. One aid man had caught a broadcast from London on his hand radio and had told him, "They say that in the invasion everything is going according to plan."

Skeets moved right in on him, saying, "Pick up your force. We're all going down to the lock. You'll have to fold and come with us."

"I can't," said Allen. "We'd be overrun. How long will you last at the dock if we don't hold here? What good is that position down in the bottoms?"

Johnson fairly screamed, "Allen, don't talk to me like that! You do as I say!"

Allen replied, "Think it over."

Johnson did—in a way. On the SCR 300 radio, he raised Lieutenant Colonel Ballard, commanding the 2nd Battalion, and put it to him: "You join me at the lock." But Ballard and his people were fully engaged in an attack at Les Droueries, and he couldn't break off, even to please Johnson. Of that refusal came lasting hurt feelings and personal friction.

Johnson did a fast burn; everyone was letting him down. But Ballard was out of reach, and Allen was right at hand. So for the moment his active anger was vented on Allen.

So he laid it on the line: "Most of this force will move with me now to La Barquette. From there, we will try to go to the bridges. You will be left with enough people to cover your own withdrawal to my position after dark comes."

Allen had gone as far as he could. He didn't believe in the order. He had challenged it. His ears had been pinned back. No soldierly alternative remaining, he saluted and said, "Yes, sir!"

Though a more painful exchange than this among fighting men would make angels weep, Skeets forgot it once Allen had bowed compliance. Allen was entitled to a warm embrace for all he had accomplished; he had fought while Johnson had wandered like Hagar in the wilderness; but he had been skinned and discountenanced, and he could still say, "Yes, sir!" It takes a soldier.

Lieutenant Fred A. Owens, the personnel adjutant, moved out with a patrol of four men ahead of Johnson to reconnoiter the route and get a quick take of the situation at the lock. The main body followed at noon. Most of the demolitions platoon had collected at Addeville after collecting enough explosives around the drop zone to cook the Douve bridges. They went along. Allen was left in the hamlet with about 50 men. The column re-threaded the marsh and the canals, harassed only by some wild shooting from the heights which it had departed. Its point came in time to the dirt lane leading to La Barquette, a narrow track well-screened on both sides by heavy foliage. From there it turned into the last intersection, at which place, according to Johnson, "all hell broke loose," which is a phrase frequently used by American soldiers when the hell is relatively minor but highly local and intensely personal.

Back in Addeville, Father Sampson, the Catholic chaplain, a jolly man and deeply loved by the regiment, went from pallet to pallet checking the casualties. One thought tormented him, which he chose not to load on Allen. He counted 14 men either wounded or hurt so critically that they could not be moved.

So he put the problem to Major Francis E. Carrel, the surgeon, a congenial and efficient healer who detested war but respected its requirements. "I'll leave an aid man with them," said Carrel; "that's the best I can do." His duty lay with the regiment.

"I'll stay," said Father Sampson.

"The Germans will come in as soon as we clear here," said Carrel. "I understand they're shooting prisoners."

"Shooting these prisoners," said Sampson, "is what I'm staying here to prevent."

Carrel shrugged. Allen, overhearing the conversation, tried to make Sampson change his mind, last and reluctantly pressing what he thought was the clinching argument: "If you don't go, Colonel Johnson may think you disobedient." The priest simply nodded gravely as if reflecting on Allen's scaling of the relative importance of life's values. When the rear guard pulled out later that day, they left Father Sampson standing at the aid station door, holding a white flag, serene, ready to be taken prisoner, readier still to battle unarmed for the stricken.

The "hell" into which Skeets trudged was a small, crudely set ambush. From the high ground, the Germans had seen his force go out and had guessed it would be back. So their machine guns, mortars and 88s were zeroed in on the spot where the point moved into the open. The blast was nerve-shattering because it was so sudden. The point went flat while the main body sought cover in the lane. Crawling, Johnson worked his way forward to the point. He was shaking with the thought that, having retraced his own footsteps, he had condemned the whole force to be fitted for wooden crosses.

But things were not really that bad. There being no way to fight back against the distant heavy weapons, he ordered his men to advance singly to the perimeter near the lock by crawling along the roadside ditches. Since it manifestly was no more dangerous to move than stay, they needed no urging. Amid the exploding shells, they pushed on toward the river and had their first lesson in how much steel and powder can be wasted in war to the despoliation of earth and foliage with almost no one getting hurt.

Private Campos went too far. A mortar shell caught him at the canal bank, one fragment cost him an eye, and another shattered his right arm. Otherwise, the statistics of hell-broke-loose prove disappointing.

For the others, it was a drag through the frying pan to plop in the fire. The enemy shells lifted from the road and followed them right into the foxholed perimeter. Skeets felt himself tied between the devil and the sea. He had no counter to the 88 and heavy mortar batteries. Too late and somewhat overweeningly, he convinced himself that "if we try to move now, it could prove more deadly than staying."

His force was still spread out. The rear of the march column had not ventured to cross the field beaten by the shellfire. At the tag end was Lieutenant Farrell, USN, who by rare chance had found his 609 radio after the drop and lugged it to La Barquette.

Johnson crawled on back to Farrell to ask him, "Do you think we can get some ship fire dropped on St. Côme-du-Mont and Carentan?" They crawled forward together into the exposed area so that Farrell could get a better look at the targets on the high ground and be in position to observe and control the shooting.

Quickly, Farrell got through to the U.S.S. *Quincy*, which was steaming in figure eights not far off the coast. From the *Quincy* he got a "Roger." Five minutes later the first salvo of eight-inch shells screamed over La Barquette on the way to high ground. It was short of the mark; the necessary adjustments were made. Thereafter the fire was uncannily accurate, playing right along the ridge line as Farrell watched. The mortar batteries in St. Côme-du-Mont lost their rhythm; the 88s in Carentan tapered off; crews had fled to cover.

Maintained for 30 minutes, the ship fire at last silenced the enemy heavy weapons. But Skeets, as he checked back over his men, counted 11 fresh casualties.

Captain Sammie N. Homan, good soldier and blithe spirit, had come with the force from Addeville. At this stage, Johnson was set to pass command of the local situation to him, while he turned attention to the larger affairs of a regiment consisting for the time of fragments which were already fully committed.

He said to Homan, "It will be your mission to hold the lock and blow up the Douve bridges."

Lieutenant Billy A. Turner, also fresh to the scene, would accompany Homan and lay the explosives.

Both officers wanted to talk it over, pointing out to Johnson that they hadn't any idea how to deploy the troops, since they had no knowledge of the German strength or positions.

Just then, Lieutenant Owens and his patrol came in. They had overshot La Barquette and advanced 500 yards closer to

Carentan. Said Owens, "I think it is impossible to move any large portion of this force to the west. We made it by crawling along the ditches. But we were under intense small-arms fire all the way."

That was that. For once Johnson listened, and Owens's words gave him caution. He said to Homan, "Strengthen the force at the lock, extend position in both directions along the north bank of the canal, push toward the Douve when it proves practicable." That was more like it. Johnson then moved the greater number of his men into the farmhouses east of the canal. There they would have roof-wall cover, which against artillery is better than a foxhole in flat ground.

Farrell tried to put fire from the *Quincy* on the Carentan causeway, hoping with luck to destroy a bridge or two. The shells exploded on both sides of it into the marsh and finally stonked the civilian houses at Pont-de-Douve.

Captain Charles G. Shettle, of the 506th Regiment, arrived, cap in hand. After a valiant, stand-up fight at the Le Port bridgehead with too few men, he was feeling terribly hard-pressed for holding power. In view of the high strategic value of his ground, could Johnson spare a few people?

Johnson said, "We're one force. I'll keep contact. If you're in danger of being overrun, I'll move to assist you with all available troops."

Since Shettle knew that he was in present and pressing danger of being overrun any hour of the day, and was holding by the skin of his teeth, Skeets's answer didn't help his case a bit.

So he asked, "Can I get naval gunfire support when I need it?" The request was passed along to Farrell, who couldn't answer with a straight "yes," not being admiral of the fleet. The one grain of comfort was that Johnson arranged for constant patrolling between Le Port and the lock.

Shettle, one of nature's silent men, was too solid a soldier to draw the oblique contrast between the two situations. He was holding an anchor position with a scant crew, desperately short of ammunition. There was no joined fight at the lock. Johnson had manpower to spare, held immobilized, armed all around and not a target within range.

Yet Shettle had no more than departed La Barquette than Johnson was on the radio to Allen, telling him to relay this message to Ballard: "Tell him I want him to get his ass down here. Tell him we're being wiped out. Tell him anything you want. But see that he gets here."

There being 250 men on hand, Johnson set about rounding out the position. For the first time, the perimeter was extended to the far side of the canal. Four squads of riflemen, with their usual weapons, and three machine guns, were deployed in a crescent about 100 yards deep. There were no Germans, either in the fire pits or houses; no German, then or later, died for the lock or reacted as if believing that it retained any operational importance.

The position on the near side of the canal was extended east and west about 400 yards, with the flanks curved back to the embankment. One strongpoint, heavy with machine guns, faced north across the marsh. There was no food or water on hand. The munitions supply averaged a little more than one basic load per weapon.

Allen arrived at dusk with 30 more men. A few miles away at the Addeville aid station, Father Sampson was preparing dinner for the wounded whom Allen had left behind. He had planted the white flag in the center of the door while occupied with other things. There was much to be done. One soldier was close to death, having lost the greater part of a leg when a hand grenade accidentally exploded in his pants pocket. Sampson kept giving him plasma. But after much struggle, the man died. There was no chance to bury him. The priest wrapped the boy in the shrouds of a parachute and carried the body to a nearby barn. Still, the Germans did not come; the waiting and wondering frayed men's nerves.

"Do you think they will shoot us, Father?" asked one boy.

"Not while I'm here," said Sampson.

He continued serving the rude meal—cocoa from the K-ration packs and tinned hash. From a Frenchwoman down the street he had begged a few bottles of *vin rouge*; it would help cheer the men whose wounds and breaks were such that they were certain to pull through. At midnight he read a prayer with them. Then he returned to the doorway and resumed his vigil, waiting, flag in hand, for the Germans. He knew they would come.

From the La Barquette perimeter, Homan, Turner and Craighill made one last sortie under cover of the dark, trying to get to the first bridge on the Carentan causeway. Turner took along explosives just in case the way was open. The 50-man patrol went 600 yards, ran into a wall of fire as it approached the highway from St. Côme-du-Mont to Carentan, lost a few men and recoiled to the perimeter.

Other patrols were sent by Johnson to seek division headquarters, make contact with the 506th Regiment and keep in touch with Shettle's force at Le Port. The shuttle to Shettle worked smoothly. The other patrols never returned. Of these losses from the vanishing patrols, coupled with the casualties at the lock inflicted by an enemy artillery which fired through the night, the force was again down to 250 men at sunrise on the second day.

23

At Les Droueries

Second Battalion of the 501st was so fond of a large bronze bell and green electric lantern on which it was accustomed to assemble that they were hand-carried by two paratroopers in the night drop.

The two yeomen vanished on the jump. Men continued to mourn for the missing bell and light. Thus was love's labor lost.

Lieutenant Colonel Robert A. Ballard hit earth right where the beacon should have been and, uniquely among the officers in the night drop, instantly knew his own whereabouts. Why he knew he could not tell himself for certain, except that the land lay as he had dreamed it.

If his hunch was right, then his target, St. Côme-du-Mont, was not more than a short walk away. So ran his thoughts as he stayed sprawled in mid-field, wondering about his next move. In easy crawling distance was a hedgerow. Still, he did not go to it. Tracers had followed him on the way down. Machine-gun fire chattered not far away, and mortar shells exploded within a few rods of his couch. Therefore, except to loosen a grenade, he lay perfectly still ten minutes to test whether he had been spotted.

When the agonizing interlude passed safely, he shook loose from his harness, ran to a ditch and got out his map and flash-

light. There was no doubt about it: the map checked with the
earth pattern and his horizons. His mood of self-congratulation
was cut short when a machine gun opened fire lengthwise of
the hedgerow where he squatted. That reminded him of the
SCR 536 radio strapped to his leg; he called and called but got
no answer.

Crawling down the hedge a few yards, he heard a cricket
chirp. The signal came from Sergeant William H. Jackson, of
Dog Company. Said Jackson, "I landed in a swamp south of
here, saw high ground in front of me, went to it and hit the
jackpot."

At the last field just before joining Ballard, Jackson had
passed Major Raymond V. Bottomly, the battalion executive,
down with a broken ankle. Together, they headed for him.

Ballard asked, "Can you walk at all?"

Said Bottomly, "No, but I can do a damn good job of
crawling."

So they went on all fours. And that involved a special
torture. The ditches of Normandy were loaded with nettles,
which stung nastily and worked insidiously into a crawling
man's clothing. Next to German fire, it was the worst affliction
of the campaign. They crawled past one field, collected a sergeant from Easy Company, and by then Ballard had had enough
of the nettles.

He said to Bottomly, "You return to the drop zone. We'll
split up, go three ways, collect men and send them back to
you."

Ballard struck east. More men moved to him from out of
the hedge shadows as he walked, and cheered by the collecting,
he pushed them along to Bottomly. Then suddenly, it was
neither dark nor easy any more. Flares fired from around St.
Côme-du-Mont almost continuously lighted the scene, hurting
more than the banging of the mortars. Snipers infested the
hedges, and with the illumination, he was drawing men to him,
only to have them shot down before he could tell them what
to do. He decided it was time to break off the roundup just as
it got rolling.

Of supply, he still had only a token. The men he had mon-
itored didn't know what had happened to the bundles. Some
of his soldiers had come down in the Carentan marshes, made
the shore by swimming, after cutting away all equipment, and
reached him sopping-wet and empty-handed, but otherwise un-

hurt. It was their guess that most of the bundles were drowned out and irretrievable.

Ballard got back to Bottomly at 0330. Already formed up were four machine guns, one bazooka, one 60-millimeter mortar, 125 rifles and more than enough men to carry them. This, then, was the battalion. Every rifle company commander was missing, and the only radio had arrived in Normandy strapped to Ballard's leg.

Dawn was cracking as the force quit the field and started for St. Côme-du-Mont, holding closer to the hedgerows. Some minutes earlier, Ballard had sent a patrol—Lieutenant Sefton and four men—to find Skeets Johnson and tell him, "Second Battalion is moving against St. Côme-du-Mont." But now he was less certain. Intelligence had reckoned that only a platoon of enemy held the village. But more than three machine guns had been spotted just outside the village by Ballard's own soldiers. Another trooper on his way to the drop zone had seen several Germans vanish into a large building at Les Droueries. So Ballard concluded that the target village was covered by a much stronger force than was supposed, while at Les Droueries was another hostile force on his flank.

There was no sense in deploying weaponless men. Since the platoons did not have machine guns enough to operate independently, the extra gunners were used as runners. Other unarmed men were sent bundle hunting. What worried Ballard above all was the dazed reaction of most of his men. Only the soldiers who had landed in the marsh seemed relatively alert; soaked and shivering, they had to keep moving for warmth. It was different with the men who had landed dry; some of them fell asleep standing, while Ballard talked to them, then fell headlong. When the formation pulled away from the assembly area, then paused briefly, Ballard saw men fall in their tracks and hit the ground with their eyes closed.

Pondering these things (of which no one had warned him), Ballard, a phlegmatic Reservist from Florida who would one day command the regiment, suddenly switched plans. He said to his operations officer, Captain William E. Pelham, "We'll attack Les Droueries." Pelham wrote the order. They would go with two companies abreast. Easy, on the right flank, would hit the farm buildings, while Fox Company, on the left, would advance to the crossroads. Becomingly, Dog Company would chase after Fox. Each "company" numbered 30 men.

When the column marched at 0530, the morn was bright enough to afford personal recognition. Ballard marveled at the effect of the growing light. The hiatus had passed. The human spirit, and seemingly body energy, leaped up with the sun. But it was not a felicitous transformation. Daylight brought euphoria. It was as if the mass reeled in a debauch. Men slapped each other on the back, giggled immoderately and cheered for no reason. Watching them, Ballard said to Pelham, "You'd think it was all over, and we'd won the war."

This mood lasted while they marched 200 yards. Then fire came against them. The sobering shock of the first bullet flattened them, instantly restoring reality.

Two additional light machine guns, borne by Headquarters Company men, overtook Ballard as the firing began. He placed them at a hedgerow forward of Easy's line. That company had gone gaily to a bend in the road. Right there, it was checked by machine-gun fire from amid the farmhouses. The men recoiled to the ditches and stayed there inert, pinned by shock, not raising their heads to answer fire with fire. Fox Company, on the left, got no farther; it, too, was prone and actionless. While the Americans stayed thus paralyzed, the Germans dropped a curtain of mortar fire on both positions and the field between.

Ballard, following along with Dog Company, had no more idea of what was happening to his line than of the positioning of the automatic guns which had stopped it. So he moved up to the hedgerow corner on Easy's left flank. From there, he could spot a few enemy riflemen, but the heavy weapons stayed hidden. It went on this way for 90 minutes. The two companies would not rally. Ballard's portion was to gaze for a few seconds through gaps in the hedge, duck back to avoid aimed rifle fire, then move right or left a few yards to another gap and come up for a new look. The enemy rifle pits seemed to be from 60 to 70 yards away. But the bullet rain was more persuasive than his example. The other men would not get up to look, much less fire. Lieutenant Edward A. Allworth, the adjutant, began evacuating casualties, using a farm cart to clear wounded to an improvised aid station in the chapel at Angoville-au-Plain. Both companies had lost about one-third strength—mainly to mortar fire—without yet striking a blow.

At 0800, Ballard said to Pelham, "These Germans intend to stand their ground and will not be scared off." Both com-

panies had made a halfhearted try to advance along the lateral
hedge banks and recoiled after a few men were hit by bullets.
Ballard thought of using smoke but could find only orange
grenades—the friendly signal. No more mortars had come up,
and the one bazooka was short of ammunition.

The attack was futile. A few Germans in the forward rifle
pits had been killed. There had resulted no abatement of the
fire. The companies still drooped. So Ballard felt himself be-
twixt the devil and the sea. He did not dare go on to St. Côme-
du-Mont and leave this other enemy force on his rear. On the
other hand, the Les Droueries position blocked the road to that
part of the regiment which supposedly was concentrating around
La Barquette.

While he was wondering what to do next, Lieutenant Walter
W. Wood arrived with 20 men. He was from 1st Battalion,
501st, and his crew were all from 506th Regiment. But they
were willing to follow him because he promised, "I'll show
you a fight." Ballard and Wood talked things over. It was
agreed that Wood and his group would make a wide swingout
to the right against the farm, moving on such a line that a broad
field boxed by hedgerows separated them from the battalion
front during the approach. (See map on page 279.)

Wood moved cautiously, hugging the hedge banks, taking
a full hour to close. By the end of that time, he had taken the
crossroads and the first house beyond. Ballard for the first time
had a little leverage, but it cost high. Easy Company, lifted by
Wood's action, joined the rush against the farmhouse. Lieutenant George S. Schmidt was killed, and five of his men were
wounded. Lieutenant Vern Merz took over the command. Fox
Company moved up later, helped by fire across its front from
Easy's weapons. Then the Germans came down the lateral
hedges in counterattack. The brunt of this onfall landed against
Wood's men, who beat it back with rifles and hand grenades.

While this action was at white heat, Ballard got Johnson's
radio order, telling him to break off, move via Bse Addeville,
pick up Allen's force and reinforce the position at La Barquette.
Ballard decided that he dared not comply, though he knew
Johnson would fume and call him insubordinate. To order a
withdrawal with an attack going could only confuse his men
and make them vulnerable to counterattack. Then there was a
second reason for delay. Lieutenant Frank Gregg had reported
in with information that Captain D. A. Brown, of Easy Com-

pany, was two kilometers away with 75 men who had not yet engaged. Ballard had told Gregg, "Get Brown and bring him to Les Droueries," and there was no way to countermand this order by radio. So he said "No!" to Johnson.

Forty minutes after getting the order, Ballard was ready to obey it, not because he felt it wise, but because he was less tied. Brown had not come up, but Wood's capture of the hot corner had momentarily dampened resistance at the farm. Pelham and other officers bucked the decision, saying, "We've got to mop up here before we turn our backs." Ballard answered, "Our backs are already turned to St. Côme-du-Mont, and if it's one or the other, we'd better go straight at it." But he had not convinced himself.

Lieutenant Denver R. Bennett was sent with 15 men of Dog Company to Angoville. The mission: "See if you can reconnoiter a route through the marsh to Bse Addeville." The main body followed slowly, losing more than an hour in clearing the ground of casualties. Half of Easy and Fox were left at Les Droueries to contain the Germans. At high noon the force reached Angoville.

That place was jumping. Through the morning, an enemy detachment and a scratch force from the 326th Airborne Engineers had fought for the hamlet, which changed ownership three times. Allworth had stayed free and alive by running whenever the Germans came back. His aid men stuck by the wounded in the church. The Germans stomped in, noticed that a few of their own wounded were also getting attention, nodded their heads, then stomped out again.

Leading the force to the edge of the marsh, Ballard saw Bennett scouting ahead of him, in deep water, head down among the reeds. Machine-gun fire from Les Droueries was lathering the surface all around him.

Ballard sang out, "How many men you got?"

Bennett replied, "Six left."

Until then Ballard hadn't seen the riflemen wiggling along through the water 200 yards forward of Bennett. He yelled to Bennett, "Keep going! Move up to your men!" Bennett did, not knowing that by now he was being used for bait. Ballard wanted to see whether the fire would follow him, thereby testing the accuracy of enemy observation. Well, he made his point without killing Bennett; rare luck, and the inability of machinegunners to see beyond 550 yards where their bullets are beating, account for that. By watching the bursts track after Bennett, Ballard knew that a body of men could not make the same passage and live. So he sent Pelham scouting beyond Angoville to see if there was a way around the swamp. The S-3 reported back: "Not a chance. The ground is all but impassable, and on that side we would have to cross a deep canal under enemy fire."

Came a radio message then resolving Ballard's dilemma: "Major Allen withdrawing from Bse Addeville to La Barquette." That meant that the nearest "friendlies" were pulling still farther away, and the information forced his decision. He would try to slip up on and past Les Droueries by toe-dancing the battalion in file right down the edge of the swamp. That way lay hedges and ditches affording good cover. The approach was toward the extreme left of the enemy position, and there was just a chance that they might make it unobserved and knock out the forward guns in a sneak play. Ballard reckoned the Germans had four heavy machine guns but couldn't even guess at their rifle strength. His own force counted six light machine guns, almost out of ammunition, and two 60-millimeter mortars, with ten rounds apiece.

They started at 1445 and had just begun walking the marge when Captain Brown arrived with 45 men. There was enough space that as they moved they could fan out in thin successive skirmish lines with scouts out one hedgerow in front. At first, all was tranquil, though a few wild bullets droned overhead. So it went—almost monotonously—for 300 yards. Then a storm of small-arms fire lashed them from front to rear out of a fortified front which ran parallel to their own line of advance. They had walked right into it. Either the Germans had hastily re-entrenched toward the indicated new direction in Ballard's attack or Les Droueries was a perimeter, set for all-around defense, right along.

Fox Company, which was leading the column, right-faced, then found itself fighting for the same crossroads which it had assailed that morning, though going at it on a new tack. The German mortars opened fire before Fox could re-form. The machine-gun blast was heavier, and the range closer, than in the opening round. Still, the company did better, charging to the last hedgerow short of the enemy guns, and losing four men, killed in the closing dash across open ground. There, cheek-to-jowl with the Germans, Fox Company became immobilized, spent of energy, feeling its wounds, fretted by its empty bandoleers and awed by the barrier hedge. With Fox held, so was the battalion, gripped on one side by the enemy and on the other by the marsh. The 60-millimeter mortars went into action near the water and winked out within a few minutes, from lack of shells. Easy Company was moved up on the right of Fox and spread along the hedgerow. The position was sound enough—a sunken road with steep, overhanging banks, shrouded by tall trees, in so close to the enemy that there was no need to fear the mortars. (See map on page 279.)

These things done, Ballard had one more task. At 2200 came a message from Allen that he had quit Bse Addeville. But he saw no point in answering; Allen's departure and Johnson's anger had become irrelevant. The force was down to its last machine-gun belt, and either that situation would be remedied by another tour and search of the drop zone or there wouldn't be any battalion. So a large party of tired soldiers went forth at midnight to redo the roundabout journey. Four hours later they were back with enough ammunition to see the battalion through another day of battle.

The night was quiet. The men slept in relays, half on, half off.

In nearby Bse Addeville, Father Sampson also waited until his worn charges fell asleep. With the dawn came the tardy Germans. He was waiting for them with the white flag.

"Here they come, fellows," he said to the wounded. "I'll deal with them and be back in a few minutes."

They led him away—two German privates. They lined him against a wall. Father Sampson said a prayer. At that moment a German officer walked into the scene. He saw the silver crosses on the shirt, the Red Cross brassard on the sleeve.

The priest was returned to his aid station. The officer checked to make sure that all the Americans were casualties. Thereafter the enemy molested Sampson not at all. But his worst trials still awaited him.

24

Call on "Poopville"

===

Except that it is one of World War II's more perfect illustrations of how unevenly fate distributes her favors to men in combat, the little fight at Pouppeville which won the southernmost exit from Utah Beach could be handled as a footnote.

This is not to say that it was ill-conducted. To the contrary, it was managed to the hilt, for never before or after did so many brilliant military brains collaborate in the staging of one small skirmish. And in the end, as the old song goes, "there was glory enough in that for boys with a little red drum."

But uniquely among the forces in the night drop, the band of sky soldiers who took Pouppeville operated virtually as if they had happened into a vacuum and were privileged to stage a little show of their own, with minimum interference from the enemy while in isolation from their friends. There is no explaining it; the gods, whose seeing mind is not as ours, simply ordained them a beautiful solitude.

By the hour of their adventure against fire, the Germans were fully alerted. The doubts which assailed them in the critical hours when the first-arriving parachutes bloomed overhead—doubts intensified by the faulty work of the carrier pilots who misdropped their passengers—are indelibly reflected in the war diary of the German Seventh Army High Command.

The earliest entry—0130 on 6 June—notes that "parachutists have dropped since 0105 hours in the area east and northwest of Caen, St. Marcove and Montebourg, both sides of the Vire and on the east coast of Cotentin." At 0200, there is this entry: "Heavy fighting reported at Le Ham." Several of these points were far outside the limits of the airhead. The command was misled by the desperate action of little groups of paratroopers cast too deep into enemy country. So it marked time on the pivot for several hours, waiting to get a more accurate reading of the danger.

By 0240, the debate was still going. The acting Commanding General of Group West contended, "We are not confronted by a major action." His Chief of Staff replied, "It can be nothing less than that in view of the depth of the penetration of the 84th Army Corps area." Then at 0400, the commander of LXXXIV Corps called the Chief of Staff, Seventh Army, to report his conclusion: "The general plan seems to be to tie off the Cotentin peninsula at its narrowest point." At last they were on the beam; but still another hour passed before the Germans knew that they were also about to be hit from the sea. It was then too late to shift a force which could block off the southernmost exit; and the flat land directly adjoining it was ungarrisoned.

Since melodrama does not become General Maxwell D. Taylor, the personification of the ever controlled, tightly disciplined life, his entry into Normandy was appropriate. He dropped routinely into a pasture a little way from Ste. Marie-du-Mont, with only cows for witnesses. His accommodating stick descended out of sight in an adjoining field, giving him VIP privacy for all of 20 minutes—the time it took him to shake free of his harness and deploy rapidly toward human company. So moving, he tramped an area pitted with fresh-dug rifle trenches and gun emplacements. But not one gun or enemy soldier gave it respectable martial dignity. The commander of 14,000 men couldn't have had it softer on a dry-run exercise. But when at the corner of a hedgerow, after his lonesome maneuvering, he saw his first trooper—a bareheaded rifleman of the 501st—they warmly hugged each other, than which the night provides no more surprising entry.

But if you "gotta have heart," you also need luck. Coming into this same area, the serial carrying Lieutenant Colonel Julian J. Ewell's battalion of 501st did not encounter truly thick flak. Still, three of its planes were shot out of the skies, and 36 troopers died.

Ewell, a handful of his own men (the battalion was tabbed for the division reserve) and about 60 men from Division Headquarters came down squarely, smoothly, uneventfully, on Drop Zone C. Out beyond the boundary hedgerows, they could hear fire. But it was like July 4; all noise, no pressure. Their assembly was conducted by rote—with blue lights and a police whistle.

Not far away, Major Larry Legere, of the G-3 section, and Captain Thomas White, General Taylor's aide, ran into an enemy group who mistook them for Frenchmen. Asked to account for himself, Legere answered in perfect French, "I come from visiting my cousin," then flipped a grenade among them and cleared away. Private Ambrose Allie had a closer call. He landed on a roof top in Ste. Marie-du-Mont and was grabbed by a party of Germans when he made the street. They lined him up against a wall and formed as a firing squad. While Allie sweated and prayed, two other Americans whipped round the corner and gunned the Germans down. But these were the only shreds of combat for the men assembling out of Drop Zone C.

Until dawn, Ewell's truncated battalion stayed just south of Ste. Marie-du-Mont, under no compulsion to get mobile and fight because it was the general reserve. But here is the baffling note: Not one man was able to identify any feature of the landscape, and though they were in exactly the right location, they didn't know it until dawn.

Not far away, Max Taylor was having the same trouble. He could not get oriented. Unable to guess his direction, he got on the path to Ewell through some sixth sense. En route, he picked up a few more of his soldiers, then in the dark, physically collided with his artillery chief, General Tony McAuliffe. Tony didn't know where he was going, either.

One-quarter mile farther on, they ran into Ewell's sit-down position. The field was already outposted. Patrols were sent out to check on road signs or interview countrymen. Driven back by fire, they returned no wiser than before.

Colonel Gerald J. Higgins, division chief of staff, thought he knew the ground for two miles around Drop Zone C like the palm of his hand. In the weeks preceding the invasion, studying the air photos, he had assiduously "counted the trees of every orchard within that area and memorized the exact pattern of each." Then when he jumped he landed just 100

yards off the terrain etched in his mind and was as completely
lost as the Babe in the Woods. The more he walked, the less
he knew. Having only a .45 Colt, he coveted strongly armed
company. When at last he heard a cricket, his deliverer proved
to be only a medical corpsman carrying a curette. This pair
simply wandered into Ewell's position.

As Higgins arrived, so did Lieutenant Colonel Pappas, division engineer. Then all the brains got together in a ditch.
That way, the banks screened their flashlights. Then they went
over and over the air obliques of the Drop Zone C neighborhood, checking for recognition points. It was as futile as had
been the leg work by the patrols. Nothing looked familiar; they
knew they were in Normandy, and that was about all.

So they gave it up and waited for first light. Then Taylor,
looking north, saw a glint on the church spire of Ste. Marie-
du-Mont and said, "I know the shape of that one; we're right
where we belong." Of the episode comes one shining value.
It redeems the pride of every buck soldier who kicks himself
because he was lost for a few hours among the hedgerows.

Talking things over, Taylor and Higgins agreed that the
division had been badly dropped—this because no one present
had yet seen anyone from the 506th Regiment. Taylor said, "It
remains for us to help the 4th Infantry Division in every way
possible." Amid uncertainty, the one logical move was to start
east looking for a causeway.

Taylor ordered all of the people present to fall in with Ewell
and go for Pouppeville, wryly remarking, "Never in the history
of military operations have so few been commanded by so
many." The force had one radio, belonging to the division
artillery, but every attempt to get in touch with friends met
failure. Some few of Ewell's people were told off, along with
a few headquarters hands, to install the division command post
at Hiesville.

The remainder—including the generals—hit the trail at 0600,
marching cross-country until they came to the main road into
Pouppeville. It was practically an uncovered march. No flank
patrols were used but only a few flankers. The column picked
up a few more men as it slogged along. Right at the start, it
drew blood without losing any. A foolish German sentry cried,
"Halte!" From an isolated bunker behind him seven other Germans came running. Two of Ewell's scouts shot six of them,
and the others ran away. Thereafter the advance on Pouppeville

was an uninterrupted breeze. They reached its limits at approximately 0900.

Immediately their presence was honored by a scattering rifle fire. But the village was poorly organized for defense. South of it was a complete field position, observation tower in the center and a rim of foxholes, machine-gun emplacements and bunkers. The Germans fled this prepared ground and got in among the houses of the village, where there were neither barricades nor slotted walls. So there was no place to stand. As promptly as Ewell's men drew to the nigh side of a wall and moved through or around it, the Germans jumped to the next house beyond. They fired back as they ran. Ewell's worst affliction was his own lack of numbers. He counted only 40 men from his line companies, and the headquarters specialists were a drag in house-to-house fighting. The Germans pushed small patrols around his flanks, and he did not have enough strength to outcircle them. Most of his losses came of the oblique pressure.

Major Legere was downed by a dum-dum bullet, which tore away most of the flesh from one thigh. In that way, Higgins lost his only staff officer.

Sergeant Meryl W. Tinklenberg knocked off one German machine-gun crew; Corporal Virgil Danforth did as well with another but got his skull creased with a bullet. Private James F. Hubbard started through a garden gate and was shot down by a sniper. Private Jesse C. Garcia heard a group of Frenchmen laughing and shouting inside another garden and stepped inside to investigate. A German waiting beyond the fence put eight bullets into Garcia.

So it continued, slowing the advance without stopping it. A few men dead, and the Germans lost heart for the contest. By 1100, Ewell was at the German CP in the center of the village. That was enough for the enemy commander. He surrendered with 38 men of the 1058th Grenadier Regiment, having lost 25 dead and wounded. The two-hour fight cost Ewell 6 killed and 12 wounded.

Lieutenant Luther Knowlton and a sergeant walked on to the far side of Pouppeville. They saw a medium tank churn toward them around a bend in the causeway.

"German?" asked the sergeant.

"Damned if I know," said Knowlton.

"To hell with it, I'm firing," said the sergeant. And he did.

Then an orange panel fluttered on the side of the tank.

Knowlton replied by tossing an orange tank grenade on the road.

The tank came on, and with this meeting between its riders and two infantrymen, the link-up at Pouppeville was complete. Ewell already knew, from questioning the villagers, that the bridges along the causeway had been mined for demolition. A few of the Germans had escaped in that direction. But Ewell could hear the forces of 4th Division coming toward him only a few hundred yards away, and he knew the runaway Germans would come bouncing back on him before they could blow up any bridges. So he set up his machine guns and waited.

Taylor and Higgins stayed with Ewell's force until the seaborne troops nosed west out of Pouppeville. They had kept hands off, leaving Ewell free to run the fire fight. When the first tanks and line companies came past, they talked to the junior officers who were loaded with information about how smoothly the landing had gone.

Though Taylor had still heard nothing about how his own division was faring anywhere save at Pouppeville, he turned to Higgins and said, "The invasion is succeeding. We don't have to worry about the causeways. Now we can think about the next move."

It was a snap estimate, based on fragmentary intelligence. But it was right as rain.

25

Other Screaming Eagles

Colonel Bob (Robert F.) Sink landed gently in a small field, felt good about it and realized too late that he had buckled up too tight. The harness cut into his flesh, and as he struggled with it, there came a feeling of suffocation. He tried his knife; it wouldn't cut through. The struggle gutted him; the sense of loneliness intensified as did the fear he would be shot before he could break free. So he lay perfectly still, and of the brief rest came quick recovery and easy delivery.

Then he saw silk billowing from the far corner of the field. Under the canopy he found Lieutenant Samuel S. Burns, of 1st Battalion.

Burns said, "I'm bad hurt; it's my leg."

Sink said, "Well, see if you can walk on it; we've got to find some men."

He gave Burns an arm up and pushed him through the nearest hedgerow. There Burns fell away from him, saying, "It's no go; the leg is broken."

Sink said, "Then I'll have to leave you."

He found a hole in the field, which the farmer must have used for wintering apples, put Burns in it, covered him with duff, which lay about, and said, "Now you stay there until we send someone for you."

Checking his compass, Sink walked east. He went one-quarter mile before, coming to a side road, he learned that all

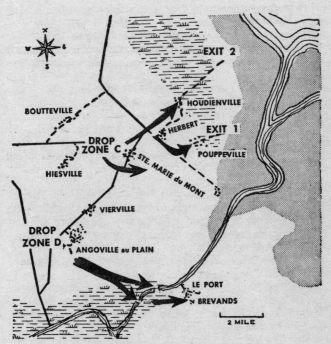

Figure 21. 506TH REGIMENT'S PLAN

the while he had been walking parallel to a main road, 20 yards from it, inside the hedge.

At the intersection he met three of his staff and the head-quarters commandant, Captain Edward A. Peters.

Peters said, "I'm sure we're on the right road."

Sink nodded in agreement, adding, "But how far east or west?"

How they sensed that they were on the main line eluded them. They simply knew.

They were opposite a small cottage. A dog barked loudly. That one break in the stillness disconcerted them.

Sink and Peters ran to the cottage and hammered on the door.

Sink yelled, *"Fermez la porte! Fermez la porte!"*

Peters said, "That means close the door."

Sink replied, "Well, what do you know? So it does."

From the second story, a Frenchman in a nightcap leaned from a window, shrilling questions.

Sink, who really did know some French, borrowed a pat line from the phrase book, saying impressively, "The invasion has begun."

The man answered, *"Très bien!"* then came on down. Though he shook all over from fright, when Sink unfolded his map, the Frenchman put his finger on the spot: they were just 250 yards from the spot chosen for Sink's CP next the drop zone.

Sink asked about Germans.

The Frenchman said, "They are all around. There are many, many at St. Côme-du-Mont."

Walking from the cottage, they picked up eight more men. Yet on arriving at the drop zone, they found no one.

Sink said, "This is it! We're where we belong. Now just beat the bushes and bring in the people."

But it wasn't that easy. At the end of two hours the in-gathering which was supposed to assemble the greater part of a regiment had netted only 41 men. They had found no radios and no one from the 2nd and 3rd Battalions.

Sink talked it over with Lieutenant Colonel William L. Turner, of 1st Battalion. They decided to head for Culoville with what they had. When they got there, not yet having heard a shot, Sink routed out another farm family to double-check his location.

The Frenchman shook his head; he had never heard of Culoville.

The wife shook her head; she didn't know it, either.

So Sink pointed down one road after another, asking, "What lies that way?" They told him, until finally the compass was boxed. There was no doubt of it: he was at Culoville.

Sink said to Turner, "There you've got it. These people have been living here all their lives and don't even know its name. That's the way things get loused up in war."

But it is also true that whimsical episodes in combat center on this man (later a lieutenant general) in the same way that lightning goes after a lonesome oak. There are a hundred good Bob Sink stories in the Army, and they are not fables.

While the night lasted, Sink kept sending patrols to check on the orchard where 2nd Battalion was supposed to rendezvous. But they returned empty-handed. That outfit, under Colonel Strayer, had been dropped far to the north in Pat Cassidy's territory and was doggedly moving south toward the assigned mission.

But this, Sink didn't know. He had heard nothing from anyone about anything. So far as he knew, he was fighting alone in Normandy. But he was still better off than Master Sergeant Lloyd E. Wills, who dropped within 300 yards of the assembly orchard, yet did not get to Culoville until noon of the second day. Most of this time Wills wandered around meeting no one, unable to see more than 150 yards in any direction because of the hedgerows. He was never more than two miles from Culoville; still, he couldn't find it. At last he joined a group of 25 men, mainly from Headquarters Company. The group drew German fire repeatedly but also kept moving in circles. Said Wills, "There's the hell of it. Get with people and you get shot at. If you got to be lost, you're better off alone."

A few minutes before dawn, Sink made his decision. Calling Turner, he said, "You'll have to take over Strayer's mission and march on the southern causeways." Turner had less than 50 men. So he was instructed not to spread his force but to concentrate on the Poupeville exit. The force took off at first light. Once again, Sink was alone. But he felt good about it; he had started something.

The irony was that the battalion ticketed for the assignment, though misdropped far off course, made a rapid and powerful assembly, and then through no fault of its own, spent its leg power and the precious hours fighting on a sidetrack. Much of its frustration came out of the mixed fortunes which availed it a smooth and strong collection; its initial togetherness was due to the shining wisdom and diligence of one soldier.

Captain Clarence Hester, battalion operations officer, saw much as he floated toward earth. Looking down, he knew that he was descending into the wrong landscape. Looking back, he saw the other parachutes and made a quick calculation that his stick of troops had stretched out more than a thousand yards.

Then what luck! As he touched ground and took his first look around, near him was a bundle of beacons. So Hester cut back 600 paces, which should have put him at the center of the stick, climbed a tall tree which grew from a knoll, and rigged it with the string of amber lights. It worked. Men moved in on him from all directions.

To Lieutenant Lewis Nixon, Hester said, "That village over there—go and find out the name."

Nixon went, "knocked up a Frenchman," as the British say, and asked his question.

The man said, "Foucarville!" and slammed the door. So that was it. Nixon, the one-man patrol, who was only seeking information, entered the enemy-garrisoned town well before Captain Fitzgerald and Lieutenant Hoggard got there and tried to take it with nine men. But he was a little more discreet.

In 40 minutes, Nixon rejoined Hester, bringing the answer. Hester wasn't having any of Foucarville either; it wasn't his pigeon.

Nixon rubbed his eyes when he saw the force assembled on Hester. In that brief interlude, there had come to him the communications platoon, the machine-gun platoon, 80 men from Headquarters Company, 90 from Dog Company, 8 from Easy, 6 from Fox and a handful of strays—the most phenomenal hit-or-miss assembly in the night drop.

By 0330, this body was joined by Colonel Strayer, his initial group of 15 men from 506th, and a few castaways from other units. Having parted company with Cassidy because of the urge to get on with his own mission, Strayer still had lingered, and now at last he had a fairly solid battalion in his hands.

What came of it is a case study in the relative value of surprise as against concentration. Cassidy, moving fast with a small party, had slipped through this same strip of country on greased heels. Strayer, taking off later with a formidable array, got nipped and blocked every foot of the way. To quote Sergeant Wills again: "There's the hell of it!" If you get too big, you just can't duck.

The battalion started moving at 0430. The Germans had wakened. Their skirmish parties had closed in on the assembly. So before Strayer could get his column on the road out of Cassidy's territory, he was beset directly amid it and compelled willy-nilly to join in clearing the Irishman's sector, which was the last thing he wanted.

There ensued a slow crawl fight, hedgerow to hedgerow. Though not numerous, the enemy force was dogged and well supplied with automatic weapons. After four hours of tedious infighting, during which the Americans had knocked off four machine-gun nests by moving grenadiers along the ditches, Strayer felt fairly free to move again. He had lost a dozen or so men while killing 25 Germans and capturing as many. And he was still within whistle range of Foucarville.

So the column hit the road—briefly. At about 0930, its van was stopped at St. Germain-de-Varreville by an artillery battery which was blocking its right of way with an accurate, unremitting shellfire. Strayer passed Dog Company around the battery's rear with instructions to "hurry south to the Houdienville causeway." The main body lost another three hours engaging and destroying the battery. Hearing nothing from topside, wholly in the dark about how the invasion fared elsewhere, Strayer stayed fixed on his mission. And he was still helping Cassidy! Already by that hour, Pouppeville had been taken, and Turner and friends, sent by Sink to do the job when he failed to get word from Strayer, arrived too late for the party.

But the labor was not all lost. Dog Company, having skirted the German battery, arrived opposite Exit No. 2 soon after the noon hour. It was first on the scene, but alas, the Houdienville causeway didn't need to be captured: there were no Germans there. The company's lot was to sit next the sands and enjoy the salt air. In this bucolic quiet, it was joined in midafternoon by Strayer and the main body. As to what had taken so long, the deployed battalion had but kept the German battery entertained at long range while Captain R. D. Winters, of Easy Company, hiked to Utah Beach, borrowed four Shermans from

4th Infantry Division, and sicked them on the enemy guns. When the armor wiped out the battery, the battalion arose and went. But such waits as this never rest troops.

The planned use of 3rd Battalion, 506th, was elementary. With one platoon of the 326th Engineers and two demolition sections, it was to hit on Drop Zone D, south of Vierville, east of Angoville-au-Plain. Thence it would march south and grab the two bridges at Le Port beside the mouth of the Douve River. The bridgehead would be expanded by advancing to the high ground near Brevands, where would occur the link-up with the V Corps spearhead moving north from Omaha Beach.

Estimated as a task for one day, it might have proved so if the gods had not frowned. Perversity took over to make 3rd Battalion's delivery as unlike 1st's as possible. It was dropped almost on the button. Then it was diffused and fragmented by unbeatable circumstance. But out of the night scramble, little trickles of men moved to labor like giants.

When its serial passed over the Carentan flood plain, heavy flak enveloped the carrier formation and dissolved it, as the planes took evasive action. The ground fire flamed up around the chutes as the troops obeyed the jump signal. It had flashed just a moment too soon. The sticks descended just short of Drop Zone D, west and north of it.

By this slender margin, the mistake which strewed them across the wrong ground and thereby balked an easy assembly also saved them. From where they touched earth, they could see a conflagration raging where they should have rendezvoused, and its fire and fury kept them at a distance, since initially, they were all responding as does one man when frightened and alone. Square amid Drop Zone D, the Germans had prepared a giant torch by drenching a farmhouse in gasoline, which was lighted as the serial came on, brightening the countryside.

But that was not all. The battalion pathfinders got in 30 minutes before the main body, to find that the Germans had foreseen that the airborne would use this ground, and had rigged and ringed it for a deadfall. It was dark when the pathfinders dropped—seven of them. But mortars and machine guns from three sides were already playing on the fields. The seven knew their stuff; they were a small packet, but mobile and bold. Using hand grenades, they bombed out two machine guns without getting hurt. After that, flares were lighted by the Germans all around the field.

The enemy fire built up steadily. Sticking to the shadows, the pathfinders watched the performance. The ground was too bright for further movement. They were both shocked and fascinated by what they saw. With every advantage in the situation, the Germans were not making good use of it. They did not have their heads up. The shooting was wild. They fired from cover. There was no movement; not one soldier came seeking them. As elsewhere in the Cotentin, the enemy behaved as if gripped by terrible fear. Still, the pathfinders knew that if the battalion descended into this, the ring of weapons could not miss the wholesale target. So they, too, knew fear; and there was no way to flash a warning.

Their heavy suspense ended when the battalion dropped short. Only two or three sticks jumped for the right ground at the wrong time. Their fate betokened what might have happened had the whole serial come straight to the mark; about 20 were shot as they floated down. For the seven early birds, the spectacle was a torment. They had done their work beautifully and had raised their feeble beacons but to have them eclipsed by a holocaust. They had tried to light the path in; it remained to the pathfinders only to find the path out, helping the other survivors. Out beyond the blazing perimeter, other troopers, scattered singly through the orchards, noted the glare and wondered what to do next.

One who had already made up his mind was Captain Charles G. Shettle, Battalion operations officer. Shettle is like that; loose-jointed, rangy, good-humored, with "country boy" written all over his map, he belongs to the Old Frontier and would have shone in the company of Boone and Harrod. He is never beset by fanciful fear. Yet when he struck earth, it seemed to Shettle that from every bank round about mortar and machine-gun fire came right at him. So he crawled to a ditch and lay there 15 minutes studying his compass and thinking of the next move. Out of reflection, he got his bearings. Angoville-au-Plain must lie to the northwest; from that direction he heard the heaviest fire; that meant that, by walking southwest a few hundred yards, he would find Les Droueries and part of 501st Regiment.

Traveling on azimuth and avoiding the road (a rule he followed undeviatingly that night), he walked straight to the rendezvous area but found no one. So he headed for Angoville-au-Plain and en route picked up two officers and 12 men of the regiment. They too had jumped short of the drop zone and had converged while looking for other people. There followed a brief council of war. Some of the men felt that the party must tarry longer and try for a larger assembly. But when Shettle said, "I'm in favor of going for the objective right now," no one gave him an argument.

Thus it was settled and they marched. From the fields over which they traveled, they collected 16 more men and two officers, one an engineer. He had them halt briefly while he cut the Carentan power line, the only action taken during the advance.

At 0430, the "battalion"—five officers and 28 men—reached the canal bridges outside Le Port. Fire came against them from beyond the far bank. But they closed upon the nigh-side abutments without getting hurt, and as first light broke, their weapons were firing across the treadway of Bridge No. 37.

Then arrived a timely reinforcement—five officers and 15 more men.

Encouraged by this increment, Shettle said, "I think we ought to force a crossing and establish the bridgehead." He called for volunteers. The job: to crawl to the far side with a light machine gun and pour out the fire which would cover the crossing for others.

Two enlisted men spoke up. Somehow they made it to the far bank though two enemy guns were zeroed in on the bridge. Both men were later killed. They were never identified. The deed remains anonymous.

Helped by the gun on the far bank, Lieutenants Kenneth H. Christianson and Rudolph E. Bolte, of How Company, also crossed, each followed by a five-man patrol. But even as the light grew, so did their wisdom. The 12 made it like gymnasts, bodies dangling, hand over hand along the girders under the bridge floor.

On the far side, the two patrols consolidated quickly as they were joined by Lieutenant Richard P. Meason, who led How Company. They then deployed as a body against the German positions which had the bridge under fire. It was slow work—a flattened inching along the ditches to get on the enemy flank and grenade the strong points at the closest possible range. At the end of two hours, they had destroyed three machine-gun emplacements and killed 13 Germans. But they had also discovered that the enemy could bring up fresh guns faster than they could proceed against them. However, that wasn't what stopped them: they had run dry of ammunition. So Meason had no choice but to halt the patrol and fold back on Shettle.

The force had no communications, and Shettle knew nothing of what was occurring elsewhere in Normandy. Such guesses as they made were far, far wrong. There was one pathetic incident. On talking it over, Shettle and his friends concluded that help might be closer at hand among the Omaha Beach forces to the southeast than among the paratroops to the north. So Lieutenant Fred T. Broyhill, of Headquarters Company, was sent forth with two men to break through the German lines and look for friends from the American V Corps. A more forlorn hope could not be imagined. At that moment V Corps was gasping for life on the Omaha sands.

At noon Shettle took an inventory. There were 30 rifle rounds per man, one Hawkins mine per man, 130 rounds for the Browning light gun, 6 rounds for the bazooka and 250 pounds of explosive.

He said to the others, "No, it's not a favorable situation. But let's not sweat too much about ammunition. As long as we stand here alive, the ground is ours."

Their position neither improved nor worsened through the day. From the reinforcement which had arrived in early morning, Shettle learned that Johnson was busy around La Barquette. So he went calling in midafternoon. Two enlisted men accompanied him. When Johnson said that he could spare no men, Shettle took his word for it but also concluded that he would get no help from that source even if the Le Port position was overrun. The one thing accomplished by his visit was that, via Lieutenant Farrell's radio link with the fleet, he reported what he had done that day, for relay to General Taylor.

In early evening, 40 more men from the regiment arrived at Le Port. They had dropped east of Carentan but had taken all day to find their way. Two bundles came with them, one loaded with rifle ammunition, the other with K-rations. As dark fell, the demolition team of engineers with Shettle worked their way downstream and within a few minutes prepared both bridges for destruction—just in case the ammunition shortage should prove fatal.

At 0200 the Germans counterattacked across Bridge No.

37. They were driven back by automatic fire which crumpled a halfhearted rush. But the repulse emptied the one machine gun.

Throughout the day, Bob Sink, in magnificent solitude at Culoville, had sweated out the Le Port situation and the failure to hear from 3rd Battalion. That bothered him no more than the radio isolation, which deprived him of news of the "big picture," or the shortage of 506th people at his elbow, which denied him local security. In fact, he thrived in a vacuum.

No sooner was Turner and his group on the road to Pouppeville than Sink got rid of his few other retainers by shaping them into combat patrols and projecting them outward with instructions to "track down the hostiles and engage them on sight."

Under Lieutenant Salvi H. Matheson, the personnel officer, one patrol went through Hiesville after prowling Vierville without ever smelling a German. Matheson didn't know it, but Hiesville had been "occupied" by Lieutenant Colonel Harry W. O. Kinnard. That nonpareil, one of the gentlest and wisest soldiers ever to school on the Hudson, was once compared by a fellow officer to Goethe's portrait of the Prince of Orange, "his thoughts are far-reaching, he is reserved, appears to accede to everything, never contradicts, and while maintaining the show of reverence, with clear foresight accomplishes his own designs." On his first go at battle, it wasn't easy. He was dropped almost eight miles from his own jump field and had walked alone from Ste. Mère-Église, "scared as hell, expecting to find a German behind every bush, but meeting no one and experiencing nothing." At Hiesville, he ran into 12 paratroopers from 12 different units. Instead of clinging to their company, he oriented each man and sent him along to seek his own group. Kinnard kept walking toward Culoville.

Another of Sink's patrols, under Captain Peters, went south and bumped into a German machine-gun nest. Two of the guns were knocked off by hand grenades. Peters was killed charging the third gun. Nothing but grenades and machine pistols seemed to work well at this business. The hedge banks compelled the duel at close quarters.

But Sink grew restive sending other men out to risk and die while he sat still. His three patrols had gone and returned without finding a trace of 3rd Battalion. The strain of waiting and not knowing finally became unbearable.

At 1100, Sink said to Major H. H. Hannah, his operations officer, "Don't you think we better go take a look?" Hannah nodded; action in any form would relieve the intolerable suspense. Besides, a soldier had just driven a jeep into Culoville, and this boon to mobility should not go wasted.

So light as air, this three-man patrol (counting the driver) got on the road and started for St. Côme-du-Mont, not knowing it was a German stronghold. They hadn't planned it too well. Sink and Hannah had only their .45 Colts; the driver handled the wheel with one hand and kept a carbine ready cross his lap.

One mile beyond Vierville, they whipped by a large enemy horse park. The driver yelled, "Look at the animals!" There wasn't time. At the main gate stood a sentry, raising his rifle.

Sink yelled, "Let him have it!"

They fired together and the man dropped. The driver stepped on the gas to speed past the enemy camp.

As the jeep leaped ahead, Sink and Hannah were suddenly aware of Germans, many, many, rising from the ditches on both sides of the road. They rose out of earth behind them, and they thronged the shoulders forward as far as the eye could see. The jeep was careening right down the center of an enemy regiment which had fallen out for rest while on a road march.

Sink yelled, "Powder River, let 'er buck!" He and Hannah worked their pistols. The driver plied his carbine, shooting from his lap. Not a shot came from the other side; the Germans either ran or jumped back to the ditches.

So it went for 200 yards. More Germans lined the ditches forward. They approached an intersection. The road ahead was partly blocked by artillery. Sink knew his luck was running out.

He said to the driver, "Turn the jeep around—fastlike—and go back!"

They sped back through the gantlet, still firing their weapons. Then they were past the horse park and blessedly delivered into country quiet. Not one German had pulled trigger on them. So ended Sink's only patrol; it had proved only that he wasn't born to die foolishly, too young.

Some minutes later they all got the shakes. By then Sink was back in his Culoville CP.

A runner came to tell him, "There's a mixed force of about

70 men, some from the 82nd, fighting Germans at Holdy, and we ain't doing very well." He explained that the enemy force was deployed around a battery of 105-millimeter guns, which no one had expected to find in that area.

Seventy-five more men from 1st Battalion had collected at Culoville, under Captains Knut H. Raudstein and Lloyd E. Patch. Sink sent them along to Holdy. The timely arrival of 50 men from the 502nd, under an apple-cheeked lieutenant, enabled the sending of a second reinforcement.

Patch and Raudstein saw the Holdy situation at one glance. The scratch force of Americans (about 20 men) had trapped a German battery of four guns by sealing the exits of the field where the guns were emplaced. About 60 enemy artillerymen were defending with hand weapons from shallow holes dug among the emplacements. The gunners couldn't stand to fire their pieces because the American rifles were too close. The Americans were too few to rush the position.

Splitting the force, the two captains worked out a routine plan—double envelopment. Following the hedge line, Patch led half the group via the right flank one field, while Raudstein took the other half an equal distance left.

Oh, yes, it was sure-fire stuff. But just as the 75 skirmishers began turning toward each other for the pinch-out, one lone-handed bazooka man (unidentified) who had been sitting on this ground for hours rushed to the hedgerow next the guns and from 30 yards' range banged in six rockets. Two exploded ammunition piles; the others ripped into a mass of soldiers in a ditch behind the guns. Resistance died with the blast. Patch could hear the bazooka man screaming, "Come on! All you got to do is kill the rest of them." He proved a good prophet.

The 502nd group arrived in time to count the corpses and mount guard over the guns.

Patch led his people to Ste. Marie-du-Mont, someone having passed him the word, "We'll find a real fight over there." Getting one foot in the village, the Americans had to back away fast. Mortar fire came in big doses, following them with too great accuracy to be accidental. Patch wondered why, then noticed the tall spire of the village church. So he backtracked to Holdy, bore-sighted one of the captured guns and in two rounds knocked the German observation post out of the steeple—fair shooting for a doughboy.

The apple-cheeked lieutenant of 502nd was feeling nervous.

He said to Patch, "I better destroy these guns."

Patch said, "No, damn it, we need these guns."

The lieutenant: "But if I don't destroy them, they may be recaptured by counterattack."

The captain: "Leave that up to me."

Patch returned to his force at Ste. Marie-du-Mont. The loss of the observation post had unhinged the Germans. They were already quitting the village, and Patch's men walked right in.

Sink heard by runner of the windfall at Holdy and sent the jeep flying with instructions to start towing in the four guns. But a few rounds of mortar fire had fallen near the battery, further fraying the lieutenant's nerves. He said to his men, "We'll have to blow up the guns." The jeep arrived just in time to save the last gun.

When Sink heard of this piece of idiocy, he was too harassed by other things to care. His command post in the stone farmhouse was on low ground between two gentle ridges. Enemy snipers had sifted through to the hedge banks of this high ground. Bullets buzzed like wasps outside the door; walking in the open was no longer fun. Sink sent out a few riflemen to scout the ridges, but the buzzing continued and grew louder.

In midafternoon, the buzz became a rattle and roar, as if several platoons had come calling. Sink passed out rifles to his wounded, formed them with the few officers present, and led them out to do a little shooting. After trading fire for 30 minutes along the hedgerows, the two sides recessed. The Germans came again at dusk, in greater numbers, pushing harder. Once more Sink rallied his headquarters crew and beat them back.

To the aged Frenchman who owned the stone house, Sink explained the situation, saying, "After dark, they will really try. You'd better seek safety elsewhere."

The Frenchman asked, "Where will I go? Where could I sleep? Do you know any safe place?"

Stumped by that last question, Sink merely shrugged, and the Frenchman stayed.

But instead of the Germans descending on the CP, night brought Generals Max Taylor and Tony MacAuliffe, with their headquarters entourage, riding on the wings of victory back from Pouppeville. They talked over plans for an attack which Sink would lead the next day. Then General Taylor went on to his CP at Hiesville to get a good sleep. General Taylor always got a good sleep.

Having started the day more thoroughly lost from the larger elements of the command than any of the big hats, Sink was ending it with most of the division dropping into his lap. "Beatitudinal" is the word for it; to the meek is given the earth.

But he was no wiser than before about the fate of 3rd Battalion or what was happening at Le Port. The "D" in D-day could stand for "disillusion." Shettle had depended on the United States Navy to pass along to General Taylor the word about how he was battling for the glory of the 506th at Bridge No. 37. Taylor would then get it to Sink, and somebody would bust a gut to get help to him. But Old Faithful—the Navy—had somehow let him down. The only gain from the message was that momentarily it uplifted Shettle, who didn't know it wouldn't be delivered.

Sink did get a rundown on the victory at Pouppeville—yes, the troops called it "*Poop*ville," accenting that first syllable. That bit was slightly galling. The southern exit should have been Sink's own prize. It had fallen to another regiment because of the dispersion which kept Sink's battalions from answering the bell on time.

26

Westward Ho!

Night must fall, and it did, with Bob Sink still hearing nothing from his 3rd Battalion. His strength, ready for the work of the second day, counted 227 men from 1st Battalion, 301 men from 2nd Battalion, 101st Division strays approximating one company, 40 soldiers from the 82nd Division and one attached platoon of antitank guns.

Here were riches for the man who had played solitaire through most of D-day. But Sink continued to count chickens before they were hatched. One of the glider battalions, scheduled to arrive at Utah Beach very early, was supposed to head straight for Sink and Culoville. So Sink published his order for the attack through Vierville toward St. Côme-du-Mont. The 401st Glidermen would jump off at 0430, and his own troops and attachments would follow.

The glider outfit failed to show. Sink, anxious to start on time, blew the whistle on his own 1st Battalion, and the attack opened raggedly. There were few German riflemen and machine-gunners present; but they buzzed so persistently around the column flanks, firing long enough before falling back, that it became impossible to keep the battalion on the dirt road leading into Vierville. The sniping from behind hedges and from within the farmhouses forced Lieutenant Colonel William L. Turner to extend his troops over a broad front while they still saw little or nothing of the enemy. Turner used a few men

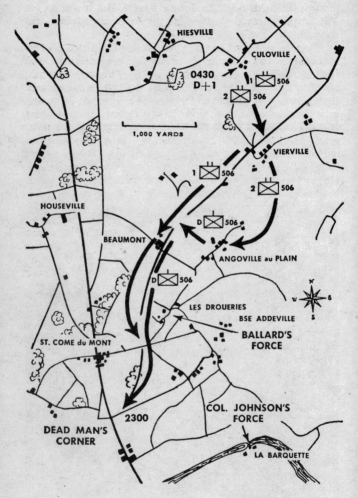

Figure 22. SINK'S OPERATIONS THE SECOND DAY

in the road simply to draw fire so that his skirmishers working through the fields might find some targets. But it was no go. The Germans stayed elusive, and the American advance was frustratingly slow.

Turner's men were bucking not die-hard, isolated pockets of resistance, but highly agile small groups of skirmishers, who fired and fell back, clinging to cover. They knew the ground, and they had well prepared it for just such a movement, with foxholes and rifle pits in depth. An uneven curtain of ground mist helped them. They never held long enough to become cornered, and when they ran back and slid into another hole, it was done too quickly to permit a fair shot at them. Coupled with the slow pace, the wraithlike nature of the enemy rubbed Turner's nerves raw. He complained bitterly to Captain E. H. Howell, the operations officer: "What in hell gives? These krauts beat us at playing Indian."

Four hours after the start, the battalion got to Vierville. Turner was in the village church when Sink and General Taylor overtook him. Sink said to him, "You will continue the attack toward the crossroads south of St. Côme-du-Mont." Without asking for clarification, Turner took this to mean that the cross-roads would be his objective for the day. So he was off once again, the fated traveler with a half-packed bag of instructions, and luck was not riding with him.

But the slow-motion advance and the German evasiveness had powerfully impressed other minds. Sink had warned his people, "Don't fire into hedgerows or buildings except to return fire." It was a precaution taken in the interests of his own forces. So many of the paratroopers were still on the loose and looking for company that he thought indiscriminate fire was as likely to kill Americans as Germans.

Lives were saved, perhaps, but at the cost of opportunity. Shortly after Turner had departed, Sink, looking south, saw several hundred troops milling around boldly in the open. At 2000 yards, they were beyond effective machine-gun fire, and too distant to be identified by uniform even when Sink and Taylor looked through field glasses. "They must be our troops," Sink said. "Germans would not be so God-damn dumb as to move around like that."

But the gnawing doubt remained. So without changing his battle plan, he sent a small patrol to investigate this body of exhibitionists along the marsh edge. The patrol got close enough to make sure they were Germans. By then, Sink had already lost them to sight, and the enemy battalion was formed and starting on its roundabout march towards Colonel Skeets Johnson's small garrison at the La Barquette lock.

Turner could barely get in motion again. While his men were still among the Vierville houses, Charley Company was hit by a line of enemy skirmishers formed along the first hedgerow south of the village. Driven back slowly, the Germans refused to disengage. They defended from hedgerow to hedgerow and moved only when at last the flankers were about to enfilade them. In three hours, the battalion advanced only 1000 yards. When it paused to reorganize at the crossroads below Vierville, things changed slightly for the better.

A platoon of six Sherman tanks, which had come on from Utah Beach, began to run interference for the dog-tired infantry. That didn't help Baker Company, strung out along the hedge line to the right of the main road; the Germans, foxholed in the orchards or firing from inside the farm buildings, refused to give way. On the left of the road, Able Company was confronted by open fields. The presence of the tanks in column prevented any German displacement to the roadway to get on Able's flank. So the armor and the one rifle company rolled right along together into Beaumont, capturing it at high noon. When the Americans gained the road intersection, the resistance in front of Baker Company dissolved, and its people came abreast near the village. But Sink had already concluded that Turner's force was too thin for its task and had ordered Dog Company to break off its action at Angoville-au-Plain and join Turner. The march took two hours, and it robbed Peter to pay Paul.

Second Battalion, approaching Angoville, was also wallowing in the ruck. Strictly speaking, it was following 1st Battalion in what was labeled a support, mop-up role. But Sink had shaken it out on the left of the main road with instructions to "clear the enemy from the vicinity of Angoville." When 1st Battalion bucked its narrow path through Vierville, however, the slippery enemy rolled off and around Turner's flanks and again clamped a hold on the village, regaining the foxholes and slotted walls from which they had been beaten one hour or so earlier. Of this Turner knew nothing; no small garrison had been dropped off to clinch Vierville; no one had deemed it necessary.

Consequently 2nd Battalion advanced on Vierville, unwarned that it was once more in enemy hands. It got the news when a demoralizing fire crashed all along its line from the village buildings and the entrenched positions on both sides thereof. There were heavy losses in the first few moments of surprise. Then the men took to the banks and ditches, from which they returned fire, though they could not regather to assault. Second Battalion stayed hung-up until four of the six Shermans which had gotten up to Turner doubled back to threaten the Germans from the rear. After a three-hour fight Vierville was cleared for a second time, and a "large number" (they were never counted) of Germans passed into captivity.

Caught between these two situations, Sink was at the mercy of his information. He was hearing only fragments from Vierville, while the ample messaging from Turner was almost totally dark. "The Germans are moving around both of our flanks along the hedgerows." That was how Sink heard it, and he rode for Beaumont to see.

In fact, the troops in Beaumont were at that time enjoying a brief respite from fire while reorganizing for another start. Before they could get going, the Germans lashed back in counterattack. Baker Company met the thrust at the edge of the village and drove the Germans back about 500 yards, killing 20 of them. The remainder sideslipped toward the farmsteads along the high ground on the right. Again the battalion gathered itself on Beaumont and moved forward a quarter-mile toward St. Côme-du-Mont. Again the Germans counterattacked, with their flankers pressing Baker Company from both sides so fiercely that the line had to fall back on Beaumont. The leading Sherman was hit by a rocket and withdrew around a bend in the road to escape the line of fire.

Colonel Turner climbed to the turret to direct the tank's fire. Again the tank nosed forward. As it rounded the bend, three rockets hit it dead on. It stayed there 20 minutes, seemingly out of action. Then it slowly backed around the bend again.

This was the situation when Sink came abreast of his forward line. Turner was already aboard the tank and messaging for an artillery observer to come up to him. Sink motioned him to come down. They sat in a ditch and talked things over.

Turner said, "It's machine-gun fire that's killing us. My main chance is to get this big gun turned on those positions."

Sink replied, "It's OK to go on with the tanks if you think

there's no other way." And then he added, "For God's sake be careful."

The tank crept forward again. It gained 30 yards. Turner suddenly rose up in the turret. As he turned to look back at Sink, a sniper's bullet drilled him through the brain in clear sight of most of his men. That one blow at the psychological moment ended the advance.

All this time, Baker Company was being engaged from its right rear, and most of Headquarters Company was beset with it. Taking over the command, Major Franklin E. Foster decided that he was in no condition to renew the attack; he ordered Able Company to fall back on Beaumont. Ordinarily, Sink might have argued with him. But Sink had already turned rearward. Seeing Turner die had hit him hard, and besides, he was worrying about 2nd Battalion. On its own, Baker Company, in late afternoon, made another try against the fortified farm buildings on the right flank, under orders to "forget rifle fire and close with grenades and bayonets." The Germans didn't flinch; under a hail of automatic fire, Baker Company recoiled to the village. Major Foster was hard wounded by a bullet, and the battalion command passed to Captain Patch.

Taking the road to 2nd Battalion, Sink ran into Dog Company and a platoon of light tanks, fresh from Utah Beach. That chance meeting recatalyzed action. Sink led them back to Beaumont. He was still bent on getting to St. Côme-du-Mont, and the strength of Dog Company made him feel big again; it counted 94 men—the largest assembly of the day. As the column entered Beaumont, it found the men of 1st Battalion clustered tight together in a courtyard at the village center— not a healthy situation. The newcomers were met by a clobber of mortar fire from the distance, mixed with machine-pistol fire from the near hedges. The huddled 1st Battalion, off line from the shelling, watched it listlessly. Dog Company marched right on past them and, hardly checking its stride, rooted the Schmeisser crews out of the hedges, drove them beyond range of Beaumont, and started down the road to Carentan. Only one light tank paced the company. Dog Company's passage was like the priming of a pump. The wearied units of 1st Battalion picked themselves up and took to the road again, following— at a distance.

Dog Company jogged along in two files on either side of the road, the men walking the ditches and pressing close to the banks, while 40 yards in front, the light tank churned along, raking the hedgerows on either side with its machine gun. Every yard gained was wrested from deployed Germans; the shoulders of the road as well as the hedge banks were pitted with manned emplacements and foxholes. Yet Dog Company lost only one trooper, shot through the groin. "Because of the tank's machine gun, they couldn't get their heads up; that was what did it." So the men said. But they also fired with rifles, carbines and BARs as they marched.

Now they were approaching the countryside near Les Droueries, where Colonel Ballard and his battalion were conducting their fight in isolation. On ahead was La Barquette, where Colonel Johnson and his party were at grips with the unknown. That stimulated the feeling of urgency; it was the reason Sink kicked them along. On General Taylor's authority, he had already countermanded Johnson's order to Ballard to break loose and march on La Barquette. Ballard was in no position to comply in any case, and Sink wanted to use Les Droueries as a springboard for the attack toward the Douve bridges. If he smashed through, he would relieve the pressures against both Ballard and Johnson and might win the objectives around the Carentan bridgehead which so far had eluded the 501st Regiment.

But despite the rush of Dog Company, the attack was already reeling and about to collapse. Dog Company was leg-fresh and not yet hurt; owing to the battle-weariness of the rest of the column, it had outrun its nearest support. There would have been difficulties enough in keeping the column closed up; the resurgent and spotty character of the opposition, the twisting of the road and the curtaining hedgerows kept each component of the column from sight and feel of any other. Dog Company had been so impressed with the need for speed that it had dismissed all normal precaution. Here was momentum amid mental fog. The men knew that friendly troops were supposed to be somewhere on ahead, though exactly where, no one had bothered to tell them. So as they drew onto the crossroads east of St. Côme-du-Mont, they threw out orange flares—the friendly signal. Immediately they saw columns of orange smoke rise from amid the trees. Hearts leaped up. The word went around: "We've got it made; our fellows are on both flanks."

So they stepped out more freely, increasing pace and porting their weapons. Suddenly fire came at them from both sides, and they bolted to get on past it, emerging from the trap with the loss of only five men. But they were still unaware of their narrow escape; they thought that some of their own comrades had fired in error.

While they ran, they heard heavy firing off to their left. It meant nothing to them because they did not know that Ballard & Battalion were embattled at Les Droueries. And they were equally innocent of knowledge that they had skinned right through the jaws of an enemy force, part of it fighting Ballard, the rest, including an antitank battery, positioned around the crossroads they had so recently threaded.

It was left to Captain Patch & Battalion to uncover what Dog Company had missed. The stretch-out of the march had already gravely disjointed that command. Thirty men from Able Company and 40 from Headquarters had pushed rapidly ahead of the main body so that they virtually played pigtail to Dog Company when it entered the crossroad. A light tank chugged ahead of them, and they had outstripped the other men out of a desire to stay in the lee of its protection.

As the tank entered the intersection, a German rocket hit it dead on. The tank stopped and its gas tank exploded. That one shot finished 1st Battalion for the day, except for a few hands from Able and Headquarters who ran on past the flaming derelict. Immediately, machine-gun fire came against the road from the fields on both sides of it. But most of the men had already jumped to the ditches when the rocket hit the tank, and the bullet hail drew little blood. From where they lay, the Americans returned fire. In time the enemy rat-tat-tat slackened. It sounded as if the Germans were pulling back. But curiosity was dead. The tank still blazed, and 1st Battalion stayed ditched.

The few bold spirits who had run on past the block got as far as the high ground directly southeast of St. Côme-du-Mont. There they drew fire from an outpost line on the skirts of the village. It stalled their movement but not their weapons ardor. They engaged where they lay, killing a few Germans and capturing four. Ahead of them was a covered road, its hedge banks rising from 10 to 12 feet and having unusual thickness. Unless the enemy was roosting in the trees, they might have gone that way with impunity. But they paid no heed.

If Dog Company had been pushing its luck, at least it had been pushing, and so far, velocity had carried it through and past the dangers which had stalled the main body. The reward remained constant—or nearly so. The company came at last to the crossroads south of St. Côme-du-Mont, from which the land runs flat all the way to the River Douve. This was the goal post—the objective which Sink had given Turner in the church hours earlier.

So the company halted, expecting that support would quickly come. In that second, its fortune changed. The tank which had run interference all the way from Beaumont was hit by a rocket, killing the vehicle, incinerating the crew. For several days thereafter the ruined hull stood at the intersection, a dead man sitting upright in its turret. From that, the troops gave it a name, and the country folk of the Cotentin still call it "Dead Man's Corner."

But the blow didn't flatten Dog Company. The men knew they had made a big score and figured they could hold what they had gained. It didn't occur to anyone that their reinforcement had fallen by the wayside.

In the gloaming, Captain Joe F. MacMillan espied a convoy of eight trucks parked a few rods ahead. They looked like U.S.A. vehicles. He walked that way and found it so; the eight were loaded with quartermaster supplies, including razor blades, shaving cream and candy.

By an accident, the convoy had become lost; by a miracle, it had driven from the beaches through St. Côme-du-Mont without drawing one bullet. The lead driver had his flashlight out and was studying a map when MacMillan came alongside.

Macmillan asked, "Don't you know you're the spearpoint of the American advance, out in front of the whole army?"

The driver said, "Captain, don't kid me."

"You better stay with me if you expect to get out alive," MacMillan replied. Then he turned to his own officers, saying, "It looks like a field problem back home—nice trucks waiting to haul us to camp."

Sink, now at his CP in Angoville-au-Plain, got no word that Dog Company had reached the crossroads. But when he heard by radio from Patch that his battalion was sprawled north of St. Côme-du-Mont, his hunch told him that he was overextended and had better pull in his horns.

Patch told him, "I have no information on Dog Company, but I think I'm strong enough to spend the night here." That left MacMillan out on a limb, but he was too wise a soldier to stay there. At 2300, he concluded that no support was coming to him, and with some of the men riding the trucks and others walking as escort, Dog Company fell back on Patch. The Germans slept.

Patch and MacMillan talked it over. Having tasted a little victory, they preferred to risk their chances on the forward ground rather than wear their men out marching. Both felt hot about it when Sink called at midnight and said they would return to the starting point. He couldn't explain the reasons over the radio. But Sink had his points. He worried that these troops were overexposed, and he felt a pressing need to tidy up his front.

At the crossroads, the sleeping troops were hard to rouse as kids on a school day. It took Patch and MacMillan 40 minutes to rout them out and get them on the road again. By 0200, they were pounding their ears in Beaumont—with one notable exception. The last touch of irony was that when the order for retirement was passed around, most of the men of Dog Company took it to mean that they were to return to their own battalion. So they slogged on through the night to reach Angoville-au-Plain, not knowing until they got there that, according to the order, they were to attack before dawn from a line of departure parallel to Les Droueries, which meant that they must double back to Beaumont. So they turned about, having lost so much time and energy on the treadmill that the wink or two of sleep afforded them in the brief pause at Beaumont was just an added torment. This was the fault of a command and staff so concerned about battle that it lost sight of troops. Dog Company Primed became Dog Company Pooped.

27

Comes the Artillery

At 0430 of the second morning—one-half hour after his ammunition party returned—Ballard ordered a stand-to by all hands in the sunken road near Les Droueries.

It was a well-timed hunch. Immediately, the enemy began punching at his front with small patrols. The parties advanced, firing. But when fire was returned, they faded back, though no blood had been drawn. Ballard guessed that they were probing to determine the limits of his position. So he sent patrols out flankward in extension of his own front to keep them guessing. But it was tit-for-tat small-change maneuvering, and nothing important came of it. At dawn the German mortars resumed fire in salvos of six to eight shells. It was wasted on the countryside in "overs" because the battalion was too close-locked to the enemy position.

At 0630, Ballard gave the order: "Resume the attack." As a force maneuver, it withered at once. To charge up and over the bank was physically impossible. The only way of advance was a belly-crawl through the ditches along the vertical hedgerows. The Germans had sited their four machine guns to fire straight down the ditches. They shot the first files. Others who followed had to raise themselves slightly to get past the corpses. So doing, they were gunned down. Gradually, the pile-up of bodies blocked the ditches. Yet somehow, as the morning lengthened, a few rugged spirits, luckier and braver than most, managed to make this fiery passage and crawl to the nigh side of the hedge bank from which the four guns were firing. Having closed, but lacking grenades, they could still do nothing but cling there and hope. It was gallant, but it didn't make sense.

Their presence simply circumscribed the fire opportunities for the line in the sunken road. Ballard saw the futility of this fingerhold; but temporarily, he was stuck with it.

The first break came when his radio cut through to Lieutenant Colonel Harry W. O. Kinnard, 501st's executive officer, who had arrived at Angoville-au-Plain with Colonel Sink, of the 506th Regiment. This is the same Kinnard who months later at Bastogne first suggested that "Nuts!" would be a proper reply to the German demand that the American garrison surrender.

Kinnard said, "I can give you artillery on Les Droueries if you can observe and adjust it."

Ballard replied, "Well, let it come." Then he gave Kinnard the co-ordinates of a lone house on the far left of the position which he guessed was the enemy CP because of the constant traffic in and out.

But 45 minutes passed before he could be certain that he was looking at the right explosions. Mortar fire was active all around, and the U.S.S. *Quincy* was again throwing shells at St. Côme-du-Mont, eight-inchers, some of them falling short. With so much boom-boom in the neighborhood, it took a wise son to recognize his own pop.

But at last Ballard got it. Then he asked, "Now after you shell the house, will you bring it back 100 yards closer to my own lines?" That gave him a safety margin of 250 yards.

What he next saw lifted him like the "Hallelujah Chorus." Three salvos—12 rounds hit the house dead on, smashing roof and walls and sending Germans flying. He said to Pelham, "We've got it made." Then the second concentration—the same number of shells—landed squarely on his own lines, being pulled back a full 350 yards.

The blow fell on Fox Company. Five men were killed instantly, and eight others were terribly wounded. Coming from the blue that way, it spun the rest to the verge of panic.

Ballard saw three men of Fox—light-machine-gunners— break and run for the rear. He sprinted at an angle to intercept them.

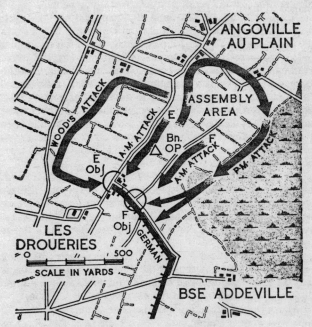

Figure 23. BALLARD'S MANEUVERS

When he cut them off, to his amazement, they seemed neither stunned nor demoralized.

But he was a little excited himself. He said, "You're going back there; you're sure as hell going back there."

They all gave him the horse laugh. One said, "Sure we're going back—sir!" Then they saluted and turned about.

Ballard yelled out to his officers, "Get the word spread among the men. There won't be any more shorts. I'm calling for the same concentration, and we'll make the right adjustments. But we've got to have artillery."

Came a shout from all along the line, "Fire away, Colonel, fire away." Hearing the words, quite suddenly he felt light; if there was any glory in the day, this was it.

So he called for the artillery to come in again, and together they returned to the serious business of killing people.

But his feeling of becoming all square did not long last. There came another insistent call from Johnson. It didn't warm the order that the regimental commander had left it to a junior S-2, Lieutenant Hoffman, to get on radio and give the word. Hoffman said, "You are directed to march the battalion to La Barquette, along with ammunition, food and medical supplies." Johnson was not under pressure at the time; there was as yet no sign of an enemy build-up against the lock. About these things Ballard didn't know; but he did know that he had been fought to a standstill, and that his own cupboard was almost bare. If the guns of insubordination had to explode in his face, he still stood by them.

He called Kinnard to tell him about the order, and Kinnard, in turn, consulted General Anthony C. McAuliffe, the artillery commander, who said, "Tell Ballard to stay put; there's a plan in the making." Kinnard called Ballard, saying, "Leave the battalion in place; you come back to Angoville to talk things over."

Right after Ballard took off, a German infantry battalion began to cross the marsh past the American left flank. (This was the same battalion that Colonel Sink had seen pass in the distance and which, later in the day, was to hit Johnson.)

Major Bottomly, sitting near the edge of the marsh with 15 men who were operating the CP, saw them first. The Germans waded in line right across his front, as if he were reviewing a parade, the closest ones just offshore, the extreme end 600 yards out. The enemy was taking the same risk which Ballard had adjudged fatal the day before.

Pelham came up at that moment. The sight shook him. One thought flooded his mind: If they swing in now against the shore, we're trapped.

Excitedly, he said to Bottomly, "I'll run for the battalion and get two machine guns. No, I'll get four machine guns. No, by God, I won't. We can't spare that many now."

Bottomly answered, "Take it easy, boy, and we'll just give them a little local fire."

To Pelham, Bottomly's reaction made little sense; with machine guns at 200 to 300 yards, they could make a big score; aimed rifle fire would scare the quarry, but not scathe it.

But he was given no time to argue. Coming along the bank

toward them, as the battalion had moved the first afternoon, in line with the men in the water, was a party of 20 Germans— a flank patrol. They were nicely within range, moving conspicuously in the open, and if their job was to divert fire from the larger force, they got it done. Bottomly's two squads, using carbines and M-1s, opened fire on them. Thirteen of these pigeons were killed. Seven came in with their hands raised.

That was more than enough fire to make the big formation shy off. The wading line struck off half-left, moving deeper into the marsh. No hurt had been done it. The Americans were roused by the success of their small foray but hardly content with it. And in their excitement, not one person thought to call Johnson and warn him that a strong body of Germans was advancing by water directly toward his lines. The lapse might not have happened but for Ballard's absence.

At Angoville, Ballard was dealing with Colonel Sink, of the 506th Regiment, who told him, "I want you to continue the attack."

Ballard said, "Then I've got to have tanks."

To his surprise, Sink said, "You've got 'em." Four Shermans were put at his disposal. Then Ballard was told that the 506th would come abreast of him before dark; by then he was expected to have taken Les Droueries. Sink was already setting the stage for a main attack which would be mounted from the same ground before dawn.

The armor returned to Les Droueries with Ballard, and he went with the tankers for a fast conning of the forward ground. "I'm sure there are no tank-stopping weapons here," he told them. A first-round knockout of the four machine guns which had stalled the foot fighters all day was to be the key maneuver; Ballard was still unaware that the enemy rampart counted 15 such guns all told.

The one factor enabling the armor to co-operate was that there were low spots in the lateral hedgerows where the tanks could bull through. This done, they would pivot and move slowly against the frontal hedge bank, spread out so that each gun would be overrun. The infantry would spring from the sunken road, be abreast of the tanks as they pivoted, surmount the barrier with them and then mop up. Between the screening metal and the cover of the banks running to the position, the foot force should be fairly well shielded. So went the plan.

But before blowing the whistle, Ballard took another look

at his own people. What he saw convinced him that Fox Company was *hors de combat*; the blow from the friendly artillery was the last straw; the men were down and shaking. Lieutenant Wood's detachment of 506th strays and 15 Dog Company men under Lieutenant Richard Snodgrass were substituted. This scratch company, with Bottomly commanding, would attack on the left.

Tedious, cautious, methodical are the words for this assault, made so by the difficulties of the uneven ground, the fatigue in troops and the deliberateness of the armor. Though the tankers stayed unbuttoned, thereby buoying the infantry, they rushed nothing. It was a "charge" in slow motion, the best measure of which is that the tanks spend 50 rounds of 75-millimeter fire and 15 boxes of machine-gun ammunition on the strongpoints and buildings before closing on the German main line. By sheer fire volume, the armor dominated the action, and what they did reacted on the spirits of Ballard's men "like rainfall on a desert."

Easy Company, on the right, took the road juncture, then came under fire from the same house it had captured the first morning. But it was halfhearted resistance. Some of the enemy force fled. A few tried to surrender. The fight had gone on too long for that. Also, the conditions of combat made acceptance all but impossible. The other sector still gave battle, and a local surrender by one group did not lessen the menace from the others. To try to handle it only made the American side more vulnerable. Almost to the last man, the Germans who stayed were killed.

Bottomly's scratch force got right to the hedge bank, then was driven back by heavy fire. The Germans on the right flank had put ten tunnels under the bank, and the foxholes and fire pits both sides of it were interconnected. Bottomly's men caught it from gunners who first volleyed from the near side then pulled back through the tunnels.

Automatically, they recoiled to the nearest tank. Bullets splattered from the hull as they advanced again, using the armor as a shield. The tank stayed with them till the hedge was past and the grapple was final. No bayonets were used. The Germans were gunned down in their positions at arm's distance. Not one prisoner was taken. No count was made of enemy dead; in its sweep, Bottomly's small outfit captured eight machine guns. The cost: four men killed, six wounded.

From Sink, Ballard got the message: "Battalion will hold the intersection; you report back for further orders." The tanks were released so that they could laager on more secure ground before dark. Water, ammunition and rations came up to the position at the same time—1930.

Although the battalion's right flank still dangled, Ballard at last felt easy. His left was solidly anchored on the marge of the marsh, he had won his first fight, and in the distance, somewhere around Beaumont, he could hear the sounds of fighting, which signaled that Sink's regiment was moving toward him.

But since Fox Company—now down to 16 men—had missed the last skirmish because of its beat-up look, when the position was at last reorganized, it was posted on the extreme loose end just to keep the risks of the day in balance.

There was no balance, no reason, in what happened on beyond. The American guns resumed speaking, softening the enemy front prior to the predawn attack. At nearby Bse Addeville, Father Sampson heard the friendly barrage creep closer. He got his wounded out of the cots and pallets and placed them on the floor near the wall. Then he led them in prayers.

In seconds, the shellfire rained on Bse Addeville, a wrecked village, where only the American aid station remained intact. Sampson worried about the effect on the two men in the next room; they were near death, and he had set them apart to lessen the strain on the others.

And it worked out in the end. One shell hit the building. There was a great flash, flame and rocking. Sampson was knocked flat. But the round had exploded in the next room. The priest groped his way through the dust and acrid smoke. He tore at the wrecked beams and rubble. The head and shoulders of one man came clear. He gasped "Father" and died. The second man was already dead.

28

Call It Hell's Corners

Johnson's grievance with his subordinate, and the mounting anger which clouded his judgment, came of his feeling that Ballard was not engaged in a real fight.

It did him no credit that he accorded Ballard so little. But Ballard had neither time nor disposition to feed him a blow-by-blow account, and Johnson was hardly unique among senior officers in doubting that the heat on anyone else compared with the fires which blazed around him.

This tendency in combat to imagine one's self at dead center of the pressure circle, which paradoxically comes of the ego but never inflates it, is intensified by isolation. Being a dramatic type, Johnson had to release his feelings about the desperation in the unfolding play.

By the second morning, he no longer spoke of the lock. He said to his few people, "Hereafter we will speak of this position as Hell's Corners." Though things were a bit wet for that, the others had the word.

A first check of his ammunition supply made him feel no better. There were no orange panels on hand to attract a re-supply plane, so he put out orange smoke. Soon after dawn, an American bomber laid its eggs on Carentan, flew straight on toward Johnson's lines strafing, and at the last moment veered. One hour later an Air Corps resupply mission came

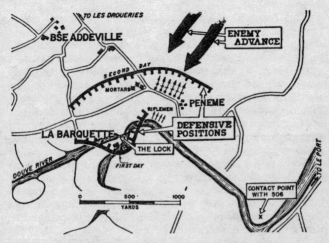

Figure 24. ACTION AT HELL'S CORNERS

over and dropped all its bundles in the marsh almost a mile away. It was good-by to all of that.

Hell's Corners sizzled hotter as the morning wore on. From Carentan the 88s resumed their whiz-bang pounding; they drew no blood but made nerves jumpy. The snipers, who had faded back during the night, crowded close again. The Americans quit walking upright and either crawled or sprinted from position to position. But it was clever sharpshooting, and ten of Johnson's men were taken out by bullets. At high noon American planes bombed Shettle's ground at Le Port. Johnson saw the bombs fall, guessed that Shettle was taking it on the chin, and yelled, "Get out more orange smoke!" They did it just in time. The planes came on straight toward the lock, saw the signal and pulled off.

In late afternoon, Johnson saw a body of troops advancing in line straight toward him through the marsh. Still expecting Ballard, he raised his glasses and looked. But it didn't help. He said to the others, "By God, I can't tell if they are friend or enemy. The uniforms blend perfectly with the water and grass. The rest of you take a look." They did, and were equally mystified.

This observed approach continued for an hour. Johnson passed the word to his officers: "Have every man go flat and stay under cover. Nobody fires until I give the order." Already, he was reversing his position, just in case it wasn't Ballard's force. Six of the eight machine guns were shifted to the northeast corner and grouped in one strongpoint. Most of the men were faced about and sent that way. They went crawling, dragging the weapons. The mortars were already set in deep pits at exact center of the perimeter. It took 40 minutes to shift the strength, owing to the care taken, and at the end of that time Johnson knew what he was up against.

Some of the moving men came out of the water and onto a flat field near the lane over which Johnson had walked to the lock. It was a German battalion, seemingly bent on a straight march to the river. They walked about so unconcernedly as to make it obvious that they didn't know a hostile blocking force was squarely across their path.

The word passed from man to man: "They're krauts." Oddly enough, the news relaxed them. While they had waited silently amid the prolonged doubt, nerves grew more taut. Now that they knew, the tension eased off. Men whispered and smiled again, if a little grimly.

Johnson sent the word up the line: "We will use one machine gun to signal the start of action. I'll say when. When the gun fires, everybody joins in." Still prone, he posted himself on the left flank of the advanced position, next the signal gun, and waited.

Their targets came on slowly, laboriously. The enemy waves seemed to ripple as they struggled through the last stretches of the marsh, stumbling over hummocks, slipping, sliding, wading the canals which laced the badlands and winding in and out of the hedgerows. As the Germans zigzagged to take advantage of the few patches of firm ground, they became more bunched. But they put out no point or advance guard, and the Americans could see no flankers.

Then about 800 yards out, a patrol detached itself from the main body and swung out wide to the left. Johnson at once launched a counter patrol of five men, telling them, "Get those men before they come even with our lines." But because the Johnson patrol had to go out crawling, lest it be seen, it was slow business, and long before the patrols could come to grips, the engagement was in full swing, which canceled both missions.

By 1600, the forward groups of Germans were within 350 yards of the machine guns, coming on, heads up. That was the interval Johnson wanted. He was measuring the delicate balance within a clearly defined tactical problem. The Germans should be brought close enough that the first volleys could sweep them with a killing fire. But they should not be permitted so close that by charging they could overwhelm his force by sheer weight of numbers. Did he err on the side of caution? At 350 yards, mixed machine-gun and rifle fire must have a few fleeting seconds to find the target. It can be done if the enemy is moving over country as flat and bare as a billiard table. That was not the case; every German had ample cover within sliding distance. Too, this was a leg-weary force after its extended struggle in the marsh. It could not have charged.

But he'd settled on 350 yards, and he said to the signal gunner, "OK now, let 'em have it!" Two bullets from the signal gun, and already all hands were blazing away. Major Allen, who from a spot near the CP was directing the fire, was delighted by the speed and volume of the response. Then he turned to look at the enemy line. He saw Germans fall, or rather, go down, and he cried aloud, "Hell, at this range I can't tell whether we are hitting them or they are diving for cover." While he gazed, the force disappeared by magic. Within a few seconds, not one German was to be seen. The hedges, canal banks and hummocks had swallowed them. Maybe a few of the enemy were out there bleeding, but clearly the deadfall had missed the quarry.

Making the most of its reprieve, the flattened battalion poured small-arms fire into Hell's Corners. Seeing a red rocket rise from the marsh edge, the Americans wondered what it meant. Soon they knew. The enemy mortars at St. Côme-du-Mont and the 88s in Carentan resumed their pounding of the ground around the lock.

Johnson's men kept pumping their weapons. Being unable to see any sign of the enemy, he, Allen and the other leaders couldn't know whether any of the bullet fire was hitting flesh. So after 30 minutes of the unremitting fire fight, Johnson worried that he would run out of ammunition. He called out to his men, "Slow down! Take it easy!" But the words were gone with the wind. Brought to white heat, his men paid no attention. However, some weapons seemed to be paying off. The mortars were plunking their rounds in, and the explosions raised a screaming in the marsh. Staff Sergeant Lester A. Patty, a wire man turned rifle grenadier, was working his weapon from well out front and doing it expertly. Between rounds he listened. Occasionally he heard weak cries of *"Kamerad! Kamerad!"* in the distance, and he carried the word to Johnson.

Johnson said to a group of his soldiers, "Maybe we can work out a surrender by the whole force."

One of them answered, "To hell with that, Colonel, we intend to kill these bastards to the last man."

The others chorused assent.

Johnson shook them off, saying, "And what if the ammunition doesn't last?"

He called then for a couple of volunteers to accompany him, one to carry a flag and the other to interpret. Private Leo F. Runge and Technician William F. Lenz stepped out. Johnson told his officers to pass along the order: "Everybody cease fire."

Then he walked toward the German lines, Runge beside him with an orange flag lofted on his rifle. The enemy fire stopped at once except for the shelling from the distant towns. But as the party walked on, rifle fire persisted from Johnson's own lines. So he stopped, switched the flag from the rifle to a tall pole and himself carried it onward. Still, the rifle fire from behind increased.

Johnson asked Runge, "Are they trigger-happy, or do you suppose they didn't get the order?"

The private simply smiled back.

Johnson said to Lenz, "If this keeps up, the Germans will fire on us."

The technician smiled, also.

That put it up to the colonel. Because of the perfect calm of these enlisted men, he knew that he had to keep going.

They made about 100 yards before the fire ceased. A few Germans arose and moved toward them. While the cease-fire lasted, they advanced another 30 or so yards. Then in an instant, the Germans who were coming forward went flat, and small-arms fire broke out all along the enemy line. Runge was knocked down by a bullet in the arm; Johnson was hit in the hand. They were flat now. The people at Hell's Corners were again blasting away. Under this canopy of bullets from two directions the three men crawled back to their own lines. From first to last, Runge and Lenz hadn't spoken a word.

The fight flared another half hour. Then the Germans broke off fire quite abruptly. The lull encouraged Johnson to make another try. He disliked asking Runge and Lenz to take the risk a second time, but they had proved to be such steady hands that he wanted their company. To his surprise, they were quite willing.

The front quieted. Getting 150 yards out, they saw two Germans coming to them, and so they waited. The enemy pair were privates, one shot in the groin, the other in the arm. After talking with them, Lenz said, "Most of the enlisted men want to surrender, but the officers and some of the NCOs won't have it. Several of the men have already been shot for crying *'Kamerad.'*"

Johnson told Runge, "Go back to the farmhouses (by the lock) and get a white tablecloth or sheet." In a few minutes, Runge was back with a fabric that would pass for white.

Then speaking through Lenz to the German with the lesser wound, Johnson said, "You are to go back and tell your commander he has thirty minutes to make up his mind. If he decides to surrender, he must ground all weapons and helmets. The men will form in single file, hands behind their heads, and move into us behind their leader, who will carry the tablecloth aloft. On filing into our lines, your wounded will get prompt attention. If this is not done, our superior force will annihilate you utterly to the last man."

Though the close-off may sound a bit stuffy, besides redundant, those are the exact words and they got the work done.

Johnson and his friends returned to Hell's Corners, supporting the German who was hit where it hurts worst. Firing resumed from both fronts. After about 20 minutes the enemy action tapered off. Among his men Johnson passed around news of the parley and ultimatum, with the cautioning order, "If you see Germans stand up, under no circumstances fire."

One eye on his watch, the other on the enemy ground, he looked, sweated and waited. At exactly 30 minutes, he saw a few men arise in the distance, then a few more.

From right behind him came a rifle shot. He whipped around. Lieutenant Owens stood there, finger on trigger. Johnson kicked him in the tail so hard that he went flat.

"God damn it!" he yelled. "What are you doing?"

"God damn it, Colonel," Owens blubbered, "those bastards have been killing my men all day, and now you won't let me shoot them."

For this otherwise stout fellow, it was breaking point; face in hands, he sobbed like a stricken child.

Said Johnson, "You get your ass in the CP, and you stay there the rest of the day."

The bullet had gone wild, and the enemy paid no heed. Their last walk as soldiers—only one small group came in at first—ended at Hell's Corners at 1800. The procession went on for hours, some of the foot draggers not quitting the marsh till dusk. By that time Johnson had bagged the bulk of 1st Battalion, 6th German Parachute Regiment.

Midway in the movement arrived the commander who, Nazi to the core, refused to organize it, but still chickened out, while pretending otherwise. This light colonel said to Johnson, "I am not a prisoner. You will not search me or strip me of weapons. I have a right to parley under the Geneva Convention. Then I will decide whether I wish to surrender." Johnson didn't bother to answer him, but turned to his own adjutant, Captain Altus F. McReynolds, and said, "Just treat this commander the way you've been handling his boys."

The full bag was 350 prisoners. About 150 more Germans had been killed or badly wounded during the fighting in the marsh. A relative few made their escape to Carentan.

Johnson's losses through the afternoon fight were 10 killed and 33 wounded. Though the comparison looked good in the box score, the day was not yet over.

Preparatory to moving the prisoners into some nearby farm buildings for guarding, they were formed on a road by the CP while McReynolds made a double-check for concealed weapons.

They had one at great distance. Another 88 round came in and exploded right into the pack, killing McReynolds and 20 prisoners and wounding a dozen more. The survivors whimpered and cried.

Lenz said, "They are begging us to send up a white rocket."

Johnson replied, "We don't dare do that; we don't know what it means."

Then he called to the guards, "If any man tries to break from this column, shoot him."

Another round hit the CP tent, missing Major Allen narrowly but wounding Major Carrel, the surgeon, in the knee. Carrel patched himself up and continued his work with the other casualties.

Patrols were sent from Hell's Corners to search the marsh for more Germans. They found many—the majority immobilized by their wounds. When they were littered in, the work load fell wholly on Carrel. The German battalion had come through the marsh without doctors, aid men, or medical supplies. Quickly, Carrel ran out of bandages. The Americans improvised some from their undershirts and scrounged sheets and other linens from the nearby farms. Sulfa and blood plasma ran low and were conserved for the truly desperate cases.

Late in the evening Johnson talked on radio to Kinnard and heard for the first time that higher headquarters had countermanded his order to Ballard to march to him. Johnson had great visions of moving up the canal and blowing up the Douve bridges, provided reinforcement came. But that hope died when he knew Ballard wasn't coming. It was too lofty an ambition in any case; his force was worn small, and besides, whether the Douve bridges should be blown up was a delicate question.

Kinnard promised him that his critical need of ammunition, medicine, water and food would be quickly relieved. The force stayed on at Hell's Corners through the next day, and with the heat going off and the supplies coming in, Johnson felt much better. In fact, it might have been Happy Hour for the Squire of Hell's Corners but for his bitter reflections about Ballard. On that subject he continued to brood, and when cooler heads told him that he was dead wrong, it didn't change his mind a bit.

29

The Snafu Engagement

When dark closed down on Les Droueries the second night, Ballard & Battalion still swam in a sea of Germans.

No less likely experience than theirs may occur in war. For two days they had hammered away at a minor, well-positioned enemy force. Americans and Germans had fought to a finish for a patch of indecisive ground. At the end, the enemy was annihilated and Ballard's people were reeling from exhaustion. There would have been no knockout blow, however, but for that little freedom of movement which enabled Ballard to bring up the reinforcement of armor.

Yet throughout this time, and into the second night, much larger enemy groups than either side which contested possession of the farm were all around Ballard, close enough to bowl him over after one stride. A rip tide of retreating German units, any of which might quickly have changed the balance at Les Droueries, slogged past the farm, westward bound. Not one paid any attention to the small bickering.

The force of marsh birds trapped at Hell's Corners was only one such threat that waned. Other battalions, flushed southward by the advance of Colonel Sink's column, marched head down on St. Côme-du-Mont, right past Ballard's flank, while the fight crackled, without pausing to give the farm a passing glance. Seeing them go by, Ballard's people on the right shivered. But always the Germans plodded on. These were tactical

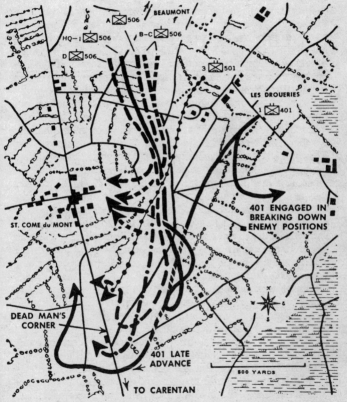

Figure 25. ATTACK ON ST. CÔME-DU-MONT

forces, armed, parachute infantry, artillery and many odd-
ments. Yet they did nothing.

Their lemminglike behavior was one of the enigmas of the
situation. Demoralization, apathy and sometimes panic are familiar features of retreat. But more than that was involved here.
Soldiers formed and under command were deliberately ignoring
the sound of the guns, leaving friends to a fate they need not
have suffered. With some exceptions, the Hitler Germans engaged by the Ridgway-Taylor troops did not perform with that
ruggedness which is expected of disciplined forces. To march
on, not even sending a patrol to see whether timely intervention
might help a comrade, was incredible, discreditable.

Some of the disarrangement—the numbness to tactical opportunity—may be laid to the planned disruption of their communications. But not all. As damaged as were their channels,
the Germans were still better linked than the Americans. The
82nd and 101st started literally with no communications, owing
to the loss of most of the radios and the malfunctioning of
those few that were recovered. After two days, the contact
between groups separated by any distance continued to be feeble and intermittent. Even so, while every hour brought
greater cohesion to the Americans, the rate of disintegration in the
German tactical forces accelerated far more rapidly. German
losses in the early hours cannot account for these contrasting
effects; they were trifling. Therefore, shock from massive surprise must have been the genesis of collapse. It put the Germans
within the airhead in an emotional spin from which they could
not recover. The enemy was temporarily victim of an acute
terror which numbed response. There is no other way to explain
the survival of Ballard & Battalion.

When Sink's column from Beaumont got down to Les
Droueries long after midnight, it deployed in a line outward
from Ballard's right. But the battalion which had won this
ground was hardly more than a mark to guide by as the other
forces moved to the starting gate. Sink, at Beaumont, had
already scratched this entry. Ballard, too, was convinced that
his men were used up and must have a respite. But in the
circumstances, this was a choice between Tweedle and Deedle.
Ballard and his people knew the ground; moreover, they profited by a few winks that night while the upcoming forces were
shagging themselves into a torpor. None toed the mark in con-

dition to think clearly, and when energy is that far gone, there is no leg push either.

Having come in over Utah Beach that morning, 1st Battalion, 401st Glider Infantry was still toiling on the road to Beaumont. It was due to arrive at the front sometime after 0400, move through Ballard's sector, jump off at once and, staying well to the left of St. Côme-du-Mont, attack to the Carentan causeway and blow up its bridges.

It came on slowly and arrived late, after the whistle blew. That belated start was nigh symbolic and appropriate to the mission. By now the whole division command was sweating out the defensive task which Johnson could not complete because of the enemy strength deployed around the approaches to Carentan. But this was protection covering an escape route rather than a shield over a sally port to counterattack. The momentum of the German pullout to the westward might have suggested that there was no longer need to blow up the Douve bridges.

Next in line, to the right of the sector held by Ballard's force, the shrunken 3rd Battalion, 501st, under Colonel Ewell, would jump off. That outfit, too, was long on the road and arrived just in time to spread over its 400-yard sector before getting the word "Go!" Ewell had been instructed to attack straight through and get his troops astride the main highway below St. Côme-du-Mont.

The two battalions of 506th on the right wing were to move by the shortest line and capture the town. Sink put his weight there, figuring (correctly) that most of the Germans would be in or around the houses, even though, by the grace of God, one of his units had breezed past the village without attracting any real fire. The physical state of this right wing was near nadir. Of the two assault companies, Able and Dog, the latter had spent nearly 24 hours and most of its energy in futile marching. After probing almost to the Carentan causeway, it had been recalled to Angoville-au-Plain. Then it doubled back to Beaumont to join the advance and finally arrived abreast of Les Droueries just in time to deploy and grind forward.

Because of all this traveling, it had missed connections with Sink at Beaumont; then it came into line facing St. Côme-du-Mont too late to hear about the battle order or receive instructions about its own mission.

In the absence of orders, the men huddled together, and on their own came to the most natural and comforting of decisions —they would strike for the same road intersection where they had been the evening before. Since Ewell, who had just come up in the next sector, was pointed on the same object, a traffic snarl was already in the making.

In this way, the hammer aimed at St. Côme-du-Mont took shape as a patched-up wooden mallet with the glue still sticky. Its parts stumbled in and formed a battle line at the last minute, facing ground which they had never seen in daylight. They were dull-eyed, bodily worn and too tired to think connectedly. Even a 30-minute flop on the turf with the stars for a blanket would have doubled the power of this body and quickened the minds of its leaders to ideas on which they had blanked out. But no one thought to take that precaution. The United States Army is indifferent toward common-sense rules by which the energy of men may be conserved in combat. These men had too little time to find their positions and check their weapons. Said Captain Patch of his people on the far right, "They were so beat that they could not understand words even if an order was clearly expressed. I was too tired to talk straight. Nothing I heard made a firm impression on me. I spoke jerkily in phrases because I could not remember the thoughts which had preceded what I said."

Yet compared with the infantry *pêle-mêle* in this befogged array, the artillery preparations were almost ostentatious. The guns had registered on 15 targets around St. Côme-du-Mont and Les Droueries somewhere around midnight. Suspected strongpoints and road intersections would be initial targets for the opening fires in the morning. Then the shellfire would pull back toward Sink's infantry line, blast the foreground for a time and move forward again in a rolling curtain ahead of the assaulting battalions. The barraging of the foreground would hold ten minutes to afford time for the infantry line to close toward the fires. Thereafter the shell curtain would jump forward 100 yards every four minutes.

So the gunners had an elaborate design and a clear-cut order, though not on paper. In this, they were somewhat better off than the infantry, which had nothing in writing, and nothing by word of mouth which transcended the chance of confusion. Sink's orders at Beaumont were all given orally and off the cuff. The Bold Cavalier was not at his best that night. He was too rushed, too bushed by the exertions of the day, to write a plan and double-check its detail. In Sink's hand, the pen at best never fitted like the sword. Dumas and Fenimore Cooper collaborating might have shaped just such a character. Nature fashioned him to fight people, not paper. No American soldier of his time has more flair than this drawling, brawling North Carolinian. His way with a regiment is to say, "Come on, gang, there lay the hostiles, let's have at 'em," and the troops love it. The best measure of their affection toward him was that the 506th called itself the Five-O-Sinks. As for his close comrades, one of their precious memories from war is Old Bob, rolling his eyes, and singing, "Beautiful Dreamer."

But as he wearily tried to square away toward St. Côme, Sink had too little time for full co-ordination, even if the command had been bright-eyed and bushy-tailed. As it was, the command was midway between somnambulism and catalepsy, and Sink wasn't far behind. He told the battalion leaders their separate objects in the attack—that he did all right. But since the orders were given verbally, he failed to define for the battalions the boundaries within which each would cover the ground to the assigned target. In the face of such an omission, the Normandy landscape becomes a tactical trap, because of that first law of nature which forces a soldier to walk in the lee of a line of sumac twigs rather than advance totally shorn of cover into enemy fire.

First light broke, and the softening-up heavy fire—high explosive mixed with white phosphorus—crashed on St. Côme-du-Mont and its outworks. To the watching infantry (most of whom were seeing their first barrage) it looked powerful and accurate enough to crush resistance.

At 0445 the rolling barrage started. Ten minutes later some of the troops arose and moved forward uncertainly along the hedge banks and ditches. But the rolling forward of the shells did not synchronize with the pace of men. At first, the artillery lingered too long. Some of the infantry groups had to pause to avoid running into their own fire. The stop made it harder to start again. Then before there could be any adjustment, the shellfire lifted, bounced forward a couple of times and disappeared into the distance. The infantry fractions farthest forward were still stalled. The artillery lost them before it could uplift them. At 0500 the Germans threw up a heavy smoke screen north of St. Côme-du-Mont. Sink guessed that it was intended to cover the withdrawal of outposts before they could be steam-rollered, and he felt good about it.

But by that time, his attack was already twisted far out of control, though he did not know it. On the extreme right flank, some 506th men didn't get the attack order, and so held their ground. In the other sectors, there was so little fire from the hedgerows in the foreground that, all other things being equal, the attack should have proceeded straight forward with the line in balance, as Sink had envisaged it. But because things were not equal, the whole attack careened toward the left in an oblique shift which at first slowed movement and later stalled it wholly. This contortion came of several factors which together made it an inevitable and natural drift.

Ewell's battalion in the center joined its neighbor on the right at the Beaumont-Carentan road which bypassed St. Côme-du-Mont to the east. Several fields, bordered by stoutly banked hedges, lay between this road and the town. The road itself was partly sunken, and its off-shoulder banks were immensely thick and higher than a man's head. So here was a relatively shellproof alley by which the attacking infantry could, with impunity, draw even with the town.

Patch, who led the battalion, was in an aberration, in doubt of his objective as of the route to it. When he saw his men bend automatically toward the protected road on the left, he went with them, unprotesting. In the absence of clear orders from Patch, their deviation to the most promising avenue in sight was instinctive. Dog Company had traveled this same road the evening before and, not having been given a target or boundary, was pulled as by a magnet to the familiar path. The take-off by Dog Company—beelined to the covered road—increased the pull on Patch and Able Company.

Once again, Dog Company marched straight for Dead Man's Corner, unbrushed by bullets as it breezed along. A clear track, but the wrong destination! By 0700, its left flank rested on the intersection—Ewell's objective—some minutes before any part of Ewell's force entered upon the same road. Thereafter, Dog Company moved a little way north along the road to St. Côme-du-Mont, then stopped, not because the shot was falling full and fast, but because it felt lonely. Finding a suitable hill south of the town, it sat down like Ferdinand to smell the sweet flowers and await whatever came. The enemy didn't, nor did friends. Both sides were stewing in their own juice.

The involvement of Ewell & Battalion in this off-season Maypole dance was involuntary. The effect of the cross buck by the 506th companies was, first, to mask his own field of fire, then to pinch his battalion toward the covered road, since it was impossible for the whole line to give way to the left. The glider battalion, which had arrived in Ballard's sector and was coming through, couldn't displace into the swamp, and its front was already drawing fire from German positions in the subridges southeast of Les Droueries. So Ewell had no choice about where to go. By weight of numbers, his battalion was gradually shoehorned into the covered road leading directly to its objective—the crossroads already taken by Dog Company.

Briefly, at the start, Ewell went unsqueezed because his line was deployed to the left of the road. That was fortunate. During the night a company of German paratroops had crept upon Les Droueries and dropped into a line of foxholes extending west from Ballard's perimeter. So doing, they fastened their own noose. Through the convergence on the covered road by Patch's companies from the right wing, they were blocked across their rear before they could be smitten from Ewell's front, and if they had intended to back away, it was already too late. Ewell's advance came on more gradually because it was well controlled. The battalion advanced with companies in line, each company with its platoons in column, because this was the best way to use the hedge bank cover. The rolling barrage covered the attack until it had passed the main buildings of Les Droueries. It also shook the krauts from their ground holes and drove them to the hedgerows. Ewell's men lost the cover of the barrage when the first fire from these scattered skirmishers came against them. It was wild on-the-run shooting, but at least it threw them off stride. With no place to go, the Germans still backed away, dropping behind a bank just long enough to get off a few rounds. In the circumstances, volley firing was useless, and the dissolution of one force disjointed the other. Ewell's people darted through the fields as individuals, zigging, then zagging, as they hunted down Germans. The shootings occurred at ranges running from 50 yards down to one foot. Without closing to bayonet point, Ewell's troops killed approximately 50 Germans while still in the shadow of Les Droueries. None of this foolhardy group got away. With it died the last German attempt to retake ground east of the Douve River.

But it was right after the battalion mopped up and squared away again that the complications arose. On its left, 1st Battalion of the 401st (an attachment of the 327th Glider Infantry), after marching through Ballard's sector, was getting its nose bloodied by Germans fighting back from prepared positions outside Bse Addeville. That unexpected pressure drove its right flank wide till it trespassed on Ewell's sector, thereby pressing his men toward the sunken road.

They had become scrambled during the brief melee in the fields. So he had to stop at the crossroads beyond Les Droueries to get them sorted out again. Just then, the right flank of the 401st bumped him from the left and, simultaneously, the troops of 506th, pouring into the road, compressed him on the right.

Up the road some distance, he could see some of his own men. But such was the traffic jam that he knew he could not recall them. The question was whether he could prevent his whole battalion from being pinched out.

Calling a halt, he walked over and said to Captain Howell, "You know, there isn't room on this one cowtrack for the whole damned Army. I think you better call higher authority and get the mess straightened out." In battle, Ewell always talks like a country bumpkin, a trait which endears him to all within earshot.

Howell called Sink and tried to explain a snafu which by then was already incomprehensible to its most ingenious participant. The opportunity for a fresh start by which the troops that had set out on the right flank might be repointed toward St. Côme-du-Mont via the shortest line was already lost. To reassort and realign troops amid battle and under fire is the devil's own job even when they know where they should have gone and how they have strayed.

Sink got some glint of the problem, though its parts necessarily eluded him. He said to Howell, "Well, at least get the battalion moved to the right of the road, and there take up a defensive position. That should stop the Germans from attacking out of St. Côme." Aware that the scramble had made him suddenly vulnerable, he also knew that unscrambling would be no easier than if he were handling an omelet.

But the howl from Howell still couldn't bring off a patch by Patch. The battalion couldn't be put together again. Parts of Able Company had followed Dog Company to Dead Man's Corner. Other parts had tried to move through the fields east of the town. At first it was plain sailing. Then as they came even with the outlying houses, German artillery fire found them and they stopped. They had killed a few snipers as they crept forward along the banks and ditches. But once put down by the artillery, and held low for half an hour, they could not get going again. They stayed in the ground east of St. Côme, and when they felt any menace close at hand, they fired rifles or threw grenades. This was their portion for the day.

Baker and Charley Companies of 506th, which had not been in the first wave, became immobilized in much the same manner. East of the town, they engaged in hedgerow fighting with small enemy groups, widely scattered but well dug in. There they stuck, so far dispersed and flattened by fatigue that the effort to collect them died a-borning. The great part of Able Company was strung out along the covered road, content with the fact, and not at all yearning for action.

So when Howell got the order to gather the battalion and block St. Côme on the east, the best he could do was gather some of Headquarters Company, which was sitting in a field on Ewell's side of the road and boot it along. This pint-sized detachment moved right through the ground where the men of Baker and Charley Companies were taking a day-long breather. So doing, it was lured by the peaceful look of the houses on the town's outer fringe, and went for them, thereby oversliding instructions.

Quickly as they entered, the Americans saw two enemy patrols come at them from opposite directions. No hurt was done. But Headquarters Company had no ambition to whip Rommel all alone that day. So it back-pedaled fast. But there stayed one slightly soiled feather in its cap: In a four-battalion attack which should have crushed the target like an anaconda, this detail of clerks, cooks and wire men made the day's only penetration of St. Côme-du-Mont.

Coupled with the lethargy of Sink's forces, the kicking it took from the German guns produced nearly total stagnation. The shells which ranged in on Able Company and kept it planted were not a stray salvo. The enemy artillery stonked the whole place. Captain Jerre S. Gross, who led Dog Company, pitched his CP in a field east of the covered road while his men slogged on to Dead Man's Corner. Major Foster, who led the battalion, leaned on a tree as they conversed. Gross asked, "If we get the town before tonight, do we then go on to the

Douve bridges?" Down came the shellfire. One round hit the tree, struck down Gross with a disabling wound, killed Foster and almost decapitated an unidentified captain of engineers who was listening in. That was the worst hurt to Dog Company during the day—hardly a crippling blow. The German artillery kept coming. It dealt few mortal blows, for the troops had gone to ground. But it was an excuse for not getting up and moving.

Ewell's battalion lost six men to the shellfire, waiting in the open field while he sought guidance from Sink. The order Sink gave Howell helped him little. It cleared some 506th men from his path without markedly increasing the fighting mobility of that regiment. The companies had become so wrapped around one another that unity had dissolved with movement. On Ewell's left, the glider battalion was doing a lot of firing, but getting nowhere. Nobody knew why. It was enough for Ewell that the glidermen were crowding him out. So at 0800, he said to the battalion, "I guess we better hitch up and get on the road to the objective." He didn't know that Dog Company was already sitting at Dead Man's Corner. He assumed that forward lay only enemy country and that the knot tied in 506th meant he would be unsupported on the left and right.

It was his kind of fighting situation—as for that matter, what wasn't? Ewell, then in his twenties, had the dynamism and imagination of a "Billy" Sherman, with the phlegm of his own kinsman, Dick Ewell, minus the petulance. The most accurate thumbnail sketch of him was done by a fellow officer of Normandy days:

> He is not interested in making people better; he expects them to be better. He is tall, has a pronounced drawl, an ironic sense of humor and a standard of appreciation so high that he seems bored with the scramblings of average human beings. Men and officers respect him. His drawling humor is much appreciated. Years later men will repeat his classic lecture on the military message book: "It's a very simple form, gentlemen, the simplest form the Army ever devised. But every dumb son-of-a-bitch always screws it up—and nobody ever keeps a copy."

The messages were not flying this day. Ewell & Battalion elbowed their way to Dead Man's Corner only to realize that they were runner-up. Still, just a handful of Dog Company men were at the intersection, and they didn't know where the rest had gone.

Looking up the road to St. Côme-du-Mont, Ewell saw wagons pulling out to the westward, and skirmishers wending the hedgerows, going the same way. He knew then that the Germans had begun to pull out. Blocking the exit was the logical move, but he figured he had too little power present to do that. So he said to his officers, "We'll get on down the road to the [Carentan] causeway. If we can't keep them from getting out, we may at least block them from surging back."

It was easily said, and the battalion, on starting, bounced right along. Then it ran into heavy fire from the houses around Pont-de-Douve. Two machine guns, one antitank gun "and quite a slew of riflemen" forced a deployment and made Ewell undecided. From Carentan the 88s opened fire on his front. He tried to call for friendly counterfire, but his wire had gone out and the radio wouldn't cut through. Then his radio operator turned toward him. The left side of his face was a red blob. A bullet had taken out his eye. He was gone before Ewell ever learned his name. With that, he made up his mind and ordered the battalion to retrace its steps.

They got back to Dead Man's Corner, started to deploy and right then were hit by Germans streaming down both sides of the St. Côme-du-Mont road in counterattack. The action opened with a crackling of rifles and Schmeissers, the bullets flying well overhead. The sounds grew louder, the aim surer, as the enemy skirmishers advanced via the banks and ditches. Dog Company, idling in a field east of the road, escaped this thrust, which went right past its nose. So did all other forces in the American "assault." The enemy counterattack was aimed exclusively at Ewell. It is easy to see why. Moving first south, then north, the battalion became the main threat to the enemy's planned withdrawal, since the other troops lay dormant.

The fire fight opened at 0930. From then until 1600, Ewell & Battalion knew no quiet. Six attacks were beaten back, each better organized than the one preceding. Every attack closed to within one hedgerow of Ewell's forward line. There the Germans would lose a few men as the Americans loosed weapons against the thorn and the dirt bank. Then the survivors would fade back, only to return with heavier fire power.

As the show opened, Ewell was deploying men on the east

of the road. He was there when the first counterattack hit. That
part of the German force which came through the fields and
orchards west of the road seized a small ridge opposite the
battalion flank.

Ewell said to the others, "That's the key. The hill dominates
the road. Either we get that or we won't hold." When the
counterattack was beaten off, a German detachment stayed atop
the ridge, holding. That lasted five minutes. Ewell put 25 men
across the road, and they stormed the ridge top, killing the
Germans. The seizure of the ridge gave the battalion a north-
south line straddling the road, and anchored on several stone-
walled farm buildings set in apple orchards. For the remaining
hours, the hill position was the pivot of the defense. The Germans kept coming, attacking from three sides. But the battalion
was compactly enough positioned to keep fire concentrated,
and the Germans lost power by spreading too far.

By 1430 came the strongest attack, the enemy at last concentrating main weight against Ewell's right flank. It buckled
under the fire, and the men fell back one hedgerow. Ewell was
then west of the road, standing at the base of the key ridge.
He saw at a glance that the whole position was on the verge
of collapse.

Sprinting to the top of the ridge, he yelled to his men on
the solid flank, "Follow me! Follow me!" Then he turned at a
run, and they followed him down the hill. Together, they closed
on the hedgerow where his men on the right were being pushed
about, and then the whole body swung round the hedge and
charged in on the flank of the German line.

Three American light tanks arrived out of nowhere amid
this crisis. They moved in frontally against the enemy line,
raking the hedges with their machine guns, while Ewell and
his people fired from the flank. The stragglers of Ewell's right
flank fell in as skirmishers, moving with the tanks. A few
Germans got away, leaving their dead and wounded.

It was over by 1500. There was still no sign of support,
apart from the happy intervention by the armor. Ewell knew
that casualties over the general front had been heavy. He had
evacuated 273—mainly men from other units—through his
own aid station that morning. Alone, he walked rearward to
check the situation. While he was gone, came another counterattack, taking the heaviest toll of the day, including the tank

commander, three battalion officers and 20 men. But no ground was yielded.

Ewell found the glider battalion flank just where he had left it that morning. That outfit had perforce committed itself to a day-long go against the enemy positions at Bse Addeville.

Ewell asked Sink, "What about pulling them out, getting them forward and deploying them on my right?" Sink said, "Go ahead." But by the time the glidermen got to Dead Man's Corner, the German withdrawal from St. Côme-du-Mont was already long gone. The German trains and people could be seen in the distance, moving along the railway embankment.

The Germans blew up the Douve bridge at 1400—the bridge which Johnson, Ewell and so many others had been straining to get at—the ultimate proof that the Americans shouldn't have been trying for it. Some aid men, combing the ground for casualties, saw the explosion and reported it.

Ewell got on his pet ridge again. Then the two battalions moved on, but contact with the enemy was not regained. Some of the German regimental trains—40 wagons carrying part of the equipment for a parachute outfit—were captured on the road to La Croix by Able Company of the 506th, which swung around to west of the road when the two battalions advanced. By then, all resistance had ended within St. Côme-du-Mont.

Soon after 1600, 1st Battalion of 506th sent a patrol into the town from the north. Not a shot was fired. The place was empty. On this quiet note ended the great snafu.

Ewell had started the day with 160 men. He lost 41, killed and wounded along the way. Most of them had taken a bullet while plying a weapon from behind a hedgerow.

Their opposition was the 6th German Parachute Regiment. At the same hour that Ewell and the others were moving into St. Côme-du-Mont, Field Marshal Rommel was conferring with three chief subordinates in the near neighborhood. They agreed that "the main factor in the situation is that the enemy . . . has not yet established contact with the Carentan bridgehead."

The 6th Parachute Regiment was ordered "to defend Carentan to the last man." To offset that dolorous directive, the Field Marshal gave the boys a bouquet: "They are fighting better than I expected."

30

Reconnaissance

By dark on 8 June, Taylor's division had completed all missions assigned it in the landing plan and was holding a defensive position along the western and southern limits of the area where it had engaged the enemy during the first three days.

Johnson's 501st Regiment was at Vierville in division reserve. Sink's 506th held a line from Les Quesnils along the River Douve to La Barquette. The 327th extended from the locks to the mouth of the river, and the sector of the 502nd, under Michaelis, ran northward from Les Quesnils.

Late that same day an engineer reconnaissance party toured the front and reported to Taylor that an advance from the north, via the main highway running from St. Côme-du-Mont to Carentan, might be possible. It was a tentative opinion which changed the whole form of operations. Taylor pondered the proposal for some time. It seemed daring to the point of rashness, and another undertaking was already in the works. The division spent 9 June refitting and working on the defensive line. Orders were issued to the 327th Regiment to cross the Douve at 0100 on 10 June and take the high ground around Brevands. Engineers from VII Corps brought forward assault boats along concealed routes during the day.

The trouble with the idea of a power play direct through center to Carentan was that the citadel was covered by a broad stretch of marsh under deep water. The main highway became

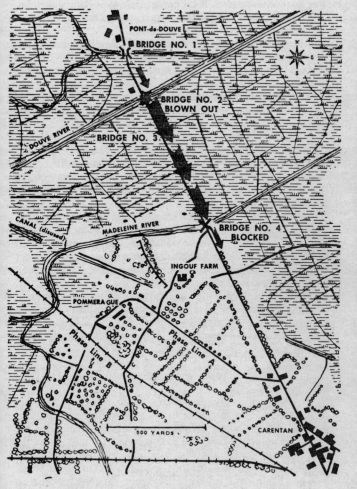

Figure 26. ADVANCE BY COLE'S BATTALION

a causeway running through a lake, and for the last half-mile was a wholly exposed, level defile, devoid of natural or man-made cover. Troops moving across it were as ducks in a shooting gallery.

After the fight at St. Côme-du-Mont, Sink's regiment outposted the eastern abutment of this passage and the first two bridges beyond. On the afternoon of 9 June, Sink went forth to take a look.

The lieutenant commanding the outpost was huddled with his men in the houses at Pont-de-Douve, leaving the bridges unguarded.

Sink asked, "Why?"

The lieutenant said, "That's the way the people we relieved were doing it, and we thought it was good enough for us."

Sink said, "God damn it, they were under fire and fighting krauts on this side of the river. God damn it, you get your men up there right now."

He then went forward with his own recon party—nine men. At first, they heard no sound, saw no sign of the enemy. Beside the second bridge, the shattered span of which was half down in the stream, they found a battered bateau. Using two-by-fours in place of oars, they paddled across the stream, and continued along the bank, still drawing no fire.

Beyond the third bridge at the right of the road there is a 40-yard stretch wholly barren of trees or shrubbery. As they trudged into this clearing, two .30-caliber machine guns, one deep in the marsh to their right, and one planted on the solid ground forward, cut loose on them. They went flat; the fire was high.

"God damn it," yelled Sink, "those are Brownings. They must be Americans."

He threw out an orange smoke grenade. At once, there was an answering orange signal from the bank ahead. The fire quieted. Sink withdrew the patrol, leaving two men on the far side of the wrecked bridge. The two guns were now centering their attention on the gap where the span had been. So heavy was the fire that three of the men opted to swim to the far bank. Sink and the others tried the bateau again. He quickly regretted it. This time the gun upstream had the range and the line. The bateau was riddled, Sink found himself paddling with his arms, while his men beat the water with their two-by-fours; the party barely got out. They ran through the first bridge with the fire still dogging them.

At Pont-de-Douve the lieutenant was gone.

Said one of the men, "He moved out to look for some artillery to counter those machine guns."

Being already sore enough to spit, Sink let it go. He called division and reported, "We put up orange smoke. They raised hell with us. If they're Americans, they need to be shot."

This intelligence was then relayed to 502nd Regiment. But as its substance was entered in the journal by Captain Henry G. Plitt, the operations officer, the message became this: "Sink put out orange smoke and was lightly fired on. The town seems to be lightly held." This was not the impression Sink wished to convey, but on the other hand, his own survey was inconclusive and his account of it was equivocal.

One hour later, Lieutenant Ralph B. Gehauf, intelligence officer of 502nd's 3rd Battalion, flew toward Carentan in an L-4 plane, looking for the best road to the village of La Billionnerie, which was to be the battalion's objective, if it got the green light. The unlikely name of that hamlet is no stranger than the mission. La Billionnerie was on the far side of Carentan. By gaining Hill 30 right beside it, the battalion could block the enemy escape route from the city. The assignment, if it came, therefore premised that the battalion could somehow breeze through or around a citadel not yet taken. There were some reasons for so thinking, though they proved not good enough. In any case, Gehauf, on his sky tour saw nothing to cloud the rosy prospect. If the Germans were in strength around Carentan, his eyes missed them. The G-2 estimate that less than one enemy battalion stood guard therefore held.

Michaelis's headquarters were at La Croix Pans, four miles northeast of the causeway. At 2100 on 9 June, he got the order from Division to attack toward Carentan; so he put the 3rd Battalion, under Colonel Bob Cole, on the road. It should hold to a schedule which would get it to Bridge No. 2—the ruined span—by 0300.

The metaled road from La Croix Pans is quite straight, about 40 feet wide, with a strong dirt shoulder, and has the same solid character where it becomes a causeway crossing the marsh at the confluence of the Douve and Jourdan rivers. The road runs levelly the entire distance, with the crown averaging eight feet above the surface of the water. Both ways from the road, the marsh extends far more than rifle-shot distance. Reeds and marsh grasses are thick amid the water, but stand too low to screen the embankment. In the marsh to the westward, between the causeway and the railroad, are large hummocks of ground solid enough to base machine-gun pits or snipers and give them fair cover. The causeway bank on that side drops sharply to the water's edge. A rifleman may cling to it, but he cannot walk along it without risking a ducking. There is too little dirt to permit troops to dig in. The embankment on the left is wider and less steep. The earth is wide and tight enough to support the cutting of two-man foxholes, though they must remain open to flanking fire. The road proper is naked to fire from any direction. Its drainage ditches are less than six inches deep. Men moving along its surface are as exposed to grazing rifle and machine-gun fire as to artillery bombardment. There is no place to hide.

The four bridges are simple, one-span affairs. The Douve, Jourdan and the canals all run swiftly with drowning depths. All are narrow streams. Only Bridge No. 1 is obscured to fire from the far shore. Past it, the causeway takes a sharp right turn and then runs straight through the other three. On Bridges 2 and 4, the Germans had erected heavy road blocks; iron gates of great weight, and standing higher than a man, had been moored by steel cables to concrete pillars four feet thick. The blowing up of Bridge No. 2 had knocked out one block; but on No. 4 the barrier remained, imposingly solid. The stunted poplars along the roadway were hardly leafed at all, and the trunks were too thin to shield a man. The broken span remained down, and the gap would have to be closed before Cole's infantry could cross.

Such were the risks that awaited, once the whistle had blown. With only 30 minutes of light remaining, at 2130 on 9 June, Captain Henry G. Plitt, the regimental operations officer, flew from Houesville in a Piper Cub to look for a feasible alternative. He followed the railroad line until he found a water gap where a 20-yard section of the right of way had been blown out clean. So he knew that was no go. Then he flew low, back and forth across Carentan. Not one bullet or shell reached up for the Piper. So he returned and reported that the advance would have to be via the causeway and that "Carentan has been evacuated." Third Battalion was already on the march when he landed; it never got the news that it would be unopposed.

Gehauf, worried about his own optimism, and not trusting the intelligence gained from his air trip, was already off on a road reconnaissance. The night was fair, and a thin mist partly obscured the full moon. With Gehauf were ten men, under Sergeant Robert P. O'Reilly. They were armed with pistols and rifles, and they marched well ahead of the battalion.

On the basis of Plitt's report, with its forecast of unopposed entry, Michaelis decided to put the whole regiment forward. The other two battalions got on the road after Cole and finally arrived at St. Côme-du-Mont by 0530, ready to barrel along if ordered.

All of these great expectations were based less on the hope that the Germans had fled than on a reasonably solid faith that if they stood their ground in large numbers and fought like wildcats, other Americans would bear the brunt of victory at Carentan.

According to plan, the 327th Regiment was to leap the Douve near Brevands at 0145, advance on Carentan and capture it forthwith. Also, the spearhead of 29th Division, coming from Omaha Beach, was due to arrive in the neighborhood at about the same time, and would probably lend a hand. But nothing turned out as it should. The 327th was clobbered by friendly mortar fire at the river crossing and took heavy losses. On drawing to within 600 yards of the city, it was beaten to ground by the enemy's 88-millimeter batteries and got no farther. As for the 29th, no one from Omaha arrived in time to help Cole and his friends one bit.

Gehauf and his patrol reached the wrecked bridge at 0130. They found bridge beams, ropes and other matériel piled high on the bank; but not one engineer was at work. The party from the 326th Engineer Battalion had taken cover behind the embankment.

Gehauf snorted in disgust when the engineer sergeant told him, "We had to quit; the 88s have found our range." He saw no dead or wounded lying about and heard no sounds of fire. But when he started to put his men across the stream, three at a time, using a small boat, the big guns opened fire, and eight rounds broke around them before they were reunited on the far side.

They proceeded single file, five men on each side of the road, through the third bridge to Bridge No. 4, where the iron gate stopped them. By budging one end of it about 15 inches, they barely wiggled through, one man at a time, with Privates James Roach and James R. Pace leading.

Fifty yards beyond the gate, Gehauf overtook Roach, saying, "We better hold it and let the battalion catch up. I don't know what we're walking into."

Roach said, "It sounds like you're scared, too."

Just then, a mortar shell landed five yards from them but spent its force in the embankment dirt. As they went flat, flares from all around made the night incandescent. Timed to the signal, mortar batteries and machine guns from their front and right showered metal their way. They saw the muzzle flashes of two machine guns on the road shoulders 50 yards ahead. O'Reilly counted seven machine guns firing from the high ground beyond. Gehauf counted five more in the marsh on their right.

Pace fired one burst from his Tommy gun. O'Reilly yelled to him, "Stop it, you damned fool, they're just guessing where we are." He reasoned it so because the party had been flat when the flares went off.

Gehauf talked things over with O'Reilly. They agreed that the party should risk holding for a few minutes to see if it could get a better line on the enemy gun positions.

Gehauf said to Private Willis N. Nichols, "Get back and tell the lead company that it must get its mortars forward to deal with these machine guns."

Nichols said, "I'd like to have company."

So Private Roy F. Hilton went along with him. They slipped through the gate at Bridge No. 4 while machine-gun bullets bounced off the metal. At Bridge No. 2, they found their small boat under water. But they bailed it out, and Hilton plugged the hole with his backside while Nichols paddled across.

On the far side, Nichols met Colonel Cole and said to him, "Lieutenant Gehauf says don't bring the battalion through because the fire is much too heavy." There is no explanation of why this runner almost exactly reversed what Gehauf had told him, except that out of excitement he forgot. Hilton listened but did not correct him; his fear, for the moment, made accuracy of statement unimportant. Under extreme stress in battle this is a not abnormal reaction. Nichols was a brave man and better-than-average trooper. But because Army training has ever put too little emphasis on the imperative of absolute accuracy in oral communications, reiterating it daily from the hour when the recruit gets his first lesson, errors of this kind are a prevalent cause of operational miscarriage.

Nichols did no damage. The engineer failure at Bridge No. 2 spared him. Fed up and frustrated, testy Bob Cole had already called Michaelis on radio, and the regiment had advised Division that the attack could not go. The canceling order came in at 0400. Cole's battalion slogged back to Les Quesnils and slept for two hours in an open field. Trucks had been promised for the withdrawal. But the convoy failed to show up.

That immaculate soldier, Gehauf, wasn't advised that the battalion was pulling out. His shrunken patrol, hammered from front and right, clung to the causeway embankment beyond Bridge No. 4, flattened out, but persisting in its task of observing and fixing the German fire positions. There is no more shining example than this of Americans doing their duty without limit.

But the light was coming, and Gehauf knew that he could not hold much longer without sacrificing the patrol. The men talked it over. O'Reilly said, "If we don't get out, then all we've learned is for nothing." At 0500, Gehauf sent Private Allen W. Bryant back to ask what Cole intended. He carried with him a carefully drawn sketch, the work of Gehauf and O'Reilly, showing the probable location of enemy fire positions, which document, in the circumstances, was beyond price.

In the interim, Private Roach, on his own initiative, crawled to Bridge No. 4, examined the understructure, found it wired for demolition, cut the wires away, and took them back to Gehauf for a souvenir.

Finding the battalion gone, Bryant returned to Gehauf, but he did it in the grand manner, standing erect and walking right down the middle of the road in broad daylight. It was sheer bravado, but the effect on Gehauf and the others was as a good Martini on an empty stomach. O'Reilly hugged him and said, "You funny son-of-a-bitch." Then they took off.

The small boat at Bridge No. 2 was now so full of holes that it couldn't be floated. O'Reilly swam across and shunted a 3-by-12 bridge spar across the gap. The others danced over on this catwalk. They got back to the battalion at Les Quesnils without drawing one round of enemy fire on the way. Cole belatedly remembered and was just dispatching an officer to bring them in. No one had time to say, "Well done."

31

Approach

Cole got word at 0930 that the battalion would go again sometime in the afternoon. This time, said Division, it would be supported by a "substantial" artillery.

The adjective scarcely fitted. The 377th Field Artillery had lost all but one of its 75-millimeter tubes in the drop and was by this time thrice-armed only because it had captured two German guns. (One of them blew up in this action, killing a captain and several other hands.) The 90th Battalion, a glider outfit, had 12 pack howitzer 75s. Then there was the 65th Armored Field Artillery Battalion with 18 self-propelled 105s. Putting them all together, they hardly composed one good Sunday punch.

These batteries were near St. Côme-du-Mont on high ground which promisingly dominated the Carentan marshland. Most of the shellfire, conforming to the pattern on Gehauf's sketch map, would be delivered against the Germans left in and around Pommenauge, south of the fourth bridge. The place is deserving of some regard. It is spelled "Pommeranque" on the military maps, which has led to the misnaming of one of the bloodiest small affairs in our fighting history.

By high noon, having checked the ammunition and digested Gehauf's target data, the gunners said they were ready. Cole and Gehauf went back to the causeway to see if the road was once more solid.

Figure 27. THE CARENTAN CAUSEWAY

The engineers had done nothing. Cole grabbed hold of a rope and said to Captain Robert L. Clements, "Use two of your enlisted people and move that planking up to me." He wanted no more than that lest a bustle of activity draw fire from around the Pommenauge farms.

Working together, the colonel, captain and two privates jury-rigged a rude footbridge. In two hours, it was complete, though wobbly. The heavy fence of iron, which the Germans had used for a block, had been torn loose and was used as a flooring, supported by wooden beams. At 1500, Gehauf and Private Bryant crossed Bridge No. 2 ahead of George Company's 1st Platoon. Bryant yelled back, "This will work, if we're careful." Still, the men had to cross single file. The structure was too uncertain for more than that, and besides, if any thicker target was offered, an 88 round whiz-banged toward the bridge from somewhere around Carentan. So they had to remain thinned after they had passed the water.

That was how Cole's battalion was fed onto the causeway, bound on both sides by the marshes and insecure in its rear; one shell would have demolished its line of retreat. The intermittent sniping by the 88, which had flushed the engineers the night before, harassed the infantrymen, but could not stampede them because the bridge stayed loaded with upcoming men, jockeyed forward by Cole. Gehauf watched it, marveling that they were getting away with it. He was choked by a terrible fear, not for himself, but for the battalion. He knew that the boom would be lowered and that it would drop hard. But he kept that to himself. Of his own choice, he would have stopped the operation, being convinced that there was some better way to do it. But Cole had been so preoccupied with other details that they had talked hardly two minutes about the situation.

Off to the right of Bridge No. 2, a hummock of solid ground, fronted by a hedgerow, jutted from the marsh. From there, a sniper threw a burst of bullets at Clements's mortar squad, all wide of the mark. A narrow ridge of solid earth, thick with grass, ran toward the hedge from the causeway. Private Claude A. Williams wiggled out on his belly until he got close enough to heave a grenade over the hedge. It exploded, Williams waited, but nothing happened. Staff Sergeant A. L. Zeroski came crawling behind Williams. Like a jack-in-the-box, a German popped up from behind the hedge. Williams arched another grenade, and Zeroski fired his carbine three times. They heard a horrible scream as the German toppled.

"I got the son-of-a-bitch!" yelled Williams.

"The hell you did," said Zeroski; "I shot him."

What remained indisputable was that the Americans had drawn first blood. Only one man, Private Gerald Johnson, was knocked out by the 88 fire while crossing Bridge No. 2; he was knocked cold, he looked dead, but he was up, whole-skinned and clear-headed within five minutes.

"Now, God damn you, break it up, don't bunch; listen to me, won't you, for Christ's sweet sake, thin out?" Knowing what one shell concentration would do to his men, Cole moved among them, chattering away, exhorting, pleading, cussing. He could have saved his breath. They kept herding together, and as fast as he broke them up, they returned to each other. But it was not fear that turned them inward; they huddled casually, noisy as magpies, as if feeling no apprehension of danger. The 88 rounds, arriving every five minutes or so, cracked like a whiplash. But most of the bursts were wide of the bridge, and most of the men were getting on beyond it. Otherwise, the enemy seemed to be paying no attention to the advance. To Gehauf it was clear enough that the battalion was tuned up, not for battle, but a grand entry.

In three hours, the whole battalion, except the rear of How Company, crossed on the iron grating, and the van squeezed through the block at Bridge No. 4, the men having sprung the cables there slightly by sheer body weight. George Company, under Lieutenant David Irvin, was in front, still solid, fairly fresh and unhurt. The files trudged forward, slowly, steadily, moving along both embankments next the water's edge. Especially on the right bank, it was tricky footing. When the men came to any stretch where the reeds thinned in the direction of the solid banks ahead, they crawled belly-down on the earth or waded through the water. For the entire length of the causeway on the right there ran a foot-deep drainage ditch a step above the marsh. Some of them went forward along this ditch, on their haunches or crawling. The cut was no real protection, but it looked good.

Gehauf and his intelligence section, with five men forming the point for George Company, were on the far side of Bridge No. 4. Even the pessimistic lieutenant was feeling better now, mystified that they had come so far and felt nothing, slightly irritated about his early alarms. Irvin's men were all past Bridge No. 3. The rest of the battalion was strung out as far back as the solid ground at Pont-de-Douve. Cole stood at Bridge No. 2, prodding the men across. But the illusion of safety was rising in him, and he had knocked off the stock instruction: "Keep low. Keep going. Stay scattered."

Thus was the column when the Germans opened fire. It began casually, erratically, with a buzz of bullets from front and right which was at first merely distracting. A few rifles, a few machine guns, that was all. These weapons were somewhere on the high ground forward of Bridge No. 4. Three hundred yards ahead of Gehauf a grassy bank rose sharply from the march. Amid this high ground was a capacious farmhouse, screened all around with hedgerows affording ideal cover. Its rightful owner, M. Désiré Ingouf, had had the good sense some days earlier to clear away to the distant village of Fontenay.

Around Gehauf the bullets zinged off the pavement or whined overhead. Some kicked up the embankment dust a few feet from his head. He was already crying out, "Keep moving! It's our best protection." There was hardly need. His men, flat in the embankment ditches at the first sound, were already wiggling forward. Most of the bullet swarm was wasted on the roadway above them. It was astounding, encouraging, that Germans were such bad marksmen. Then from among the reeds, snipers seared the column's flanks.

They had picked their spots carefully—the wide gap in the reeds at Bridge No. 2 and a like opening on the left, forward of Bridge No. 4. The bank there was almost sheer, and the wet clay afforded no hold even for crawling men. The point, moving with Gehauf, slithered along flat to the ground.

Corporal Martin Washko saw an enemy machine gun spitting at him from a platform 100 yards out in the marsh. He couldn't fire back; he was clinging to a shrub to keep from sliding into the water. Private Tony Diaz de Leon, fourth man in the point, looked back and saw no one coming along behind him. He yelled to the men forward, "Hold it! For Christ's sake, hold it."

Privates Carl Deyak and James E. White, the two scouts, were 15 yards ahead on the right embankment. White sat up in the drainage ditch to get a better view. Deyak stayed flat. A shell—the first mortar round in the fight—exploded between them. The next round exploded shards into Deyak's face and shoulders. A bullet creased White through the hair.

On the other side of the road, De Leon, five yards behind Washko, took a bullet through the arm. He yelled to Washko "Hurry! I'm hit. I'm going to bleed to death." Washko crawled back and applied a tourniquet. He saw then that they had advanced too far. The enemy machine gun could search the ditch and get all of them, whereas behind De Leon there was a bulge in the bank that would give them some protection. So he called to the others, "Follow me!" and they wiggled toward his position. A lone German, firing a machine pistol, came right after them, crawling along the embankment. He was turned back by his own machine gun, which also got two members of the point before they could close on Washko.

They acted on their own, neither hearing from Gehauf nor thinking about him, amid the encompassing need to press their bodies into the shallow space afforded by the one bulge in the bank. For the moment, the lieutenant had other business. Sergeant Delwin J. McKinney, who commanded the point, had been coming through the iron gate on Bridge No. 4 when the shooting began. But he was a big man, and the squeeze was too tight. McKinney saved himself by jumping into a ready-made German foxhole beside the gate. The rain of bullets on that barrier told him that the enemy guns must be zeroed in on it.

Gehauf, seeing McKinney spin out of sight, and thinking he was shot, crawled back to him. They talked. Said Gehauf, "I know now it's this place and not Bridge No. 2 that will kill us." The cable had given a little bit, but still not enough. And there was another point. Gehauf put it to McKinney: "I got up far enough to see what our own shells are doing. We're way over. Artillery must lower its fire 200 yards."

McKinney, from his foxhole, passed the word by shouting back to Irvin, who was still waiting to come through the barrier. Irvin put it on radio at once. But it was 2200 before the guns got the word, by which time Cole's battalion had already been held in check four hours.

The head of the stretched-out column had no choice but to stay where it was, since the bullets beating on the iron gate at Bridge No. 4 closed off retreat. The men on the right-hand embankment were pinned and punished by the snipers and machine guns in the marshes. The main body could not fall back. Bridge No. 2 was still a one-man passage. The battalion could not crowd that way without becoming a fat target. So there was a general paralysis through the remaining hours of daylight except as men individually, or squads singly, under a bolder-than-average leader, crawled slowly forward, extending the advance toward Bridge No. 4.

Cole stayed at Bridge No. 2, not so much to urge men forward as to block any return. He was at last fully aware of the stark danger in the situation. He knew that the battalion would be destroyed if the Germans hammered the causeway with artillery. The one limited safeguard was to keep men from bunching.

Both ways from the bridge, he walked among them, trying to make them understand it. The tough San Antonian was never a gentle talker, and this day he was at his cussingest best, all sulphur. "God damn you, listen, spread out; how many times must I tell you?" and then a boot in the tail. It was that kind of thing. But it wore his own nerves fine without changing anything.

As promptly as he turned his back, they converged, fear and the old herd instinct drawing them together. He fumed, too, because his men lay in the grass along the embankments, muttering, "That God-damned sniper!" every time a bullet zinged by, but doing nothing about it. They returned fire only when given a direct order. "Start shooting at those hedgerows and they'll quit" was his argument. But it wasn't wholly reasonable. Men sprawled on a sharp incline may easily fire forward; but volleying flankward is against gravity.

So the reply was left pretty much to the guns based on St. Côme-du-Mont. Their role was little enough. One forward observer, Lieutenant Spruel, of the 377th, was up with George Company, but had no radio. He put his sensings over Irvin's radio to Cole, from where it was relayed to the batteries by Captain Julian Rosemond. The guns worked over the opposite shore from 1600 until 2330. But if Gehauf's eye was accurate, six hours of that shoot was directed to churning up unoccupied fields beyond M. Ingouf's homestead.

When the last light died, the guns went silent. The word then reached the causeway that the artillery could not put over any night fires. No explanation was given, and Cole never learned why. But the reason was elementary: temporarily, the ammunition cupboard was bare.

Where the banks were firm and spacious enough to support it, the men burrowed in during dusk, using entrenching spades, jump knives and bare hands. No order was given; they simply sensed that the battalion was stuck for the night. In George Company sector, the 2nd and 3rd Platoons had closed on Bridge No. 3. There, a broad dike eight feet high confined the canal on the left of the bridge. Riflemen and machine-gunners dug in along this rampart at right angles to the causeway. Their fire line faced forward. Echeloned behind the line on the right of the road one machine gun was sited to fire on the farmhouse.

This force opened fire. Under its cover, the other men advanced to Bridge No. 4. Six of them filed through the gap in the iron gate while the enemy stayed heads down. The seventh, Sergeant Joe L. Clements, took a bullet in the chest while trying to squeeze through. At that, Captain Robert Clements yelled, "Hold everything!" With ropes and levers, they went to work on the gate; it didn't budge. So Clements redeployed them along the banks behind the bridge while 2nd Platoon continued its fire from the muddy dike. It was returned in such good measure by the enemy machine guns on the high ground that the NCOs crawled on their bellies in moving between foxholes. In less than two hours 2nd Platoon spent its ammunition. Its riflemen saw not one living target, but the winking tracers from the enemy guns gave them a fair line on the positions.

Two 60-millimeter mortars from the dike worked over the farm hedgerows. Private Allen Emery, of Headquarters Company, lugging an 81-millimeter mortar, pushed to within 30 yards of Bridge No. 4, and loosed 18 rounds against the farm positions. He opened at 400 yards, pulled back to 350 yards, then advanced to 400 again. By then, he had three shells left. A German mortar round exploded into the embankment seven yards from where he sat. Muffled by an earth bulge, the blast knocked Emery and his weapon over. Unhurt, he moved the tube back 100 yards, set up again and fired the last three rounds. Heroism? No, it was nothing but one man's indomitable instinct to arise to the practical needs of the moment.

Cole left Bridge No. 2 with his executive, Major John Stopka, a taciturn soldier from Wyoming, who later died bravely at Bastogne. Then he worked forward through the column to the van of George Company. Along the way, he raised hell with Item Company. The men were hugging the low spots at the foot of the right embankment, hoping to stay hidden by the reeds. He yelled at them, "God damn it, start firing and keep firing or I'll bust your asses." He didn't expect the fire to do much hurt, but he figured that inaction would prove fatally demoralizing.

The gunner on the right of the road at Bridge No. 3 displeased him. The boy was spraying ammunition like mad. Cole said, "Can't you see that if you just tap that trigger and give them a few shots at a time while you traverse, you'll last longer and may hit somebody?"

Some of Clements's lead platoon was dug in around the angle of the canal bank and the road shoulder behind Bridge No. 4. At the corner, Lieutenant Irvin was firing a bazooka at the farmhouse. Being at extreme range, it was an outright waste of ammunition. Though the men were all in foxholes, the German bullet fire caroming off the iron gate and concrete posts took its steady toll of the fire line. Cole was up there four hours, and while he watched, wondering what to do, eight men were hit by bullets. There was no way to beat the block at Bridge No. 4, if the enemy guns held on the iron gate. He said to Clements, "I think you better make ready to swim your company across this last stream." Then he walked left along the dike, seeking the best spot for a crossing. It was in his mind that if he could get one company on the far bank, he could throw ropes to them and pass the rest of the battalion forward hand over hand.

Worse still was the ordeal of Item Company, on the right bank beyond Bridge No. 3, though Cole had skinned it for slackness. The bank was almost perpendicular, with too little dirt to permit digging. It was Hobson's choice that the men tried to hide behind the reeds. From out in the marsh, 20 or more snipers were flailing Item's naked flank. One-quarter mile away a solid neck of land rose above the water, like the prow of a destroyer. Some in Item Company thought this the source of their misery; others believed the bullets came from boats concealed in the rushes. One sergeant said, "You're all nuts. There's no boat and no snipers out there. We're getting it from the high ground forward." What the men knew for certain was that the barren bank beyond Bridge No. 3 had become an alley of death and the prime target of the enemy. After 17 of its number were hit, Item Company sickened of running this gantlet, and of the day. An aid man, Private Tkcyzka, was shot through the brain. Lieutenant George A. Larish, leader of 1st Platoon, was shot through the heart. Lieutenant John P. Painschab died the same way.

Blessedly, the rest of the battalion had some insulation against the shock of these losses. So stretched out was the column that it felt nothing as a whole. Juniors knew that their seniors were casualties only when someone passed the word along the line that they must take command. The men on the right bank suspected that the men on the left were faring a little better— a good guess—and would have crossed to the other side had it been possible. Bullets were scratching the asphalt from two directions, with no letup. The men crawled when required to move. They were prone when hit. Those who remained ablebodied could see little of what was going on except the heels of the man in front of them.

Corporal Lloyd King and Privates Wesley Jackson and Thomas A. Pinon worked up to Bridge No. 3, carrying a machine gun. The air above crackled with rifle fire. They crawled under the bridge and crossed the stream, hand over hand, on the struts. In mid-passage, Pinon's ammunition carrier was hit and dropped into the water. Another bullet exploded a box of matches in Jackson's pocket, and he made land with his tail blazing. Pinon set up the gun in a foxhole beside the bridge and fired rightward at an angle of 90 degrees from the road. That dampered the sniper fire from the reeds through the rest of the evening. Bridge No. 3 began to cool off, though Pinon's action was the only counter to the bullet fire from that direction. The men of Item Company, after four hours of it, were numb with shock.

Under Captain Cecil L. Simmons, How Company began the passage of Bridge No. 2 in early evening, while the heat was on. "Keep your heads down, follow the leader, and I don't give a damn if you shoot," Simmons told his men. The rear platoons were still not over the bridge when the dark closed. Five rounds of mortar fire exploded on or near the bridge while 1st Platoon crossed, wounding Lieutenant Robert L. Mc-Laughlin and three troopers. Five more men were hit by stray bullets while trying to hug the ditch on the right embankment. Still, Simmons & Company came off better than any outfit on the causeway. When Cole got back to How Company, he said to Simmons, "If anyone has to swim the Madeleine this night, I'll move you up through Clements and let your people take the beating for a while." He still had no idea how bad things were in Item Company, nor could he guess that worse was coming.

32

Long, Long Night

At first the night was kind only because the Germans could no longer see their targets worming along the causeway banks. Their weapons kept going. Up front, George Company lost some more men to bouncing bullets as the people on the right tried to crawl across the road to the left bank, more neglected by the enemy.

Midnight neared. Private Hans K. Brandt made it to Bridge No. 4. He saw that men were tightly bunched around the barrier, with as many as one squad in a ten-yard space. It angered him.

From somewhere off in the reeds to the right (he thought it not more than 70 yards) an enemy machine gun opened fire. The bullets grazed the pavement and ricocheted from the bridge beams. If that continued, the bunched men would be picked off. Brandt borrowed two grenades and waded out through the reeds.

At the same moment, men farther back on the causeway, being less closely engaged, saw a plane flying toward them from Carentan. Its wheels were down; they knew it was a dive bomber. It came straight on along the line of the road, not more than 400 feet up. No one yelled or said a word. They saw, but they didn't understand.

Brandt was ten yards into the marsh. He looked up and saw the dive bomber. In that instant, he went flat near a stunted tree. To his eyes, "the whole earth seemed to strike fire." The explosion lifted him, and he dropped with a splash. But he had felt the jar wrench his left leg, and landing, he blacked out briefly from the pain. Six men on the bank were knocked cold by the same explosion. Brandt arose, limped on through the water, got within 30 yards of the machine gun and threw his two grenades. He wasn't sure he hit anything; he had gone deaf, and his other senses weren't clear. But no more fire came from that point. By the time he reached the bank, two of the men stunned by the bomb had slipped into the water. He carried them ashore. The men at the barrier were no longer huddled tight. The concussion of the bomb, whipping across the causeway, had parted them like chaff. One group of wounded was stacked in a grotesque pile. He got them spaced out; that was the best he could do. Then he started back for first aid. So many bullet-riddled men clogged the embankment that he couldn't travel it. So he walked rearward right down the middle of the road. The enemy didn't fire.

After unloading one egg right near Brandt, the dive bomber had flown straight on, and unloaded eight personnel bombs along the stretch of bank where Item Company stayed low behind the reeds. In a split second, Item lost another 30 men, most of them hit by the bombfire. Of that number, eight were killed or mortally wounded.

Yet here was a curious thing. The men strung out along the causeway thought, without exception, that only one plane had attacked them. They had flattened so swiftly after the first bomb exploded that they had no real view of it. The few observers who witnessed the strafing from behind Bridge No. 1 on the road to Les Quesnils saw clearly that two German bombers had crossed above the column at right angles in an instant of time. One came with bombs; it disappeared across the marshes. The other attacked mainly with its machine gun. It followed the road. The distant watchers saw its tracers "bouncing like ping-pong balls off the pavement." The plane Brandt saw was not the one that hit him; the two axes of attack crossed directly over Item Company.

Private Paul J. McKenna was on the left embankment. Bomb fragments hit him in both shoulders, the right leg and right hand. He walked on back for first aid. Private Glenn A. Moe was three feet down and still digging his foxhole when the bombs hit. Shards got him in the left hand and shoulder. Two men burrowed five yards from him were also wounded. He finished digging the foxhole. Then he walked back to Pont-de-Douve, carrying one of the wounded. His wounds dressed, he asked for the help of a stretcher bearer, returned to the spot and brought in the second man, his labor taking four hours.

Item was down and out. Flattening when the bombs fell, its men could not rise again, save for a sturdy half dozen, whose first thought was to evacuate the worst of the stricken. The great number fell victim to the deadly drowsiness that overtakes infantry after calamitous shock losses. They had no interest in what had happened to them; they expressed no curiosity about who had been hit. Lieutenant Robert G. Burns found he could not keep his men awake no matter how he tried. Some were in heavy sleep within two minutes of the bombing. It confused Burns; he could not tell which were the sleepers and which the wounded and dying. He saw men who, having tumbled down the bank, lay still with their bodies half in water. He went to them, thinking they had been hit, then discovered they were sleepers who had rolled down the bank and had not awakened when they slipped into the frigid marsh. Others lay there in their jump suits, wet through and through, yet sleeping the torpid sleep of utter exhaustion. Officers gave over any attempt to rouse these men. Item Company had become a cipher in the column. Burns, a burly, redheaded bruiser who had served as division athletic officer, saw far more than he understood, which but made him wonder more why none of the experts came forward to explain it to him. Burns said, "By God, it's funny. Here I had just been worrying about how we would get some sleep."

One more such blow just then could have broken them. But it didn't come. The enemy also must have been gutted of strength finally. The battalion lay open to him, and his guns knew where to fire. But he abruptly suspended all action. The night was fair and the air chilled. The sky was cloudless and starlit, a faultless dome affording good visibility. Then the moon rose, fully illuminating the scene, but not changing the situation. Over the marsh lay a great quiet.

It was time for another go at Bridge No. 4. As Cole was pondering which company should be tapped for it, there came a call from Clements. It was 0130. Stopka took the message and, turning to Cole, said, "Clements says all his men have gone through the gate except a handful right around him."

Cole said, "OK, tell him to move every last man through."
It was not a final decision. Clements's men were pretty beat-
up, and Simmons's company was comparatively fresh. But he
had to have at least two companies on the other side of the
barrier if he was to attack. So he would pick the front runner
after Simmons also got past the gate.

Simmons had already figured that he would get the nod and
was taking his company forward, via the pavement. He overtook Clements some minutes after the call to Stopka. To his
surprise, Clements and most of George Company were still
waiting short of the iron gate.

Clements said to him, "I'm not sending any more men up
there. There's no cover."

Simmons replied, "Hell, there must be some cover if you've
got men up there."

Simmons squeezed through the gate and crawled forward
on the left embankment until he heard Germans talking 20
yards beyond where he lay doggo in a drainage ditch.

Then he crawled back to his radio at Bridge No. 4 and called
for artillery support. The fire-control center replied, "The guns
can't fire tonight." The time was 0200. It was right then that
Cole called him on radio to say, "Go on past Clements and
take over the lead." Simmons replied, "I'm already past him,
and the men are coming as fast as possible." He was not happy
about it; his brief reconnaissance had shown that Clements was
right in saying the ground was barren of cover.

Perplexed by the conversation, Cole went forward to see
how Simmons could have leapfrogged Clements without an
order, if Clements was already past the gate.

Cole got there at 0300. He found Simmons and one platoon
beyond the barrier, along with a five-man patrol from George
Company, under Lieutenant Cortez. Clements and the rest of
George Company were behind the iron gate, right where Cole
had left them six hours earlier.

Wounded soon after, and removed from the battle, Clements
never had an opportunity to answer Cole's charge that he misre-
ported his position. Cole said, "I couldn't have been mistaken;
I harassed him seven times about it." This is probably the key.
Cole gave his juniors a hard ride. When a commander practices
that, excessively optimistic reports meant to mollify him are
the likeliest consequence. Clements was reasonably reluctant
after his experience of that day. It is remarkable that any of

his men survived the passage. Telephone and electric wires were down in a tangle over the gate. When each man made his run, diagonally through the narrow breach, those watching saw scores of sparks fly up from the gate and metal bridge as bullets bit the metal. "It was like watching a fireworks display."

Cole doubled back to Regiment. He wanted it made clear beyond doubt that the plan was still on, and the attack had to be made.

Simmons again scouted forward. From his better 'ole in the ditch he heard wagons creaking along the road, coming toward him, and he wondered whether the Germans were bringing in field mines or more machine guns.

At 0400, Cole returned with the order to go. Simmons's men were still feeding through the barrier breach at the rate of one per minute. He had ordered that spacing, lest they be caught bunched when the Germans resumed fire.

Cole said, "To hell with that. Line up, all of you! We've got to take the risk or we'll never be ready." The results justified him. All of How Company and of George, which followed, got through the breach without hearing one bullet. Cole, after looking over Item Company, ordered it to the rear. Only 21 men and 2 officers were left of the 80 and 5 who had marched to the causeway.

How Company, in the lead, counted 84 people. There were only 60 left in George Company. Headquarters brought up the rear with 121. They advanced in split column, men in single file on each side of the road, moving straight toward the solid knoll on which rested the Ingouf farmstead. Drawn toward that object, the pacemakers had suddenly to veer right, making for a tidy meadow bounded by hedgerows.

Private Albert W. Dieter, the lead scout, advanced boldly in the thin light to within five yards of the first hedgerow running at a right angle to the road and bounding the farm. The platoons were strung out behind him for at least 200 yards.

As Dieter took his last steps to close on the hedgerow, German fire—rifle, machine-gun and mortar—opened full against the column. The enemy had not been surprised. The synchronizing of weapons bespoke that they had waited until the Americans got within easy range. But they must have been overly excited or afraid, for the first volley, heavy in volume, did little damage.

Dieter, well out front, couldn't be missed. His left arm was shredded from wrist to shoulder by a machine-gun burst. Without ducking or quickening his pace, he walked back through the storm to where Simmons had taken cover in a ditch. Along with every other American, Simmons had gone flat.

The boy stopped. He said to Simmons, "Captain, I'm hit pretty bad, ain't I?"

Simmons said, "You sure are."

"Will I make it?"

"I'm not sure."

"Captain, they've always called me a f——up in this company. I didn't let you down this time, did I?"

"No, you sure didn't."

"That's all I wanted to hear."

Head up, Dieter walked on toward the causeway, looking for someone who might dress his wound.

Cole, who, only a moment before the opening fire, had said to Simmons, "The company's too bunched. Those God-damned Germans are here. They know we're here. Now thin out," looked around to survey the damage.

Two men who had followed Dieter were dead from machine-gun bullets. Six members of the lead platoon were wounded and had crawled off to the roadside ditches.

Simmons crept over to attend their wounds. One boy's arm was shattered and shredded much like Dieter's. Simmons needed some kind of table on which to work while applying rough splints. There was a dead German in the ditch, cold and stiff, who didn't need his pack any more. Simmons removed the corpse's pack, rested it on the stomach and went to work with his first-aid kit.

From the far side of the road a sniper poured fire at him while he worked. From rearward, a light machine gun was passed forward. Simmons positioned it on the ditch bank, and Staff Sergeant John T. White got on the gun and worked over the hedgerow which he thought concealed the sniper.

Private William Penden came running from a nearby field and flopped down beside Simmons. He lay there, shaking as if convulsed by pain.

"Are you hurt, Penden?" Simmons asked.

Penden answered, "Hell no, they haven't got me yet."

Simmons said, "Well then, let's keep firing at the dirty devils."

It was stilted language, but it got Penden in motion for a

little while. He crawled up the ditch a few yards beyond Simmons and opened fire with his carbine.

That gave Simmons an idea. His own carbine was empty. He'd better load it. While he was fumbling with the clip—his hands were sweating, and the fingers were not as responsive as usual—he noticed that Penden had stopped firing.

He called out, "What's the matter, Penden? Has anything gone wrong?"

There was no answer.

White shook Penden, then turned to Simmons, saying, "Penden's dead. That sniper got him. The left side. One in the heart."

Another boy crawled into the ditch with a bad arm wound, spurting blood from an artery.

Simmons said, "I'm sorry, but I have no tourniquet."

The boy said, "You better look at this private medical kit I've got in my pocket. It might help. I come prepared."

Simmons found a hemostat in the kit and promptly pinched off the flow of blood.

The German sniper kept on banging away.

33

Charge

Cole crawled back along the ditch, about 50 yards.

He said to Rosemond, the artillery liaison officer, "Get some shellfire on the farmhouse and the hedges."

Rosemond made his call, then told Cole, "We can't give you any fire; the artillery commander isn't present with the guns to approve the request."

Cole said, "God damn it! We need artillery, and we can't wait for any general."

The shells started coming in less than 15 minutes.

Cole clocked the first explosion at 0530. For the next 25 minutes the artillery pounded the hedgerows around the farmhouse. Cole and Rosemond watched the bursts. The stuff seemed to be getting in where they wanted it. Still, there was no slackening of the enemy weapons. Rather, the roar and rattle built up higher.

By Cole's order, the artillery switched from air bursts to delay and then changed back again. It made no difference. Bullets whipped through the thorn above the ditches and tore into the embankments in as great volume as before.

Simmons was too busy with his wounded and the defense of his narrow ditch to pay heed to the artillery. Still, he wondered about Cole. His was the lead company. He was expected to carry the action. But if Cole gave any thought to his infantry,

331

he hadn't indicated it since his first exchange with Rosemond.

Cole, momentarily, was stumped. Though he confessed it to no one and sought no counsel, he had no idea what to do next. For one fleeting moment, he considered withdrawing his men the way they had come. Then he wondered about trying to advance them a few at a time along the main road to Carentan. Or as a last alternative, what about charging the farmhouse to win or lose it all in one throw?

He spent no time weighing these options. Nor did he look to his battalion again to see how it was spread. The decision was made on impulse, not as a well-reasoned thing, but with almost explosive force. It was like a quarterback picking a play number without thinking of the formation or remembering where goes the ball. The Texan was that way in battle. By nature, one of the gentlest and most lovable of men, he tightened up under fire, never personally afraid, but haunted by the nightmare that he would somehow let down his people. His rashness, irritability and failure to talk things over all came of that disturbance.

Major Stopka lay in a ditch across the road. Cole yelled to him, "Hey, we're going to order smoke from the artillery and then make a bayonet charge on the house."

Stopka answered, "OK!" raising not one question.

Then Cole turned back to Rosemond and told him what he wanted.

Within a few minutes the smoke shells were falling in an arc which had the farmhouse as its center, extending past the Madeleine River on one end and curtaining the main road to Carentan on the left.

Cole waited beside Rosemond while the smoke was being laid. Fifteen to 20 minutes passed. He called to Rosemond, "Adjust to leftward to meet the wind." That the curtain should be exactly right was his sole concern.

George Company, deployed and pinned in a narrow meadow on the left of the main road, was getting hit by a machine gun and a Schmeisser from a covert in the hedge bounding the field's south end. Clements's men tried to crawl to the hedgerows as the bullets found them. The company's tail, which had not gained the meadow, was sent scurrying to the roadside ditches as the fire swept all the way to Bridge No. 4. They dug in next the road and remained foxholed while the fight thickened around the farmhouse.

First Sergeant Hubert Odom, of George Company, an indomitable soldier, the moral pillar of the outfit, worked along the hedgerow bounding the main road to the hedge shielding the German strongpoint.

Three men were with him. They moved so far crouched over that their fingertips trailed the embankment as they followed the ditch. Odom objected to crawling; it obscured the view of what lay ahead. His three helpers carried a machine gun.

While Odom prowled forward, Private Emery, the mortar man, went to work on a house 500 yards down the main road from which machine-gun fire was spilling into the meadow. He hit dead on with his third round, setting the building afire, then looped in two more rounds for good luck. Picking out a second position, he fired again, still working the weapon alone.

Odom, 15 yards ahead of the gun crew, saw a German rise from behind a hedge, 20 paces ahead. Before he could raise his weapon, the German loosed a burst from a Schmeisser and dropped out of sight.

Private William P. Evans, behind Odom, cried out, "He got all of us." He was right; every member of the gun crew had been winged in the arm or shoulder. But Evans, flopping, got the gun in action. Odom crawled on through a water-filled ditch which cut through the hedge; he was so low on his belly that the enemy fire couldn't find him.

He yelled back to Sergeant Anthony L. Zeroski: "Throw me your grenades." With his good arm, Zeroski tossed him three. Odom flipped them around the corner of the hedge. A German screamed. Another German jumped from a foxhole and disappeared so quickly that Odom had no time to fire his carbine. Zeroski crawled up and covered Odom while he rounded the hedge. One of his grenades had destroyed the machine gun. But the crew had slipped away through an angling communications trench toward Carentan. Odom knew there had been four men. He had interrupted their breakfast, and the pork sausages on the four plates were still warm.

While Odom worked over the forward ground, an artillery round exploded into the meadow, wounding Captain Clements in the shoulder. He bled terribly and was half-conscious. It couldn't have happened at a worse moment. With Odom absent, and Clements down, the company was now leaderless.

Cole had passed the word to Stopka, and the word was

supposed to have been passed on down to the company commanders and from them to the men: "Everybody fix bayonets and reload rifles with a full clip; be ready to go at the sound of a whistle."

Three companies—George, How and Headquarters—were supposed to have received the order. With every part of the command far-stretched, pinned and under unrelenting fire, it would have taken extraordinary diligence and a shipload of luck to get that order circulated and understood.

Stopka, his mind on other things, merely walked to the hedge on his side of the road and, seeing some riflemen under the lee of the hedge opposite, shouted Cole's order to them until they nodded as if they understood.

That was all Stopka did. Cole stuck fast to Rosemond, regulating the artillery, never looking at his battalion. At 0615, Cole gave an order to Rosemond. Responding, the guns lifted their fire to Phase Line B—the railroad track beyond the farmhouse.

When he heard the killing shells come screaming over, Cole blasted on his whistle and, not saying a word, took off at a trot across a ditch. It was a small miracle that all of 21 men followed him as the charge got in motion.

Too late, Stopka had recognized his own error. Dashing across the road, he was in an instant among the 40 or so men in the small meadow, exhorting them, "Come on! Let's go! Over the hedge! Follow the colonel!"

But collection was no longer possible. Stopka couldn't in one moment of excitement clarify what was wanted. Only the men nearest him rose and ran toward the farm. A picket squad trailed after Cole. Headquarters and How Companies were represented by only a man or two.

Cole looked back over his shoulder, and what he saw almost stunned him. In agony of mind, he concluded that his battalion had quit cold on him—and he was dead wrong.

Back in the ditches and behind the hedges, men were talking like this:

"I heard someone yell something about a f——whistle."

"Well, what about the f——whistle?"

"Damned if I know."

And another pair talked:

"They say we should fix bayonets."

"How do they figure to use them?"

"I didn't hear."

Like the order, the signal couldn't be heard except by a small circle, and where it was heard, few understood what it meant. In the confusion, the few to whom the message was passed heard it halfway or garbled. The words couldn't rise above the sounds of battle. The majority heard nothing. The minority knew something was afoot, but didn't know the charge was on until they saw a trickle of men running across a field. Then a few of the bolder spirits raced after, trying to catch up.

Cole ran halfway across the meadow. His wind gave out. He stopped, knelt on one knee and looked back again. Bullets were clipping the grass all around him and whining overhead.

He saw that his men were trailing him single file. So he pumped both arms at them, yelling, "For Christ's sake, spread out." Instead, they hit the dirt, one behind the other. Then he worked them over individually, booting them and shouting, "Get up and go on!"

His Colt .45 was in his hand. He pointed it wildly in the direction of the farmhouse, shouting, "God damn, I don't know what I'm shooting at, but I gotta keep on."

His aimless trigger-pulling and the wild yelling broke the spell. There was laughter from among those flattened forms able still to squeeze it out. Six were killed by bullets as they lay there with Cole exhorting them.

Private Robert E. Doran, Cole's radio operator (later killed in Holland), came running forward, his SCR 300 radio strapped to his back. His bound restored motion to Cole, and they trotted on together. The smoke barrage was clearing, and through rifts in it, they saw the farmhouse.

Stopka overtook them and ran on, screaming, "Let's go! Let's go!" He hurdled a broad ditch. Cole, on a different course, jumped a low hedge and came down in the same ditch, like a fouling point-to-point chaser, in water up to his neck. He yelled back to Doran, "Don't follow me!" But Doran was already in mid-air and made the same jump, landing dry.

Others caught the leaders and passed them. Stopka saw two men shot down ahead of him. He yelled to one of them, Private Edwin S. Pastouris, "How are you?"

Pastouris, hit through the chest, yelled back, "I'm OK. You keep going!"

Fifteen men from How and Headquarters Companies, arriving belatedly, ran on along the main road to the hedgerow forming the rear boundary of the farm, then turned and ran down the hedge on the outside till they came even with the house. Never pausing, they disappeared into the orchard.

That was how Cole wanted it. By now he was standing by the building, waving his men on. There was no other way to do it. They all had the impulse to stop and duck under cover.

Dead Germans lay thick over the ground and in the foxholes. The only live ones in sight were mortally stricken. Survivors of the machine-gun crews had quit their stoutly fortified bunkers along an earth mound just beyond the farmhouse and pulled back through the orchard toward the railroad; only a few got trapped before they could leg it. The American artillery kept on firing toward the railroad. Battalion had lost contact with the guns, and they held on the last assigned target.

As the men came along, Cole, with Stopka's aid, distributed the token forces so that the battalion could again be brought in hand as the manpower deployed forward. How and Headquarters Companies were to assemble on the right of the farm before continuing the action. George Company would collect around a brush pile behind the house. Item Company's remnant, which was now filing through Bridge No. 4, would form on George Company.

"After we see what we've got left," Cole said to Stopka, "we'll know better what to do."

But what had been lost to the battalion during its ragged charge could no more be counted in bodies done in or mangled than its collective torment may be expressed in words attempting to describe the shock experience of each man.

It is enough to recount the step-by-step ordeal of Private Bernard Sterno, a runty lad from Ohio, not the brightest soldier in How Company, possibly not the bravest, but just an average trooper, born south of the tracks, who, because war came, was diverted to a school where he learned the meaning of hard duty.

Sterno was one of the few who heard Cole's order clearly, being just a few feet away. He made ready to follow, though his Garand had jammed, and he had no bayonet.

But being short-legged and no athlete, he couldn't keep pace with Cole, and was losing out until the formation foundered for a time in mid-field.

When Sterno went flat, he saw a dead German sprawled in a slit trench back of a clump of bushes. Set in the foliage was a Schmeisser with a cord leading back to the body. The foolish

German had wanted the best of two worlds—active fighting and maximum protection.

Sterno merely coveted the machine pistol. But fearing that the cord might be a booby trap, he slashed it with his jump knife. With his knife hand in mid-air, he felt something "bump into a finger" of it. But his gloves were on, and he didn't realize that a bullet had cut his middle finger clean away. He didn't look. He got the pistol and crawled on, crawling because, trying to stand again, he found his legs were caving.

Crawling not more than his own length, he bumped into another body, a friend from How Company. He was bleeding from a bullet wound just above the heart, and Sterno could tell that he was near death.

An aid man came along. He said to Sterno, "Don't you know you're all bloody? You've lost a finger." The medico stopped and bandaged the finger stump, then continued on.

Sterno followed him on all fours. He heard a voice cry, "Help me! Somebody help me!" It was a sergeant from his own company. He was shot through the stomach and leg. Next him was the medico who had just bandaged Sterno. But he was dead from a bullet right through his temple. Sterno stripped off the medico's kit and gave the sergeant rude first aid. But his own mangled hand made it difficult, and he spent much time, lost his bandage and had to redress his own wound.

By then, heavy enemy fire was again breaking around the farmhouse, and Cole, standing at the corner of the CP, was yelling to the troops, "Move out! Get away from here or we'll all be killed."

Sterno crawled on, got 30 or so yards beyond the house, saw some skirmishers lying in a water-filled ditch, and joined them. They were firing loosely toward the orchard. Sterno borrowed an M-1 from a dying private, and fired also, though he had no notion what he was firing at.

Again his bandage worked loose. Another aid man passed by, looked at the bloody stump and said, "You get to the rear." It was an order, so Sterno crawled back to the road. Its ditches were filled with unattended wounded, and Sterno figured he'd best stay a while and help them. One man said to him, "Maybe you can flag an ambulance for us; none of us can stand."

Road and ditches were being raked by 88-millimeter fire coming straight down the gut from Carentan. The man lying near Sterno had only a bloody hole where his right eye should have been. He wasn't sure the eye was gone.

Plaintively, he asked Sterno, "What about it? Is my eye gone?"

Not wishing to tell him the truth, Sterno replied, "Well, even if it is, you should be glad you have the other one."

Sterno marveled at these new comrades. There was no GI talk in them, no profanity, no complaining. They spoke simply as if every word had to be squeezed out.

Sterno prepared a sulfa pad and put it on the man's empty socket. Then he went to work on the other wounded. There was a sudden swish from another 88 shell. Sterno jumped from the ditch but didn't quite make it. He "felt something terribly hard and heavy" land against his back, jarring him, as if he had been "kicked by a mule in the spine."

He wasn't sure whether he had been wounded again or had only felt concussion. In fact, a shard had ripped into his back and stopped in his groin, though this wasn't known until he was examined aboard an LST (Landing Ship, Tank) the following day.

The man who had lost an eye was now crying, "My arm, my arm, oh my arm." Sterno was groggy for a few seconds. When he looked, he saw that the man's right arm had been torn off at the socket.

Another man near him, who had been alive a minute before, had lost half his head.

It felt to Sterno that blood was running down his own back, but he couldn't be certain. He thought it might be shock and imagination.

Then he looked at the others in the group of wounded. One man five feet from him had blood streaming from his ears, nose and mouth. He was conscious. He tried to talk. But the words wouldn't come. He babbled on, sounding like an infant.

Sterno figured that most of these men were beyond his power to help. He crawled on rearward to Bridge No. 4, and by then his arms and legs wouldn't work any more.

So he dropped into the foxhole next the concrete pillar. Thirty seconds later a mortar shell exploded against the pillar, and one slug of it hit Sterno in the neck, while a second slug mortally wounded a lieutenant lying next him.

But Sterno didn't know that. He had finished his bit for one day and was no longer conscious.

34

Life on the Farm

There are other flashbacks. First Sergeant Kenneth M. Sprecker and that omnipresent soldier, Private Roach, of How Company, reached the farmhouse 30 yards ahead of Cole. Roach shot the lock off the back door, and they dashed inside. The place was empty. Roach stopped, seeing a toilet that would flush. Sprecker ran outside. From the brush pile, he saw two German riflemen under the apple trees, raising their rifles. Sprecker got off a burst from his Tommy gun. They died 'neath the blossoms.

Second Lieutenant Edward A. Provost, of How Company, had nine men with him when he heard Cole's whistle, not quite knowing what it meant. But he saw men running in the direction of the enemy, and he took off after them. The nine soldiers went along because an officer moved into danger. Provost was a little man, dandyish in look, hesitant in speech. He had Cole's active contempt and knew it.

Five of Provost's nine soldiers were shot down, crossing the field. He ran on with the other four. They dodged around the road, skirting the right side of the farmhouse. It was paralleled by a hedgerow. Opposite the farmhouse was a solidly built machine-gun nest dug deep into the bank overlooking the Madeleine. The men crept in behind the cover of the stone wall set as a flying buttress to the farmhouse. Provost wasn't giving them any directions; they moved in silence.

Private James O. Brune, the mail orderly, looped a grenade

over the wall toward the nest. There were five Germans either at the gun or in the V-shaped trench behind it. The grenade exploded amid them. One or two were stunned; the others stood there screaming.

That was how Brune and Provost saw them when they bounded up the eight crude steps between the road and the gun position without giving the crew a moment in which to recover.

Brune's M-1 was at his hip. He started to pull the trigger.

Provost screamed, "Don't waste bullets! Use the bayonet!"

That was what they did. Such was the excitement of the moment that later they could not remember how many of the five they had run through. There are things best forgotten by warriors wishing to stay square with the rest of life.

Call it a minor footnote to the national history: Cole's was the only bayonet charge ordered by an American officer in World War II. Provost, the unwanted shavetail, was the only leader to insist on closing with the bayonet. Maybe it was his moment of hysteria. Brune was the only soldier, on his order, to apply cold steel. One week later, Cole shucked Provost off.

The two men carried on, picking up a few hands from the forward detachments—ten men altogether. Drawing abreast of the orchard, they looked leftward and saw "about two squads of Germans milling around" as if making ready to pull out.

Provost's group propped themselves behind a hedgerow and fired. They were shaking. Not more than four of the enemy fell from the first volley. The others flattened at once, formed a line and returned the fire. Provost thought they were too far away for grenading. But a rise in the ground covered them. So he pulled a pin and got ready to throw.

Then a bullet, cutting deep, slashed him through the cheek. Blood spilled all over him. He returned to the farmhouse in search of an aid man. There he met Sergeant Sprecker, who was looking for other men from the company.

Provost said, "I left some men up that lane. They're fighting. You better take over." Sprecker did. The five men had quit shooting. Sprecker, leaving it that way, called out, "You krauts—come in—*kamerad*." Five Germans popped up with hands raised. That ended the skirmishing around the orchard for a little while.

What remained of Item Company had come forward because Lieutenant Burns wouldn't quit. When the farm fight opened, his little band was just behind Bridge No. 4. They heard the noise of battle up ahead. But in the same moment, the German machine-gun fire again engulfed the iron gate, and bullets struck fire from it as on the evening before. The men of Item ran for the narrow opening amid this hail of steel. They did it one man at a time, heads down. The lucky ones who got through then jumped down to the protection of the embankment.

Lieutenants Burns and Gleason, the last two officers, were hit trying to get through the gate. So were 7 of the 21 troopers who had survived the ordeal on the embankment. The few who made it went on leaderless, attaching themselves as individuals to any group they could find. Item, as a company, no longer operated. It made little difference. The German barraging of the farmhouse had spoiled Cole's pattern for reassembly. All of 3rd Battalion was by now inextricably scrambled, and the junior leaders fought on with small scratch groups, wherever it became possible to collect them.

Fire had not lifted from the meadows between the farmhouse and Bridge No. 4. Men who had taken cover there when Cole and his immortals charged the farmhouse remained pinned. Most of the Germans were behind the hedgerows on the other side of the road from M. Ingouf's property. From them came the automatic fire which swept the meadows and kept the main body flattened in the ditches or near the banks. The charge led by Cole had moved off obliquely to the right, away from the line of fire, though the original movement, extended through the orchard, would have outflanked it.

So far as command of the causeway was concerned, the German center of strength had been on the barren earth mound between the farmhouse and the Madeleine. Cole's charge had routed the garrison there, and Provost's bayonet had snuffed the last flicker of resistance. But none of this had disturbed the enemy's main strength. When the smoke barrage cleared away, their weapons could again volley into the fields where the tail of the column had sought cover. It was their natural line of fire. Where they held, they were on axial lines pointed directly toward the meadows where flattened Americans were wondering what to do next and how to rejoin their commander.

It was their characteristic pattern. Behind the hedgerows, the Germans dug their foxholes in perfect geometric proportion, square-walled and deep. In fact, they were so deep that a man of average height could stand erect in them and just see over. When two Germans stand to within a foxhole, they maintain themselves in a half-crouch, back on their haunches, with heads erect, facing one another. Each man has a rifle slung at his hip and pointed up over the edge, so that one man sees whatever comes at the back of the other, and both have a fair field of vision. In Normandy, the machine-gun strongpoints were usually at a corner where the hedgerows converge. So placed, they could cover the roads or a sweep of country. The foxholes were in line directly behind the hedges, spaced more or less evenly between the machine guns. The battle's complexity came of the cut-up nature of the country. Its tactics were as simple as an end run—flank the hedgerow line, and the whole section of front must then form on the next convenient field to the rear.

Captain Simmons and Sergeant White hadn't heard Cole's order. Simmons, working over his wounded, heard someone yell something about a whistle. He said to White, "Can you hear what it's all about?" White didn't reply. Simmons continued to apply first aid.

An 88 shell exploded near the ditch, knocking Simmons cold. Some minutes later he revived. White was shaking him by the shoulder.

"What's happened?" Simmons asked.

Said White, "I think we missed the boat. The battalion was ordered to charge the farmhouse. Some of the men are already there."

Said Simmons, "We better get the hell out of here."

He was still groggy. He motioned to the men around him to arise and follow. A group got up. He didn't notice how many. They advanced straight up the ditch and toward the corner of the hedgerow which ran back of the farmhouse.

One German machine gun was still firing from that corner, toward the field Simmons's men had just left. It felled four of them in mid-air as they hurdled the irrigation ditch. The others ran on, firing their rifles. One grenade knocked the gun out; the crew died from bullets. Setting up a Browning light machine gun on the same spot, Simmons pointed it in the opposite direction. The Americans prowled around the vicinity for a few minutes.

One hour after the charge, Simmons reported to Cole at the farmhouse. Cole said, "Get your men over there in that cow yard and see what you've got." Simmons had started with 84 men; he finished the day with 30. He had lost the greater number before ever getting up to Cole.

Momentarily, around the farm, the fire fight dwindled. Provost and others had collapsed the enemy left front. Simmons, by knocking off the last machine gun, had cleared the immediate right, though the question remained whether the Germans had pulled back any farther than the next field.

Since Cole's mission remained unchanged, and he was still to make the long circuitous march to Hill 30, he was no longer do-it-yourself sanguine. Much earlier he had called Michaelis, suggesting that Regiment had better put another battalion on the road. Michaelis agreed. Pat Cassidy and Outfit were told to start marching.

That decision raised a unique command problem for Michaelis. His 2nd Battalion was the Regimental Reserve. Taylor had directed him not to commit it in any case. Moreover, the road between Les Quesnils and the fight was strongly interdicted by gunfire.

So once Cassidy got on the road, where was the fate of the regiment at stake, and how should the front be commanded? Guiding on "the book," Michaelis stayed put with his Reserve—which couldn't be used. So did his executive, carrot-topped Major "Pinky" Ginder, a no less resolute man. They were frankly puzzled, and what they should have done is a good question in view of the outcome—that the attack as a whole was never centrally directed. At the moment, from where Michaelis sat, however, the distant fight seemed to be subsiding.

Cole thought so, too. When he called Private Doyle Bootle and said, "Go back over the causeway, find Colonel Cassidy and tell him to bring 1st Battalion up," he was thinking about the march to Hill 30. His own men were pooped and leg-weary. He made this random estimate of his own strength without leaving the farmhouse to see. Actually, the situation was far worse than he knew. His meager parties, which had closed on the hedge banks near the farmhouse, counted too few men to form a thin fire line. But because the battle noise had grown less, Cole believed he had the Germans on the run.

Bootle started out walking, then spurred by sniper fire, sprinted to the Carentan road. To his passing glance, the fields now looked clear of Americans except for the dead and wounded. Cassidy and his battalion were still toiling toward Bridge No. 4. But Bootle didn't get that far. Tuckered out, he gave the message to Sergeant Joseph H. Gillion, of How Company, who sent it by radio to Regiment, which relayed it to Cassidy.

Doran's radio was again working, but he had neglected to tell Cole. So when a few minutes later Lieutenant Provost showed up at the CP still looking for an aid man to patch his torn cheek (there was none), Cole said to him, "You go to the rear, find Cassidy and tell him to get up here." He wasn't sure Bootle would make it.

Provost took the message as far as a sergeant leading the first platoon in Cassidy's column. He met him at Bridge No. 4. At long last the engineers had torn away the iron gate at Bridge No. 4 and installed a solid span at Bridge No. 2. Provost said to the sergeant, "Cole wants 1st Battalion forward as quickly as possible."

But quickly wasn't possible. Seeing one of his own men lying in a ditch, wheezing from a chest wound, Provost stopped by Bridge No. 4 to patch him. When he noticed a group of How Company men hugging the dirt nearby, he called out, "Why aren't you up front?"

"We're pinned down," several of them replied.

"The hell you are; you're afraid," said Provost.

Then the machine gun cracked down on him, and quite humbly, he crawled back on hands and knees to carry the word to Cassidy's men that Bridge No. 4 was still hot. It was wasted energy. The front of the column had already jumped for refuge to the embankments.

Ten minutes later it was moving again. When the front ranks entered the meadow beyond Bridge No. 4, rifle and machine-gun fire from far down the Carentan road cut into them. The column marched on through a field littered with the dead and dying.

Cole, in the farmhouse, already had his hands full. His only two aid men were attending the wounded in the roadside ditches and the field of the charge. That deprived the fight forward of medical attendants. Private John W. Pike, a mortar man, came to the CP with a bullet through his shoulder. Cole and Sprecker bandaged him. Private James W. Evans, How Company rifle-man, arrived hopping, his right leg broken by a shell burst. Private Joe Jiminez, of How Company, came with two bullets in his shoulder. Cole got on radio to Regiment, saying, "Send us all kinds of ammunition, an ambulance and every aid man you can lay hands on."

After patching Jiminez, he laid Evans down on the pavement

of the courtyard and splinted his leg with a pick handle. As he straightened from that job, he saw an unfamiliar face—a private from 1st Battalion—his first news that Cassidy was arriving. The boy sat by the door, his shoe off. He was methodically applying sulfa powder to a blister on his heel.

"Get the hell out of here right now, fellow," said Cole. "This is a dangerous spot."

"I want to be safe, Colonel," said the boy. "If I don't fix this, I might get blood poisoning."

As he uttered the last word, he was hit dead on by an artillery shell, which smashed him up against the stone building and scattered his brayed flesh across the flagstones.

The ambulance arrived—an ordinary truck for want of a Red Cross vehicle—loaded with ammunition. Hit a dozen times on the way up, it raced back through fire, bearing a double-deckload of wounded, 20 in the body of the truck and others in stretchers across the top. This same shuttle was maintained through most of the day, and two jeeps were added to the service.

Cole's staff at last got up to him. They had been busy with this and that. Gehauf, dead beat from 48 hours of patrolling, had fallen asleep in a ditch along the causeway, and Cole had let him lie. He stormed into the CP, cursing Cole for being so considerate. Lieutenant Ralph L. Watson, the personnel officer, had remained behind with the radio section. Captain Edward J. Barrett, of operations, had stayed at Bridge No. 4 until the iron gate was cleared away (he knew Cole could not last unless the road was opened) and had then walked to M. Ingouf's service road to help organize the fire line.

By pure coincidence, they arrived in a bunch and together entered the kitchen. Cole was in the next room doctoring his wounded. An artillery round landed on the doorstep outside. The steel sprayed in through the open door.

Gehauf, Watson and Barrett were all hit. So was an enlisted man. The staff had to be hauled away on the next run of the ambulance.

35

Support

To the eye of Cassidy, as his battalion started forward on the last lap, it looked as if there were more good bodies drifting back over the causeway than were moving up under his command.

Some of Cole's wounded added to the congestion. They shuffled along, eyes staring vacantly into space with that set expression peculiar to unattended and mobile casualties who have bled too much. But there was also a heavy flow of men who seemed to have nothing physically wrong with them.

Cassidy was spared little time to reflect on that. Suddenly shot and shell and the swarm of bullets struck all around the column, and the column broke for the embankments and the marsh.

Cassidy found himself standing in water waist-high, pushed there by the press of men fleeing the road. He felt "scared as hell." The crack of small-arms fire round about him was terrific. More men came tumbling down the banks and into the water.

One of them was Private Dowson, Cassidy's orderly and a battalion favorite. When General Eisenhower had inspected the outfit just before it mounted up for Normandy, he had stopped beside Dowson to ask the popular question, "What do you plan to do when you get out of the Army?"

Dowson, chuckling, replied, "General, I don't hanker to do

anything but get back to Georgia and eat black-eyed peas and greens."

Little Dowson—he joined Cassidy in the marsh just a moment too soon. An artillery round came along and, without exploding, cut his head off at the neck without touching his body.

Cassidy got out of there and ran on up the road to the bridge. The bullet fire was still thick but going high. So he stood in the middle of the bridge, yelling, "See, that fire is way overhead; it won't hurt you."

Somehow, he got them to believe it, and he put most of them through the bridge within the next half hour. Yet to the senses of Lieutenant Robert Rogers "that bullet fire was so thick that a man didn't dare raise his head." It was coming from well-concealed positions amid the marshes on the right rather than from the high ground. Rogers set up his two machine guns at Bridge No. 4 and threw traversing fire over the marsh. His guns, and Cassidy's bravado, got the battalion through. But it was touch and go. Baker Company, leading the battalion, lost eight men, going through Bridge No. 4, and three of them were killed.

Rogers led Baker Company on up the fire-swept road, still dreaming that he would break through a thin crust of enemy and then make an easy march to Hill 30. The column turned into the meadow where Cole had charged; its sward was calm as a millpond. But at the far end the farmhouse was a bull's-eye of mortar and artillery fire. Rogers said, "Let's keep clear of that." So the company swung around to the right of the farmhouse and went into position on the far side of M. Ingouf's service road. No one had told Rogers what to do, but it was an inspired guess. He was astonished to see that 3rd Battalion "was just a scattering of little knots of men with no continuous defensive position," and he knew that his dream of reaching Hill 30 in a romp was best forgotten.

On the march-up, no two companies fared alike. As had happened with Cole's battalion, they spilled onto the forward ground raggedly, convulsively, in small groups or singly, depending on how the meadows were erupting at a given moment.

Take Able Company, which followed Baker. Mortar and artillery fire knocked off five of its men at Bridge No. 4, and somewhere along the causeway, six were lost to bullets. Cassidy followed along with Able from the bridge, figuring that most of the regulating job was done and his place was now forward.

The two lead platoons started across the meadow stormed by Cole. (Baker Company had made it without a scratch.) Midway of the field, right out of the blue, mortar and 88 shells in salvo landed among them. Fifteen men were hit while still marching. The shock scattered the others in all directions. The irrigation ditch was just ahead. Some dived into it and stayed submerged, only their faces out of the water. Others ran back all the way to Bridge No. 4. Two hours were lost in re-collecting them and bringing them forward. The mortar shelling continued, though in lesser amounts.

Behind the company, Cassidy had gone flat with his radio operator. Seconds later, a mortar shell exploded near the radio man and killed him instantly. Cassidy got to his feet and tried to talk the others into moving. "Follow me! It's safer forward." But this time the inertia was nearly absolute. Only three or four arose and tried to run forward. Rather than be killed at the wrong place, Cassidy continued on to the house to talk to Cole.

Third Platoon of Able came up, started across the field and got caught in the same meat grinder. It dissolved as the men ran, looking for a shielding bank or tree trunk. But cover was no longer easy to find. The more convenient ditches and foxholes were already filled by the dead, wounded and stragglers in the backwash of the battle. Third Platoon lost nine men in this one field. So Able had paid with 30 men before getting to the fire line.

From out of Baker Company's position on the right flank, Lieutenant Homer J. Combs led a patrol of six men all the way to the railroad track. This party crossed trails with another detached group of ten men, who advanced a machine gun to the crossroads south on the Ingouf farm, then searched the nearby houses. Its leader was Private Redmond Wells, one of the real stalwarts of the day.

Combs's party saw a group of Germans off to their left 100 yards. The Americans were already under sniper fire. It is not surprising that their aim was bad and their own musketry achieved nothing except the vanishing of the German group. So they held a council of war. The others wanted to scout after the Germans. Combs said, "Look, we're already so far out on a limb that I can smell the blossoms. I propose to stay here, and we can do it if we establish a fire line now and stick together." That was what they did, and they held all day—a little isle of Americans in an enemy sea. It was a nub of a position anchored amid ditches and hedge banks.

The Germans came back to the road as soon as Combs settled. Thereafter he knew no quiet. The enemy fired from a ditch just 20 yards away. Combs survived only because on that side he was partly protected by a brick wall. Thus locked, and virtually isolated from the main body, the men maintained themselves mainly with grenades, though twice they beat the Germans off with bayonets. Their one machine gun was set up to fire diagonally at the crossroads and into the field beyond. For a time, it kept the enemy from crowding. That they stayed, however, was a triumph of the human spirit, for this forlorn outpost had no link with the main body.

Soldiers are superstitious, especially infantrymen, and one small incident had fortified them. They had found a grim tableau at the crossroads when they first came forward. In one corner was mounted a German machine gun; the dead gunner sat there, hand on trigger. Sprawled across gun and gunner was a dead American paratrooper. He'd been dead many hours but near his hand were two boxes of U.S. machine-gun ammunition. Someone said, "He seems to be saying that we've come to the right spot." The men took his gift along, and before the morning passed they had need of it.

At first there were only 13 men in Combs's outpost, including some from Wells's patrol who had attached themselves. The others, after searching the houses and finding only a few frightened Frenchmen, had returned to the farm. But as the morning wore on, men singly out of 1st and 3rd Platoons, hearing heavy fire forward and feeling curious about it, infiltrated toward them until finally Combs commanded about five squads.

Little else of this piecemeal front was solid at midmorning. But along the low hedgerow by the house, there was power pointing toward the orchard. There, Staff Sergeant Harrison Summers, the one-man army from Cassidy's battalion, had planted two machine guns, one aimed toward the apple trees, the other sited so it could sweep the road. Summers had chosen his spot and didn't intend to move.

Able Company had been downed in the field about 1100. The same barrage engulfed the farmhouse where Cole sweated it out, regulating the shellfire and trying to locate his own flanks. The guns were now working over the fields beyond the railroad and banging away at Carentan. It had to be so. Cole knew that some elements of 1st Battalion had come up but couldn't be sure where they had gone. Of how the battle lines were forming, and whether any of his men or Cassidy's had made contact and were now fighting, he had little or no idea.

When Cassidy got to him, the big clobber was on, and direct hits were rocking the building.

Cole looked up and said, "Let's get the hell out of here!"

They did. Cassidy went out the side door and into a wood-pile. Where Cole went, he didn't see. But that was about the extent of their conversation on how to co-ordinate forces and plans. There was none. When Cassidy got out of the kindling, he hiked back to Bridge No. 4 to collect his runaways and burn the tails of the fainthearts. But he didn't stay long.

Their failure to communicate is one of the anomalies of the battle. They were close friends in a Damon and Pythias way, and also roommates. But each was having his first experience with joined battle, and each was overly preoccupied with his own foreground.

A deviation from sound command behavior, their aloofness, on balance, made little difference because of the unique situation. Empirically, 1st Battalion's role became one of building up on the same ground on which 3rd Battalion had exhausted itself. Without relieving 3rd, 1st took over, got its shoulder in the door and there became wedged. Cole's remnants merely filled in along Cassidy's defensive line. Nobody reconnoitered the front in detail. Had anyone tried he could have quickly died, for the positions were not contiguous, and movement from one to the other meant full exposure where the fire was thickest. Lacking information to the contrary, Cole hugged the illusion that his men had the lion's share of the fight while Cassidy's companies, along the edges, were freeloading on a glory ride.

The Irishman already knew what he needed to do. Cole, at the farmhouse, could oversee the left flank. Cassidy would therefore guide things on the right wing near the road, where nobody was commanding. He felt it of no consequence that half of his soldiers would be under Cole.

Five men of Able Company got together after the clobber in the meadow. On their own, they figured that the worst enemy pressure was perforce developing along the high ground near the Carentan road, and that Cole's mop-up of the farm was turning the German weight rightward, threatening an outflanking movement which might close the escape route. So they changed direction and pushed southward to the intersection of the fourth hedgerow and the highway.

There they reinforced Cole's leftmost element—four riflemen and a light machine gun. The gun had stopped. Two gunners had been driven off, successively, by bullets bouncing off the barrel and hitting them in the face. Losing blood, they became too weak to handle the weapon. The other men didn't know how.

When Cassidy's men reached the position, Cole's four men were all in the ditch, all wounded, all bleeding badly, too worn to help each other, but unwilling to crawl away.

The newcomers propped themselves behind the hedge—and had time for nothing more. From their right, the German machine-gun fire came at them so accurately and in such volume that not one fired a shot. About noontime they withdrew, having accomplished nothing but the evacuation of the four wounded.

Holding the most advanced ground of any Americans, they had seen not one German. It was typical of the day. The enemy was a phantom. Staying covered, he advanced along the perpendicular hedgerows and ditches, then moved to the flank on the inside of the hedgerows running approximately at right angles to the road. The Germans were skilled at this manner of advance and rarely exposed more than a shoulder or helmet tip. Give them not too much credit. The battle scene in modern warfare is commonly an empty landscape. To feel fire all around, see comrades fall by the score, yet note not one living target in sight is the average lot of the infantryman.

Men with Cassidy and Cole knew that a new fire line was building up opposite them only from the rising rattle of weapons hidden by the banks and greenery. Had they withheld fire until they saw an enemy soldier, their try would have been hopeless. That day, 70 per cent of the American skirmishers around the farm saw Germans only after the Germans had become corpses. Still, they fought, blasting the banks and bushes with their hand weapons; if rarely the bullet found a mark, the volume discouraged a mad rush. The Garand was their best friend. Only 13 of them could remember using a grenade on that day: only six could say they killed an enemy with it. More by accident than design, nine used a bayonet to stick a man during the scurrying around the hedgerows.

Squad and company scrambling, brought about by the way the two battalions were committed, was made worse by the geometric pattern of the countryside. The fields around Carentan are of all shapes and sizes: triangular, trapezoidal, oblong. Their outline, instead of the rise and fall of ground, determined the paths of advance and points of resistance. Units had to accommodate themselves to it. Large groups could not be put forward together, or kept intact on the defensive. To strengthen the force behind any stretch of hedge was to multiply the chance that more men would be killed. Small groups, going out on different missions, sometimes advanced on converging lines and merged, or returned to the old spot to find their comrades gone.

As Cole and Cassidy both knew, the flaw in the general position was that it had no rear. The progressive diffusion of forces aggravated that weakness, killing the chance for a reorganization which would allow for a local reserve. So there was nothing on which to fall back. If the front cracked, the people who could still move would have to leg it for the causeway.

Captain Rosemond, trying to adjust the artillery from the top floor of the farmhouse, was plagued by the hedgerows. They curtained the fields, and he couldn't see where the shells were falling. So he had to play it by ear in the manner of jungle warfare, judging by the sound whether the shells were dropping where he wanted them.

Cole said to him, "We need more delay fire, something that will get in at the base of the hedges and root these krauts out of their holes. Most of your stuff is blowing off in air."

"If we had it," said Rosemond, "you'd get it."

But he was plagued with more problems than that. In fact, this wasn't his task at all. Lieutenant Spruel was the assigned forward observer. But Spruel had been killed during the charge. He must have had a hunch about it. Just before jumping off, he said to Rosemond, "I didn't want to ship back to England anyway; they'd just give us another training schedule."

So Rosemond had taken over, a substitute forward observer with no communications. The radio operator had gone down in the same ditch as Cole, and his set had been drowned out. That was how things stood for three hours. When the heavy clobber was on in midmorning, threatening to blow the house down, Rosemond wasn't sure whether the Germans were hitting true or his own guns were shooting short.

The first ambulance arrived, bringing ammunition. There was an SCR 609 radio aboard. He changed the crystals to his own dead radio set, and it worked. That was near noon, and for several hours thereafter he did his stuff with no hitch.

By 1200, neither infantry battalion had enough feel of the Germans to be sure whether they were standing or preparing to cut and run. Several times there was a heavy rattle of burp guns as the Germans crept closer. Men said to one another, "They're coming now." Always the threat faded.

Bridge No. 4 stayed enveloped by machine-gun fire from positions along the Carentan road. Part of How Company was deployed along the hedgerows by the road. Falling short, the fire cut into them, killing six, wounding eight, in a bad quarter hour. A man from George Company had a dud mortar round land on his head while he lay flat in a ditch with arms outstretched. It wrapped the helmet around his head, and he had to crawl to a medico to have it pried loose.

Simmons sent eight men on a patrol beyond the first farmhouse on the right side of the road. Three were hit by mortar fire. The others jumped into a water-filled ditch. A German machine-gunner had them covered and put down a band of fire above the stream. They stayed submerged for more than an hour praying for him to quit.

He tired. So did others. A lull held the front.

36

The Cabbage Patch

That noontide pause in the battle goes unexplained. Such things may happen in combat from phenomenal coincidence. At a given moment all hands feel the need of a respite; or ammunition runs low everywhere at once; or a squad knocks off to split a ration, and the example carries far and wide, like a pebble tossed into a pool, flank to flank, front to rear and across the void of disputed ground. Armies are not machines; amid inferno, they will sometimes react to one touch of human nature as capriciously as children on a playground. No one knows why it happened.

So there was only the silence and a furnace heat. The air quivered with it. A warm wind blew the smoke away. Its grime and the embankment dust had caked every face. Men were masked like copper miners. But for one racing hour tension fell off.

No greater boon came to the Americans that day. Cassidy's battalion, which until then had been unable to take firm hold of anything, having been exploded into the scene by the surprise barrage, could at last complete a semiunified defensive arrangement.

All of this time, Charley Company had been held on the causeway because Cassidy saw to it, not wishing to have another unit chewed up and scattered by the enemy artillery. It now marched forward into ground directly forward of the sec-

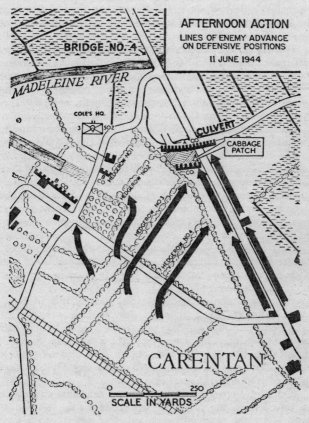

AFTERNOON ACTION

LINES OF ENEMY ADVANCE
ON DEFENSIVE POSITIONS

11 JUNE 1944

BRIDGE NO. 4

MADELEINE RIVER

COLE'S HQ.

3 502

CULVERT

CABBAGE
PATCH

HEDGEROW NO.1

HEDGEROW NO.2

HEDGEROW NO.3

HEDGEROW NO.4

CARENTAN

0   250
SCALE IN YARDS

Figure 28.   GERMAN COUNTERATTACK

ond hedgerow running to the Carentan road through the Ingouf farm.

The deep irrigation ditch forming the boundary of the field between the road and the farmhouse turns about evenly with the second hedgerow, the stream flowing under the road through a culvert. Beyond the ditch and extending to the third hedgerow was a broad cabbage patch.

There amid the cabbage heads, Charley Company's rifles and machine guns were so distributed that they could put a flanking fire on the Germans as they crept down the far side of the third hedgerow, or with equal facility, pouring a flanking fire on them if they came down the inside ditch, and the hedge-row paralleling the road.

Able Company was pulled back from the position beyond the farmhouse and built up along the rear of Charley Company, so that its weapons covered the base of the cabbage patch and could fire toward the fringe of the orchard and against the third hedgerow frontally. Its line extended across the Carentan road and bent around the far end of the culvert. So placed, the weapons there could snuff the attack if the Germans came forward along the ditches of the Carentan road trying to envelop the two battalions.

Thus deployed, 1st Battalion became a wall directly blocking the lines over which the Germans were in that same hour planning their counterattack. Its pattern varied hardly at all through the afternoon hours.

Yet it was all fortuitous, sheer bullheaded luck. Cassidy and his officers had not recognized the decisive nature of the cabbage patch. Nor had Cole or anyone, except the five-man patrol from Able Company which had roamed up the road, stayed at the hot corner for more than an hour, and been unable to fire. They saw its importance but only vaguely, and they spoke of it to no one else.

Charley Company spread itself among the cabbages because the men felt that the young cabbage heads and the scooped-up earth along the rows afforded fair concealment and a little protection. To an infantryman, even a shielding cabbage head is preferable to nothing. But these riflemen did not realize that their ground was a hub at the center of the spokelike hedgerows along which the Germans would have to come.

During the lull, Cassidy talked with Cole briefly. Charley

Company was then coming forward, a fairly solid body. They discussed where to place it.

Cassidy said, "The fields next the road are the least manned, and that makes us more vulnerable there."

Cole agreed. In the event of a strong counterattack, the right flank would probably hold, and the enemy strength would shift toward the vacuum on the left. On this rather casual basis, the decision was taken, and the gravity center of the two-battalion front was shifted from the farmhouse to the road, where it belonged. The prime importance of the cabbage patch was unmentioned; no one had studied it. Cassidy went on back to feed his platoons into the appointed ground in conformity with the general idea.

But the quiet had made Lieutenant W. A. Swanson, that usually phlegmatic soldier, unusually restless. Taking Sergeant Jay Schenk, of Charley Company, Sergeant Stanley Czarnick, of Headquarters, and two machine-gunners of George Company, he scouted up the Carentan road to the first group of farmhouses on the left of it.

. Their prowl took them beyond the fourth hedgerow. They ducked into the first dwelling and saw a party of Germans peering from the windows of the house beyond.

Both groups fired at once—rifles and machine pistols. Two Germans were cut down. Czarnick got a bullet through the face.

Czarnick said, "I guess I better go back for a dressing."

Swanson had emptied his Tommy gun and had no refill. He said, "I guess we'd all better get the hell out."

The Germans on whom he had fired had vanished. He saw no others around. But as he doubled back to the battalion, he saw other enemy troops in large numbers moving into the third and fourth hedgerows. He said dryly, "It doesn't look like they're getting out." From among the cabbages, Lieutenant George R. Cody looked to his front and saw these same activities. But the Germans were not firing, and reluctant to break the calm, Cody withheld fire.

Unwittingly, on his prowl, Swanson had passed within a few yards of Sergeant Odom and his two companions. After knocking out the enemy machine gun in early morning, this trio stayed put, a lonely outpost, by the farmhouses, way out ahead of the American front. Odom clung there because no one else seemed to be guarding. He missed Swanson's thrust because one hedgerow intervened. Also obscured to Odom, Private Allen C. McLean, of George Company, was manning a lone post in the same field between the road and the houses. Not far from him, though neither McLean nor Odom knew it, Corporal Leroy Drummond, of How Company, with half a squad, maintained a third post. In the absence of orders, these several fragments had disposed themselves where they thought they might be useful. Yes, it's called initiative.

Drummond had been drawn to the field on hearing someone crying. It was a friend, Private Claude F. Fletcher, with a shell fragment through his stomach. He carried Fletcher to the rear, then returned to the field.

Without knowing what it meant, Drummond heard the exchange of fire between Swanson and the Germans. It made him uneasy. So he walked to the road and saw the enemy groups feeding into the hedgerow lines, which put them on his rear. He counted about 50 of them, then said to his men, "I think it's time for us to move back."

The detachment fell back not more than 150 yards. Drummond was stopped by the sight of a Browning heavy machine gun, set up in firing position where two embankments met. There was no one anywhere around it. "I think this is our spot," said Drummond: "now we can go to work on them." He spread out his four men in a rifle line along one bank, got on the gun and sprayed fire on the Germans sneaking down the third hedgerow, killing a few of them, forcing the others to turn tail. It crimped the counterattack just a mite before it could start rolling. Odom and his companions stayed where they were; they had chosen their ground and they liked it.

Far over on the right of the two-battalion front, Private Robert I. Boyce led five other riflemen up the service road running from the farmhouse. An enemy machine-gun squad walked toward them. Two women marched in front of the squad. It gave Boyce the idea that the Germans wished to surrender. Then one member of his party saw the gun, carried by two soldiers and almost hidden by the women's skirts. He yelled, "Get down! It's a trap." They fired. Two Germans were shot dead. Magically, the two women disappeared, and no one noted how or where.

Simmons's five men who had been pinned in the water-filled ditch along the Carentan road congratulated themselves on being well out of it when the lull came. They beat it back and flankward to the bank of the Madeleine, just in time to see two squads of Germans emerge from a shelter which no one had searched. It was such a sudden thing that the Germans ducked behind an earth bank before the Americans could raise weapons. From behind the bank the enemy Schmeissers and rifles spewed so much fire at them that the Americans had to get amphibious again. Having spent one hour in the water of the ditch, they passed most of the afternoon immersed in the waters of the Madeleine. Theirs was the cleanest experience of the day.

Swanson's insatiable curiosity again got the better of him. Having finished his sight-seeing tour beyond the left flank, after earlier visiting the far outpost on the right where Combs and mates put fire on the crossroads, he craved another look at how things were going there.

But the pitcher went once too often to the well. Before he could lay eyes on Combs, he collided with a party of Germans, who swarmed over him after bursting through a gap in the hedgerow.

They pinioned, slugged and blindfolded him. They said nothing. He said nothing. But he felt very silly.

So held, he inevitably missed the next freak turn in the situation. The brief soldier's peace of the noontide quickly phased into an even shorter-lived Generals' truce. McAuliffe, who was running the battle for Taylor, got the idea, and probably it was suggested to him by the sudden silence over the field.

Nobody along the front quite understood what was going on, and the greater number of both Americans and Germans, far scattered and not joined with higher command by radio, were wholly ignorant that any parley was being attempted. Cole got the mysterious word over radio: "Have all hands cease fire. Somebody wants a truce." It left him slightly puzzled. There was no way to suspend fire; it had stopped itself. As for getting the word to the men, he knew the locations of only the few he could see from his upper-story window. But he did try to comply by sending a few runners forth. His own information was so vague that when he tried to pass it on to the messengers, one of them asked, "How do you stop shooting until you get a truce?" The same problem has bothered several UN commissions in the years since.

Not feeling like playing hero that day, the runners spread the words only to the few tactical groups right around the farmhouse. From this circle, it spread outward, swiftly but irregularly, according to the pattern invariably followed by rumors and reports along a battle front.

Along the Carentan road, one American yelled, "Hey, they've surrendered," and the cry sped on its way. Another story went the rounds: "We've captured a German field marshal; that's what it's all about." However, the optimists and whopper spreaders were given little credit. Most of the men were simply disposed to wait and see, and few of them believed that the battle was over. The wiser NCOs and the more cynical privates took note that the Germans were using the cease-fire to strengthen their forward positions. They saw a few more men walking forward and none going back. They felt sure that the truce talk was a trick pulled by the Germans to achieve a build-up without paying.

At the crossroad where Combs and his party held forth, neither Germans nor Americans got the word, and the war kept going. The Germans in the ditch battered away at the brick wall with percussion grenades and machine pistols—a glorious waste of ammunition. In the distant field, Combs saw Germans concentrating with greater abandon than at any time during the day and wondered why. But he couldn't fire on them. He was hoarding his ammunition against a final rush by the Germans in the ditch. So they sweated out the regrouping, and not having a radio, they couldn't tell Cole about it.

Only along the Carentan road, troops could see what was going on, though they stayed mystified about the object and how the thing was started. An American officer carrying a Red Cross flag came through Bridge No. 4, and was shortly met by two Germans carrying white flags, who led him toward the city. The American was Major Douglas T. Davidson, regimental surgeon of 502nd, a lanky character with a hayseed look and drawling voice, who loved fighting more than healing and was forever grousing about man's inhumanity to man.

Davidson was taking his ride to ask whether the Germans were ready to surrender Carentan. Actually, McAuliffe had no such hope when he sought a truce and sent Davidson forth. But he wanted an hour in which to clear the field of wounded, and he thought this the best way to get it.

The German commander in Carentan wouldn't even see

Davidson. But while the American was getting the cold shoulder, a chaplain arrived at the Ingóuf farm, collected about 50 casualties in jeeps and trucks and led the convoy back over the causeway.

Davidson was back within the American lines by 1300. The men didn't see him return. But they knew. As he crossed Bridge No. 4, on his way to Regiment, the Germans cut loose with everything—rifles, machine guns, mortars, artillery—in the heaviest concentration of the day.

It landed with power and precision against the length of the American front, catching many of the troopers in the open and causing as many casualties as the chaplain had cleared away.

Cole called Regiment: "I must return fire."

Regiment objected; so far as it knew, Davidson wasn't back.

The barrage continued. Cole called again and was told, "No, we can't give you permission to fire."

Just then a shell hit the roof above Cole's head. He yelled, "God damn it, did you hear that? Now can I let my men shoot?"

The answer was, "No, you must wait."

Well if that was what Regiment thought, it was cuckoo. The soldiers had already taken the decision out of its hands in this matter. Behind the rows and cabbages, they were blasting away. When at last Regiment called back to sanction fire, Cole didn't bother to pass the word along. All hands felt pretty droopy when the fight began again. The lull and truce had lasted just long enough to bring on an almost overpowering drowsiness. Simmons had to waken several of his men after the shoot started. One of them said, "I guess these bastards have got to get it the hard way."

Anyhow, Swanson profited from the truce. The Germans who had captured him, thinking they had violated a high-command agreement, removed his blindfold and booted him back into the lane. Having not the slightest idea why, he felt sillier than before, and more mystified than relieved.

37

Rout

Swanson and Combs had seen them forming.

Drummond and his few riflemen had intervened at the psychological moment to bloody their noses and turn them briefly. His machine gun was their first warning that the gap had been closed.

But they were momentarily deflected, not stopped. Their plan was a double envelopment, and one horn of it only had been snubbed. Of a sudden, the fight flamed along the hedgerows running through the orchard toward the farmhouse. Blasting with machine pistols and rifles, they came crawling and running near the banks, half-hidden by the flowering apples. Their fire converged toward the hedge where Harrison Summers commanded two machine guns.

Lieutenant Clarence A. Thompson, Jr., moved along the second hedgerow, trying to round up a few more men. There were only five or six troopers within sight or sound. He could feel the heat as the Germans sifted toward him through the trees. But his men were not yet hurt or especially alarmed. The bullets—a few of them—plunked into the bank. Most of the fire droned high overhead as if the Germans were shooting at the house. Thompson trotted on down the hedgerow looking for idle rifles.

Came one bullet to the mark. It hit Sergeant William A.

Grant in the arm. The blood spurted. He knew it was an artery, and he would either get aid quickly or die. Not saying a word, he turned and ran toward the farmhouse.

In combat, here, ever, is the seed of panic—unexplained flight toward the rear. Seeing Grant go, the two men nearest him jumped from their foxholes, slipped a few steps leftward and then bolted, not following Grant, but running blindly down the hedgerow toward the main road. Thompson, seeing their flight, ran after them, screaming, "Come back! Come back!" His frantic cry but made matters worse.

Lieutenant Rogers, propped against the first hedgerow near the house, heard and saw these things happen. He heard another shout go up from close around him: "The order is to withdraw." It passed from man to man, a swelling chant: "Withdraw! Withdraw!"

A second lieutenant, a few paces from Rogers, echoed it: "Withdraw!"

Rogers yelled, "Damn you, don't say that unless you're sure."

Seconds later Rogers was biting his own tongue. The shave-tail turned back to face the Germans, and a bullet got him through the brain.

The bailout along the main hedgerow dropped the weight of the German attack squarely on Harrison Summers's two guns. Fire from the Schmeissers ripped the trees and beat up dust all around him. Being with Summers, the gunners stuck it, gave back everything they had, raking the orchard and the gaps in Hedgerow No. 2 with steady fire. Summers stood there, shouting encouragement. The contest went on, 10, 15 minutes. The Germans closed to within 30 yards of the gun. Then the survivors faded back. The same man who won the fight at WXYZ near Utah Beach could stake a claim on having saved the day on M. Ingouf's farm.

For what Thompson and Rogers feared most had happened. The sudden run by three men at the second hedgerow and the cry, "Withdraw! Withdraw!" stampeded the sector. Stragglers and wounded lying in the fields arose and fled. The able-bodied joined them. Short of the cabbage patch, the front was picked clean. Out of control, the mob raced for Bridge No. 4.

There it was stopped by a knot of supply and communi-cations officers and NCOs who, seeing men in flight, got out their pistols, blocked the road and stemmed the tide. But the fugitives were spent. Some lay down on the embankment and vomited.

None of this delirium was felt within the cabbage patch; the soldiers there didn't know about it till long after. They were too busy killing krauts. Recoiling, the Germans had bounded rightward again, and Charley Company slaughtered them as they came down the rows.

Cole, running his fight from within the house, did not know his front had been breached. He felt a vague uneasiness. From the way the enemy fire built upward and from the sustained barking of Summers's two guns, right under him, he guessed that the enemy counterattack was rolling. He said to Rosemond, "Give us more artillery."

Nothing much disturbed Private Allen T. Emery, of Cole's Headquarters Company. He had worked like a Trojan with his heavy mortar in the night stalemate on the causeway. When Grant got shot, Emery, looking through the brush of the first hedgerow, saw him come on at a run. The men with Thompson were a little to his left at the hedgerow beyond. He saw the group break and run. He heard a man near him cry, "The Germans are coming; get behind the bridge!" Then several men picked up the cry, and he heard, "Withdraw!" He saw men from both battalions get in motion, first a walk, then a trot, then a dead run. It was as if they started with a doubt that they were doing the right thing and then became swept along. All of this seemed a little unusual, but he couldn't do anything about it.

He and Private Eugene W. Saver, of How Company, his buddy of the day, watched them go. Saver said, "Well, what do you know about that?" Emery had an M-1, Saver a BAR. It didn't occur to either of them that their weapons were needed or that they were in real danger.

A few feet away was a square-cut, German-tooled foxhole, six feet deep. They jumped in to get out of the line of fire. So placed, being small men, they couldn't see over the top. Occasionally, they boosted one another to see what was happening. Soldiers were still running toward the bridge. Mortar fire, which had been falling at intervals along the hedge line was now exploding "in right big bunches." Emery could also see that the traversing enemy machine-gun fire was clipping the shrubbery like a scythe. None of this being pleasant, he dropped back into the hole.

The Germans had cut two neat ledges in its walls. In one was a bag of sausage, bread and butter. The other held a box of homemade fudge.

They were hungry and they first demolished the solid food. Then they wolfed the fudge. Naturally, they saw no Germans. They didn't believe that anyone could overrun their position. So eating on to the last crumb, they wondered why their friends had run away to the bridge.

"That's good candy," said Emery; "I didn't know Germans could do it."

The breaching of the line was survived because, where the panic had stripped one sector, the enemy still had no thoroughfare. Either the Germans had to come through the orchard toward Summers's guns, or they had to move along the lateral hedgerows toward Charley Company in the cabbage patch. The embankment pattern blocked a move through center.

Some of the runaways returned sheepishly to the ground they had quit. The defenders continued playing it by ear. When they heard the Schmeissers barking from 100 yards off, then from 60, then 40, they knew that the danger was tightening. The b-r-r-r of the machine guns would double, then treble— not more shots, but more sound. The working of rifle bolts, the falling of empty brass, were plainly audible. The nearer the enemy came, the more accurate grew the fire.

At the crossroads position where Lieutenant Combs fought, the German onfall, when the truce ended, came fast and furious. Enemy skirmishers swept in numbers around the curving line, coming on with rifles, grenades and Schmeissers, closing up tight from behind a mortar concentration. Only the machine gun, answering, kept their numbers thinned at close range.

The Germans won the crossroads, dug in along its ditches and turned three machine guns against the brick wall. Combs and the few others crouched under its protection weathered this steel tempest. The 30 men of 1st Battalion, who had filtered forward to join the outpost, were driven off.

Not far from the farmhouse there is a square-cut indentation in the bank of the Madeleine, filled with stagnant marsh water. A few rods from it is a small bay, also excavated in Napoleon's time. The men retreated to the neck of land between and set up a new defense. Missing Combs and seven others, they concluded that this fraction was either overrun or shot down in flight. But the eight stayed by the stone wall. Embattled thereafter, and surrounded by a force many times their size, they stayed there and fought back. It seemed safer than making a run, and when Combs yelled, "We won't give up!" that settled it for the others. This small blister on the German rear kept the enemy from giving undivided attention to the attack on Cole's line. The mortar fire had already shifted to the cabbage patch and the hedgerows nearest the house and did not shift back again.

The pounding was hellish. Many mortars, unlimited ammunition and uncannily accurate fire. Comparatively, the German artillery was a small nuisance. Only three 88s were shelling; getting off several rounds apiece at intervals, they would then break off for ten minutes. But the mortars and the machine guns had the range and stayed with it.

Already reeling from the mortar fire, ten men of Baker Company at the second hedgerow were taken unawares by a German with a machine pistol who crawled through the hedge and blasted them from the flank. Seven were hit by bullets. The other three quit the line, helping the wounded back. Near this gap in the line, ten men from How Company were deployed. One of them shot the German firing the Schmeisser. That quelled the worst menace. But more than a squad of Germans had made it to the far side of this same hedge. This put the antagonists six feet apart, separated from each other by a bank of earth. The brush was too thick to permit firing through the hedge at this point. Both sides tried to grenade over the hedge. But Germans and Americans were clinging too close to the protecting bank, and in this deadly game of ante-over, the throwing was wild.

From the gap where the Baker men had been, one German pushed a light machine gun through the foliage. Its first burst struck Harrison Summers's machine gun guarding the left flank of the hedgerow by the house, destroying the gun and killing its crew of three. The right-hand gun, under the hand of Private William A. Burt, kept on firing straight down the service road, and without knowing it (he had no idea there were any Americans up ahead), he helped save Combs and his friends. That fire from the flank pinned the Germans who were dug in at the crossroads. Burt had seen a few of them trying to cross the road. Later he said, "I zeroed in on that spot because it seemed like a good idea at the time."

But the luck in that outpost couldn't last. Combs got hit in the head, a grazing bullet which knocked him cold. There were three dead and 15 disabled wounded already at the stone-wall position. Privates Luther Davis, James Parham, Burton Petit, John Kokrugga, Anthony Foglia, Redmond Wells and Sergeant Ted Kaus now held the fort.

Wells, the most forceful personality and, though a private, a leader of the same cut as Combs or Davy Crockett, took charge.

Not long after, a bullet got him in the right shoulder and cracked the bone. There were no dressings present. By lying still and squeezing, he could stanch the blood flow.

"I think that's about enough," Wells said to the others. "Leave me here. I'll surrender the wounded. The rest of you better run back and try to make the hedgerows."

The other six said not one word in reply. They looked at him one by one and shook their heads. There was no leader now, just six soldiers with one fixed idea. The fight went on, and they were still together when it ended.

With Summers and Rogers in the positions guarding the farmhouse, there had been 28 men when the truce ended. Now 12 remained in the fight, and four of them had flesh wounds. The others were all dead or wounded and disabled by bullet fire.

Charley Company and the remnant of Able were still deployed among the cabbages, having held their ground more than six hours against counterattack which, recoiling repeatedly, never stopped. Alone among the units scattered over the front they had maintained a semblance of tactical organization. But the cost came high. Charley, which had the more advanced position, had lost 20 men to bullet fire and the mortar shelling before the afternoon waned. Able was present with 30 men and three machine guns. How many men it lost in the cabbage patch was never calculated, since, unlike Charley, it did not give that sector undivided attention.

The position was never for one minute dented. As consistent as was that showing, so was the pattern of the enemy's effort to dissolve it. The Germans continued to advance in parallel lines down the hedgerows to the cabbage patch. But always other enemy riflemen pressed forward along the ditches of the Carentan road. The twin lines of advance were maintained through the afternoon. Toward the close, the thrust along the ditches slowed because the enemy was blocked by the pile-up of his own dead. Even so, the Germans kept trying, and in the last stage the machine guns covering the ditches were slaughtering enemy riflemen as they came on over a heap of the slain within 25 feet of the muzzle blast. On the right-hand ditch, Privates Charles L. Roderick and Franklin E. Cawthon kept their gun going six hours.

Roderick took a hit on the operating handle while firing. It drove a piece of the handle through his shoulder. He refused evacuation, called for a new handle, and continued firing.

Privates Leroy C. Nicolai and Alfred A. Fitzsimmons worked the gun on the left ditch. Shooting in bursts of six or seven, they burned up 20 boxes of ammunition during the afternoon. When the fight ended, they counted ten dead Germans within 25 yards of their gun. The banks of the ditch were greatly irregular. It was possible for the Germans to crawl almost to the gun before Nicolai could get a bead on them.

Through the afternoon, the Carentan road could not be traveled by jeeps or by men bearing ammunition, such was the intensity of the fire. To the rear of the guns, the ditches were solidly clogged with American wounded and the ammunition carriers could not come forward over their bodies. Yet one of these obstacles was self-liquidating.

Men—the wounded, the faltering and all of those who for any reason could no longer face the fire—were strung out along the ditches and part of the causeway for more than a mile on both sides of the Carentan road.

These two chains of battered humanity served as a conveyor belt. Ammunition boxes were given into one pair of hands back at Bridge No. 4. They passed through scores of hands on the way up and arrived blood-soaked. But always, they came along. The wounded crawled the few yards necessary to get the upcoming ammunition and then crawled to where another pair of feeble hands could take hold and pass it along. That was how the battle line and the guns on the ditches stayed supplied.

Congestion at the Carentan road got worse as the afternoon lengthened and new wounded from the fire fight pressed to the ditches to await an ambulance. As the flow to rearward increased, the need for new hands along the fire line grew more acute. Spares were rounded up from work crews along the causeway. Some of these men got stalled in the ditches as they tried to come up. In some way, the traffic block had to be broken.

Sergeant Charles R. De Rose, had fallen into a hole and broken his leg, when he first moved up to Able Company's position at the cabbage patch.

He undertook the job. Standing in the same hole where he had broken his leg, and leaning for support on his arms to lessen the pain, he directed traffic for five hours. He shuttled the wounded back. He urged the able-bodied forward to the cabbage patch.

This soldier could do much with his voice, even when his limbs were of little help.

To every American who saw him in action, the memory is indelible. He was one of the most splendid figures of the day.

But fate had already engraved his number on one special shell.

38

Crisis

It was six o'clock. Rosemond stood at a second-story window for a minute looking out over the meadows. Cole joined him.

He noted the pitifully scant number of his men scattered along the first two hedgerows. They were firing as fast as they could pull trigger. But compared with the racket and roar arising from the field beyond, the noise of his own fire sounded like a death rattle. He knew then that his line was going.

He said to Rosemond, "It isn't enough, not nearly enough."

Rosemond nodded his agreement. There was nothing worth saying.

Captain Simmons crawled along the inside of the vertical hedge on a last trip, carrying ammunition to the ten men who were holding out along the second hedgerow.

Their machine gun had jammed from overfiring. Only rifles and a few grenades were left to them. Simmons dropped the supply and crawled back. Talk didn't serve any purpose.

Then he collected six men and built up a fire line along the hedgerow near the house. This was the last reserve. When the Germans made the second hedge, and his squad forward had to fall back over the last field, it might partway cover the withdrawal.

There was no longer any attempt to evacuate the wounded. They came back along the ditches if they could crawl. If they couldn't, they stayed where they had been hit. Via the ditches, the remaining aid men tried to get to these cases and bandage them on the spot. Such was the rain of fire on Bridge No. 4 that ambulances and litter men could no longer come through.

Watching these things, Cole and Rosemond knew that the play was ended. They could see nothing of the enemy, but they could feel his presence all around.

Rifle fire was buffeting the house from two sides and knocking slates from the roof overhead. The silent communion continued, with both men shaking their heads. Neither was willing to use the words, "We've lost." But each read the other's thoughts.

In Rosemond's mind there was a question. Was it better to stay and go down fighting or attempt to withdraw via the causeway, with all the horror that such a retreat entailed?

He couldn't answer. For lack of an answer, he said a prayer.

In Cole's mind there was no question at all. Abruptly, he found his voice, saying to Rosemond, "There's nothing left. These men have already fought to the last. I can't ask any more of them."

It was his duty to pull out; that was how he read it. But he would have to leave his wounded, those in the fields and the ten or so in the house. He called an aid man and told him, "Tell other aid men that if I order a withdrawal, they will go out with us and not encumber themselves."

One-half hour passed. Then he called Colonel "Pinky" Ginder at Regiment, using these words: "I've had enough for the day. The rest of the regiment had better get set so that we can be covered when we withdraw."

He asked that 2nd Battalion be rushed forward to form a fire line along the dike by the Madeleine. The artillery should be ready with white phosphorus shell to smoke the farm area and the Carentan road when the battalions headed for the causeway.

But after he had warned Ginder, he marked time, waiting for a sign that the battle was turning more radically against him. Stopka, moving around the farmhouse to watch the fighting, could hear the Germans working their rifle bolts behind the hedgerows. He turned to Cole, saying, "Do you know it's getting God-damned hot?"

Few local arrangements were needed. Cole thought the best thing was to go out fast, and to hell with a rear guard. He'd regulate the center, Stopka the right, and Captain James H.

Hatch, of 1st Battalion, would be in charge of the left flank. Cassidy was at the causeway trying to round up people.

One chance remained—the American artillery. But Rosemond's radio was still jammed. The men had been working at it frantically but couldn't shake the enemy jamming. A few shells were coming over. But they were too few, and the bursts were too far behind the lines to worry the Germans. Rosemond knew that nothing but a real "stonk" brought in right near the farmhouse could turn the tide.

Then as if by magic, the jamming ceased.

Rosemond found himself talking to Captain Charles Aldrich at the fire-control center.

Cole cut in: "Tell him either we get fire now or we're going to get the hell out."

Rosemond told Aldrich what he wanted.

Aldrich replied, "We're out of ammunition."

"Then, for God's sake, get some!" Rosemond was pleading as a man pleads for his own life. "Get it! Please get it! We must have it!"

Aldrich closed off for just a moment, then returned to the instrument. He said, "I see trucks of ammunition just now coming into the battery positions."

The barrage screamed over; there was never any sweeter music. Through the day, the batteries had rotated fire in support of the farm position. Now every gun was speaking. Without asking Cole what he wanted, Rosemond pulled the fire back so close that it just missed the roof and exploded in the first field beyond.

For a few, it was too close. Sergeant De Rose was still standing in the hole by the road, leg broken, doing his duty. A shell broke 25 feet in front of him. He said to the men around him, "Watch! The next one will fall here."

But he stood fast, waving the men on. The next shell landed within five yards of him and blew him apart. Lieutenant Frank Magrie, already close to death from a bullet wound, was put out of his misery by the same round. Swanson and Cody escaped death by a few feet. Hearing the shell whistle, they dived headfirst into the water-filled ditch.

Later, the men of Able Company talked of these things. They did not have the normal reaction of infantry that has lost men to its own artillery fire. "We lost good men, but we had to have that fire," one said, and the others agreed. They had seen the last onfall as the Germans came down the approach hedgerows ready to close on the house from both sides. Better than Cole, they knew how close a thing it was.

The barrage lasted five minutes. The American infantry, saved by it, afterward spoke of it as "intense, devastating." That came of gratitude. The fields and banks were not much knocked about. A day or so later, one could walk over this ground and see hardly a sign of the shelling.

But the explosions caught enough of the advancing German infantry to turn the tide of battle. When the guns ceased, Cole's ears told him the crisis was past. Bullet fire still beat against the housetop. But it was feebler now, as if delivered from longer range.

Cole and Rosemond waited five, ten, fifteen minutes. The recessional continued. In the distance was the faint crackle of small arms. But there was nothing more than that. The enemy machine guns were moving southward.

"Listen to it!" Cole said to Rosemond. "Just listen to it!"

They went outside. Ten men were dispatched from the field to prowl Ingouf's service road as far as the intersection. Four Germans came out of a wood patch crying, *"Kamerad!"* But they still carried their rifles. Two men of How Company had been killed by this trick early in the day. So the patrol shot into them. Two were cut down, and the other pair escaped. Otherwise, the patrol found nothing but dead Germans.

Cole sent a second force of 25 men under Lieutenants George H. Craft and George E. Bean, both of George Company, to prowl the orchard. They crossed as a line of skirmishers, firing as they moved along. No fire was returned though they advanced 200 yards, covering all the ground which the Germans had used so well that day.

Cole came up to them when at last they formed a fire line along the farthest hedgerow bounding the Ingouf farm. He said, "I want you to hold here until the 2nd Battalion arrives to relieve you." They were quite content to do so. The danger was gone. Far, far away, they could hear a little musketry. But the whole front was cool along the bank of the Madeleine.

At 2000, 2nd Battalion came up. Cole ordered a roll call of his men. There were 132 left to answer. While they stayed formed in the orchard, one last salvo of shells broke amid the apple trees, killing three men, wounding eight. Now they were 121.

They marched off to St. Côme-du-Mont, under their own power and, with half their number limping from wounds and bruises, got to the village just a few minutes before midnight.

As they broke up, one of the sergeants said to Cole, "Colonel, didn't you know that today is Sunday?"

"Jesus Christ!" he answered. "Why didn't somebody remember to tell me?"

Epilogue

There remains to say how this narrative was put together, since the book is without documentation, no credit is given to any collateral sources, and the thousands of men who bore witness stay unthanked and anonymous except as their names appear in the action.

The explanation is perforce a personal story. When in April, 1944, I was ordered from the Central Pacific Theater to Europe in time for Normandy, I complied reluctantly and protesting. The reason was that we had a going shop in the Pacific, and at last had come abreast of our work after eight months of hard toil on the backlog. Further, my orders for Europe were most vague as to what duties I would personally undertake. Going there as a member of the War Department General Staff, with no authority except that deriving from my commission, I had the mission of being a spare, agreeable or otherwise, who should help where he could.

My new temporary boss, that lovable old soldier, Colonel William A. Ganoe, at once relieved my anxieties. His people could not spread far enough to cover the airborne part of the Normandy invasion and had no plan for so doing. So with his blessing, I inherited this task by default.

No greater break has ever come my way except the love of my family. Suddenly, I was among men who could both fight like tigers and later talk about it intelligently. They accepted me because we were interested in the same things. The task was one of working over every part of the force, interviewing groups and individuals almost endlessly, until we knew what had befallen the whole and why. In the nature of the case, the two divisions had almost no battle documents covering the fight in isolation. They had been much too busy moving and working weapons. So the normal historical process was reversed. What I collected became the body of the basic record. It is the main source of official history's information dealing with these operations. But such accounts merely skim the surface of the person-by-person ordeal in battle, which I insist is the Big Story.

Covering airborne as a combat historian, as to technique, is the diametrical opposite of covering line divisions in battle, as I had done in the Pacific. This, I soon enough discovered. The one moves from collected order to diffusion; the other starts with total diffusion and proceeds through assembly to solid formation. With line troops, the easiest part comes first; with airborne, one must pick up hundreds of separate threads and follow through until, out of the weaving, they compose a comprehensible pattern. That means hundreds more personal and small group interviews in the beginning, many of which lead to dead end because the individual or group did nothing consequential.

Then there was another unique problem. Both in the La Fière and the Carentan causeway fights, company units dissolved, and squads became so intermingled that the tactical give-and-take could not be clarified by mass interviewing of company components only. So for the first time I had to form battalions as a whole, and finally, two battalions together, and interview the assembly, until we had heard from every active participant, in the presence of his fellows, before we at last knew the continuity. The mass interviewing of the Cole and Cassidy battalions on the causeway fight alone took six whole days, working eight hours each. The commanders simply stood by and listened, bearing witness only when a personal action or observation was germane to the course of operations. By the end, we knew what had happened.

Many of the acts described in the book were rewarded with the Medal of Honor, DSC and Silver Star. Little or no mention has been made of the awards. It is better that the reader judge which deeds satisfy his ideal of courage beyond price and dutifulness that passes common understanding. All who read will agree that there are never decorations enough to go around. None is likely to feel that these pages reflect a younger American generation gone soft. Yet nothing has been eliminated from the record, and nothing has been glossed over. The language quoted is what was used, to the best of human recollection.

In the hour of the fight few if any of the participants were known to the country. Numerous of them have become military VIPs, if not world figures, in the years since. For example, in General Taylor's labors at the White House, Ewell and Legere work at his elbows. Captain Simmons of this book is now General Simmons, and so on. These postgraduate achievements are not spelled out. There was honor enough in what happened on these fields of their great common endeavor.

My work began under the apple bower at the Carentan farm and was concluded near the trees of Sherwood Forest, the two airborne divisions having repaired to England to reoutfit for the next jump into Europe. And that was fitting enough, for stauncher men than these never walked the streets of Nottingham, even in legend.

Index

MEN AT WAR!

Gritty, gutsy, fascinating, real, here are stories of World War II and Vietnam— and the men who fought in them.

____THE KILLING ZONE: MY LIFE IN THE VIET
NAM WAR Frederick Downs   06534-0/$3.50
____SEMPER FI, MAC Henry Berry   06253-8/$3.95